Redefining Christian Britain

Redefining Christian Britain: Post-1945 Perspectives

Edited by

Jane Garnett
Matthew Grimley
Alana Harris
William Whyte
Sarah Williams

scm press

©

Jane Garnett
Matthew Grimley
Alana Harris
William Whyte
Sarah Williams
2006

The Authors have asserted their right under the Copyright, Designs
and Patents Act, 1988, to be identified as the Author of this Work

British Library Cataloguing in Publication data

A catalogue record for this book is available
from the British Library

978 0 334 04092 7

First published in 2007 by SCM Press
9–17 St Alban's Place,
London N1 0NX

www.scm-canterburypress.co.uk

SCM Press is a division of
SCM-Canterbury Press Ltd

Typeset by Regent Typesetting, London
Printed and bound in Great Britain by
William Clowes Ltd, Beccles, Suffolk

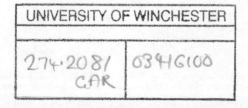

Contents

Acknowledgements

This book began with a conversation after one of the weekly summer seminars on modern religious history held in the History Faculty in Oxford. We would first like to thank all the participants in that seminar, which has been a stimulating and supportive forum for the comparative discussion of a broad range of religious issues and cultures. Out of the conversation came the idea of convening a workshop held at the research centre of St John's College, Oxford in April 2005. St John's was generous in providing a series of beautiful rooms for the meetings and in offering other practical support. We wish to thank the college, and also the History Faculty for its financial contribution to the costs. Nearly all the people whom we invited to participate agreed to come, and engaged enthusiastically in two days of intense and focused debate. We are most grateful to all of them for helping to generate such creative ideas, many of which have been taken forward in the book. The participants were, in addition to the editors: Ashley Rogers Berner, Mark Chapman, Grace Davie, Mathew Guest, Harriet Harris, Lucy Jennings, Ian Jones, Bernice Martin, David Martin, Hugh McLeod, George Pattison, Raymond Plant, Martin Spence, Robert Tobin, John Townsend and Tom Waters.

The book was conceived as a wholly collaborative project. The five co-authors/editors have worked together from the start, refining the themes which they had identified for discussion at the workshop, and drawing out points from that debate. We developed the core framework of the analysis, co-writing each of the introductory and connecting elements of the overall structure. A series of short cameo essays were commissioned to focus particular questions – a set of variations on the fugue. The authors of these cameos, many but not all of whom had been at the workshop, represent a range of disciplines – theology, sociology, history, political theory – and a wide variety of perspectives. They have helped to provide material for a real interdisciplinary debate. We thank all of them for their commitment to the book, their contributions, and their good humour and patience with our editorial interventions.

Discussions of the book as it has developed have taken place in the lovely settings of Wadham and St John's, latterly with telephone and email links to the west coast of Canada. Many friends and colleagues have been kind enough to be interested, have offered advice and given us ideas. We should like in particular to thank the following: Rob Bennett, Lizzy Emerson, Roy Flechner, Giles Fraser, Mick Gordon, Robin Griffith-Jones, Margaret and Bill Harris, Chris Hinds, Catherine Holmes, Stella Moss, Avner Offer, Cecilia Rosser, Gervase Rosser, Rafal Stepien, Nial Stewart, Paul Tod, Zoë Waxman and Paul Williams. We would also like to thank our students, with whom we have discussed our thoughts on the themes of the book, and who have, as always, asked the best awkward questions.

We are indebted to SCM Press for taking on the book, and to their anonymous readers, who made many helpful comments. Finally the other editors would like to express their enormous gratitude to Alana Harris for her magnificent efforts in organizing the workshop and the preparation of the manuscript. Her calm, wisdom, and technical expertise have been invaluable in these contexts, as has been her intellectual contribution to the whole project.

About the Contributors

Editors

Jane Garnett is Fellow and Tutor in History at Wadham College, Oxford.

Matthew Grimley is a Lecturer in History at Royal Holloway, University of London.

Alana Harris is a part-time Lecturer in Modern History at Hertford College, Oxford and completing her DPhil in Modern History as a Senior Scholar at Wadham College, Oxford.

William Whyte is Fellow and Tutor in History at St John's College, Oxford.

Sarah Williams is Associate Professor of Church History at Regent College, Vancouver having formerly taught in the University of Oxford.

Case-Study Contributors

Rufus Black is a partner of the international management consultancy firm McKinsey and Company, and a theologian, ethicist and ordained Minister of the Uniting Church of Australia.

Mark Chapman is Vice-Principal of Ripon College, Cuddesdon, Oxford.

Grace Davie is a Professor of Sociology and Director of the Centre for European Studies at the University of Exeter.

Mathew Guest is a Lecturer in Theology and Society at the University of Durham.

Harriet Harris is a philosophical theologian and Chaplain of Wadham College, Oxford.

Ian Jones is Director of the St Peter's Saltley Trust, Birmingham, having been a Research Associate for the Lincoln Theological Institute for the Study of Religion and Society, University of Manchester.

Bernice Martin was Reader in Sociology at Royal Holloway, University of London.

Holger Nehring is a Lecturer in Modern History at the University of Sheffield.

George Pattison is the Lady Margaret Professor of Divinity at the University of Oxford and Canon of Christ Church.

Raymond Plant is a Labour peer, and Professor within the School of Law, King's College, University of London.

Ashley Rogers Berner is Bielby Graduate Fellow at St Hilda's College, Oxford and a Fellow at the Institute for Advanced Studies in Culture at the University of Virginia.

Robert Tobin completed his DPhil in Modern History at Merton College, Oxford in 2004 and is now training for ordination as an Anglican priest at Westcott House and Emmanuel College, Cambridge.

Peter Webster completed his PhD at the University of Sheffield and is Editorial Controller of *British History Online* based at the Institute of Historical Research, London.

Introduction

In 2000 the Anglican clergyman and statistician Peter Brierley published *The Tide is Running Out*, a despairing account of cross-denominational Christian decline. 'We are Bleeding to Death', he declared, quoting the Archbishop of Canterbury's own conclusions about the fate of his church. Brierley's analysis is widely accepted. Indeed, many authors writing on religion in post-war Britain seem to vie with one another, competing to see who can include the most categorical statement of Christianity's demise in their book titles. Some have seen the period as characterized by *The Death of Christian Britain*.[1] Others have announced, unequivocally, that *God is Dead*.[2] Even those books that approach the issue less apocalyptically rely heavily upon the secularization thesis, a sociological model that, in its most extreme form, predicts the eventual collapse of organized religion and the disappearance of Christianity from the public domain.

Yet, despite such predictions of decay, when the British were asked in the 2001 census 'what is your religion?', over 70% identified themselves as Christians.[3] Moreover, issues of religious faith and identity seem to dominate our newspapers, and television programmes on monasticism, spirituality and religious history continue to capture a large viewing audience. Christian voices are prominent among those agitating for debt-forgiveness and protesting against military conflict. Speculations about Christianity, not least those inspired by the *Da Vinci Code*, excite the popular imagination.[4] Cutting edge contemporary theatre has identified the intersections between faith, reason and religion in multi-ethnic societies as one of the most pressing preoccupations of modern life.[5] And books on the intersections of the world religions can be found on bestseller lists and increasingly within the curriculum of university departments of history, international relations and sociology. How do we reconcile these conflicting indicators with the accounts produced by most writers on the subject? Is the tide running out – or have we been examining it in the wrong way?

This book offers a new set of perspectives on the place of Christianity in post-war Britain. It seeks to break out of the constraints of the existing debate, and to find new answers to new questions. Instead of writing an account of the decline of Christianity, we explore its transformation. Rather than simply reinterpreting the secularization thesis, we have tried to provide a different model of analysis: one that draws on philosophy, theology and the history of ideas as much as it does on sociology or social history. We believe that our key concepts – those of authenticity, generation, and virtue – can be used to redefine the research agenda. As well as setting out our understanding of the potential of these concepts and indicating new directions for research, we have asked experts from a variety of disciplines to contribute essays on changing aspects of the practice, transmission and influence of Christianity in Britain since 1945. Rather than describing, in predictive terms and self-fulfilling categories, the 'melancholy, long with-drawing roar' of the sea of faith,[6] the essays and analysis that follow seek to chart in detail its currents, cross-currents, shallows and sustaining depths.

The Secularization Paradigm: its Advocates and Opponents

In its modern form, the secularization thesis emerged in the 1960s through the pioneering work of sociologists such as Peter Berger,[7] Bryan Wilson[8] and David Martin.[9] Drawing upon the work of Weber and Durkheim, they argued that the social dislocation caused by the onset of economic and social modernization was linked to the decline of religion as a significant feature in public life. Their insights were enthusiastically taken up by a whole genera-tion of social historians.[10] The most vociferous contemporary advocate of this enduring thesis is Steve Bruce, who draws upon Berger to attribute the commencement of secularization to the Reformation.[11] This rent in the 'sacred canopy of faith', he argues, gave rise to an individualism comple-mented later by the emergence of Enlightenment rationality. The subsequent process of modernization is identifiable in social differentiation (the develop-ment of specialist occupational roles); societalization (namely the move from locality to concepts of the nation state); and an emphasis on technical rationality which supplants the supernatural for those seeking explanation or assistance.[12] These forces privatize religion and push it to the margins and interstices of the social order.[13] Bruce argues that this process has accelerated over the last century, and that 'in so far as we can measure *any* aspect of religious interest, belief or action and can compare 1995 with 1895, the only description for the change between the two points is decline'.[14] He concludes that 'we now have a society that is very largely secular, not just in the formal operations of major social institutions but also in popular culture'.[15]

Statistics and their interpretation are the chosen arsenal and battleground for much of the heated argument about secularization. Many sociologists and social historians are greatly exercised by the collation and measurement of religiosity, particularly institutional membership and practice. Contesta-tion turns on what conclusions can be drawn, and predictions made, from data on falling church membership, Sunday attendance, and use of church-based rites of passage.[16] Advocates of quantitative and predictive measurement such as David Voas, for example, have analyzed the decline of the number of Anglican baptisms per head of population to below 50% in 2001. Adding this to the loss of one million baptized believers every five years through mortality, he concludes that 'for the first time since the Church was founded, then, nominal adherents of the established faith are in a minority (and) England is no longer an Anglican country'.[17] A similarly bleak perspective is offered by Peter Brierley, who extrapolates from the current trajectories devastating losses of 23% of members from the mainstream churches by 2020, with some denominations – like the Presbyterians (42%) and Methodists (37%) – experiencing precipitous collapse.[18] From these figures, Brierley predicts that on the current, cross-denominational Sunday attendance figure of 8% of the population, by 2040 only 2% of the population will be church adherents and 65% of this figure will be aged over 65 years.[19] It is envisaged that the Church of Scotland and the Methodist Church in Britain will disappear before 2035.[20] Larger denominations are able to draw some crumbs of comfort from selected statistics which imply continuing resilience; Bob Jackson points out that one in five Anglican churches is growing,[21] while Catholic commentators are consoled by the fact that, measured by Sunday attendances, they are the largest denomination in Britain, and that Mass attendances are several times the total national attendance of the country's favourite spectator sport, football.[22] But such sanguine assessments cannot mask the fact that Catholic attendances have also dropped by 30% since 1961, to a mere 995,000 people in 2001.[23] This statistical story is just as stark for the other Catholic sacramental rites of passage, with infant baptisms falling by 61% and marriages within the church by 78% since 1958.[24] For secularization theorists, journalists and demoralized clergy alike, the pattern of decline is evident and incontrovertible: in 1851 between 40 and 60% of the British population attended church, with the figure around 30% in 1900, falling to 12% in 1979, 10% a decade later, and a figure of 7.5% in 1999.[25] On these measures, Britons are leaving the principal Christian denominations in droves, with the corollary that the influence of the churches has diminished and their prospects are dismal.

As Jeffrey Cox has recently written, the secularization thesis has proved pervasive and resilient for a number of reasons. He cites its 'promiscuous flexibility' – its remarkable propensity to absorb objections, and work them into the master narrative. He also points out 'the persuasive power of the metaphor of the downward slope' – the way that the facts of decline appear to make the whole theory unanswerable.[26] Another reason, hinted at by Cox but not developed by him, is that secularization can work as both a descriptive and a normative theory. As the latter, it appeals not just to secularists imagining the final demise of religion, but also to some Christians, particularly (but not exclusively) evangelicals, who dream of a return to apostolic purity, shorn of nominal conformists and messy compromises with the world. These two interested parties have to an extent colluded in endorsing the secularization thesis.

These are general reasons for the remarkable international appeal of the secularization thesis, but for the scholar of post-war Britain it is worth exploring why it had a *particular* purchase in 1960s and 1970s Britain, and why it has survived subsequent revisionist onslaughts. It was one of several teleological accounts which enjoyed a vogue in the social sciences at the same time – not just its 'twin', modernization theory, but also Marxism. Of course, most proponents of the secularization thesis were not Marxists, but the thesis (particularly with the emphasis on working-class agency in many British historians' versions of it) was consistent with Marxist teleology, and drew from it. The subsequent demise of Marxism and theories of modernization meant that by the 1990s, the secularization thesis was the last great teleological narrative left standing – a sort of theoretical Cuba to which old believers in other theories could continue to rally.

Moreover, secularization was just one of a number of declinist narratives which enjoyed a vogue in Britain from the 1960s onwards. It needs to be seen in context alongside other accounts of decline – cultural, imperial and economic – which provided the dominant national narratives in the media and the social sciences. But it is also important to note that these narratives were not stable and that religion played variable roles over time in their construction. Framed in the post-war period by anxiety about changes in Britain's role in the world, and about her destiny as a nation, these narratives gave way in the 1980s to a concerted attempt to root out nostalgia for the values which were held to have contributed to Britain's decline; and then to more recent preoccupations with national and world security and the nature of progress.[27] During the first phase, there was widespread lament about the perceived decline of religious belief and practice, which seemed to threaten stable moral norms. In the second phase the exercise of a different sort of energy (for some still conceived in religious and moral terms) was called for to achieve national rebirth. In the most recent period, revived (or more visible) religious belief has been figured by many as a regressive throw-back. All of these associations complicate the notion of a teleological process of religious decline.

The narrative of inevitable and empirically irrefutable decline has recently been revised by some commentators. The chief challenger to a statistically and institutionally focused approach is the historian of religion, Callum Brown, who uses insights liberally gleaned from modern cultural theory to establish his overarching category of 'discursive Christianity' – defined as self-subscription to protocols of personal identity deriving from Christian expectations or 'discourses'.[28] These discursive constructions of religiosity are expressed in various modes such as ritual, economic activity, dress and speech and, on Brown's analysis, continued to operate until 1963 when: 'really quite suddenly . . . something very profound ruptured the character of the nation and its people, sending organised Christianity on a downward spiral to the margins of social significance.'[29] This 'something' is identified as the disaffection of women, induced by second-wave feminism and wider societal changes in the 1960s. The defection of those who had been the bulwark of popular support for organized Christianity since 1800 and their denunciation of a mostly Protestant, evangelical ethos plunged 'a formerly religious people . . . into a truly secular condition'.[30] Having apparently been written out of Brown's script, secularization makes a sudden *deus ex machina* appearance at the eleventh hour. Brown thus ends up merely rescheduling the timing and gradient of secularization.[31]

In the Generation section of this book (Part II), we give an account of why we find implausible Brown's description of 1963 as a Larkinian 'Annus Mirabilis' in which 'sexual intercourse began' and everything changed forever.[32] His 'Big Bang' account of the 1960s is certainly out of line with recent historiography, which has stressed how slowly feminist ideas and changes in sexual morality percolated through society.[33] More generally, Brown is open to the accusation that his preoccupation with a single process, the 'sexual revolution', has led him to ignore other crucial social changes. Like the earlier versions of the secularization thesis which he seeks to replace, his account of religious decline is monocausal. In particular, he has nothing to say about how mass immigration led to the British population becoming religiously pluralistic, rather than overwhelmingly (if in some cases only nominally) Christian.

Nevertheless, as Bernice Martin has pointed out, the overblown claims which Brown has made for the 1960s have unfortunately obscured some important insights in his work.[34] Martin singles out his emphasis on the resilience of Christianity until the late 1950s. Along with other revisionist historians, Brown has convincingly buried the notion that urbanization, industrialization, and working-class disaffection were responsible for the onset of religious decline in the nineteenth century.[35] Moreover, his account does much to move the debate beyond the 'reductionist bipolarities' of churchgoers and non-churchgoers, believers and unbelievers, which ignored 'whole realms of religiosity which cannot be counted'.[36] It is therefore to be welcomed for the attention it pays to the language of those engaged in religious activities and to the different registers in which belief may be articulated. We feel that Brown's idea of 'discursive Christianity' can as usefully be applied to the 40 years after his arbitrary cut-off point of 1963. It can help us, for instance, to interpret the 2001 census question on religion, which yielded such a surprising number of self-identifying 'Christians'. Like the 1851 Census of Religious Worship,[37] the meaning of the 2001 Census data on religion has been heavily contested, with David Voas and Steve Bruce recently suggesting that it was simply reflective of a superficial anxiety about Islam, and a desire to assert racial difference against Asian-Muslims.[38] But by using Brown's idea of 'discursive Christianity', we might instead conclude that the fact that over two-thirds of the population chose to identify them-selves as Christian was not accidental, but indicates high levels of residual religion; on this analysis, religion is still functioning, in some form, as a criti-cal part of British identity, and 'Christian Britain' still has some meaning.[39]

Equally important in attempting to shift the debate beyond church statis-tics and squabbles about chronology is the research of the British sociologist Grace Davie, who has similarly advocated an examination of the persistence of the 'beliefs of ordinary British people and the significance of these beliefs in everyday life'.[40] Reinterpreting census data and analysis of rites of passage, and drawing on anthropological insights, Davie coined the now familiar aphorism 'believing without belonging' to acknowledge the per-sistence of the sacred despite an undeniable decline in churchgoing. She contends that while many Britons and Europeans have ceased to connect with their religious institutions in a formal, active sense, 'they have not abandoned, so far, their deep-seated religious aspirations or (in many cases) a latent sense of belonging'.[41] What Davie describes is close to the 'diffusive Christianity' which historians like Jeffrey Cox and Sarah Williams have identified in working-class communities in the early twentieth century,[42] as well as to what the sociologist and clergyman Edward Bailey has termed 'implicit religion'.[43]

In her more recent work, Davie has developed the idea of 'vicarious memory', a Christian memory which subsists within the general population, and is delegated to churchgoers and clerics for enactment until drawn upon 'at crucial times in their individual or collective sense'.[44] The movement away from regular church attendance and institutional practice is linked by Davie to broader social movements, such as changes in the use of leisure time, and rejection of institutional authorities and associational culture, rather than being seen as proof of secularization.[45] Moreover, Davie con-vincingly illustrates that these trends are not a universal phenomenon, but essentially European, and are 'extrinsic rather than intrinsic to the modern-izing process per se'.[46] In survey treatment of North and South America, Asia and Africa, Davie has described the vibrant state of the traditional denomi-nations, as well other religious revival movements. Her findings lead her to concur with the recent assessment of the former advocate of the classic secularization thesis, Peter Berger, that 'the greater part of the world (both developed and developing) is "as furiously religious as ever"'.[47] Other theorists have pointed out the difficulty of applying secularization theory to Islam, a religion which does not have a concept of the 'secular' in the way that Christianity has.[48] Commentators like Jeffrey Cox and David Martin have identified a need to escape the confines of the all-too pervasive 'master narratives', which are not only 'teleological, Eurocentric, deterministic and deceptively value-laden',[49] and reflective of their secularist ideological con-ceptions,[50] but also inadequately narrate the rise and fall of religion without allowing for the possibility of transformation.

6

A third critique of secularization has come from those sociologists studying spirituality beyond traditional Christian religiosity, particularly the burgeoning fascination with the 'holistic milieu'. In extensive field research examining the growth of New Age and alternative spirituality, British sociologists have sought to circumvent the secularization debate, pointing to the remarkable growth of mind-body-spirit spirituality,[51] the inarticulate but insistent expression of belief outside traditional formularies and Christian creeds,[52] and the gradual evolution of a new language of spirituality.[53] When conceptualized in these terms, religious (or spiritual) beliefs and practices are not so much declining and destined to disappear as undergoing a profound transition and transformation. There does seem to be a growing sociological consensus behind this identification of a 'spiritual revolution', but in its exclusive focus on an amorphous spirituality and the subjective dimensions of this spiritual questing (explored in Chapter 1 on 'experience'), this approach neglects equally important transformations in communal and institutional religious practice. By positing a massive 'subjective turn', its proponents are open to the accusation that they replace one totalizing explanation (secularization) with another, based on equally uncertain predictions.

This book has been conceived as an attempt to escape both from the constraining organizational theme of secularization, and from a contemporary sociological analysis which seems to focus almost exclusively on the subjective dimensions of a nebulous 'spirituality'. It aims to explore aspects of Christianity's continuing influence on culture in the late twentieth century which seem to be missing from most histories and sociological accounts. Jeremy Morris has lamented 'a certain constriction . . . in the meaning and scope of religion' in recent historiography, with authors being reluctant to show how Christianity intersected with broader social and political movements.[54] An unrelenting diet of baptism and Sunday school attendance statistics has left some accounts looking rather pallid. Important areas of study have been largely ignored, including discussion of the impact of changes in liturgy, education and national identity on religious practice. We have sought to offer a more nourishing and varied diet by including these themes, as well as art and architecture, children's literature, protest movements, and economics. We have also taken up, and engaged with, Callum Brown's assertion that changes in discourse are crucial to religious change. Mindful that both secularization theorists and revisionists have concentrated on private and local manifestations of religion at the expense of the public and the national, we seek to correct this by applying to Britain recent sociological insights about the global re-animation of the public role of religion.[55]

We have aimed to examine Christianity in its broadest sense, as including not just observance and belief, but its wider influence on society and culture. In describing, in historical terms and through contextualized studies, the role of Christianity as an active agent or unacknowledged foil for many of the structural changes and cultural shifts in Britain since World War Two, we hope both to contest and complicate existing narratives. Our approach takes account of the massive changes in the social, ethnic and religious composition of the country, yet argues that Christianity has continued to play an important role in debates about meaning-making and identity. What emerges from our study is not a single explanatory paradigm or 'master narrative' but a richer and more resonant plurality of voices. Nevertheless, in developing new categories for interpreting religious change and continuity, we hope to provide some tools for analysing the complex re-orientation, and even re-animation, of religion in the contemporary world.

Beyond Master Narratives

We have been impelled to undertake this study because we believe, as others before us have observed, that the stories and metaphors that we use to discuss our histories and define our identities matter. These narratives illuminate particular patterns of thought, revealing how the world is seen and how people seek to shape it. We also believe that such narratives need to be historicized in order both to be understood and to develop creatively. Some of the metaphors that have predominated in the characterization of post-war religion have obscured rather than illuminated meaning – and changes in meaning. Their very capaciousness has led to a tendency to use them reductively and predictively. This is true of two tropes which have been at the heart of the secularization master narrative: an organic analogy; and the metaphor of the liberal economic market.

There has been a strong propensity to use organic imagery when speaking about religion. In one variety, this organic analogy tends to picture religion as an organism, and to use finite, univocal and unidirectional terms such as 'birth' and 'death' to describe religious change. Building on this metaphor, the vigour of Christianity is compared to the health and vitality of the human body – an understandable, if somewhat ironic, impulse in analysing a religious system that prioritizes enfleshment through the incarnation and a conception of the church as the body of Christ. In another variant of this analogy, the imagery is evolutionary. Contemporary experimental psychology and scientific accounts of religion have both questioned whether religiosity is inherent within human genetic make-up;[56] the cognitive, neuroscientific functioning of the brain;[57] and the structure of the cosmos.[58] In the most stridently atheistic use of this pervasive analogy, religion is castigated as an irrational and extreme virus, transmitted through 'memes' (the cultural equivalent to genes),[59] and particularly infectious when passed on to children.

Organic metaphors have often been connected with the other dominant metaphor, the marketplace. There is a long tradition of interplay between biological metaphors and classical economic theory, an interplay which from the nineteenth century was both built on and vehemently contested by religious arguments. What started to develop in the late 1970s was a stronger orientation towards individual enterprise, with which the evolutionary biologist Richard Dawkins's *The Selfish Gene* (1976) seemed all too readily to resonate. The market metaphor has developed new momentum since then, as late capitalism has become consumer – rather than producer – oriented. Religious advisers and academic commentators have alighted rather too readily upon this metaphor, which, like evolutionary metaphors or metaphors of life and death, can encompass everything and nothing, and thus has limited explanatory edge. The fusion of these metaphors in contemporary debate is exemplified in the writing of Pete Ward, former adviser to the Archbishop of Canterbury on youth ministry.[60] Drawing upon Zygmunt Bauman's notion of a 'liquid modernity', he postulates that the church too must become liquid: it must flow, move and change, and reject the solidity of previous patterns of church.[61] Within this idealized and emerging 'liquid church', the believer is embraced as a consumer[62] and society conceived as an intricate system of networks.[63] While Ward's images do not always cohere – his 'liquid', for example, has 'fuzzy edges'[64] – none the less it is clear that his master narrative of the consumer market has become a predominant one in interpretations of modern religion which have tried to contest the secularization paradigm. Grace Davie has argued that a 'genuine religious market' is emerging in Europe, in which obligation is giving way to choice and consumption.[65] Richard Giles has welcomed 'humanity's rediscovery of itself as first and foremost a consumer',[66] and Lawrence Moore has maintained that from the late nineteenth century onwards American religion 'took on the shape of a commodity'.[67] Perhaps most influentially, Wade Clark Roof has sought to map the *Spiritual Marketplace* of modern America.[68] In this, he is partly drawing on the pervasive rational choice theory developed by sociologists in North America, who are seeking to dispose of the secularization thesis and to indicate the potential for revival if European religious markets can develop the diversity of spiritual commodities to be found on the other side of the Atlantic.[69] In writing on religion, it seems, the market has been everywhere.

This interest in consumption and the adoption of a market metaphor is not, of course, confined to the study of religion. In many respects, it represents nothing more than the application of discourses derived from cultural studies more generally.[70] As Conrad Lodziak has recently complained, consumption has become the dominant understanding of social meaning in much modern sociological writing.[71] 'Postmodern society', Bauman declares, 'engages its members primarily in their capacity as consumers rather than producers.'[72] If this is so, then surely it is only appropriate to examine religious 'consumption' within the same light? But the appropriation of imagery derived from the marketplace presents particular problems for those engaged in studying religious belief and practice. It was as long ago as 1967 that Peter Berger first articulated the notion that religious institutions had become marketing agencies and that religious traditions had become commodities.[73] Importantly, he saw this process as one of secularization. The need to market religion, he contended, not only changes the church but changes people's perceptions of the church; it 'plunges religion into a crisis of credibility'.[74] To be sure, other writers have been less critical of consumerism and less doubtful about its effects on institutional religion.[75] Pete Ward, again, has declared that 'rather than condemn the shopper a materialist liquid church would take shopping seriously as a spiritual exercise'.[76] Nonetheless, it is hard not to feel, given the traditional attribution of religious decline to modernization and industrialization within positivist sociological and whiggish historiographical accounts, that the marketplace metaphor is one that is inextricably intertwined with secularization theory. Certainly, we would want to suggest that it is inappropriate as an over-arching explanatory model.

In the first place, it might be objected that models of consumption are theologically inadequate.[77] As John Hull has recently noted, the Anglican Church's apparent acceptance of a consumer society surely compromises its claims to any sort of prophetic role.[78] Secondly, and more significantly for our purposes, market metaphors may conduce to bad history and blinkered sociology as well as poor theology. One does not need to accept Lodziak's attack on 'consumer culture' wholesale to feel that it may be impoverishing to limit oneself to a single image of human action or identity. How too are we to reconcile the empirical findings of writers like Ronald Inglehart, who have traced a move away from materialism at the end of the twentieth century, with those more abstract assertions about the continued importance of consumerism made by other researchers?[79] In the third place, an exclusive emphasis on the market seems historically problematic. There is no doubt that in post-war Britain, levels of wealth and quantities of consumption did increase.[80] But whether that transformed society, turning it from a cohesive system of producers into an anarchic set of alienated consumers, seems more doubtful.[81] Not only is such a narrative short-sighted – ignoring, for instance, the evidence of a consumer culture in the eighteenth and nineteenth centuries.[82] It is also one that posits dramatic social change in a way that is historically unconvincing. Just as there is evidence of consumerism before this period, so there is clear evidence of counter-consumerism during it. If this is a hegemonic discourse, it is one that seems very insecure.

Above all, the assumption that the religious field can be satisfactorily understood as a market made up of competing providers and consumers is arguably a category error. Religion may be – and perhaps always has been – in part commodified. But it is also much more than just a commodity. If religious practice and belief is to be understood as a central part of identity, then a new and rather richer interpretation is required. The importance of identity implies more than mere consumption. As Charles Taylor puts it,

The full definition of someone's identity . . . usually involves not only his stand on moral and spiritual matters but also some reference to a defining community . . . Thus it might be essential to the self-determination of A that he is Catholic and a Québecois; of B that he is Armenian and an anarchist. (And these descriptions might not exhaust the identity of either.)[83]

In other words, not only does a market model of religion make concessions to a secularizing master-narrative, and not only does it rest upon some contestable notions of (post)modern society and of British history more generally. It also offers a shallow and insufficiently nuanced sense of selfhood. If selfhood is not just about choice and consumption, but is also about values and about relationships, then the market metaphor is not able to encompass the varieties of religious experience found in Britain after 1945. But if consumption and the market are inadequate metaphors, what should stand in their place? They have become so dominant that they are very hard to escape. Even criticisms of consumerism like John Drane's *McDonaldization of the Church* rest heavily upon a market model – as he himself seems to recognize.[84] Others advocate the attractive, but arguably unattainable strategy of a compromise model, in which the church (conceived in primarily Anglican terms) seeks to be distinctive, whilst inculturated and engaged with consumerism and consumerist religiosity.[85] This confusion and lack of clarity suggest the need to ask different questions and to develop new models and explanations.

New Explanations and Voices

It was a desire to develop such questions and explanations that led us to convene a two-day workshop at St John's College, Oxford in April 2005. Bringing together a small, invited group of historians, sociologists, philosophers, and theologians, the workshop was structured around a number of themes that we identified as central to the question of the social and cultural significance of Christianity in Britain after World War Two.[86] The sessions were deliberately informal and open-ended, but we were struck by the degree of agreement among scholars from very different disciplinary backgrounds about the problems of existing interpretations, and about possible alternatives. The categories that we advance in this book are the product of these discussions, though not every contributor will necessarily endorse the editors' choice of categories, or their articulation of them. We present a chorus of voices, each broadly committed to seeking new models to address similar concerns about religious change and continuity in modern Britain, but each bringing to bear his or her own very different disciplinary perspectives. Informed by insights from intellectual history, philosophy and theology, as well as sociology and social history, we are proposing three key concepts as ways of redefining the research agenda: authenticity, generation and virtue.

Authenticity

Much current writing on post-war religion suggests that this period saw a 'subjective turn': a move from collective identities towards a privatized individualism. The idea of a 'subjective turn' is most closely associated with the writing of Charles Taylor.[87] Although, as the next section shows, he uses it in a nuanced and sophisticated way, it has been borrowed and expressed with less subtlety by sociologists of religion, who argue that this 'turn' was highly damaging to organized religion. This claim has been endlessly recycled, but needs to be subjected to scrutiny. Certainly social attitudes changed significantly in the second half of the twentieth century, but was there a 'subjective turn'? We argue that there is an absence of compelling evidence that such a definitive turn occurred; people did not suddenly turn from the collective to the private, or reject the claims of the community in an expression of simple solipsism. Instead, taking our cue from another idea of Charles Taylor's, we argue rather that the belief in 'authenticity' became a governing concern in the post-1945 period.[88] This required a reinterpretation of religious resources and practices – in particular, 'tradition' was interrogated and for some re-conceptualized throughout this period. This preoccupation was expressed in certain understandings of religious or spiritual *experience* – with some people arguing that conventional religious observance was increasingly 'inauthentic', or unable to express adequately their personal and collective spiritual searchings. As our case studies illustrate, some people rejected 'traditional' religious practice altogether, whereas others engaged in debates about what the 'traditional' required to make it more 'authentic' and expressive, through ritual, music or congregational arrangements. Issues of *performance* are another element of this category. Polarized debates have developed over the second half of the twentieth century about the relationship between Christian moral teachings and 'authentic' sexual identity, the role of the clergy in performing the liturgy and communicating a 'relevant' Christian message, and tensions between notions of authenticity and performances of public and private rituals.

Generation

The second section of the book deals specifically with the 'chain of religious memory' – and ways in which religious traditions and resources are sustained and modified. As such, it tackles the claims made by Callum Brown and others that the 1960s marked a great caesura in the religious life of Britain, particularly in respect of women's participation in the churches, the socialization of youth in religious ideals, and the challenges to the churches posed by youth culture. This section contests the chronologies and rigid categories employed in most writing about generation by focusing attention on *transmission* and the ways in which religious ideas and identities are handed on between generations – through magazines and popular music, issue-specific youth movements, and most recently the Internet. The essays in this section emphasize that tradition is neither monolithic nor static – it is handed down (or not) in partial and reconfigured ways which are informed by relations between the generations and interaction with the surrounding cultural context. Attitudes to religion and morality often zigzag between generations, as well as varying across points in the lifecycle. Analysis of religious tradition needs to move from viewing it as a commodity – to be preserved and consumed 'intact' – towards a focus on the producers of tradition: the ways in which the generations seek to imitate, or individuate, by rejecting or re-appropriating religious resources. This also involves close interrogation of the various dimensions of Christian *language*, and the ways in which religious ideals, formation and information circulate beyond the purely literary, textual and theological in architecture, art and children's literature. Moving beyond an idea of religious language as something static, we offer a distinctive account of how Christian languages and grammars were transformed in post-war Britain.

Virtue

Our final section deals with issues that are usually ignored by writers on post-war British religion, chiefly the relationship between religion and morality. Conventional accounts stress the collapse of an ethical consensus, the imposition of more rigid distinctions between public and private behaviour and the difficulties for state regulation posed by multiculturalism. They posit the emergence of a neutral state, and the eschewing by individuals and authority of a judgemental language of virtue and vice. However, this section argues that – *pace* some conservative commentators – the language of virtue has not vanished altogether. Persistent arguments about the *good life* have seen theologians and academic ethicists increasingly turning back to classical and Christian concepts of virtue and vice. Charged with enforcing a statutory mandate for religious instruction dating back to 1944 in a completely transformed multicultural society, educationalists have sought new formulations of morality and the 'good life', with contradictory and often confusing consequences for the religious curriculum. In economics, the dominance of neo-liberal theories of the market has led both their champions and detractors to address their deficiencies by recovering Christianized ideas of virtue and the good life.

The need to respond to (or resist) market economics has also been one reason for the re-animation and re-interpretation of the concept of the *common good*, which some communitarian theorists have also advanced as a way of ensuring cohesion and tolerance in a pluralistic society. There has been vigorous debate about whether this common good should be substantive (perhaps incorporating elements of different religious traditions) or merely procedural. Certainly there has been a clear transition from notions of a Christian nation, or a 'liberal Anglican' idea of the common good in 1945, to its re-configuration within a pluralistic and global context. Integration with Europe, mass migration, and globalization mean that the common good is no longer conceived in exclusively national or mono-cultural terms. This does not mean that Christian Britain has ceased to exist, but rather that it is increasingly conceived in relation to other Britains, such as Muslim Britain, and to global identities. The potential of this re-imagined community, which acknowledges the inherently and historically relational dialogue between Christianity and its surrounding culture and thereby disrupts an exclusive (and defensive) Christian identity, will be explored in the conclusion to the book.

Conclusion

In proposing these three categories for analysis, we hope to offer a new set of perspectives on the place of Christianity in post-war Britain, and to move beyond the secularization thesis, and the hackneyed and misleading analogies of life, death, or the marketplace. We do not intend our categories to be exhaustive, or to offer any overarching interpretation – they are after all a reaction against such interpretations. Our intention is merely to set the ball rolling in a new direction by indicating a redefined research agenda. We hope that our work will provoke others to refine or criticize our categories, and to suggest alternatives. Our approach escapes the legacy of interpretation of those who laud or lament the 'long withdrawing roar of the sea of faith' to offer, tentatively and experimentally, a new set of navigational tools for negotiating this constantly changing religious seascape.

Notes

1 Callum G. Brown, 2002, *The Death of Christian Britain: Understanding Secularisation 1800–2000*, London: Routledge.

2 Steve Bruce, 2002, *God is Dead: Secularization in the West*, Oxford: Blackwell.

3 This is compared with 15.1% who answered 'none'. See http://www.statistics.gov.uk/CCI/nugget.asp?ID=954&Pos=3&ColRank=2&Rank=1000, accessed 27.10.06.

4 See Robin Griffith-Jones, 2006, *The Da Vinci Code and the Secrets of the Temple*, Norwich: Canterbury Press; Nicky Gumbel, 2006, *The Da Vinci Code: A Response*, revised edn, London: Alpha International Resources.

5 See Mick Gordon and A. C. Grayling, 2006, *On Religion*, London: Oberon Books, transcript of the play first performed at Soho Theatre on 28 November 2006.

6 Matthew Arnold, 1994, *Dover Beach and Other Poems*, New York: Dover Publications, p. 87. On the pervasiveness of this metaphor within debates on secularization, see Don Cupitt, 1984, *The Sea of Faith*, London: BBC, and the television series of the same name.

7 Peter L. Berger, 1967, *The Social Reality of Religion*, London: Faber & Faber.

8 Bryan R. Wilson, 1969, *Religion in Secular Society*, Harmondsworth: Penguin; Bryan R. Wilson (ed.), 1992, *Religion: Contemporary Issues: The All Souls Seminars in the Sociology of Religion*, London: Bellew. See also Eileen Barker, James A. Beckford and Karel Dobbelaere (eds), 1993, *Secularization, Rationalism and Sectarianism: Essays in Honour of Bryan R. Wilson*, Oxford: Clarendon Press.

9 David Martin, 1993, *A General Theory of Secularization*, revised edn, Aldershot: Gregg Revivals.

10 See, for example, Alan Gilbert, 1976, *Religion and Society in Industrial England: Church, Chapel, and Social Change, 1740–1914*, London: Longman; Hugh McLeod, 1974, *Class and Religion in the Late-Victorian City*, London: Croom Helm.

11 Steve Bruce, 1996, *Religion in the Modern World: From Cathedrals to Cults*, Oxford: Oxford University Press, p. 46.

12 Steve Bruce (ed.), 1992, *Religion and Modernization: Sociologists and Historians Debate the Secularization Thesis*, Oxford: Clarendon Press, pp. 8–9.

13 Bruce, *Cathedrals to Cults*, p. 47.

14 Steve Bruce, 'Religion in Britain at the Close of the 20th Century: A Challenge to the Silver Lining Perspective', *Journal of Contemporary Religion* 11(3) (1996), p. 273.

15 Steve Bruce, 'Secularization and the Impotence of Individualized Religion', *The Hedgehog Review: Critical Reflections on Contemporary Culture*, 8(1–2)(2005), p. 45.

16 Robert Currie, Alan Gilbert and Lee Horsley (eds.), 1977, *Churches and Churchgoers: Patterns of Church Growth in the British Isles since 1700*, Oxford: Clarendon Press, p. v.

17 David Voas, 2003, 'Is Britain a Christian Country?', in Paul Avis (ed.), *Public Faith? The State of Religious Belief and Practice in Britain*, London: SPCK, p. 97.

18 Peter Brierley, 2005, *UKCH Religious Trends No 5: The Future of the Church 2005/2006*, London: Christian Research, p. 0.4.

19 Brierley, *UKCH Religious Trends*, pp. 0.3–0.4.

20 See Brown, *Death*, p. 5 and S. Bruce, 2003, 'The Demise of Christianity in Britain', in Grace Davie, Paul Heelas and Linda Woodhead (eds), 2003, *Predicting Religion: Christian, Secular and Alternative Futures*, Aldershot: Ashgate, pp. 53–63.

21 Bob Jackson, 2002, *Hope for the Church: Contemporary Strategies for Growth*, London: Church House, p. viii.

22 Michael P. Hornsby-Smith, 1989, *The Changing Parish: A Study of Parishes, Priests, and Parishioners after Vatican II*, p. 210.

23 Tom Horwood, 2006, *The Future of the Catholic Church in England*, London: Laicos Press, p. 13.

24 A. E. C. W. Spencer (ed.), 2004, *Pastoral and Population Statistics of the Catholic Community in England and Wales, 1958–2002*, Taunton: Pastoral Research Centre.

25 Steve Bruce, 'Praying Alone? Church-Going in Britain and the Putnam Thesis', *Journal of Contemporary Religion*, 17(3) (2002), 317–28, p. 326.

26 Jeffrey Cox, 2003, 'Master Narratives of Long-Term Religious Change', in Hugh McLeod and Werner Ustorf (eds), *The Decline of Christendom in Western Europe, 1750–2000*, Cambridge: Cambridge University Press, p. 205. See also Jeffrey Cox, 'Provincializing Christendom: The Case of Great Britain', *Church History*, 75(1) (2006), 120–30.

27 Richard English and Michael Kenny, 'Public Intellectuals and the Question of British Decline', *Journal of Politics and International Relations*, 3 (2001), 259–83.

28 Brown, *Death*, p. 12.

29 Brown, *Death*, p. 1.

30 Brown, *Death*, p. 1.

31 Brown had previously identified decline from 1914; see Callum Brown, 'A Revisionist Approach to Religious Change', in Bruce (ed.), *Religion and Modernization*, pp. 31–58, at p. 53.

32 Philip Larkin, 1974, 'Annus Mirabilis', in *High Windows*, London: Faber & Faber.

33 Jeffrey Weeks, 1989, *Sex, Politics and Society: The Regulation of Sexuality since 1800*, London: Longman, Chs. 12–14; Hera Cook, 2004, *The Long Sexual Revolution: English Women, Sex and Contraception*, Oxford: Oxford University Press.

34 Bernice Martin, 'The Non-Quantifiable Religious Dimension in Social Life', in Avis (ed.), *Public Faith?*, pp. 1–18, at p. 8.

35 Brown, *Death*, p. 9.

36 Brown, *Death*, p. 11.

37 K. D. M. Snell and Paul S. Ell, 2000, *Rival Jerusalems: The Geography of Victorian Religion*, Cambridge: Cambridge University Press, pp. 35–46.

38 David Voas and Steve Bruce, 'The 2001 Census and Christian Identification in Britain', *Journal of Contemporary Religion* 19(1) (2004), 23–8, at p. 26.

39 Paul Weller, 'Identity, Politics, and the Future(s) of Religion in the UK: The Case of the Religion Questions in the 2001 Decennial Census', *Journal of Contemporary Religion*, 19(1) (2004), 3–21.

40 Grace Davie, 1994, *Religion in Britain since 1945: Believing without Belonging*, Oxford: Blackwell, p. 5

41 Davie, *Believing without Belonging*, p. 8.

42 Jeffrey Cox, 1982, *The English Churches in a Secular Society: Lambeth, 1870–1930*, Oxford: Oxford University Press; Sarah Williams, 1999, *Religious Belief and Popular Culture in Southwark c.1880–1939*, Oxford: Oxford University Press, p. 5.

43 Edward Bailey, 1998, *Implicit Religion: An Introduction*, London: Middlesex University Press; Paul Badham, 1994, 'Religious Pluralism in Modern Britain', in Sheridan Gilley and W. J. Sheils (eds), *A History of Religion in Britain: Practice and Belief from Pre-Roman Times to the Present*, Oxford: Blackwell, pp. 488–502, at p. 490.

44 Grace Davie, 2002, *Europe: The Exceptional Case: Parameters of Faith in the Modern World*, London: Darton, Longman & Todd, p. 19. See also Grace Davie, 2000, *Religion in Modern Europe: A Memory Mutates*, Oxford: Oxford University Press, p. 59.

45 Grace Davie, 'Praying Alone? Church-going in Britain and Social Capital. A Reply to Steve Bruce', *Journal of Contemporary Religion*, 17(3) (2002), 329–34 and Robin Gill, 'A Response to Steve Bruce's 'Praying Alone'', *Journal of Contemporary Religion*, 17(3) (2002), 335–8.

46 Davie, *Europe*, p. 161.

47 Davie, *Europe*, p. x.

48 Talal Asad, 2003, *Formations of the Secular: Christianity, Islam, Modernity*, Stanford: Stanford University Press; Peter Van Der Veer, 2001, *Imperial Encounters: Religion and Modernity in India and Britain*, Princeton: Princeton University Press, pp. 1–20; Francis Robinson, 2000, 'Secularization, Weber, and Islam', in his *Islam and Muslim History in South Asia*, Oxford: Oxford University Press, pp. 122–37.

49 Cox, 'Master Narratives', p. 205.

50 David Martin, 2005, 'Secularization and the Future of Christianity', *Journal of Contemporary Religion*, 20(2) (2005), 154–60, p. 145. See also David Martin, 2005, 'Secularization: Master Narrative or Several Stories?', in *On Secularization: Towards a Revised General Theory*, Aldershot: Ashgate, pp. 123–40.

51 See Paul Heelas and Linda Woodhead, 2005, *The Spiritual Revolution: Why Religion is Giving Way to Spirituality*, Oxford: Blackwell; Paul Heelas, 'Challenging

Secularization Theory: The Growth of "New Age" Spiritualities of Life', *The Hedgehog Review: Critical Reflections on Contemporary Culture*, 8(1–2) (2006), 46–58; Stef Aupers and Dick Houtman, 'Beyond the Spiritual Supermarket: The Social and Public Significance of New Age Spirituality', *Journal of Contemporary Religion*, 21(2) (2006), 201–22 and Miguel Farias and Mansure Lalljee, 'Empowerment in the New Age: A Motivational Study of Auto-biographical Life Stories', *Journal of Contemporary Religion*, 21(2) (2006), 241–56.

52 Kate Hunt, 'Understanding the Spirituality of People Who Do Not Go to Church', in Davie, Heelas and Woodhead (eds), *Predicting Religion*, pp. 159–69, at p. 163.

53 See Christopher Partridge, 2004, *The Re-Enchantment of the West, Volume 1, Alternative Spiritualities, Secularization, Popular Culture and the Occulture*, London: Continuum, pp. 159–69, at p. 186.

54 Jeremy Morris, 'The Strange Death of Christian Britain: Another Look at the Secularization Debate', *Historical Journal*, 46(4) (2003), 963–76, p. 968.

55 José Casanova, 1994, *Public Religions in the Modern World*, Chicago: University of Chicago Press and José Casanova, 2006, 'Rethinking Secularization: A Global Comparative Perspective', *The Hedgehog Review: Critical Reflections on Contemporary Culture*, 8(1–2) (2006), 7–22.

56 Daniel C. Dennett, 2006, *Breaking the Spell: Religion as a Natural Phenomenon*, London: Allen Lane, pp. 138–9 and 315–17; Holmes Rolston III, 1999, *Genes, Genesis and God: Values and their Origins in Natural and Human History. The Gifford Lectures University of Edinburgh 1997–9*, Cambridge: Cambridge University Press.

57 Eugene D'Aquili, 1999, *The Mystical Mind: Probing the Biology of Religious Experience*, Minneapolis: Fortress Press; Kelly Bulkeley (ed.), 2005, *Soul, Psyche, Brain: New Directions in the Study of Religion and Brain-mind Science*, New York: Palgrave Macmillan; Andrew Newberg, 2002, *Why God Won't go Away: Brain Science and the Biology of Belief*, New York: Ballantine Books.

58 Paul Davis, 2006, *The Goldilocks Enigma: Why Is the Universe Just Right for Life?*, London: Allen Lane, p. 250.

59 Richard Dawkins, [1976] 2006, *The Selfish Gene*, 30th anniversary edn, Oxford: Oxford University Press, pp. 192–3 and 198–200.

60 George Carey, 2004, *Know the Truth: A Memoir*, London: HarperCollins, pp. 190–1.

61 Zygmunt Bauman, 2000, *Liquid Modernity*, Cambridge: Polity Press.

62 Pete Ward, 2002, *Liquid Church*, Carlisle: Paternoster, p. 65.

63 Church of England Mission and Public Affairs Council, 2004, *Mission-Shaped Church*, London: Church House, pp. 4–7.

64 Ward, *Liquid*, p. 47.

65 Davie, *Europe*, p. 148.

66 Richard Giles, 2004, *Re-Pitching the Tent: The Definitive Guide to Re-ordering Buildings for Worship and Mission*, 3rd edn, Norwich: Canterbury Press, p. 71.

67 R. Lawrence Moore, 1994, *Selling God: American Religion in the Marketplace*, New York and Oxford: Oxford University Press, p. 6.

68 Wade Clark Roof, 1999, *Spiritual Marketplace: Baby Boomers and the Remaking of American Religion*, Princeton and London: Princeton University Press.

69 See Lawrence A. Young, 1997, *Rational Choice Theory and Religion: Summary and Assessment*, New York: Routledge; Rodney Stark and William Sims Bainbridge, 1985, *The Future of Religion: Secularization, Revival and Cult Formation*, Berkeley: University of California Press; Rodney Stark and Roger Finke, 2000, *Acts of Faith: Explaining the Human Side of Religion*, Berkeley: University of California Press; and the trenchant opposition of Steve Bruce, 1999, *Choice and Religion: A Critique of Rational Choice Theory*, Oxford: Oxford University Press, p. 2 with the stated intention of putting a 'stake through the vampire's chest' of the rational choice approach to religion.

70 Robert Bocock, 1993, *Consumption*, London: Routledge, provides a good introduction.

71 Conrad Lodziak, 2002, *The Myth of Consumption*, London: Pluto Press.

72 Bauman, *Liquid*, p. 76. More generally see his, 1996, *Life in Fragments: Essays in Postmodern Moralities*, Oxford: Polity Press.

73 Peter L. Berger, 1967, *The Sacred Canopy: Elements of a Sociological Theory of Religion*, Garden City, New York: Doubleday, p. 137.

74 Berger, *Canopy*, p. 150.

75 David Lyon, 2000, *Jesus in Disneyland: Religion in Postmodern Times*, Oxford: Polity Press, pp. 77–87.

76 Ward, *Liquid*, p. 58.

77 As even Pete Ward appears to acknowledge. See his 2005, *Selling Worship: How What We Sing Has Changed the Church*, Carlisle: Paternoster, p. 181. For a sustained critique, see Jeremy Carrette and Richard King, 2005, *Selling Spirituality: The Silent Takeover of Religion*, London: Routledge.

78 John M. Hull, 2006, *Mission-Shaped Church: A Theological Response*, London: SCM Press, pp. 19–20.

79 Ronald Inglehart, 1990, *Culture Shift in Advanced Industrial Culture*, Princeton: Princeton University Press, pp. 5, 176.

80 Peter Clarke, 1996, *Hope and Glory: Britain, 1900–1990*, London: Penguin, pp. 248–55.

81 See John H. Goldthorpe, David Lockwood, Frank Bechhofer, Jennifer Platt, 1969, *The Affluent Worker in the Class Structure*, Cambridge: Cambridge University Press, p. 183.

82 See, for example, John Brewer and Roy Porter, 1993, *Consumption and the World of Goods*, London: Routledge and Judith Flanders, 2006, *Consuming Passions: Leisure and Pleasure in Victorian Britain*, London: HarperPress.

83 Charles Taylor, 1989, *Sources of the Self: The Making of the Modern Identity*, Cambridge: Cambridge University Press, p. 36.

84 John Drane, 2000, *The McDonaldization of the Church: Spirituality, Creativity, and the Future of the Church*, London: Darton, Longman & Todd, pp. 3, 83.

85 Duncan MacLaren, 2004, *Mission Implausible: Restoring Credibility to the Church*, Milton Keynes: Paternoster, pp. 176–83, drawing upon Jean Baudrillard, 1998, *The Consumer Society: Myths and Structures*, London: Sage.

86 For a full list of participants, see the acknowledgements.

87 Charles Taylor, 1991, *The Ethics of Authenticity*, Cambridge: Harvard University Press, p. 26.

88 Taylor, *Ethics of Authenticity*, pp. 63, 66–9.

Part I

Authenticity

I

Experience

Writing on the spirituality of those known as 'Generation X', which he conceived as a particular attitude to life rather than a designator of birth-date, the theologian Gordon Lynch identified the marked propensity of modern Britons to 'seek meaning that feels personally authentic to them rather than being prepared to accept "pre-packaged" truths provided by religious, political or corporate organizations'.[1] In contrast, dismissing these growing forms of spirituality outside the institutional church as 'amorphous supernaturalism', the most trenchant advocate of the secularization thesis, Steve Bruce, has asserted that:

> Individual beliefs which are not regularly articulated and affirmed in a group, which are not refined and burnished by shared ceremonies, which are not the object of regular and systematic elaboration, and which are not taught to the next generation or to outsiders are unlikely to exert much influence on the actions of these who hold them and are even less likely to have significant social consequences.[2]

The essays in this section collectively seek to escape the Scylla of an excessive reliance on institutional calibration and quantitative indicators of religiosity, and the Charybdis of a wholesale endorsement of the 'subjective turn' in religiosity – which has postulated a definitive movement from collective, mostly church-based spirituality towards privatized, individualized beliefs and personalized practice.

This introductory chapter proposes a more qualitative, empathetic and nuanced hermeneutic to discern the persistent meaning-making strategies employed by British women and men within a Christian framework,[3] and to describe the transformations in the forms, both within and outside traditional church structures, through which this exploration takes place. The three case studies on liturgy, church music and congregational life are situated within this conceptual framework, and seek to elucidate the ways in which institutional churches across the denominational spectrum have reacted to considerable changes in social attitudes in the second half of the twentieth century. Employing the insights of Charles Taylor, this chapter endorses Gordon Lynch's identification of 'authenticity' as one of the governing concerns of the post-1945 period, with a corresponding emphasis on an expressive and experiential spirituality that has challenged some forms of conventional religious observance. At the same time, it questions the existing research on so-called 'progressive spirituality' and the New Age milieu which, it is often claimed, will replace 'traditional' Christianity by offering predominantly individualistic and unstructured forums for the development of a tailored, experiential religiosity.[4] As such, it takes up Taylor's insight about the need to expand upon a purely subjectivist understanding of 'authenticity' in analyzing the mechanisms through which the mainstream churches (with varying degrees of success) have sought to re-emphasize a personally apprehended spirituality in ways that are consistent with inherited traditions and habitual practices and thereby reconfigure the communal dimensions of worship, song and prayer. This introduction to the more detailed studies that follow concludes with a brief vignette describing the unexpected and seemingly counter-intuitive forms in which this contemporary quest for meaning may be expressed – namely the much-reported mass-phenomenon of pilgrimage to Lourdes. Displaying the curious and confusing fusion of both individualist and communalist impulses and experiences, as well as dimensions of the 'traditional' and 'habitual' intermixed with elements of 'postmodernity' such as tourism and consumption, this example of a rapidly growing form of religious exploration at a time of falling church attendance illustrates the need for a more complex framework of analysis. An approach that focuses on the interpretation of such religious experiences, or the complicated dynamics of 'lived religion', offers flexibility and subtlety in seeking to describe and interpret religious changes and continuities in Christian belief and practice in the post-war period.

Within an extensive study in 1947 of 'popular attitudes to religion, ethics, progress and politics in a London Borough', Mass-Observation's sophisticated sociological survey concluded:

> All these symptoms point in much the same direction – religion with God relegated to the background, the stress on everyday actions . . . belief in standards of behaviour acquired through personal experience . . . a philosophy rather than a theology, a coherent way of life rather than a faith.[5]

This influential snap-shot of post-war England, with its emphasis on the individual as an increasingly important locus for the determination of attitudes to religion and ethics, and the primacy of personal experience as the litmus test for decision-making,[6] seemed to identify many of the broader societal changes which were taking place during the period. In a similar vein, Gordon Allport's popular tract *The Individual and his Religion* (1950) was also representative of contemporaneous assessments of the 'decline' of formal religion – and the exponential growth of psychology as one of the most influential master narratives of the second half of the twentieth century. Stressing the emerging importance of an individual 'philosophy on life' and 'democratic' individualism in the practice of religion, Allport characterized the religious changes of the immediate post-war period as an escape from the 'forces of culture and conformity' peddling a 'second-hand . . . immature religion', which should now be replaced with a reflective freedom of choice in the individual's 'religious quest'.[7] As such, these contemporaneous socio-logical assessments of post-war Christianity built upon a particular under-standing of religion, articulated most famously by William James in his *Varieties of Religious Experience* (1902), which discounted institutionalized religion and prioritized a subjectivist assessment of spirituality as 'the feelings, acts and experiences of individual men in their solitude'.[8]

Surveying these shifts in self-definition and identity-construction, histori-ans of twentieth-century Britain have largely taken at face value these assessments of religion, correctly discerning a perceptible shift towards 'the subjective life' in post-war society, while more oblivious to the counter-vailing signs of the vitality of certain forms of institutional religion in the 1950s.[9] Instead of recognizing within the post-war period a new phase in the longstanding debate about the intersections between institutional practice and individual religious experience, they have emphasized a decisive break with the old order. In a variety of studies encompassing political parties and personalities,[10] governmental policy agendas,[11] and the growth of popular affluence and leisure,[12] a number of scholars have identified a growing preoccupation with issues of individual autonomy, self-expression and resistance to 'traditional' structures and authority figures. Indeed, some historians have argued that within this period there is a shift from the con-cept of 'character', informed by societal demands and external projections of 'respectability', towards the concept of the self as 'personality'.[13] This grow-ing understanding of the self as a reflexively organized endeavour, drawing upon internal referents and individual appraisal rather than external rules and societal estimations was, of course, facilitated by the language of psychology which provided a new grammar for speaking about the 'self'.[14] The effect of this increasingly dominant intellectual framework, in the estimation of the historian Nikolas Rose, was that 'From now on, all our practices for the management of life, all our systems of spiritual guidance . . . and all our judgement of ourselves and others, will be obliged to make reference to this psy-shaped space that inhabits us'.[15] Building on these foundations, other social theorists have traced these developments through to the present, to assert the emergence of the 'postmodern being' and an associated, much-lamented crisis of certainty – in which the individual 'swims in ever-shifting, concatenating and contentious currents of being'.[16] Assessing the results of these trends on the landscape of our present-day Western societies, Zygmunt Bauman has lamented the absence of stable patterns, codes and rules to which individuals can conform, resulting in disorientation and despair caused by an individual's endemically and incurably underdetermined labours of self-construction.[17]

Sociologists of contemporary religion have tended, rather uncritically, towards the wholesale adoption of this 'subjectivist' thesis. Abraham Maslow's classic 1964 assessment that 'all the paraphernalia of organized religion . . . (are) secondary, peripheral, and of doubtful value in relation to the intrinsic and essential religious or transcendent experience'[18] has continued to be endorsed in more recent studies of spirituality. Terms such as 'Sheilaism' (after the private faith of one of his interviewees, Sheila Larson), were coined by Robert Bellah to describe these forms of an individualized, atomized and amorphous faith.[19] Metaphorical descriptions of the movement from 'dwelling' to 'seeking' to describe the shift away from regular institutional church attendance[20] and the certainties of religious authority, have also become ubiquitous.[21] In a British context, the influential sociologist of religion Paul Heelas has characterized this transformation as a form of 'detraditionalization', which he has defined as the shifting of authority from 'without' to 'within' and the displacement of external sources in identity formation and decision-making.[22] In a more recent collaboration with Linda Woodhead which examined Christian congregations, New Age practices and holistic groups in Kendal, both authors extended upon this analysis in describing a 'massive' turn away from 'life as', which acknowledged a transcendent system of meaning, goodness and truth, towards the reliance on 'subjective life', informed by states of consciousness, memories, passions, conscious and unconscious sensations and bodily experience.[23] Gordon Lynch has also written about this movement 'beyond religion', in which the search for meaning abandons abstract conceptions and instead values 'the physical and non-verbal as much (if not sometimes more) than the cerebral and verbal as a source of meaning'.[24] Assessing the capacity of these forms of privatized spiritualities to promote wholesome ethical values and a broader social ethic, Jeremy Carrette and Richard King have charted the loss of the communal dimensions of religion and their transmutation into a solipsistic system for 'self-comfort and self-consumption'.[25] While not completely 'disenchanted', on the assessment of these historians and sociologists of religion, the spiritual landscape of post-war Britain is one in which there is a cacophony of diverse and dissonant melodies. Moreover, the persisting strains of the sacred are seen to bear little resemblance to the master-score of yesteryear, which is nostalgically conjured as harmonically coherent, performed in a communal setting and celebratory of religious continuity.

In his monumental survey of the philosophical and theological sources underpinning the modern understanding of selfhood, Charles Taylor has charted the evolution of the persistent, post-Enlightenment distinctions between the 'natural' and 'supernatural'[26] and the fragmentation of shared frameworks for meaning-making. In partial agreement with many of the discussed sociological assessments, Taylor has identified the emergence of an increasing emphasis upon subjectivity,[27] arguing that our contemporary understandings of 'identity' are an extension of the Romanticist preoccupation with the search for a 'self' understood as unique, individual and heroically distinctive.[28] This intellectual and cultural impetus, further developed in the twentieth century by theorists such as Derrida and Foucault, underpins what Taylor has identified as the contemporary imperative given to personal 'authenticity' – conjuring in the popular realm certain understandings of self-fulfilment and individual freedom as a counterpoint to associated notions of social conformity.[29] Taylor has identified this axiom of 'authenticity' as an overwhelmingly pervasive ideal within present-day Western societies,[30] yet one that is ill-defined as a form of moral imperative.[31] Moreover, he has argued that a closer interrogation and elucidation of 'authenticity' as a 'sentiment de l'existence' suggests that 'we can only achieve it integrally if we recognize that this sentiment connects us to a wider whole'.[32] The stories and indeed the strategies we employ to actuate this personal project are defined in connection with, or opposition to, other people and our past.[33] Therefore while Taylor, and other philosophical ethicists such as Alasdair MacIntyre, have acknowledged the much-touted 'subjectivist' imperative in contemporary spirituality and indeed its designation as a form of 'quest',[34] they break ranks with many social theorists and sociologists of religion in arguing that this societal transformation should not be defined as contradictory to, or to the exclusion of, the concurrent and continued operation of the 'communal'. For as Taylor has observed most explicitly, the self cannot 'be itself' on its own: humans exist within 'webs of interlocution',[35] and therefore subjectivity must be understood as inherently and irrevocably 'dialogical'.[36] Taylor has identified a framework that does have a strongly individualist component, but need not be individuating in content.[37] On his assessment, and that of his fellow communalist philosophers, an individual's interrogation of faith and search for the spiritual will not necessarily lead to the trumping of traditional religion by the holistic movement and cannot result in isolated and totally individualized life-philosophies. Taylor rather contemplates the continuing attraction of 'extremely powerful religious communities, because that's where many people's sense of the spiritual will lead them'.[38] The description in the following essays of growing mega-churches, re-configured congregations and the plethora of church off-shoot communities, utilizing resources both within and outside 'traditional' religion, seems to confirm this assessment of the continued possibility of interrogatory religious questing within both communal and institutional settings.[39] However, what does seem to be a constant in this characterization of contemporary spirituality is this emphasis on seeking or questing – which is an inherently active, experiential and engaged activity.

In acknowledging the emphasis on expressive individualism as a key factor in modern-day spirituality, but moving beyond the limitations of a purely subjectivist analysis, Taylor has concluded that 'religious experience' has become the key consideration in spiritual searching and affiliation.[40] Acknowledging William James's prescient identification of this element as the key factor in modern-day religiosity,[41] Taylor expands upon and redefines this notion of 'experience' to acknowledge and encompass the communal and sacramental as equally important sites of encounter between the believer and the divine.[42] Nevertheless, within these moments of 'collective effervescence', there may also be identified a concern for the voluntary, the chosen and the expressive which seem to be common factors within this framework for analyzing the diverse and divergent trajectories of contemporary spiritual life.[43]

The flexibility of this framework, which acknowledges the premium placed on authentic religious experience but moves beyond the individualizing and de-institutionalizing narrative of the 'subjective turn', has been increasingly appreciated by historians of popular or lived religion drawing for their sources on material culture, popular tracts and oral history.[44] Sociologists of religion and social commentators are beginning to adopt this approach also, for example in the sociological surveys of Andrew Yip, which have explored the 'lived experience' of gay, lesbian and bisexual Christians within various Church of England congregations. Writing on the dynamic 'co-existence' of traditional beliefs and contemporary preoccupations within the identities of these practising Christians,[45] Yip has explored the ways in which their positive experiences within the church allow the development of both a personal and communal spirituality. In describing this reliance on individual religious experience for the construction of personal identity, he has concluded that, 'ironically', an ethic of authenticity, integration and self-determination 'often facilitated their continued presence in the churches, instead of leaving a potentially stigmatizing and exclusive community'.[46] For such Christians, their experience of God within the church and in community with other Christians necessitates a reconstruction or adaptation of traditional theological resources in ways that accommodate their personal circumstances and affirm their self-wrought identities. In a similar way, Wade Clark Roof's influential studies of contemporary American spirituality have acknowledged the continuing role of religious communities in facilitating an engaged, inquisitive and individual spiritual searching within, as well as outside, the congregation.[47] Roof's focus on the complexities and adaptability of this 'reflexive spirituality'[48] is also valuable for illustrating the ways in which this emphasis on 'experience' and self-authenticating, lived religion operates across the social and theological spectrums.[49] In a British context, while an ethic of authenticity and experiential Christianity may animate the socially and sexually liberal stances adopted by the Christians studied by Yip, an appeal to a personally apprehended and experiential Christianity may be also identified within a more conservative, charismatic agenda.[50] An obvious example is the ways in which themes of spiritual questing and an expressive Christianity feature prominently in Nicky Gumbel's phenomenally successful Alpha programme, which commenced at the Holy Trinity Church, Brompton,[51] now encompasses over 7,000 churches[52] and has evangelized over eight million people in many denominations across the world.[53]

Another important insight offered by the utilization of 'religious experience' as a thematic category for evaluating the vitality and diversity of contemporary spirituality is the potential it offers for re-evaluating the place of 'habit' in religious life. Habitual actions such as the liturgy, religious ceremonies, and structured prayer rituals have been overlooked in many accounts of contemporary spirituality, which assume that these corporate actions are the obsolete accoutrements of an outdated, univocal institutional practice. However, an appreciation of the ways in which habitual religious experiences may lodge in the memory of the believer and become available for personalization and re-activation as a necessary underpinning for meaningful choice and an integrated identity, has been acknowledged by David Martin[54] and Rowan Williams.[55] Habitual skills and practices have also been identified by the sociologist Colin Campbell as 'part of any programme aimed at producing a rational, reflexive actor', whether that be the performance of a deliberately chosen act in a habitual manner, or the habitual decision to do something in a self-conscious and deliberate fashion.[56] Participation in religious services may be viewed as a 'habitual act' in either of these senses, but on neither definition need this adherence to ritual, order and the 'pre-packaged' be seen as necessarily contradictory to, or curtailing of, expressive individuality, religious experience and personal subjectivity. These intriguing intersections between contemporary spiritual searching and communal, habitual practice, and the premium placed on religious experience may be identified in the unexpected 'reality-TV' hit, *The Monastery*.[57] One of the participants in this filmed, 40-day immersion at Worth Abbey was the 29-year-old, non-religious Londoner Tony Burke. Upon leaving the Abbey, Burke reflected on the ways in which his engagement with the Christian scriptures and the ordered rhythms of monastic life led towards the discovery of a personal, deeply experiential spirituality.[58] Resonating with over three million viewers, *The Monastery* uncovered a mechanism for structured self-exploration that was disarmingly 'modern' and yet deeply historic – and provided a tangible example of Nikolas Rose's genealogy of the psy practice of the self, expressed both within the therapeutic and holistic milieu and within 'the ancient spiritual exercises'.[59] Spurring an unprecedented interest in monastic life and an exponential growth in retreat programmes, *The Monastery* and its spin-off *The Convent* have challenged the institutional churches to reflect on the resources within their traditional practices that may chime with contemporary desires for an interior-focused, expressive spirituality.[60]

Another illustration of the ways in which attention to, and analysis of, lived religious experience in its individual and communal dimensions might complicate existing descriptions of contemporary spirituality is a consideration of the much-reported mass phenomenon of religious pilgrimage within Europe.[61] One of the most enduringly popular sites of such pilgrimage is the Pyrenean town of Lourdes, renowned as a place of Marian apparitions and spiritual healing and visited by over six million pilgrims each year.[62] The number of British visitors to the shrine has recently been reported to be at its highest level ever, with the most marked growth observed among young people undertaking the pilgrimage and travelling to help the elderly and sick at the sacred site.[63] The composition of a pilgrimage group from the Lancashire Diocese of Salford is representative of this trend, with over three hundred young people among the nine-hundred strong contingent that journeyed to Lourdes in July 2006.[64] In written responses and interviews undertaken with the 37 young pilgrims attending under the auspices of St Gregory's Deanery, Burnley, virtually all the young people wrote and spoke of the pilgrimage as a time of 'personal journey', to explore 'many questions' about their faith and to 'grow spiritually and socially'.[65] Individual accounts stressed the importance of the pilgrimage as a time for reflection, thinking about life direction, getting in 'touch' with God and deepening their experiences of faith. However, just as marked in the written responses following the pilgrimage was the importance placed on the social dimensions of these experiences – with one aspect of this being the sense of sociability and community aided by the nightlife, despite some sensationalized newspaper reports juxtaposing these 'impious' pursuits with the solely sacred elements associated with pilgrimage.[66] In contrast, the youth accounts stressed the importance of these opportunities for meeting other young people, making friends and building confidence in a collective and counter-cultural practice of faith. As one English university student described it on his third return trip to Lourdes: 'I love it, I love the idea of working your pants off all day and having a great drink afterwards. There's a sense of community, of family, here that I've never found anywhere else.'[67]

These reported reflections also resonate with the Lancastrian youth (aged 16 to 23) interviewed, who highlighted the importance of the pilgrimage in providing a practical and communal expression of faith. These young people spoke at some length about the challenging impact of intergenerational contact with the sick and elderly pilgrims and the effect of these interactions on their reflections about their own lives and spiritual identities. Articulating the importance and strength of these communal aspects, many also wrote explicitly about feeling part of an extended 'family', which encompassed both the diocese and (for some) the 'universal' Church, given the multitudinous nationalities also gathered at the shrine during this peak season. This metaphor of 'family', and associated linguistic descriptions to describe a sense of intergenerational community, belonging and acceptance, were reiterated by many of the youth (and indeed older pilgrims) throughout the week-long stay in Lourdes.

Virtually all of the 27 written responses collated placed considerable emphasis on the sense of purpose, fulfilment and self-worth that involvement in the hospitals and with the sick pilgrims provided. Many of the young people explicitly reflected on the ways in which this social ethic and opportunity to serve counteracted their initial repulsion at the overt commercialism of the Pyrenean town, transforming this from a 'holiday' to something both 'fun and social' but also meaningful through 'the building of relationships, a sense of being needed, and (the creation of) a whole new view on the way (we) look at things'. Part of this 'new way of looking at things', which a large number of the young people reflected upon, was the overtly religious, habitual and ritually structured components of the pilgrimage – with some writing about the sense of history evoked by participation in the torchlight processions, the sense of the 'sacred' and the 'holy' within the Grotto, the use of statues and candles to aid prayer, and viewing the liturgy in a deeper way. One young man spoke of learning 'to pray properly, instead of praying alongside the monotonous drone of the mass', with many other young people praising the tailored, interesting sermons and the 'emotionally affecting' services like the ritual anointing of the sick, which had a particular resonance given the volunteers' close acquaintance with and assistance of the ill pilgrims. Within all these accounts, there may be discerned an estimation of the pilgrimage as a form of spiritual quest along the lines of Roof's contention that contemporary spirituality is most effective when it engages the 'emotions and impulses, involving not just heads and hearts but bodies'.[68] The religious inheritance of over a century of pilgrimage to this place, and the structured liturgical dramas of the Domain were not only the setting, but also a partial stimulus for this exploration of what was, for some but not all, an inherited faith – but which became, for most, a personal, subjective experience that also animated, or re-activated, collective spiritual energies. There are clear parallels to be drawn between this form of overtly spiritual pilgrimage, and the impulses underpinning the collective, counter-cultural movements emerging from the 1960s, such as the Campaign for Nuclear Disarmament 'marches' which are explored by Holger Nehring later in this book.

In seeking to account for the revival of pilgrimage in our contemporary religious situation, Timothy Radcliffe OP has characterized this form of spiritual seeking as a particularly important and flexible means for religious expression, as it may be 'expressive of deep conviction, but also give(s) space for the unsure, those who travel hoping to find something on the way or at the end'.[69] In the period following World War Two, the historic churches themselves metaphorically embarked on a pilgrimage, harnessing new mechanisms and reconfigured historical means for the expression and exploration of Christian faith within post-war society. In her essay on the substantial similarities between the reform of the Roman Missal and the updating of the Book of Common Prayer, Alana Harris illustrates the confused plurality of strategies employed within both the Catholic and Anglican churches in trying to balance the demands for a communal yet personally expressive liturgy, and the perplexed response of the practising laity when confronting these changes. The complexities of this renegotiation of liturgical authenticity, as well as the tensions between habitual and experiential worship are explored within her account of the continuing controversies about ritual language. Similarly, the passions generated by competing preferences in church music in the post-war years are examined by Ian Jones and Peter Webster in their contribution exploring the changing aesthetic and pastoral assumptions within Anglican and Catholic hymnology in the post-war period. This essay also charts the church's re-evaluation of traditional Christian resources against increasing demands for a personal and emotionally engaging faith, with a shifting emphasis from detached assessments of appropriate music to an approach more focused on the attitudes of the worshipper. The churches' well-intentioned initiatives and general responsiveness to the needs and shifting demands of worshippers also forms the subject of Mathew Guest's broad-ranging survey of congregational forms and parochial life in the post-war period. Guest describes the creative and innovative strategies employed across the denominations in the last few decades, and the mixed success greeting such diverse reconceptions of forms of congregation life. Within all three essays, there is a recognition that for pilgrimage churches 'on the move' there is a premium on adaptation and flexibility – for allowing sufficient 'space' for religious questioning and development, as well as scope for the expression of communal commitment, in an environment that prioritizes experience as an ultimate point of reference.[70]

Notes

1 Gordon Lynch, 2002, *After Religion: 'Generation X' and the Search for Meaning*, London: Darton, Longman & Todd, p. ix.

2 Steve Bruce, 1996, *Religion in the Modern World: From Cathedrals to Cults*, Oxford: Oxford University Press, p. 59.

3 See Avis, *Public Faith?*, p. xi and Bernice Martin, 'Beyond Measurement: The Non-Quantifiable Religious Dimensions in Social Life', in Avis, *Public Faith?*, pp. 1–18.

4 See Heelas and Woodhead, *Spiritual Revolution*; Gordon Lynch, 2007, *The New Spirituality*, London: IB Tauris (forthcoming).

5 Mass-Observation, 1947, *Puzzled People: A Study in Popular Attitudes to Religion, Ethics, Progress and Politics in a London Borough*, London: Victor Gollancz, p. 147.

6 Mass-Observation, *Puzzled People*, p. 92.

7 Gordon Allport, 1951, *The Individual and His Religion: A Psychological Interpretation*, pp. vii–x.

8 William James, 2002, *Varieties of Religious Experience: A Study in Human Nature*, Centenary Edition, London: Routledge, pp. 28–30.

9 For a discussion of the Billy Graham religious 'revival' of the 1950s, see Brown, *Death*, pp. 170–5; Adrian Hastings, 2001, *A History of English Christianity 1920–2000*, London: SCM Press, pp. 453–60; and Patrick Pasture, 'Christendom and the Legacy of the

Sixties: Between the Secular City and the Age of Aquarius', *Revue d'histoire ecclésiastique*, 99(1) (2004), 82–116. For an exploration of religious and gender transformations across the denominational spectrum, see Alana Harris and Martin Spence, '"Disturbing the Complacency of Religion?": the Evangelical Crusades of Dr Billy Graham and Father Patrick Peyton in England, 1951–54', *Twentieth Century British History* 18(3) (2007) (in press).

10 Martin Francis, 'Tears, Tantrums and Bared Teeth: The Emotional Economy of Three Conservative Prime Ministers, 1951–1963', *Journal of British Studies*, (2002), 41(3), 354–87.

11 Pat Thane, 1999, 'Population Politics in Post-War British Culture', in Becky Conekin, Frank Mort and Chris Waters (eds), *Moments of Modernity: Reconstructing Britain 1945–1964*, pp. 114–33, at p. 133.

12 Mark Jarvis, 2005, *Conservative Governments, Morality and Social Change in Affluent Britain, 1957–1964*, Manchester: Manchester University Press, p. 4.

13 Richard Sennett, 2002, *The Fall of Public Man*, London: Penguin; Heather A. Warren, 'The Shift from Character to Personality in Mainline Protestant Thought, 1935–1945', *Church History*, 67(3) (1998), 537–55.

14 Frank Mort, 1999, 'The Commercial Domain: Advertising and the Cultural Management of Demand', in Conekin, Mort and Waters (eds), *Moments of Modernity*, pp. 67–8.

15 Nikolas Rose, 1997, 'Assembling the Modern Self', in Roy Porter (ed.), *Rewriting the Self: Histories from the Renaissance to the Present*, London: Routledge, pp. 224–48 at p. 238. See also Nikolas Rose, 1989, *Governing the Soul: The Shaping of the Private Self*, London: Routledge.

16 Kenneth J. Gergen, 1991, *The Saturated Self: Dilemmas of Identity in Contemporary Life*, New York: Basic Books, p. 80.

17 Bauman, *Liquid Modernity*, p. 7.

18 Abraham Maslow, [1964] 1970, *Religions, Values and Peak Experiences*, Hamondsworth: Penguin, Ch. 3.

19 Robert Bellah, 1996, *Habits of the Heart: Individualism and Commitment in American life*, Berkeley: University of California Press, updated edn, pp. 221, 235. See also Thomas Luckman, 1967, *The Invisible Religion: The Problem of Religion in Modern Society*, London: Macmillan, pp. 107–14.

20 Robert Wuthnow, 1998, *After Heaven: Spirituality in America since the 1950s*, Berkeley: University of California Press, pp. 6–8.

21 Anthony Giddens, 1991, *Modernity and Self-Identity: Self and Society in the Late Modern Age*, Cambridge: Polity, pp. 194–6.

22 Paul Heelas, Scott Lash and Paul Morris (eds), 1996, *Detraditionalization: Critical Reflections on Authority and Identity*, Oxford: Blackwell, p. 2. In a similar vein, see Eileen Barker, 1995, 'The Post-war Generation and Established Religion in England', in Wade Clark Roof, Jackson W. Carroll and David A. Roosen (eds), *The Post-War Generation and Established Religion: Cross-Cultural Perspectives*, Boulder: Westview Press, pp. 1–25.

23 Heelas and Woodhead, *Spiritual Revolution*, pp. 2–6.

24 Lynch, *After Religion*, 119–20. See also Gordon Lynch, 2005, 'An Ethnographic Approach to Studying Popular Culture: The Religious Significance of Club Culture', in *Understanding Theology and Popular Culture*, Oxford: Blackwell, pp. 162–83.

25 Carrette and King, *Selling Spirituality*, p. 68.

26 Taylor, *Sources*, p. 11.

27 Taylor, *Sources*, p. 17.

28 Charles Taylor, 1992, *Multicultural and 'the Politics of Recognition'*, Princeton: Princeton University Press, p. 28.

29 Taylor, *Ethics*, pp. 63, 66–9.

30 Taylor, *Ethics*, pp. 17–18.

31 Taylor, *Ethics*, p. 65.

32 Taylor, *Ethics*, p. 91.

33 Taylor, *Ethics*, pp. 105–6.

34 Alasdair MacIntyre, 1984, *After Virtue*, Notre Dame: University of Notre Dame Press, pp. 203–4.

35 Taylor, *Sources*, p. 36.

36 Taylor, *Sources*, p. 38. See also MacIntyre, *After Virtue*, pp. 221–3.

37 Charles Taylor, 2002, *Varieties of Religion Today: William James Revisited*, Cambridge: Harvard University Press, p. 112.

38 Taylor, *Varieties*, p. 112.

39 Cf. Paul Heelas and Linda Woodhead, *Spiritual Revolution*, pp. 60, 67 in which the authors contemplated, but did not expand upon 'the vitality of subjective-life spirituality in the sacred landscape as a whole'. For a more detailed consideration of the role of Christian communities in identity formation, ethical questing and questioning, see Robin Gill, 1999, *Churchgoing and Christian Ethics*, Cambridge: Cambridge University Press, pp. 197–260.

40 Taylor, *Varieties*, p. 116.

41 Taylor, *Varieties*, p. 116.

42 Taylor, *Varieties*, p. 23.

43 Taylor, *Varieties*, p. 87.

44 See Thomas Kselman, 1991, *Belief in History: Innovative Approaches to American and European Religion*, Notre Dame: Notre Dame Press; Katharine Massam, 1996, *Sacred Threads: Catholic Spirituality in Australia 1922–1962*, Sydney: University of New South Wales; David D. Hall, 1997, *Lived Religion: Towards a History of Practice*, Princeton: Princeton University Press; Ann Taves, 1999, *Fits, Trances and Visions: Experiencing Religion and Religious Experience*, Princeton: Princeton University Press; James M. O'Toole (ed.), 2004, *Habits of Devotion*, Ithaca: Cornell University Press; and most especially Robert A. Orsi 2002, *The Madonna of 115th Street: Faith and Community in Italian Harlem 1880–1950*, 2nd edn, New Haven: Yale University Press; and 2005, *Between Heaven and Earth: The Religious Worlds People Make and the Scholars who Study them*, Princeton: Princeton University Press. For a comparable study in an English context, see Williams, *Religious Belief*, and Timothy Jenkins, 1999, *Religion in English Everyday Life: An Ethnographic Approach*, Oxford: Berghahn Books.

45 Andrew K. T. Yip, 'The Self as the Basis of Religious Faith: Spirituality of Gay, Lesbian and Bisexual Christians', in Davie, Heelas and Woodhead, *Predicting Religion*, p. 144.

46 Yip, 'Self', p. 143.

47 Roof, *Spiritual Marketplace*, p. 75. See also Jackson W. Carroll and Wade Clark Roof, 2002, *Bridging Divided Worlds: Generational Cultures in Congregations*, San Francisco: Jossey-Bass.

48 Roof, *Spiritual Marketplace*, p. 75.

49 Roof, *Spiritual Marketplace*, pp. 167–77.

50 Stephen Hunt, Malcolm Hamilton and Tony Walter (eds), 1997, *Charismatic Christianity: Sociological Perspectives*, Basingstoke: Macmillan, pp. 5–6 for a discussion of the role of human experience of the divine as the starting point for religious reflection within the Pentecostal movement.

51 Nicky Gumbel, 2001, *Telling Others: the Alpha Initiative*, Eastbourne: Kingsway.

52 For example see Danny Kruger, 'There's plenty of life left in the churches', *Daily Telegraph*, 13 October, 2005, p. 18. For more a more detailed exploration of the Alpha phenomenon, see Stephen Hunt, 2001, *Anyone for Alpha? Evangelism in a Post-Christian*

Society, London: Darton, Longman & Todd and 'The Alpha Programme: Some Tentative Observations of State of the Art Evangelism in the UK', *Journal of Contemporary Religion*, 18(2003), 77–93; Martyn Percy, 'Join the Dots Christianity: Assessing Alpha', *Religion and Theology*, (May) (1997), 14–18 and Tony Watling, '"Experiencing" Alpha: Finding and Embodying the Spirit and Being Transformed – Empowerment and Control in a "Charismatic" Christian Worldview', *Journal of Contemporary Religion*, 20(1) (2005), 91–108.

53 See http://alpha.org/ – accessed 01.09.06. On the impact of Alpha on church growth and evangelism, see Bob Jackson, 2002, *Hope for the Church: Contemporary Strategies for Growth*, London: Church House, pp. 81–3.

54 David Martin, 1973, *Two Critiques of Spontaneity*, London: London School of Economics and Political Science.

55 Rowan Williams, 2003, *Lost Icons: Reflections on Cultural Bereavement*, London: T&T Clark, pp. 56–63.

56 Colin Campbell, 'Detraditionalization, Character and the Limits to Agency', in Heelas, Lash and Morris (eds), *Detraditionalization*, pp. 159–64.

57 See for example Robert Shrimsley, 'Abbey life may be the answer to viewers' prayers', *Financial Times*, 29 May 2005, p. 13; Gillean Craig, 'Being in the open' *Church Times*, 20 May 2005, p. 24 and Nicholas Buxton, 'What I got from the Brotherhood', *Church Times*, 12 August, 2005, pp. 16–17. On the follow-up 'The Monastery Revisited', which caught up with the original men, and the spin-off 'The Convent' see Ian Johns, 'Getting back in the Abbey Habit', *The Times*, 8 June 2006, p. 27 (Times 2).

58 See http://www.bbc.co.uk/religion/programmes/monastery/tony_story.shtml – accessed 31.08.06.

59 Nikolas Rose, 'Assembling the Modern Self', pp. 240, 243.

60 Editorial, 'Lessons from The Monastery', *The Tablet*, 28 May, 2005, p. 2 and Cormac Murphy-O'Connor, 'A Time to Show the Way', *The Tablet*, 26 August, 2006, pp. 12–13; Bill Bowder, 'TV Monks spark interest in the faith', *Church Times*, 20 May 2005, p. 7 and 'Changed Lives emerge from TV Cloister', *Church Times*, 27 May 2005, p. 4.

61 See Danièle Hervieu-Léger, 1995, 'The Case of French Catholicism' in Roof, *Post-War Generation*, pp. 161–2 and Davie, *Memory Mutates*, pp. 157–62.

62 For a scholarly history and sophisticated study of the phenomenon of Lourdes, see Ruth Harris, 1999, *Lourdes: Body and Spirit in the Secular Age*, London: Penguin.

63 Christopher Lamb and Josephine Siedlecka, *The Tablet*, 5 August 2005, p. 42; Yves Lambert, 2004, 'A Turning Point in Religious Evolution in Europe', 19(4) *Journal of Contemporary Religion*, pp. 29–46.

64 See http://www.salforddiocese.org.uk/reports/2006/060804_lourdes_pilgrimage.pdf – accessed 01.09.06. For a report on the Diocese of Westminster youth pilgrimage, see Bernard Lavery, 'Youth's heroic ministry', *The Tablet*, 20 May 2006, p. 16.

65 Quotations are from interview notes and written reflections collated by one of the editors (AH) in Lourdes between 27 July and 6 August, 2006. Grateful thanks are extended to Patrick O'Dowd, Marcia Dixon, Fathers Simon Firth and Christopher Gorton and the Burnley youth pilgrims for their enthusiasm and generous assistance with this fieldwork. This fieldwork forms part of a more extended study on pilgrimage – see Alana Harris 'The Pilgrimage Project: A Study of Motivations and Experiences in Sacred Spaces' (Fundação Bial, Bursary for Scientific Research, 2006–8).

66 See Peter Allen, 'Drunk Britons shatter the peace of Lourdes', *The Sunday Telegraph*, 20 August, 2006, p. 5; cf. Mick Brown, 'A Different Kind of Miracle', *The Age (Good Weekend)*, 12 August, 2006, pp. 42–7.

67 Brown, 'Different Kind', p. 47.

68 Roof, *Spiritual Marketplace*, p. 46. See also John Fulton (et. al), 2000, *Young*

Catholics at the New Millennium: The Religion and Morality of Young Adults in Western Countries, Dublin: University College Dublin Press; Dean R. Hoge, 'Core and Periphery in American Catholic Identity', *Journal of Contemporary Religion*, 17(3) (2002), 293–302.

69 Timothy Radcliffe, 2005, *What is the Point of Being a Christian?* London: Burns & Oates, p. 10.

70 Yip, 'Self', p. 143.

Case Studies

'The Prayer in the Syntax?' The Roman Missal, the Book of
Common Prayer and Changes in Liturgical Languages,
1945–80
  Alana Harris

Expressions of Authenticity: Music for Worship
  Ian Jones and Peter Webster

Reconceiving the Congregation as a Source of Authenticity
  Mathew Guest

CASE STUDY

'The Prayer in the Syntax?' The Roman Missal, the Book of Common Prayer and Changes in Liturgical Languages, 1945–80

ALANA HARRIS

But clearly any new services or translation must be more than the transference of one language (Latin – or archaic English) into another (modern English). New services must give to the whole Church a strong sense of its own, meaningful liturgy. The lay people must be clearly and intelligently brought into an active and corporate act.

('Anglican Views on the Liturgy', *The Tablet*, 19 December 1964, p. 1442)

I am not convinced that the Cranmerian style of prayer comes closer to the ineffable mysteries of Christian faith . . . The idea that God must be addressed in different, more dignified and more archaic language than everyday speech is slightly dangerous, if it unduly emphasises the transcendent at the cost of the immanent . . . It is hard to relate to that God as an intimate being, even less so a lover, when the language used to communicate with him is so rare and strange.

(Clifford Longley, 'The Language of Prayer', *The Tablet*, 17 November 1979, p. 1114)

Introduction

Among theologians, historians of religion, liturgical scholars and indeed the worshipping laity, there is widespread agreement that the Roman Missal (1570) and the Anglican Book of Common Prayer (1662) collectively constitute the two most influential compendia of public liturgy in the history of Western Christendom.[1] In their different guises, these liturgies were the means by which generations of Christians learnt not only to 'read, mark, learn and inwardly digest' the truths of Scripture but also to experience the sacramental presence of Christ, commemorated or re-enacted each week in the Eucharist. It is therefore highly significant that both these repositories of Christian tradition were subject to extensive scrutiny, and ultimately supplanted, in the two decades following the Second Vatican Council (1962–5). Neither were such correspondences in liturgical developments across the denominations lost on contemporary commentators. As an anonymous Anglican contributor to *The Tablet* in 1964 observed, ostensibly with the Council reforms and contemporaneous Anglican Prayer Book revision in mind, the need to go beyond mere linguistic revision to ensure lay ownership of a 'meaningful liturgy' was seen as a pressing imperative in both churches. More than a decade later, when the Catholic Church had weathered not just the introduction of the vernacular but the sweeping changes of the Missa Normativa (1970), *The Times* religious editor Clifford Longley wrote in this same Catholic weekly about the agitation in Anglican circles preceding the introduction of the Alternative Service Book (1980). Drawing upon arguments well-rehearsed in a Catholic context such as the need for active participation and an everyday spirituality, Longley placed a greater emphasis on the relationship between ritual language and liturgical change. In his analysis, ritual reform required linguistic change to make the liturgy in either communion not only more meaningful and expressive, but also personal and intimate.

These two commentaries, representative of the theological critiques and pastoral considerations operating within both denominations in the decades immediately following World War Two, offer an insight into the common preoccupations and complex issues articulated in the continuing debates around liturgical reform. Central to this debate was the issue of liturgical 'authenticity'. Might this be guaranteed through adherence to traditional forms sanctified by centuries of consistent practice, or should this be evaluated by the function of the liturgy in facilitating worship that was personally expressive and broadly accessible now? Similarly, the debates about lay involvement in the service, invoked particularly in the Roman Catholic context by the catch-phrase 'active participation', involved similar questions about the mode and manner of worship. With an increasing societal emphasis on 'experience' over dutiful adherence, liturgists considered how the changes could facilitate greater corporate understanding and engagement with the divine. Another concern was how these priorities for communal worship might relate to potentially contradictory individual preferences in prayer. Underpinning all these debates, and also indicative of a broader societal preoccupation, was the larger issue of language itself. Was a Christian vision or imagination purely a 'linguistic achievement' and therefore safeguarded by the historic liturgy as a 'massive prior objectivity, historically given, (within which) the self can be forged'?[2] Alternatively, as theologians reading Bonhoeffer, Tillich and Kierkegaard were arguing in the same period, could a 'deeper immersion in existence',[3] facilitated by everyday language and an informal, adaptable liturgy, be the manner in which contemporary humanity should be drawn to God? This case study will seek to illustrate the complexities of these issues as articulated within both communions and the ambiguities inherent in the strategies proposed to address these changing circumstances. Commencing with a necessarily brief explanation of the liturgical developments, it will explore the issues of authenticity and experience identifiable within the debates, and argue that while the churches correctly identified the shifts in the spirituality and liturgical propensities of Christians in England across the course of the twentieth century, neither communion formulated an adequately sophisticated response to the rapid and multifaceted transitions in post-war society. The result of this confused liturgical strategy within both communions, and the overarching theological ferment of the 1960s explored in Mark Chapman's essay in this book, was to unsettle the faithful in the pew yet remain unattractive (or inaccessible) to the unchurched in the street. Three or four decades on from these debates, with the continuing decline in church attendance, both communions have recently revisited these common issues of liturgical authenticity, experiential worship and the language of prayer. Whereas there were commonalities in the strategies they adopted in the 1960s and 70s to address these issues, there are now signs of divergence in the search for a form of Christian prayer that will move the heart, engage the mind and lodge in the memory of the committed, while also offering a flexible tool for mission.

Background to the Liturgical Changes

While the most profound changes to the Anglican and Roman Catholic liturgies were effected in the 1960s and 70s, scholars of the modern liturgical movements within both denominations have increasingly traced the historical and philosophical foundations of these reforms as far back respectively as the Oxford Movement and the work of the Catholic Benedictines Dom Guéranger and Dom Beauduin, expressed in conferences at Malines (1909) and Maria Laach (1914).[4] Within an Anglican context, the passionate intensity and intersections of politics and piety encountered in the proposed 1927–8 changes to the Book of Common Prayer were certainly precursors to the debates about the Series I, II and III revisions later in the century.[5] Moreover, liturgists and churchmen responsible for the reforms would acknowledge their intellectual debt to the Anglo-Catholic Benedictine Dom Gregory Dix.[6] His monumental 'fat green book', *The Shape of the Liturgy* (1945), meticulously marshalled patristic sources to argue for the ongoing and organic development of the liturgy, and has been deemed so influential that virtually 'every rite that has been compiled since manifests the work of Dix in its revised structure'.[7]

For Roman Catholics, this increasing interest in the intricacies and ancient underpinnings of the liturgy was also encouraged by publications such as Adrian Fortescue's *The Ceremonies of the Roman Rite Described* (1917), and was institutionally endorsed in Pope Pius XII's encyclical *Mediator Dei et Hominum* (1947), which identified the liturgy's organic nature and sought to strike a balance between liturgical 'archaeologism' and genuine development consistent with the traditions of the church following the last substantive reforms of the Mass under Pius V. These publications, and further liturgical congresses at Lugano (1953) and Assisi (1956), set the stage for the Constitution on the Sacred Liturgy, *Sacrosanctum Concilium* (1963), the first document to be agreed by all the Catholic bishops of the world gathered for the Second Vatican Council. Anticipating many of the ecclesiological changes that would follow throughout the conciliar discussions,[8] the Constitution opened with the stated intention that the rites of the church should be 'revised in the light of sound tradition, and . . . given new vigour in order to meet today's circumstances and needs'.[9] While the Constitution endorsed the retention of Latin for the Latin rites (§36), the emphasis of the document on the laity's 'full, conscious and active part in liturgical celebration' (§14) and the scope for increasing use of local languages (§36) resulted in the immediate introduction of English to parts of the Mass and the swift revision of rubrics, culminating in an entirely new rite in 1970 and sweeping changes in church architecture.[10] Pope Paul VI's Missa Normativa was implemented in English parishes in 1970, accompanied by vociferous protests from some quarters,[11] and promoting a petition to the Pope for the retention of the old Missale Romanum of 1570, signed by prominent English Catholic and non-Catholic personalities under the auspices of the Latin Mass Society.[12]

At the same time, Anglicans and Catholics were drawing increasingly closer through ecumenical dialogue,[13] and these theological conversations and liturgical convergences formed the backdrop to the more far-reaching Series II revisions to the Prayer Book (1967), which were similarly motivated by the articulated priorities of promoting better corporate and vocal prayer.[14] However, it was the revisions of Series III (1974), rendering the liturgy in direct, colloquial and modern English that created the greatest controversy and spurred the formation of the Prayer Book Society (1975). Agitated by what was thought to be the demise of the 1662 Prayer Book, members of this Society organized a high-profile and prominently supported petition to the General Synod in 1979,[15] but, despite such protests, Series III was also incorporated into the Alternative Service Book (1980) on the premise that 'new understandings of worship should find expression in new forms and styles . . . (and) unity need no longer be seen to entail strict uniformity of practice'.[16] For many Catholic and Anglican laity, unaware of the historical background and theological justifications for these revisions, these quickly implemented changes represented a 'profound incision and cauterization of religious consciousness'.[17] As the Catholic Bishop of Leeds (and Chairman of the Liturgical Commission for England and Wales) had acknowledged in 1965, 'the Mass is the most intimate and personal act of our religion (and) associations of a lifetime have gathered around it'.[18] And yet, one of Vatican II's stated objectives for these reforms was to enable 'Christian people . . . to understand (the holy) things easily, and to enter into them through a celebration that is expressive of their full meaning, is effective, involving, and the community's own'.[19] There is a remarkable correspondence in the opinions voiced by the Anglican Liturgical Commission on the ASB launch, which concluded that 'the task of the liturgy is to create resonances with people's experiences and to identify with people where they are'.[20] Articulated within all these commentaries, spanning a decade and the denominational divide, are similar tensions and shifting reinterpretations of what an 'authentic', 'expressive' and 'experiential' liturgy might now require. The complexities and contradictions encountered in these transformed understandings of the form and function of the liturgy will be explored through the remainder of this essay.

Authentic and Relevant Ritual

As Charles Taylor has persuasively elucidated, a preoccupation with 'authenticity' and subjective experience has emerged as an overarching ideal in Western societies after World War Two.[21] Within this explanatory framework, Taylor has identified a resistance to models 'imposed from the outside, by society, or by a previous generation',[22] giving rise to a suspicion of authorities and time-honoured traditions. This scepticism included greater reflexivity about the forms and expressions of religious faith – questioning the relationship between the 'manner' and 'matter' so that identity was no longer imparted within a set framework.[23] This led to a widespread dismissal of conventional religious observance as inauthentic unless chosen, personally expressive and customized. The debate about these shifting understandings of what an 'authentic' liturgy might require is tantalizingly signalled in a *Times* editorial in November 1975 discussing the liturgical reforms. Entitled 'Freedom of Worship and Doctrine', it reflected on the increasing ritual experimentation in the Church of England and hailed the 'cautionary example' of 'recent liturgical infidelities' in 'the Roman church in the British Isles', to opine:

> The zeal of the liturgical reformers has to be admired and deplored. They over-value the place of contemporary idiom, plain statement, and relevance to secular concerns in the language and ceremonies of the liturgy, and they undervalue familiarity, consistency, antiquity, and the 'pious resonance' of traditional forms. They also set aside too lightly the devotion with which many who are habituated to the traditional liturgy of the church cherish what has been handed down to them. Not just for the sake of its authenticity, but as a sign that the things of the spirit outlast the hectic changes of the world.[24]

In this context, authenticity is linked to continuity, time-honoured traditions, and habitual consistency of practice. It reflects very similar concerns to those voiced a little earlier by the Catholic layman Roger de Wever in his angry correspondence with Cardinal Heenan:

> whereas the Roman Mass had evolved over more than a thousand years . . . the new Mass has been willed, planned, concocted, and is therefore artificial! It is an instant Mass . . . (in) the language of the supermarket.[25]

Bound up in his criticism are understandings of 'authentic ritual' defined in opposition to novelty and self-conscious reflexivity, and implicit criticisms about the commodification of the liturgy within everyday language. For traditionalists like de Wever, and his counterparts in the Anglican communion, the very familiarity and longevity of the old liturgy made it authentic because it was removed from the contemporary, the self-constructed and the ordinary. Contesting the claim of the Vicar of Ealing that unless there was change the Church of England would become a 'jewelled corpse', the Dean of Guildford drew upon the history of iconoclasm to explain the role of worship 'to transform the ordinary into a revelation of the superordinary'. He continued by contrasting this legacy with Series III's role in 'transforming the divine into the ordinary and reducing the vision of the city of God to the likeness of a landscape in suburbia'.[26] These sentiments were, however, deplored by other correspondents as antiquarian, elitist and old-fashioned, prompting one correspondent to muse ironically: 'Will those who are crynge for the preseruacion of the woordes and orders of Archbishoppe Cranmer haue hys spellynges also?'[27] But the value placed on tradition as a guarantee of authentic worship was not just an upper-middle-class phenomenon. Anglican commentators invoked the comprehension of the Book of Common Prayer by 'ordinary people . . . for more than *three* centuries'.[28] An Irish Catholic mother similarly appealed to tradition, history and the numinous as informing her preference for the Latin liturgy when writing to Cardinal Heenan about the 'liturgical infidelities'. Chronicling the devastating impact of the changes on the faith of her 24-year-old, motor mechanic son and denouncing the claims that this 'suffering is going "to benefit future generations"', she closed by reflecting: 'He values Latin intensely as being so ancient, so loved and suffered for in the past, and so apart from the coarse everyday English that surrounds him at work. Also he values silence.'[29] Cardinal Heenan's reply, which advocated 'putting up with these new things for the sake of the ignorant and the weak', reiterated the implicit justifications of the reforms on the basis of certain understandings of class and urbanization, concluding: 'most Catholics in the cities have not the same love of the Mass as your son. They will understand the Mass much better now with so much of it being said in their own language.'[30]

These exchanges illustrate the shifting understandings of 'authentic' liturgy intensely debated in the Catholic Church following the Council. From 1962, correspondence columns in the Catholic press increasingly included letters from people like A. M. Wood taking 'a stand against the dragooning of the laity into the use of a foreign and dead language'.[31] History and tradition were also invoked by advocates of the reforms, directly to contest their opponents' appeal to past precedent. They justified the changes as authentic because they were *even more* historic, traceable back to the practices of the 'authentic' early church – invoking the simplicity of the 'ancient corporate celebration of the Eucharist',[32] or rhetorically retorting: 'did Jesus Christ at the Last supper say *"hoc est enim Corpus meum"*?'[33] This shifting understanding of authentic worship placed a premium on self-expression and informality, deemed more effective in one's mother tongue and enabling greater comprehension and spontaneity. For as A. H. Armstrong solipsistically concluded, if he as Professor of Classics at the University of Liverpool could 'neither pray nor converse easily and naturally' in Latin, how unreasonable must the church be to compel 'ordinary Catholics' to so conduct their public worship?[34] Advocates of the Alternative Service Book appealed to a similar argument, asserting:

> We go to pray, in our very inefficient, lowly and unliterary ways; for many of us this becomes that much easier when the words we use bear some relation to our mundane thoughts rather than to the high-flown rhetoric of 1662.[35]

This shifting emphasis on the need for the liturgy, whether Catholic or Anglican, to inculcate a genuinely-held, expressive spirituality that communicated truth and directly addressed contemporary concerns was explicitly articulated by James Mulligan in private correspondence to the Archbishop of Westminster in 1964. The layman from Twickenham wrote in effusive terms, welcoming the vernacular which created for his children 'a Liturgy they will see and understand, learn from and help to perform'; and which would give them 'a chance to survive as Christians in a society which is too clearly the antithesis of what we believe to be right'.[36] As the following essay by Ian Jones and Peter Webster illustrates, these same concerns played through the debates about the appropriate hymns and musical settings for this worship. The 'pious resonance' which *The Times* in its 1974 Editorial attributed to the Book of Common Prayer (and by analogy to the Latin Mass), was believed by many Christian laity and elements of the church authorities to be an inferior or insufficient instrument to articulate truthfully the 'spirit of the age'.[37]

Experiential Christianity – Individual and Communal worship

These changing societal priorities, and the perceived demands of greater missionary outreach, were also articulated by Bishop Holland of the Salford Diocese. In a series of pastoral sermons on the liturgy in 1964, perhaps articulating his own attempts to integrate the changes, Holland urged his flock to accept the reforms because:

> People are no longer supported in their faith by environment and social custom. The faith must become a truly personal possession, deeply held and of such quality that it enables each to base his life on the great central truth of the Christian message.[38]

The English Hierarchy, unprepared for the liturgical developments but dutiful in articulating the Vatican position, explained that making the liturgy accessible in the vernacular would enable 'the millions who hitherto were mere bystanders . . . (to take) an active part in the Mass'.[39] Similar issues about the intersections between the individual and communal aspects of worship, the participation of 'ordinary' Christians in the liturgy, and the importance of language to these questions also played through the Anglican debates over a decade later. Rhetorically caricaturing the perceived elitism of those academics and educated persons promoting the retention of the Prayer Book as very 'north Oxford', Reverend Martin Linskill was perhaps just as patronizing in arguing that 'if those whom the Lord has given us are Goths, it's no good being Ciceronians, not if its apostles we would be'. As a vicar in Middlesex, he sought to differentiate linguistic beauty from theological and pastoral considerations, citing the imperative that: 'The Word of the Lord should once more bite, not lull, that worship should be common, not clerical, that Prayer should be real prayer, not dutiful performance'.[40] In this series of juxtaposed dichotomies, it is possible to trace the conflicting interpretations during the period of what was deemed necessary for an effective liturgy – an active, engaging service rather than habitual recitation, and a commonplace, corporate experience rather than 'clerical' worship. As Mrs Elisabeth Montefiore articulated it, as an unabashed advocate of the reforms given her former membership of the Liturgical Commission, the Alternative Service Book enabled 'glad authentic worship' because it was 'the work of the People of God and the public expression of their relation to Him . . . command(ing) the *attention* of those taking part'.[41] These sentiments could have been articulated more than a decade earlier by a Catholic layman, B. C. Atkin, who deplored similarly the use of the Catholic Mass as 'an occasion when a large number of individuals betake themselves (for some reason) to a particular building in order to perform their private devotions; it is a public, corporate, concerted act of the whole people of God.'[42]

This increasing emphasis on attention, understanding and activity as redefined components of an authentic 'religious experience' in the post-war period could, however, give rise to ambiguous and sometimes contradictory impulses in Christian worship. For some, like the 16-year-old David Power writing to his archbishop, the changes had facilitated both increased personalized expression *and* more corporate involvement, for:

> I can truly say that I have never experienced such a great sense of communion and participation as with the Normative Mass . . . (and) the greater emphasis on being Christian than Catholic, all enhance the meaning of Mass . . . I really get quite a 'kick' out of . . . (the) experience (of) this calming and relaxing union with the ground of our being.[43]

Scarcely making allowances for youthful fervour, Cardinal Heenan expressed some pleasure that his young charge found the changes 'attractive', but sternly chastised him for using 'agnostic' expressions such as 'ground of our being' which he supposed to originate from a reading of the bestseller *Honest to God*.[44] Interestingly, those opposed to liturgical reforms also increasingly appealed to the demands of an explicitly experiential, emotional and corporate spirituality. The University of Durham theologian T. H. L. Parker reflected of the Prayer Book:

> Other people may get a Housman-like shiver down the spine under the impact of this piece of Tudor literature, but one man, at any rate, counts it a privilege and an ever dear delight to be allowed to worship in the unadulterated tradition of the reformed catholic Church.[45]

Moreover, it was not just the university-educated who found that the older rites, in their ancient languages, could also enable a communal and perhaps more numinous relationship with the divine. Writing to the Archbishop of Westminster's Private Secretary in 1969 to communicate the grass-roots' discontent and 'mournful' discussions about the 'matter of the mass', Margaret Peckham recounted a conversation with a lady at a bus stop: '*A domestic servant*, no clever degrees for her! [who] assured me that she understood the Latin Mass! But the V[ernacular] Mass was meaningless to her' (original emphases).[46] Beyond the patronizing tone of this class-ridden social commentary, this anecdote illustrated the multiple and shifting ways in which the laity might define religious 'experience' and 'participation' – with the setting of the Latin Mass for this woman providing a particularly sacred moment for prayer and participation through familiarity.[47] The power of the customary, predictable and habitual to foster communal expression and personal conviction was underestimated by many Catholic and Anglican liturgists,[48] but appreciated by Lord Denham who wrote of his difficulties with the different wordings of the 'Lord's Prayer', lamenting: 'By the time one has worked out which alternative set of the three words is being used, one has totally lost all concentration on the actual meaning of this most important of all prayers.'[49]

Going further in his criticism of the diversity of services within the Alternative Service Book, Canon George Austin disparaged the impact of this '*à la carte* menu of alternatives' on the stated reform objective of better communal worship, taking a whole-of-communion approach in his estimation that it undermined 'common prayer . . . (such that) we have now become a congregational sect'.[50] There were similar ambiguities and paradoxical consequences in Roman Catholic experiences and evaluations of the new Mass. In an early assessment of the reforms immediately following the Council, Anthony Radcliffe drew a contrast between 'what Sunday Mass used to be – rows of blank faces, people coming and going at all times, and quite a lot of talking'; compared with 'the "modern" service, with almost everyone taking an interest and following what is going on'.[51] This was not a universal assessment, however, for many like Joan Adams saw the effect of this more corporate, active liturgy as the creation of a "sheep like" congregational Mass where 'one doesn't even have to think – just to pray parrot-fashion with the others'.[52] As A. D. J. Grumett similarly observed, this stress on communal and vocal participation felt like '"regimentation" . . . (for) a frenzy of activity must bear witness to the fact that we are "participating"'.[53] The premium on 'corporate involvement' in a society of increasing, individually focused leisure and more sophisticated spectacle, placed great pressure on the liturgy as a 'performance' – as the 62-year-old, self-confessedly 'lapsing Catholic', Mrs J. Casey confided: 'One might as well be at a film show or a football match; at least in the latter there is unbounded enthusiasm which there will never be for the so-called Missa Normativa . . .'[54]

These contradictory impulses encountered in the reforms and magnified by societal change were well identified in correspondence to the Hierarchy from Miss Joan Thompson. Deploring the preponderance of drilled choruses and noise at a time when contemporary youth evidenced an attraction towards contemplative prayer and Eastern mysticism, she rhetorically asked her pastor: 'How is this form of the Mass to attract a generation which has rejected rigid patterns of behaviour, and which is determined to "do its own thing"?'[55] Bishop Holland's articulation of the need to make the faith a 'truly personal possession' correctly diagnosed an increasing demand from the faithful, across the denominations, for a liturgy that facilitated their individual, conscious and emotional involvement in the drama at the altar table. However, just how this was to be balanced with the equally prioritized objective of the liturgical movement for communal and 'active participation' remained unclear and a contentious issue for both denominations. The proliferation of experimental services, and liturgical variations (often involving contemporary music) was an immediate, but often short-lived response. In view of this confused agenda, some contemporary commentators recognized that these reforms would do little to counteract the marked trends in church attendance across the communions.[56] Nor, as was subsequently recognized by the church authorities, were the reform objectives sufficiently coherent, comprehensible or innovative to attract a new cohort of church-goers.[57]

Conclusion

At the heart of these controversies within the Anglican and Catholic communions about the retention or reformation of their liturgical rote and rite lies the ever-problematic issue of the appropriateness of traditional ritual to embody and to express, with historic continuity yet contemporary resonance, the import of Christ's historic command to 'do this in remembrance of me'. The liturgical movement within both churches, while chiefly informed by the scholarly task of recovering the ideals of early church worship, also presciently anticipated what the shifting societal understandings of 'authentic' liturgy and religious 'experience' might require of ritual in the post-war period. Nevertheless, in the implementation of these reforms in both churches from the 1960s onwards, there were contrasting and sometimes contradictory estimations of the balance between the traditional and the contemporary, the habitual and the novel, the individual and the communal. These tensions underline the centrality within these discussions of the language of the liturgy, which involved different assessments of whether it was the 'manner' or 'mode' of the liturgy which was crucial to its efficacy. In debating the 'prayer in the syntax', the liturgical commentators and agitated correspondents were articulating, sometimes inchoately, the ongoing theological debate about whether we speak the liturgy or it speaks us; whether the Sabbath was made for man, not man for the Sabbath.[58] Towards the close of the century, these debates and disagreements about the authentic form of liturgy, and its function in articulating a personally held but communally expressive spirituality remain contentious. Through the adoption of the new liturgical form, *Common Worship* (2000), the Church of England has extended the movement signalled with the Alternative Service Book (1980) towards greater variety and parochial customization of the liturgy, retaining modern language and a choice of ten different eucharistic prayers, within a broadly uniform liturgical structure. The result is a plurality and diversity of liturgical styles (and theological emphases) across parishes, and even between various parochial services.[59] In contrast, in a document entitled *Liturgiam Authenticam* (2001),[60] the Vatican Congregation for Divine Worship has signalled a return to an understanding of 'authenticity' as vested in tradition and 'truths that transcend the limits of time and space' rather than a celebration of the sacraments as a 'mirror of the interior dispositions of the faithful' (§19).[61] In reflecting on the liturgical reforms within both communions in the post-war period, the demands of 'authenticity' as variously understood and actuated lie at the heart of each communion's continuing interrogation of the relationship between 'the word and the Word'. It remains to be seen whether these churches' divergent, but definitive determinations of the demands of 'authentic' worship for today will allow for the articulation of a distinctively Christian story to those within its walls, while speaking the good news to the much greater number who now lie beyond the porch door.

Notes

* The author would like to thank Dr Jane Garnett, the Revd Dr Philip Endean SJ and the Revd Dr Simon Jones for helpful comments, suggestions and stimulating conversation surrounding the preparation of this article.

1 Barry Spurr, 1995, *The Word in the Desert: Anglican and Roman Catholic Reactions to Liturgical Reform*, Cambridge: Lutterworth Press, p. 8.

2 David Martin, 2002, *Christian Language and its Mutations: Essays in Sociological Understanding*, Aldershot: Ashgate, p.141–2.

3 John A. T. Robinson, 1963, *Honest to God*, London: SCM Press, p. 47 (citing Kierkegaard) and pp. 86–7.

4 For a general, Anglican consideration of the liturgical movement see Louis Weil, 1983, *Sacraments and Liturgy: The Outward Signs. A Study in Liturgical Mentality*, Oxford: Basil Blackwell; Paul A. Welsby, 1984, *A History of the Church of England*, Oxford: Oxford University Press and the comparative history in Bryan D. Spinks, 2006, 'Liturgy' in Hugh McLeod (ed.), *The Cambridge History of Christianity: Volume 9 World Christianities c.1914–c.2000*, Cambridge: Cambridge University Press, pp. 471–82. Comprehensive Catholic discussions of the liturgical movement may be found in J. D. Crichton, H. E. Winstone and J. R. Ainslie (eds), 1979, *English Catholic Worship: Liturgical Renewal in England since 1900*, London: Geoffrey Chapman; Aidan Nichols, 1996, *Looking at the Liturgy: A Critical View of its Contemporary Form*, San Francisco: Ignatius Press; and Alcuin Reid, 2004, *The Organic Development of the Liturgy. The Principles of Liturgical Reform and their Relation to the Twentieth Century Liturgical Movement prior to the Second Vatican Council*, Farnborough: St Michael's Abbey Press.

5 See Matthew Grimley, 2004, *Citizenship, Community and the Church of England: Liberal Anglican Theories of the State between the Wars*, Oxford: Clarendon Press, pp. 140–71.

6 John A. T. Robinson, 1960, *Liturgy Coming to Life*, London: Mowbray, p. 21.

7 Kenneth Stevenson, 1977, *Gregory Dix: Twenty-Five Years On*, Nottingham: Grove Books, p. 24.

8 See *Lumen Gentium* and *Gaudium et Spes* in Norman P. Tanner (ed.), 1990, *Decrees of the Ecumenical Councils: Volume II Trent to Vatican II*, London: Sheed and Ward, pp. 887–91; 1069–135.

9 Tanner, *Decrees*, p. 821 (§4).

10 Crichton, *English Catholic Worship*, pp. 79ff; Adrian Hastings (ed.), 1991, *Modern Catholicism: Vatican II and After*, London: SPCK; and Hornsby-Smith, *Changing Parish* and the essay of William Whyte in Part 2.2.

11 For discussion of these contestations, see Scott M. P. Reid (ed.), 2000, *A Bitter Trial: Evelyn Waugh and John Carmel Cardinal Heenan on the Liturgical Changes*, London: Saint Austin Press and Joseph Pearce, 1999, *Literary Converts: Spiritual Inspiration in an Age of Unbelief*, London: HarperCollins.

12 For a full copy of the petition, and its signatories, see *Times*, 6 July 1971, p. 5.

13 See the Vatican II Decree on Ecumenism (*Unitatis redintegratio*), and work of the Anglican–Roman Catholic International Commission, commencing in 1970.

14 Roger Homan, 'The Liturgy: Experiment and Results' in Peter Mullen (ed.), 2000, *The Real Common Worship*, Denton: Edgeway Books, pp. 31–47, at p. 33.

15 See David Martin, 'Why Spit on our Luck?' *PN Review*, 6(5) No 13 (1979), pp. 1–5, replicating the three petitions and their highly prominent signatories.

16 *Alternative Service Book (1980), with the Liturgical Psalter*, 1980, Cambridge: Cambridge University Press, p. 9.

17 David Martin, 'Personal Identity and a Changed Church', in David Martin and

Peter Mullen (eds.), 1981, *No Alternative: The Prayer Book Controversy*, Oxford: Basil Blackwell, p. 13.

18 Bishop Dwyer, cited in 'More English: The Second Stage of Liturgical Reform', *Tablet*, 20 March 1965, p. 33.

19 Tanner, *Decrees*, p. 825 (§21).

20 Cited in Mullen, *Real Common Worship*, p. vii.

21 Taylor, *Ethics*, p. 16.

22 Taylor, *Varieties*, p. 83.

23 Taylor, *Ethics*, p. 82.

24 Editorial 'Freedom of Worship and Doctrine', *The Times*, 9 November 1974, p. 17.

25 Roger de Wever, Correspondence to Cardinal Heenan, 2 March, 1970 (London, Roman Catholic Diocese of Westminister Archives (AWW), file HEI/L (b) Liturgy Letters from Laity 1969–70). Hereafter HEI/L (b) LLL.

26 Reverend Tony Bridge, Letter to the Editor, *The Times*, 23 November 1979, p. 13.

27 Reverend Eric Thacker (Vicar of St Paul's Leeds), Letter to the Editor, *The Times*, 24 November 1979, p. 15.

28 Dr Raymond F. Glascock, Letter to the Editor, *The Times*, 11 May 1978, p. 17 (original emphasis).

29 Mrs Mary Pegge, Correspondence to Cardinal Heenan, 8 December, 1964 (AWW HEI/L (a) LLL, 1964–5, 1966–8). Hereafter HEI/L (a) LLL.

30 Reply from Cardinal Heenan to Mrs Mary Pegge, 16 December 1964 (AWW HEI/L (a) LLL).

31 A. M. Wood, 'The Dialogue Mass', *The Tablet*, 29 September 1962, p. 915.

32 A. Manson *et al.*, 'National Liturgies and Catholic Unity', *The Tablet*, 18 July 1964, p. 811–12.

33 Randle Lunt, 'Language, Truth and Liturgy', *The Tablet*, 1 April 1964, p. 387.

34 Professor A. H. Armstrong, 'The Dialogue Mass', *The Tablet*, 27 October 1962, p. 1023.

35 Mr K. F. W. Doughty, Letter to the Editor, *The Times*, 25 November 1980, p. 13.

36 Mr James Mulligan, Correspondence to Cardinal Heenan, 7 December 1964 (AWW HEI/L (a) LLL).

37 E.g. Canon David H. Bishop (Norwich), Letter to the Editor, *The Times*, 14 June 1980, p. 15 who stated: 'Many of us are concerned with communicating the Christian faith . . . recognize that tools have to be changed when they wear out or when the work demanded of them changes.'

38 Bishop Thomas Holland, 'Sermon: A Conscious Faith' (18 October 1964), as part of Eight Sermons on the Liturgy (Burnley, Salford Diocesan Archives, Box 220 Marshall-Beck-Holland Papers, 1956–).

39 'Cardinal Heenan's Pastoral', *The Tablet*, 6 March 1965, p. 277.

40 Reverend Martin Linskill, Letter to the Editor, *The Times*, 22 November 1979, p. 15.

41 Mrs H. (Elisabeth) Montefiore, Letter to the Editor, *The Times*, 1 July 1980, p. 15 (original emphasis).

42 Mr B. C. Atkin, 'The Dialogue Mass', Letter to the Editor, *The Tablet*, 20 October 1962, p. 994.

43 Mr David Power, Correspondence to Cardinal Heenan, 14 November 1969 (AWW HEI/L (b) LLL).

44 Reply from Cardinal Heenan to Mr David Power, 14 November 1969 (AWW HEI/L (b) LLL).

45 The Revd T. H. L. Parker, Letter to the Editor, *The Times*, 27 November 1979, p. 13.

46 Miss Margaret Peckham to Monsignor David Norris, Letter, 14 February 1969 (AWW HEI/L (b) LLL).

47 See Crichton, *English Catholic Worship*, p. 47; Spurr, *Word in the Desert*, p. 18.

48 See Derek Brewer, 'Liturgy: Need and Frustration', *Theology* 80 (1977), p. 175 and David Martin, 'A Decade On', *PN Review*, 16(6) No 74 (1990), p. 42.

49 Lord Denham, 'Language of the Prayer Book', Letter to the Editor, *The Times*, 7 December, 1977, p. 19.

50 Canon George Austin, Letter to the Editor, *The Times*, 6 December 1979, p. 15.

51 Anthony Radcliffe, 'The Case for the Vernacular', Letter to the Editor, *The Tablet*, 21 August 1965, p. 939.

52 Miss Joan Adams, Correspondence to Mgr F. A. Miles, 1 June 1969 (AWW HEI/L (b) LLL).

53 A. D. J. Grumett, 'The Fallacy of Change', *The Tablet*, 31 January 1970, pp. 113–14.

54 Mrs J. Casey, Correspondence to Cardinal Heenan, 14 February 1970 (AWW HEI/L (b) LLL).

55 Miss Joan Thompson, Correspondence to Cardinal Heenan, 16 November 1970 (AWW HEI/L (b) LLL).

56 For a representative assessment of the reforms, see Dom Edmund Flood, 'The Nature of the Mass', *The Tablet*, 17 May 1975, p. 469.

57 For an example of these confused objectives, see Church of England Commission on Urban Priority areas, 1985, *Faith in the City: A Call to Action by Church and Nation*, London: Church House Publishing, p. 135 which speaks of the need for an 'informal' but 'incarnational' liturgy, and for 'universality of form with local variations'.

58 See Martin, 'Why spit?', p. 3 and subsequently David Martin, 'On Christian Language' in *On Secularization*, p. 173. For recent theological considerations of the analogical, performative function of the traditional (Latin) liturgy, see Catherine Pickstock, 1998, *After Writing: On the Liturgical Consummation of Philosophy*, Oxford: Blackwell; Stratford Caldecott (ed.), 1998, *Beyond the Prosaic: Renewing the Liturgical Movement*, Edinburgh: T&T Clark; Joseph Cardinal Ratzinger, 2000, *The Spirit of the Liturgy*, San Francisco: Ignatius Press; Godfried Cardinal Danneels, 2003, 'Liturgy Forty Years After the Second Vatican Council: High Point or Recession', in Keith F. Pecklers (ed.), *Liturgy in a Postmodern World*, London: Continuum, pp. 7–26, and in a Protestant context, Stanley Hauerwas, 2004, *Performing the Faith: Bonhoeffer and the Practice of Non Violence*, London: SPCK.

59 Ironically, most 8am services and cathedral worship utilize the 1662 BCP liturgy, allowing its re-emergence (almost by default) as the most commonly performed liturgy throughout England, Northern Ireland and Wales.

60 http://www.vatican.va/roman_curia/congregations/ccdds/documents/rc_con_ccdds_doc_20010507_liturgiam-authenticam_en.html – accessed 30.08.06.

61 This has re-animated 'old' discussions about the need for expressive or aesthetic language, the legacy of Vatican II, and most importantly the ecumenical consequences given a great measure of inter-denominational liturgical convergence: see Editorial 'Ancient and Modern', *The Tablet*, 1 July 2006, p. 2; Arthur Roche, 'Search for truth and poetry', *The Tablet*, 5 August 2006, p. 10–11 (Chairman of ICEL); and extensive correspondence under the headings 'Venerate the vernacular', *The Tablet*, 8 July 2006, p. 18; Various correspondents, 'Words that come naturally', *The Tablet*, 19 August 2006, pp. 18–19; 'Words of grace and dignity', *The Tablet*, 26 August 2006, p. 18 and Mgr Kevin McGinnell, 'Suffering in translation', *The Tablet*, 2 September 2006, p. 19 (Chairman of ELLC).

CASE STUDY

Expressions of Authenticity: Music for Worship

IAN JONES, WITH PETER WEBSTER

It is inherently impossible to design a form of worship which will at one and the same time 'attract' the average modern man and provide a framework in which the authentic Christian Gospel can be preached. The one gives the lie to the other.

(Gordon Ireson, *Church Worship and the Non-Churchgoer* (1944))[1]

The last few years have seen a tremendous change in the form of worship in most churches, especially in the realm of praise. Our music has developed so that we can sing about Jesus and what God has done for us in the kind of music we enjoy most.

(Advert in *Buzz* Magazine, February 1975).[2]

Introduction

Written just 31 years apart, the contrasting aesthetic and pastoral assumptions of these two perspectives reflect a revolution in Christian worship taking place since World War Two. In 1944, Gordon Ireson (then missioner for the Anglican Diocese of Exeter) looked to the coming of peace as both an opportunity and a challenge for the church as it sought to reconnect the British people with their Christian roots. This, for Ireson, was more likely to result from a restoration of tried and tested patterns than from a radical revolution in church life and liturgy. This was not least because 'an age so incredibly vulgar that it can turn majestic themes of Mozart and Beethoven into Jazz tunes, and the air of the "Hallelujah Chorus" into "Yes, we have no bananas" is not likely to produce language adequate for the worship of God'.[3] Within 15 to 20 years, however, the musical and liturgical landscape of hymn and Prayer Book, choir and organ familiar to Ireson and his contemporaries would be challenged by new sounds in both 'art' and 'popular' music, and by radically different ideas about the content and conduct of worship. Within 30 years, new orders of service heralded the arrival of a more participative style, while a greater informality in the atmosphere of worship spread even among many otherwise traditional congregations. In music, guitar-led groups were formed and contemporary pop and folk took its place alongside established hymnody. For the contemporary-minded evangelical writers and readers of *Buzz* magazine,[4] these were exciting times: the dead hand of tradition had been thrown off and a younger generation of Christians immersed in the newest pop cultures enabled to worship in language more meaningful to them. However, for those of a more traditionalist disposition, the new styles seemed an abandonment of taste, decency and history.

The divergent views of the two opening quotations reflect something of this heated debate over the style and performance of music for worship taking place within British Christianity since the mid-twentieth century. At root, this debate concerned the locus of authenticity in worship. How was God best to be worshipped through music? Was 'authentic' worship that which engaged the heart of the worshipper, or that which employed the appropriate style of music? If the latter, did authentic worship presuppose particular musical styles, or could a variety of styles be contemplated? Was 'appropriateness' a function of its organic growth out of a longer tradition, or its fidelity to contemporary 'secular' music? Would the Christian message be compromised by adopting contemporary styles or could greater attention to popular culture actually help engage new groups in worship? These were important questions: competing conceptions of worship and preferences in church music generated passion like few other spheres of congregational life in the post-war years.[5]

These were not new questions, of course: concern for authenticity in worship is inherent in the Judaeo-Christian tradition and the Bible.[6] Nevertheless, the later twentieth century saw a new chapter in this debate. The challenging of long-held conventions in the arts and music, a growing emphasis on personal freedom and the erosion of Christian influence in culture and society not only created a new context for thinking about the 'authentic' in worship, but also prompted a reconsideration of what 'authenticity' itself might actually mean. All post-war discussions about what made 'good' music for worship were underpinned by questions about the integrity, propriety or 'fitness' of particular musical styles and their performance. Regardless of theological or ideological differences, these values lie at the heart of what 'authenticity' connotes.[7] This essay therefore explores the different ways in which a concern for the 'authentic' in worship was worked out in discussions of church music in post-war Britain, predominantly within an Anglican context. Centrally, the essay charts a subtle, contested, but crucial, shift away from regarding 'authenticity' as inherent in the music itself, and towards a renewed emphasis on the attitude of the worshipper.

The Meanings of 'Authenticity'

Understanding what 'authenticity' might mean in the context of music for worship requires consideration of three particular areas of thought. The first

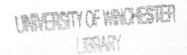

is Christianity's biblical and theological inheritance and the various under-standings of 'true worship' within it. For example, the Pauline exhortation to sing 'in Psalms, hymns and spiritual songs, singing and making melody in your hearts to the Lord'[8] has had a varied exegesis in Christian history, sometimes used to justify the most elaborate choral service, and at other times (such as in Zwingli's Zurich) even to disallow singing entirely. In theological terms, music had the potential to be both an incredibly powerful means of praise and a dangerous source of distraction or corruption.[9]

Second, discussions of 'authenticity' also have a musicological inheritance derived from aesthetics and cultural theory. In some contexts, 'authenticity' may mean faithfulness to the performance styles of a composer's lifetime, or to their original intentions.[10] However, 'authenticity' may also be a tool of critical analysis: music has often been labelled 'authentic' if it conforms to particular stylistic expectations, or embodies something meaningful for (or about) its audience or performer. Ideas of 'authenticity' have also changed over time: influenced by Kant, Hegel and others, mid-twentieth-century musicologists frequently assumed that beauty was an 'intrinsic, objective quality', implying that 'authenticity' could be measured with relative ease according to particular conventions. By the 1990s however, musicologists were far more likely to regard 'authenticity' as subjective, highlighting the power relations implicit in labelling a piece or performance as 'authentic' or 'inauthentic'.[11]

A parallel subjectivization of 'authenticity' has (thirdly) taken place in the realm of ethics and values. Charles Taylor suggests that over the post-war period in particular, a fundamental shift has taken place towards the personal, the interior and the individual as the final source of meaning and self-definition, with a corresponding critique of the ideal of a consensual (therefore externally imposed) public good.[12] Historians concerned with the cultural and religious life of Britain since 1945 have noted a similar trend, variously highlighting a decline in 'living according to the rule',[13] a shift from 'doing the done thing' to 'doing your own thing',[14] or a 'turn inwards' in the locus of moral authority.[15] Nevertheless, as Taylor notes, this 'ethic of authenticity' has by no means achieved universal acceptance – evidenced in the quotations which head this chapter, and by recent media and political debate on the legacy of the 1960s.[16] That this new conception of 'authen-ticity' has, in Taylor's words, both its 'boosters' and its 'knockers' will become clear in the rest of the essay.[17]

Choosing Music for Worship: Cultural and Religious Conventions

The early to mid-twentieth century saw the emergence of a loose consensus between influential writers and musicians on the style, performing stan-dards, and quality of music for church.[18] In hymnody, a wealth of cherished eighteenth- and nineteenth-century material was further enhanced by the addition of new work – notably the *English Hymnal* of 1906. Its musical editor, Ralph Vaughan Williams, was one of a growing number of respected composers who (since Stanford) had begun to devote serious attention to church music. Although topics of contention still existed, many church music professionals and interested amateurs nevertheless perceived themselves to be part of a stable, slowly evolving and progressively more refined tradition: as Erik Routley later reflected, 'On Christmas Day 1955, some of us thought we had Church music pretty well where we wanted it.'[19] 'Church Music' was widely understood as a recognizable genre with its own canon of greats and loose criteria for selection.[20]

For many among the English church music establishment of the 1940s and 1950s, implicit or explicit 'authenticity' meant faithfulness to these standards and expectations. Four underlying assumptions seemed particularly common: first, that church music should elevate the tastes and spirits of worshippers; second, that it would be of sufficient compositional quality; third, that it would be consonant with the longer church music tradition; and fourth, that church music should have no obviously 'worldly' connotations, reflecting the prevailing understanding that a sharp dividing line between 'sacred' and 'secular' spheres.[21] The widespread acceptance of these paradigms is graphically demonstrated in 'establishment' reactions to Geoffrey Beaumont's *Folk Mass* (1956) which, in drawing heavily on the dance and light music of the 1920s and 30s, arguably presented the first major and popular challenge to the conventions of the day.[22] Critics rounded on the *Mass* for pandering to a lowest common denominator and thus failing to lift its hearers to 'learned' conceptions of taste. For the editor of *English Church Music*, the piece, though well-intentioned, was part of a tendency 'to underrate the capacity of ordinary, humble people to think and feel finely'.[23] (As Robert Hewison has noted, the transformative potential of 'common culture' was a powerful ideal in the mid-twentieth century, but commonly with the assumption that 'common culture' meant 'western European high culture'.[24]) Second, critics fixed on what they regarded as the low compositional standards of the *Folk Mass*. One scathing editorial in *Musical Opinion* found the piece composed 'almost entirely of clichés, which does not contain one original idea from start to finish'. By contrast, the review continued, 'Modern compositions must by their musical merit and gravity be worthy of the liturgical functions'.[25]

Third, critics found the *Folk Mass* wanting in its disregard for the wider Anglican musical tradition. Mid-twentieth-century discussions of church music often displayed a strong consciousness of drawing upon a distinguished national heritage. This did not demand mere imitation, but did assume a rootedness in the work of great English church composers past.[26] By (wrongly) labelling the work a 'jazz mass', its critics found it easier to discount the work on the grounds that it did not arise from the European classical tradition from which church music traditionally drew its repertoire. Finally, many establishment voices were critical of the *Folk Mass* lest it lead people 'to despise a religion which thinks to ensnare them by decking its services with the trappings of the dance hall and variety stage'.[27] This notion that the forms and styles of Christian worship were necessarily antithetical to popular culture was a prominent feature of the 1940s and 1950s. In his much-reprinted 1948 book *The Anglican Way*, the Revd Verney Johnstone (then Director of Religious Education for the Diocese of Newcastle) reminded readers that, 'Anglican worship stands in sharp contrast to all that is "popular" and "cheap" in modern life . . . and we have to wage a constant battle against the infiltration of such "cheapness" into our services'.[28] As John Connell and Chris Gibson have argued, claims of 'authenticity' in music have often been related to music's relationship with its context, or based on 'attempts to embed music in place'.[29] The capacity to create an atmosphere conducive to (or 'fitting' for) worship was therefore a key strand of debate over new musical styles.

General agreement on what constituted 'good taste' in music was probably always more an aspiration of 'respectable' and 'expert' opinion than a reality. Nevertheless, the controversy over the Beaumont *Folk Mass* demonstrated that that by the mid-1950s, even the *ideal* of a general public consensus on musical taste was beginning to be questioned. The challenge came from two very different quarters: from the arrival of rock'n'roll (associated with the youth sub-cultures of the 1950s and 60s) and from new directions in the world of 'art music' (notably the 'avant-garde' of Cage, Boulez and Stockhausen).[30] Both forms, in different ways, challenged the prevailing Romantic conceptions of beauty and taste. However, both also extended the Romantic ideal of artistic freedom as the wellspring of creativity, emphasizing expression and experience as the touchstones of 'authenticity'. In this light, musical canons and conventions of all kinds were increasingly viewed with suspicion. The resulting change of tone was graphically illustrated in the difference between the 1951 Archbishops' Commission report *Music in Church* and its 1992 successor *In Tune with Heaven*. While the former implicitly assumed the pre-eminence of the Western classical tradition, the latter concluded that to ask, 'what is good art . . . painting . . . sculpture . . . poetry . . . music?' was 'the least satisfactory discussion in connection with any art form' and that ultimately, 'judgement depends primarily on personal taste'. Indeed, 'Who dare presume to describe the aesthetic tastes of the Almighty?' Even the phrase 'church music' – widely considered a recognizable genre forty years previously – was placed in quotation marks by the 1992 report's authors.[31] The notion that 'authenticity' might derive from faithfulness to a distinct 'church' style was by this time increasingly difficult to assert unchallenged.

Performing Music for Worship: Popular Culture and Self-Expression

Defining artistic 'authenticity' as individual expression rather than imitation was not a new idea in the late twentieth century. Nevertheless, technological change, increased social freedom, acceptance of cultural pluralism and a renewed suspicion of 'authorities' created strikingly propitious conditions for a shift towards viewing self-expression as the primary locus of 'authenticity' in the post-war period. What did this mean for church music? A helpful case study is found in the rise of a new style of charismatic and evangelical worship. Revivalist Christianity has a long history of adapting contemporary tunes for worship, and charismatic and evangelical Christians in the 1960s also began to see the potential of the new rock and pop styles in worship and mission.[32] While many existing churchgoers were happy with the existing style of public worship, others found it old-fashioned, dull and distant from everyday life.[33] Whereas the growing and cautiously confident churches of the post-war period were largely able to insist that this distance was the fault of contemporary culture rather than the church, and thus leave change in worship to a longer evolutionary process, the crisis experienced by many congregations from the late 1950s to the early 1970s appeared to demand more radical solutions. 'The church must move with the times', as the popular dictum of the day put it. One element of the charismatic and evangelical response to this situation was to seek words and music for worship that reflected popular styles.

While criticized as driven by fashion or 'gimmicks',[34] much of the new wave of experimentation was motivated by a search for a musical language that was sensitive to the experience of the person in the street and the musical worlds they inhabited. This was important if the growing gap between church and contemporary culture was to be closed, but it also reflected a wider shift in the meaning of 'authenticity' itself, as a quality residing less in the music *per se* and more in the sincerity of the individual worshipper. Besides changing the music itself, early charismatic leaders also sought a more participatory approach to church music not solely reliant upon office-holders or salaried professionals. Alongside or in place of the organ, instrumental groups were frequently formed (by 1988 an estimated fifth of all Anglican congregations had one).[35] While many of these were technically proficient, sincerity was frequently prized over technical ability. A greater sense of personal freedom was also evident in encouragements to bodily movement, a loosening or abandonment of set liturgy,[36] and a simpler, vernacular (though biblically grounded) style. As Jeremy Begbie, James Steven and others have noted, the 1970s and 1980s saw an increasing volume of songs conceiving praise and worship of God as a highly personalized, intimate experience.[37] Where *Youth Praise* contained a strong missiological dimension, *Sound of Living Waters* gave increased prominence to the gathering of believers for worship. This idea became even more prominent in the *Songs of Fellowship* collections, in which a number of songs set worship within a place of safety and refuge away from the danger and corruption of 'the world'.[38] Arguably the emphasis on the personally meaningful in worship has been further extended in the more interior, open-ended approach of 'alternative worship' services growing in popularity from the early 1990s, many of which (significantly) eschew congregational singing altogether in favour of individual reflection.[39]

This foregrounding of 'authenticity as personal sincerity' in charismatic and post-charismatic worship may reflect two much wider shifts in the religious and cultural life over the post-war period: first, a renegotiation of the boundaries between private opinion and public consensus. To sing the more objective doctrinal or credal statements of much traditional hymnody arguably represented a public consent to official religion. On the other hand, the more subjective and experiential nature of many contemporary praise and worship songs allowed more scope for the 'private' to inform the 'public'. Second, the concern for sincerity in worship arguably reflected the fact that Sunday church was increasingly the domain of a smaller band of individually committed believers rather than a wider cross-section of the devout, the half-believer and the outwardly conformist sceptic.

While the popularity of the praise and worship song reflected a genuine tendency towards interiority and expressivity in late twentieth-century charismatic and evangelical worship,[40] it was not the only trend. Evangelical song-writers also championed the renewed use of 'scripture in song', delved into an older hymn tradition and wrote prolifically of transcendence, social justice, prophecy and eschatology.[41] In so doing, they were to produce music quite different from the intimate, highly-personalized worship song. Leading exponents of the genre, such as Graham Kendrick, even warned explicitly of the dangers of 'spiritual self-gratification'.[42] Nor may 'authenticity' necessarily imply *individualized* expressivity in evangelical worship: Pete Ward notes how recordings of worship songs have established certain performance styles as definitive,[43] while the 'alternative worship'/'emerging church' movement moderates individualizing tendencies with a strong emphasis on community.

Nor has the emphasis on personal authenticity in worship been confined to evangelicalism: active participation in worship and accessible language have become more common across almost the whole spectrum of Christian worship. In Roman Catholicism, for example, the flowering of the liturgical movement in the early twentieth century and the subsequent encouragement of the Second Vatican Council from the early 1960s helped to ensure that congregational singing and formal liturgical participation became a regular feature of worship in most parishes. The speed of the transition was all the more remarkable given the lack of a strong tradition of congregational singing in English Catholicism – although some remained to be convinced.[44] Across denominational and stylistic boundaries, the late twentieth-century emphasis on participation and accessibility in worship arguably reflected a much wider partial deregulation of the worship space (for example, a widespread rejection of the early twentieth-century tendency to see hushed concentration in church as the epitome of 'reverence';[45] the decline of 'Sunday best' clothes, and a greater informality of behaviour in church).

Locating Music for Worship: Folk, Pop and World Music

While the adoption of 'pop'-influenced music has perhaps been the dominant trend, a highly significant counter-trend has been the supplementing of the established hymn, organ and choral corpus with a variety of other sources to create worship more authentically 'of the people'. Far from foregrounding the interior in worship, this movement has, in sharp contrast, placed the locus of authenticity just as firmly in the music itself as did the church musicians of the 1940s and 1950s. The rift between 'pop' and 'the popular' has been among the most prominent fault-lines for the discussion of 'authenticity' in music in the twentieth century. Influentially, the Frankfurt School cultural theorist Theodor Adorno insisted that, far from being genuinely 'of the people', 'pop music' was merely the product of a mass-produced, standardized 'culture industry' cynically manipulating the tastes and desires of the people.[46] This strong distaste for 'pop' culture as inauthentic was shared (albeit on different grounds) by a range of twentieth-century British cultural commentators from F. R. Leavis to Richard Hoggart.[47] The accusation that pop's commercial origins and 'lowest-common-denominator' approach made it an inauthentic vehicle for worship attracted some support from 'establishment' commentators on church music in the period.[48] However, this did not prevent church musicians and liturgists of more traditional preferences searching for an authentically 'popular' church music style.[49] For A. G. Hebert, modern art had effected a 'divorce between art and the people' but 'as Christian worship is the worship of the Body, its forms of music and ceremonial must be such that the people can make them their own'.[50] Here, Hebert's convictions reflected a wider awareness by the mid-twentieth century that the church's music was failing to engage with the mass of the population. In 1958, Charles Cleall, respected church musician and writer of the 'Master of the Choir' column in *Musical Opinion*, voiced his concerns about church music 'indistinguishable from that of "Saturday Night on the Light [Programme]" . . . ' but also criticized 'scholarly' hymn books of 'good music, fine poetry and splendid engraving; aesthetically unexceptionable, but so free from red blood that nobody wants to use them'.[51]

Cleall's own answer to this conundrum was to dig deeper into the plainsong tradition and combine this with the best-loved 'poignant airs' from a variety of sources from Bach to Sankey.[52] For others, such as the hymnwriter Sydney Carter and the Iona Community's Wild Goose Worship

Group, the future lay rather with *folk* music as an apparently more 'authentic' source of inspiration than pop.[53] For Erik Routley, generally an enthusiastic supporter of the development, 'what folk songs can do – as jazz and pop at present cannot – is reflect faithfully and precisely the prevailing mood of a culture'.[54] In Roman Catholicism, the use of vernacular music was given a particular spur by the Second Vatican Council, in particular in *Sacrosanctum Concilium* (1963) and the post-conciliar *Musicam Sacram* (1967). Although little of what was produced arose directly from an English folk heritage, influential early collections such as Malcolm Stewart's *Gospel Songbook* (1967) introduced Catholic congregations to a variety of new music from Sydney Carter to American folk and Negro Spirituals.[55] Though there were some misgivings (in 1969, the Catholic lay group *Unitas* publicly denounced the practice of 'mini-skirted girls . . . in front of microphones singing pop tunes whilst the Mass is going on'),[56] the uptake of folk music for the Mass appears to have been strong: one 1976 survey of the Roman Catholic Diocese of Portsmouth found a third of parishes already using a folk mass setting.[57] A similar pattern appears to have continued to the beginning of the twenty-first century, with folk and contemporary music remaining widely used despite criticism of the post-Vatican II liturgical agenda in some quarters.

With the increased ease of global exchange in the late-twentieth century, a final important development was the growth of interest in the music of African, Asian and Latin American Christianity alongside that of folk-style music from the British Isles. Among the most prodigious collectors of such songs have been the Iona Community's Wild Goose Worship Group,[58] though this represented just part of a wider assimilation of 'world church' songs into denominationally produced hymnals.[59] Although these largely resisted the temptation to fetishize 'world music' as somehow more 'authentic' than Western pop,[60] it is nevertheless interesting that Western church musicians have tended to champion *either* folk style *or* pop style music from the Global South. Enabling a general exposure to non-Western worship traditions has not therefore been the sole criterion by which new music from overseas has been selected. Nor has the use of folk or world church songs always simply been a matter of musical preference: use of an Iona songbook may be just as much an indicator of congregational style and outlook as using the *Spring Harvest* songbook or *Hymns Old and New*.[61] Rather than growing 'naturally' out of the communities which sing it, folk music is now a *style* of hymn-writing; one commodity within an increasingly globalized field of musical options.[62] This is not to deny it either musical merit or devotional value, but simply to recognize that in the pluralized, fragmentary musical sphere of the early twenty-first century, the 'authenticity' of any church music style cannot be ascribed unproblematically.

Conclusion

Though in fact a very old question, the post-war period saw a new chapter in the debate over what constituted the 'authentic' in church music. A significant renegotiation of values in religion, culture, society and musicology saw the balance of opinion shift *away* from locating musical authenticity within the music itself or in external conventions on its selection, and *towards* a greater sense of 'authenticity' as deriving from the individual or subjective. However, if this was the dominant trend, we should not only acknowledge the developments which did not fit this pattern, but also the extent to which the meaning of 'authenticity' in church music was also viewed in radically different ways. As we have seen, the pursuit of the 'authentic' could sometimes lead church musicians to reject the personal, the expressive and the contemporary, in favour of a variety of other, older sources.

Our understanding of twentieth-century worship may be helped by a careful disentangling of the variety of concerns enwrapped in the concept of 'authenticity': how should different elements of the Christian theological inheritance be weighted in the choosing of music for worship? Is mass consumer culture unacceptable for worship, or should the churches seek to connect with contemporary musical culture and, by so doing, redeem it? Does the power and value of music lie in its inherent compositional qualities (however defined) or in the ear of the beholder? How important is faithfulness to national or denominational tradition? What functions should music play in worship – to attract, uplift or both? And how does a redrawing of the boundaries between 'sacred' and 'secular' spheres affect the ways in which certain styles of music are considered? If a concern for the 'authentic' is indeed central to the story of religion in post-war Britain, tracing the different responses to these questions since the mid-twentieth century is surely an important element in understanding its significance for the life and worship of the Christian churches.

Notes

1 Gordon W. Ireson, 1944, *Church Worship and the Non-Churchgoer: A Handbook for Clergy and Teachers*, London: SPCK/National Society, p. 5.

2 'With my Hands Lifted Up: Scripture Songs' [Advertisement] in *Buzz* Magazine, February 1975, p. 19.

3 Ireson, *Church Worship*, p. 62.

4 Stemming from the Jesus Movement, and sponsored by Music Gospel Outreach from 1965, *Buzz* sold over 30,000 copies monthly at its height in the 1970s, appealing to a mostly young, charismatic and evangelical audience. For more on the magazine, see Tony Jasper, 1984, *Jesus and the Christian in a Pop Culture*, London: Robert Royce, pp. 160–62; and Pete Ward, 1996, *Growing Up Evangelical: Youthwork and the Making of a Subculture*, London: SPCK, pp. 89–94.

5 Ian Jones, 2000, 'The "Mainstream" Churches in Birmingham, c. 1945–1998: The Local Church and Generational Change', University of Birmingham PhD Thesis, pp. 248–62.

6 Contrast Colossians 3.16 and Ephesians 5.19. For an example of such disputes, see: Peter Webster, 2001, 'The Relationship between Religious Thought and the Theory and Practice of Church Music in England, c. 1603–c. 1640', University of Sheffield PhD Thesis, pp. 43–56.

7 'Authenticity' in David Beard and Kenneth Gloag, 2005, *Musicology: the Key Concepts*. London: Routledge, pp. 17–20.

8 Ephesians 5.19.

9 Webster, 'Religious Thought and the Theory and Practice of Church Music', pp. 43–56 and 68–71.

10 See Peter Kivy, 1995, *Authenticities: Philosophical Reflections on Musical Performance*, Ithaca and London: Cornell University Press, pp. 1–7 and Harry Haskell, 1988, *The Early Music Revival: A History*, London: Thames and Hudson, in particular pp. 175–88 on historically informed performance practice.

11 Beard and Gloag, *Musicology*, pp. 17–20.

12 Taylor, *Ethics of Authenticity*, p. 29.

13 Frank Mort, 'Symbolic Fathers and Sons in Post-War Britain', *Journal of British Studies* 38 (1999), 353–84, p. 364.

14 Elizabeth Roberts, 1995, *Women and Families: An Oral History, 1940–1970*, Oxford: Blackwell, p. 14.

15 Gerald Parsons, 1993, 'Between Law and Licence: Christianity, Morality and "Permissiveness"', in Gerald Parsons (ed.), *The Growth of Religious Diversity: Britain from 1945 vol. II: Issues*, London: Open University/Routledge, pp. 233–63, at p. 236.

16 Dominic Sandbrook, 2005, *Never Had It So Good: A History of Britain from Suez to the Beatles*, London: Little Brown, pp. xiii–xv.

17 Taylor, *Authenticity*, pp. 13–23.

18 For more on this consensus, see Ian Jones and Peter Webster, 'Anglican "Establishment" Reactions to "Pop" Church Music in England, c. 1956–1990', in Kate Cooper and Jeremy Gregory (eds), *Elite and Popular Religion: Studies in Church History* 42 (2006), 429–41.

19 Erik Routley, 1964, *Twentieth Century Church Music*, London: Herbert Jenkins, p. 151.

20 For historical background, see William J. Gatens, 1986, *Victorian Cathedral Music in Theory and Practice*, Cambridge: Cambridge University Press, pp. 60–5.

21 Many of these values are exemplified in Church of England, 1951, *Music in Church: a Report of the Committee Appointed in 1948 by the Archbishops of Canterbury and York*, London: Church Information Bureau.

22 For more on attitudes to the Beaumont *Folk Mass*, see Jones and Webster, 'Anglican "Establishment"'.

23 'Editorial', *English Church Music* 28 (1) 1958, pp. 1–3.

24 Robert Hewison, 1981, *In Anger: Culture in the Cold War, 1945–60*, London: Weidenfield and Nicholson, pp. 177–81. This approach is epitomized in T. S. Eliot's influential writings on culture – for example T. S. Eliot, 1939, *The Idea of a Christian Society*, London: Faber & Faber, pp. 39–42.

25 Editorial 'From Minerva House', *Musical Opinion* 963 (December 1957), pp. 149–50.

26 Thus the music of Vaughan Williams, Britten and Howells, though new and sometimes daring, each displayed a (conscious) debt to an older English choral tradition, and were quickly accepted into the canon. A parallel concern for consonance with tradition can also be seen within Catholicism about the revival of plainsong – see John Ainslie,

1979, 'English Liturgical Music before Vatican II' in Crichton (ed.), *English Catholic Worship*, pp. 47–59.

27 *English Church Music* 28 (1) (1958), pp. 1–3.

28 Verney Johnstone, 7th impression 1956 [1948], *The Anglican Way: A Plain Guide for the Intelligent Layman*, London: Mowbray, p. 75.

29 John Connell and Chris Gibson, 2003, *Soundtracks: Popular Music, Identity and Place*, London: Routledge, p. 19.

30 These twin themes were addressed explicitly by W. Greenhouse Allt, 'The Presidential Address', *Quarterly Record of the Incorporated Association of Organists* xliii (October 1957), pp. 5–6.

31 Church of England, 1993, *In Tune with Heaven: The Report of the Archbishop's Commission on Church Music*, London: Church House Publishing, pp. 67–8.

32 Peter Webster and Ian Jones, forthcoming 2007, 'New Music and the "Evangelical Style" in the Church of England, 1958–1991' in Mark Smith and Steve Holmes (eds), *British Evangelical Identities* 2 vols, Carlisle: Paternoster Press.

33 For churchgoers' and non-churchgoers' attitudes in one neighbourhood of Birmingham, see: K. A. Busia, 1966, *Urban Churches in Britain: A Question of Relevance*, London: Lutterworth Press, pp. 105–10.

34 See: Lionel Dakers, 1995, *Places Where They Sing: Memoirs of a Church Musician*, Norwich: Canterbury Press, p. 207; and also Dakers, 2000, *Beauty Beyond Words: Enriching Worship through Music*, Norwich: Canterbury Press, p. 138.

35 *In Tune with Heaven*, p. 274.

36 Although of course charismatic worship retains a strong informal script of its own – see Church of England, 1981, *The Charismatic Movement in the Church of England*, London: CIO, pp. 35–7.

37 See James H. S. Steven, 2002, *Worship in the Spirit: Charismatic Worship in the Church of England*, Carlisle: Paternoster Press, pp. 118–26 on intimacy as key goal in contemporary charismatic worship.

38 Ward, *Growing Up Evangelical*, pp. 118, 128–30, 138–9. An analysis of the songs written since 1980 and included in the *Songs of Fellowship* collections suggests that whereas in Volume 1 (1991) songs using the first-person singular and the first-person plural were roughly even in number, 'I'/'me' language predominates much more heavily in Volume 2 (1998) and outnumbers 'we'/'us' songs by more than 2:1 in Volume 3 (2003). *Songs of Fellowship* Volumes 1 (1991), 2 (1998) and 3 (2003), Eastbourne: Kingsway.

39 See the more open-ended approach to worship in two influential handbooks: Mike Riddell, Mark Pierson and Cathy Kirkpatrick, 2000, *The Prodigal Project: Journey into the Emerging Church*, London: SPCK; Jonny Baker and Doug Gay with Jenny Brown (compilers), 2003, *Alternative Worship*, London: SPCK.

40 Martyn Percy, 1996, *Words, Wonders and Power: Understanding Contemporary Christian Fundamentalism and Revivalism*, London: SPCK.

41 For an early examples of 'scripture in song' see: 'I will enter his gates with Thanksgiving in my Heart' (Leona von Brethorst, 1976) and 'Therefore the Redeemed of the Lord' (Ruth Lake, 1972) in *Songs of Fellowship*, Vol. 1. For a renewed interest in older hymnody see (for instance) Graham Kendrick's 2001 reworking of 'Rock of Ages' in *Songs of Fellowship*, Vol. 3. For social justice see Kendrick's 'Beauty for Brokenness' (1993) and for a focus on the prophetic and eschatological in contemporary song-writing see Robin Mark's 'These are the Days of Elijah' (1997), both in *Songs of Fellowship*, Vol. 2.

42 Graham Kendrick, 1984, *Worship*, London: Kingsway, p. 31.

43 Pete Ward, 'Worship and Mediated Religious Culture' (paper given to the Study Group on Christianity and History symposium on 'Worship', 19 November 2005). See also: Pete Ward, 2005, *Selling Worship: How What we Sing has Changed the Church*,

Milton Keynes: Paternoster Press. This emphasis on the worship leader and the use of modern technology in worship has paradoxically placed worship back into the hands of 'experts'; the very thing the early charismatic movement wished to avoid.

44 See Nicholas Kenyon, 1980, 'Worship', in John Cumming and Paul Burns (eds), *The Church Now: An Inquiry into the Present State of the Catholic Church in Britain and Ireland*, Dublin: Gill & Macmillan, pp. 83–8.

45 For which see: S. J. D. Green, 1996, *Religion in the Age of Decline: Organisation and Experience in Industrial Yorkshire, 1870–1920*, Cambridge: Cambridge University Press, pp. 293–324.

46 Theodor Adorno, 'On Popular Music' (first published, 1941) reprinted in Simon Frith and Andrew Godwin (eds), 1990, *On Record: Rock, Pop and the Written Word*, London and New York: Routledge, pp. 301–14.

47 Richard Middleton, 2001, 'Pop, Rock and Interpretation', in Simon Frith, Will Straw and John Street (eds), *The Cambridge Companion to Pop and Rock*, Cambridge: Cambridge University Press, p. 214.

48 For more, see: Jones and Webster, 'Anglican "Establishment"', pp. 429, 433–4.

49 Iain Chambers, 1985, *Urban Rhythms: Pop Music and Popular Culture*, Basingstoke: Macmillan, p. 7.

50 A. G. Hebert, 1935, *Liturgy and Society: The Function of the Church in the Modern World*, London: Faber & Faber, pp. 241, 212. Compare the popularity of hymns in the nineteenth century: John Wolffe, 1997, '"Praise to the Holiest in the Height": Hymns and Church Music', in John Wolffe (ed.), *Religion in Victorian Britain, Vol. V: Culture and Empire*, Manchester: Open University/Manchester University Press, pp. 59–99.

51 Charles Cleall, 'The Master of the Choir', *Musical Opinion* 986, November 1959, pp. 120–21.

52 Charles Cleall, 1960, *Sixty Songs from Sankey, Newly Presented for Voices by Charles Cleall*, London: Marshall, Morgan and Scott.

53 Following in the footsteps of an earlier generation such as Vaughan Williams and Martin Shaw – see Nicholas Temperley, 1979, *The Music of the English Parish Church*, Cambridge: Cambridge University Press, Vol. I, pp. 322–5; 333–4 and Ralph Vaughan Williams, 1934, *National Music*, London: Oxford University Press.

54 Erik Routley, 1969, *Words, Music and the Church*, London: Herbert Jenkins, p. 125

55 Malcolm Stewart (comp.), 1967, *Gospel Song Book*, London: Geoffrey Chapman; Hubert J. Richards (comp.), 1969, *Forty Gospel Songs*, London: Geoffrey Chapman; and Hubert J. Richards and Alan Dale, 1969, *Ten Gospel Songs*, London: Geoffrey Chapman.

56 Statement in response to the resignation of Brian Houghton, parish priest of Bury St Edmunds, in the wake of the replacement of the Latin Mass with English – 'Laity Share Distress', *The Times*, 5 August 1969, p. 4.

57 Ainslie, 'English Liturgical Music', p. 103

58 See, for example: John Bell (ed. and arr.), 1990, *Many and Great: Songs of the World Church*, Glasgow: Wild Goose Publications.

59 Janet Wootton, 2003, 'The Future of the Hymn', in Stephen Darlington and Alan Kreider (eds), *Composing Music for Worship*, Norwich: Canterbury Press, pp. 137–9.

60 For debates about 'authenticity' and 'world music' in the wider music industry, see: Connell and Gibson, *Soundtracks*, pp. 156–7; David Looseley, 2003, *Popular Music in Contemporary France: Authenticity, Politics, Debate*, Oxford: Berg, p. 50.

61 See Pete Ward, 1997, 'The Tribes of Evangelicalism', in Graham Cray *et al.*, *The Post-Evangelical Debate*, London: SPCK/Triangle, pp. 19–34.

62 For the disembedding, re-embedding and hybridization of religious practice within a global society, see: Simon Coleman and Peter Collins (eds), 2004, *Religion, Identity and Change: Perspectives on Global Transformations*, Aldershot: Ashgate, pp. 1–13.

Reconceiving the Congregation as a Source of Authenticity

MATHEW GUEST

The Changing Status of the Congregation

The congregation remains the axis of collective identity for most practising Christians. Yet its most obvious and predictable feature is that of decline, and those concerned with charting the secularization of modern Britain have generally referred to the shrinking size of local congregations as an index of changing cultural orientations towards institutional Christianity and all that it stands for. Indeed, claims that religion in Britain may be characterized by a tendency to 'believe' rather than 'belong' suggest we need to look beyond the traditional congregation, and instead to dispersed networks, spiritual outlets and religion on the level of the individual. The centre of gravity has shifted, and with it the dominant orientation to religion, from a form of social engagement focused on commitment to a bounded community, to a form of consumption, focused on individual needs which may change over time. According to this analysis, the congregation is at best a social relic, gradually but inevitably disappearing from the cultural landscape. To be sure, a faithful few continue to follow a traditional model, which conceives the parish church as the focus for the spiritual identity of the local community, and the priest as father, intercessor, moral advisor, and guardian of local civic interests. As Tim Jenkins' insightful study of the country church in Comberton, Cambridgeshire demonstrates, this may now equate to a past ideal rather than a present reality. But if this is so, the ideal has not entirely evaporated.[1] For many British people, however – especially in urban and suburban areas – churches are seen as marginal to public life, their pastoral functions in particular replaced by schools, the health service and friendship networks.

And yet, despite this, there appears to be room for a new sort of congregation which caters to the needs affirmed by individuals. If religion has become less about obligation and more about choice, there is no reason why congregational involvement should not be a part of that choice, and indeed, it appears to be so for many British people. Moreover, while falling levels of

regular church attendance invite arguments for secularization, this phenomenon can be alternatively theorized in terms of the problem of 'associational
disconnection'.[2] This is the argument that in a modernizing society, fewer of
its citizens tend to be formal, actively participating members of organizations. This is reflected in falling levels of membership among trade unions
and political parties, and in levels of participation in leisure activities requiring individuals to gather together on a regular basis.[3] On this understanding,
church decline indicates not declining Christian belief as such, but a lack of
trust or interest in institutions and forms of communal activity generally.

If this argument is to be believed, then the status of congregations becomes
an interesting question indeed, a barometer of cultural change rather than
the death-knell of Christian Britain. While traditional congregations gradually slip off the statistical scale, we need to consider whether more creative,
dynamic forms of collective engagement are taking their place, perhaps
offering a more culturally authentic option for the post-traditional, late-
modern seeker. The weekly service and coffee morning give way to the cell,
network, festival, and parachurch, often defined by participation rather than
membership as such. Here I refer to what sociologist David Lyon calls
'deregulation',[4] the notion that, in contemporary, late-modern society,
religion has become less rigid, less constrained, and freer to occupy novel
spaces and take on new forms. The Christian congregation has not been side-
lined in favour of this more modish form of engagement; rather, it is being
rethought and reconfigured in light of it. As Christianity itself has become
more deregulated, so those who consider themselves to be within its boundaries – and perhaps, especially, those at its very margins – venture a rethinking of the nature of the congregation: its purpose, structure, remit, and social
form as a manifestation of Christian fellowship in the contemporary world.
This case study considers some of the different ways in which congregations
have evolved in recent times as *loci* of authenticity, and reflects on the
emerging implications for Christian identity.

The Congregation as a Source of Authenticity

In the post-war period, British congregations have emerged as sites of both
continuity and innovation. The parish structure of the Church of England, for
example, has ensured that the role of the church as a focus for local identity,
while now more tenuous, is at least maintained through the architectural
presence of parish churches and the nostalgic attachment to them felt by some
parishioners. In recent years, an alternative model of the congregation has
gained ascendancy, one often referred to as the 'gathered congregation'.
According to this understanding, a church does not cater to those within its
parish boundaries, but to those who consciously make an explicit and active
commitment to the life of the congregation. This model has become most

visibly applied in large city-centre churches which attract congregants from a wide geographical radius. These are often evangelical congregations that foster high expectations with respect to lay involvement in church life, and it is not unusual for members to extend their practical commitment well beyond Sunday services. When this model of church life prevails, the congregation becomes the centre of a complex network of activities that has its own discourse and rules of engagement. Perhaps more importantly, these churches offer a supportive and extensive community of like-minded associates, a context for the transmission of common values, and opportunities for authority and empowerment consonant with one's own organizational, pastoral or pedagogical skills. Organizational structure is also matched by a concern for moral order, which partly explains an appeal to young families in a culture in which models of ethical prescription are increasingly elusive and unfashionable. Congregations like this are not restricted to the evangelical wing of the church, although they are arguably typical of it. The strong relationships between church and people that pertain in some Roman Catholic congregations can follow a similar model, although an institutionalized reticence towards affirming lay leadership means such support networks may not always be as enduring or as practically effective. When they are, these are channels for the nurturing of a sense of authenticity grounded in leadership and service – Christian legitimacy affirmed on the basis of one's active contribution to the moral and spiritual life of the collective.

While evangelicals have demonstrated a degree of pragmatic entrepreneurialism, they rarely enjoy the social and financial capital required to establish a material presence in local communities that is entirely independent from existing church structures. The British cultural landscape lacks the all-important voluntarism of the USA and the associations of grass-roots empowerment that go with it (not to mention the abundance of land and comparatively low cost of real estate). This has implications for many of those on the margins of church culture, who seek to challenge traditional conceptions of the congregation. For example, many of the most innovative church projects caught within the Church of England's 'fresh expressions' initiative – aimed at fostering 'different ways of being church in a changing culture'[5] – depend upon nearby parish churches for premises, leadership and funding. While sometimes akin in style and ambition to the Calvary-inspired 'new paradigm' churches of the USA – combining relaxed worship and informality with a zeal for mission and Biblicism[6] – they rarely achieve comparable levels of membership or sustained momentum at the popular level.

However, such initiatives mark a continued attempt to rethink the congregation as a collective experience, one whose value is often measured by its cultural engagement. A pioneering exemplar here was Sheffield's Nine O'Clock Service (NOS), which until its collapse amid scandal in 1995 combined charismatic evangelicalism with a conviction that the church can only have meaning for young people when it embodies their own 'culture'. In practice, this involved the use of contemporary dance music in multi-media services, a positive affirmation of the fashions of youth subculture, and the celebration of the Christian message both in nightclubs and using the stylized media popularized in those contexts. The material expression of a shared Christianity was further distinguished by a commitment to environmental ethics and social justice, and the mainstream church's detachment from contemporary culture was presented as indicative of its moribund future. Its appeal to a dispersed 'culture' was formally recognized by the Anglican Church, when NOS was acknowledged as the Church of England's first 'Extra Parochial Place'.

NOS was radical and inspirational to many, and while no groups have subsequently managed to emulate its attendance levels,[7] numerous initiatives have embraced a similar openness to rethinking church and many have adopted its conviction that authenticity is grounded in the extent to which a church is in tune with contemporary culture. One example is 'moot', a so-called 'emerging church' which is attached to St Matthew's Church, Westminster.[8] Moot focuses on fostering community in a variety of ways, including links with London-based artists, small group Bible study, and multi-media worship. In so doing, it combines elements of the large-scale gathered congregation with a commitment to enculturation, to the need to 'be real' if one is to be true to one's self and Christian at the same time. This builds on an evangelical tradition of separating faith from culture, only to fuse them again in a kind of postmodern take on identity, fostering a creative reconfiguration of Christian selfhood alongside a positive orientation to social engagement. Moreover, in its commitment to the artistic and cultural life of its immediate locality, moot reflects something of the more traditional parish understanding of congregational life. The emphasis here, though, is on recognizing cultural particularity and shaping congregational identity in response to it, rather than serving the community through a model of worship and pastoral care that is pre-defined and unchanging.

This approach to congregational life is not without its critics, among them the historian Edward Norman who as long ago as 1978 warned that the church was placing a misguided emphasis upon being 'relevant' at the expense of paying attention to 'eternal truths'.[9] Concerns were also expressed from non-confessional quarters, with the sociologist Bryan Wilson voicing his misgivings about liturgical experimentation on the grounds that it signals a search for exciting experiences which indirectly detach conveyers of solemn meaning from their original and proper reference points.[10] Common to both critics is an underlying assumption that authenticity is grounded in continuity of tradition, something implicitly – and sometimes explicitly – challenged by those spiritual entrepreneurs who wish to steer the congregation into new realms of possibility.

Informing this shift in perceptions is a sense, as Philip Richter puts it, that 'denominational labels have become less significant to churchgoers than shared Christian (counter-cultural) identity'.[11] With congregations to some extent catering to a generic Christian identity the question arises as to how this identity is defined and how it is made manifest in the life of local churches and chapels. We might also ask whether the quest to be 'authentically Christian' has become a more pressing concern for those who see their identities as under threat from a secularizing society, one response being to accentuate difference between themselves and British culture, or between themselves and the 'inauthentic', 'lukewarm' Christianity of the 'mainstream'. One striking example would be the Church of England's Reform group – originally established in opposition to women's ordination but remaining a traditionalist voice on a wide range of issues. Reform enjoys some success as a network-based lobbying group, and its voice was heard in the protest against the appointment of Jeffrey John as Bishop of Reading when several affluent parishes threatened to withhold their diocesan contribution on account of his living in a homosexual relationship. For wealthy evangelical congregations, social class has been rediscovered as a source of spiritual capital, a commodity for deployment in the negotiation of theological conflict and in the defence of the boundaries of tradition.

In a different kind of critique of the mainstream church, charismatic Christians ground their spirituality in a thirst for the Holy Spirit that reflects a negative judgement of non-charismatics as staid, emotionally detached and resistant to the living Word. Here, authenticity is associated with embracing a mode of experience that feeds into both the subjective and the performative, both private and public manifestations of an embodied, living Christian vitality. Churches embracing this have allowed the charismatic to infuse congregational culture. This is perhaps most pronounced in the Pentecostal denominations and independent 'new churches', although a notable experientialism is also common in Anglican and Roman Catholic congregations within the charismatic renewal movement. A focus on shared, impassioned sung worship generates a culture of emotional expression that is rarely achieved in such intense forms in individual or small group contexts. Moreover, such an experiential dimension to congregational life accounts for the appeal of some churches, so that we might speak of what anthropologist Simon Coleman calls 'conference people', i.e. those individuals who attend a particular church in order to satisfy their need for a momentary spiritual experience, usually fostered within the emotional intensity of charismatic worship.[12] Coleman finds this tendency among charismatic Christians in Sweden, and it would not be unreasonable to apply this insight in accounting for the appeal of some of the unusually popular UK churches such as Kensington Temple or Holy Trinity Brompton.

Although there has recently been evidence of a tempering of the charismatic movement,[13] perhaps as a counter-reaction to the signs and wonders theology of the 'third-wave' associated with John Wimber and the Toronto Blessing, it is undeniable that a steady shift has occurred over the past 50 years which indicates a growing interest in the mass Christian gathering – the community as a site for experience, rather than as established spiritual home. Some 'conference people' are content to derive such encounters from their regular church while others look elsewhere. The apparently significant number of people worshipping in British cathedrals, for example, may indicate a related preference for the large-scale and magisterial over the routine and provincial.[14] More obvious and more thoroughly researched phenomena, however, are the popular Christian festivals such as Spring Harvest, New Wine or Greenbelt. Such mass contexts of Christian enthusiasm carry important consequences for the traditional congregation, particularly as they are arguably better suited to respond to the changing needs of the spiritual consumer. Spring Harvest, for example, is the largest British annual Bible week, now attracting some 80,000 participants each year. Both worship and teaching are major elements of the festival, but are predominantly organized within alternative seminar streams. Individuals choose between different streams, hence building up a 'package' of sessions that best suits their interests and predilections. Rob Warner has recently argued that this produces a paradoxical situation, with Spring Harvest presenting itself as unified in its conformity to established evangelical doctrines, while accidentally relativizing these claims by fostering a diverse range of speakers and sessions. Moreover, these seminars also change over time as their conveners seek to retain their contemporaneity and, in turn, their popularity among a shifting evangelical market.[15] Warner's analysis reminds us that, bound up in the issue of mass gatherings is not just a Durkheimian notion of the intensification of collective experience, but also the pervasive influence of late-capitalist consumerism, which reconfigures the relationship between individual Christians and the institutions they draw from in resourcing their faith. The general constituency of these festivals may also reflect how evangelical Protestants continue to sit more comfortably with the entrepreneurial ethos of late capitalism than their Roman Catholic cousins. In this sense, while denominational factors appear to play a lesser part than they used to in informing how Christians consciously construct their identities, they continue to exert some influence over the shape of the religious market.

Most pertinent for an understanding of the congregation is the question of whether such experiences fostered in these contexts become priorities over and above any continued commitment to a congregational or parish community. In some wings of the charismatic movement, for example, does the congregation risk becoming a source of heightened experience alone, one which is personally satisfying, but which is not part of a more comprehensive commitment to church life? Of course, those using such large churches as 'occasional congregations' may regularly attend another church, and pledge a more enduring and practical commitment to it (indeed, their evangelical appeal may imply that this is likely). If so, then at the very least, we need to be open to the notion that congregations have acquired multiple functions, and in response to a fickle and itinerant pool of participants, some churches may find themselves serving a niche market, with some offering 'experience' while others serve the parish. One analysis might associate the former with middle-class, 'elective parochials', that increasing population of Britons who move relatively frequently between jobs and homes and who, upon arriving in their latest sojourn, seek out temporary experiences of community. Those sympathetic to the church naturally gravitate towards 'gathered' congregations because they are more receptive to them, their commitment based on choice and immediate need rather than a durable attachment to the locality. The dominance of the middle classes within charismatic evangelical churches makes this link even more likely. Alternatively, the 'occasional' or 'temporary' congregation may be viewed as one more step on the way to what Alan Jamieson has called a 'churchless faith',[16] a more palatable possibility once the congregation has been reduced to an optional source of individualized spiritual experience.

Yet even this is not necessarily discontinuous with congregational involvement. Disillusionment with the church as an institution and body of ideas may lead not to wholesale disaffiliation, but to a change in personal orientation, so that the congregation is treated as a resource, presenting various experiences and ideas which may be adopted, negotiated or rejected in light of what is felt to be authentic by the discerning individual seeker. Such a trend was found by Andrew Yip in a study of gay, lesbian and bisexual Christians, surveyed during the late 1990s. While frequently labelled as having a 'problematic sexuality' out of keeping with Christian teaching, Yip's respondents more often than not remained affiliated to the mainstream churches.[17] Here the congregation becomes a cultural resource, to borrow James Beckford's expression,[18] and something from which one may selectively draw and borrow in accordance with individual needs and identity politics. Those who feel marginalized by, or alienated from, the mainstream church may find this orientation to congregational involvement particularly attractive, especially if no alternative community options present themselves, or if personal commitment prevents a complete detachment from the institution. One suspects, for example, that many female Roman Catholics and liberalized evangelicals have adopted such an approach to their congregational commitment for some time, feeling some discomfort with the party line, but also harbouring a reluctance to sever links with the mother church that has embodied their faith, perhaps since birth. With individualization apparently outpacing institutional change among the churches, we might expect this orientation to congregational engagement to become more dominant in future years.

Community Beyond the Congregation

While many have revised their expectations of the congregation, others have sought Christian community elsewhere. Perhaps most obviously, the cell church movement has reconceived the nature of Christian fellowship as a small-scale, intimate gathering. Such a vision has a long history, not least in the early Methodist tradition of 'class meetings', which were neither an alternative nor a supplement to regular Sunday worship, but 'an integral structural part of the Methodist Society'.[19] Yet the modern cell church – inspired by evangelical writers such as Ralph Neighbour and Lawrence Singlehurst – represents a new twist on this theme. Church is reconceived as the small group or 'cell', a model that emphasizes church as close-knit and cohesive, but also united in a common focus on saving souls; warmth and mutual sharing are at its heart, but relationships are temporary in so far as cells are eventually expected to multiply as part of a mission strategy. Such objectives are often organized around highly rationalized structures and a pyramid system of leadership.[20]

The restorationist house churches – now restyled as 'new churches' – occupy in many respects the same stream of development, elevating authority by the spirit and lay activism alongside a strong ethic of internal conformity and obedience. The emerging place of 'small groups' as a low-key, more intimate alternative to a more traditional 'congregational' gathering has gained momentum through the church growth movement, with 'small groups' often hailed as 'building blocks' for a healthy and growing Christian community.[21] Outside the evangelical world, spiritual retreats, courses in Christian counselling and the '12–step' courses which have emerged in response to Alpha, such as the more gradualist Emmaus, also make use of a small group format. This perhaps offers a surrogate for the close community felt to be lacking in fast-paced consumer society, while also often feeding off secular cultural trends, such as the systematization of consumer experience, emerging concerns about which are captured in talk of the 'McDonaldization' of the church. While a search for authenticity draws on personal experience, it often achieves its goal within communal contexts, which offer an interactive medium through which meaning is constructed and sustained over time.

While the cell church embodies a shift to the small-scale, close-knit and intimate, the parachurch movement signals the rising significance of organizations like World Vision or the Evangelical Alliance which function on a national or transnational level, alongside congregations. It is difficult to gauge the precise significance of parachurch organizations for the British context. The appeal of parachurches among committed churchgoers suggests they are not treated as a surrogate for regular congregational commitment, and yet some organizations appear to foster an enthusiasm for international mission which relegates church to the status of a secondary concern. This is the case, for example, with Morris Cerullo World Evangelism, which attracted thousands among the UK's black churches to its Mission to London revivals during the early 1990s. Large-scale revival meetings centred on a health and wealth 'faith' message, with corresponding signs and wonders, but the teaching embraced by participants also focused on '"winning people for Jesus" . . . as part of an international effort'.[22] As such, parachurches offer an alternative context for Christian activism, one that fosters a space in which ordinary Christians may contribute to mission or social action on an international stage. Its appeal beyond the local and national reflects both globalized perspectives and a passion for 'world mission', particularly important to evangelicals and Pentecostals, but also among those who combine their Christian identity with a commitment to humanitarian causes. Hence, while it is true that the influence of the parachurch phenomenon is more tangible within the context of global missionary efforts than within local congregations, the latter are increasingly exposed to their allure as meta-level media for the expression of Christian identity in a globalizing world.

Finally, advances in technology have forced us to rethink the very nature of community itself. Stewart Hoover, in his *Mass Media Religion*,[23] charted the impact of the mass media on US churches, demonstrating that the diffuse audiences of televangelism reflect an experience of 'translocalism'. This sense of being a part of a wider community was fostered by a kind of vicarious religion based on television viewing behaviour; viewers feel a part of a united televised church, while remaining passive participants within their own living rooms. The World Wide Web demands we rethink the issue further, with Manuel Castells even postulating a global 'network society', unbridled by local constraints and less subject to the limitations of the nation state.[24] Religion has its place in the information age, as does the congregation, but in radically reconfigured reconceptualized forms. An excellent example of this reorientation is the 'Vurch' ('Virtual Church') website, which offers the opportunity for prayer to be typed in and submitted to 'God's private address' (available to no other user), or to 'God's public one' which allows other 'Vurchgoers to see it and put their hands together with you'.[25] In this radical overhaul of congregational reality, the church finds itself recognizing changing notions of privatized engagement, shifting authenticities in line with advanced technology, and producing an experience that is subversive, playful, exploratory and often chaotic. It opens up new possibilities in the conception of collective worship and community identity which challenge the congregation on every level.

Notes

1 Timothy Jenkins, 1999, *Religion in English Everyday Life*, New York and Oxford: Berghahn Books, pp. 43–73.

2 Martyn Percy, 2004, 'Losing Our Space, Finding Our Place? The Changing Identity of the English Parish Church', in S. Coleman and P. Collins (eds), *Religion, Identity and Change: Perspectives on Global Transformations*, Aldershot: Ashgate, pp. 26–41, at p. 28.

3 Grace Davie, 'From Obligation to Consumption: A Framework for Reflection in Northern Europe', *Political Theology*, 6(3) (2005), 281–301, p. 283.

4 David Lyon, 2000, *Jesus in Disneyland: Religion in Postmodern Times*, Cambridge: Polity.

5 Fresh Expressions website – http://www.freshexpressions.org.uk/section.asp?id=24 – accessed 20.03.06.

6 See Donald E. Miller, 1997, *Reinventing American Protestantism: Christianity in the New Millennium*, Berkeley and Los Angeles: University of California Press.

7 At the height of its popularity, NOS attracted around 600 participants each week and boasted 400 members as early as 1988, only three years after it was first launched. See Roland Howard, 1996, *The Rise and Fall of the Nine O'Clock Service*, London and New York: Mowbray, pp. 27f.

8 Moot website – http://www.moot.uk.net/ – accessed 10.12.06

9 Simon Goodenough, 1983, *The Country Parson*, Newton Abbot, London and North Pomfret: David & Charles, p. 166.

10 Bryan Wilson, 1976, *The Contemporary Transformation of Religion*, London and New York: Oxford University Press, pp. 93ff.

11 Philip Richter, 2004 'Denominational Cultures: The Cinderella of Congregational Studies?', in M. Guest, K. Tusting and L. Woodhead (eds), *Congregational Studies in the UK: Christianity in a Post-Christian Context*, Aldershot: Ashgate, pp. 169–84 at p. 169.

12 Simon Coleman, 2000, *The Globalisation of Charismatic Christianity: Spreading the Gospel of Prosperity*, Cambridge: Cambridge University Press.

13 Brierley, *Tide is Running Out*, p. 54 discussing a decline of 16% in those self-defining as 'charismatic', with a shifting preference (growing by 68%) in those adopting the label 'mainstream evangelical'.

14 Stephen Platten, 2006, *Dreaming Spires?: Cathedrals in a New Age*, London: SPCK.

15 Rob Warner, (forthcoming), 'Autonomous Conformism: the Paradox of Entrepreneurial Protestantism (Spring Harvest: a case study)', in L. Woodhead and A. Day (eds), *Religion and the Individual*, Aldershot: Ashgate.

16 Alan Jamieson, 2002, *A Churchless Faith: Faith Journeys Beyond the Churches*, London: SPCK.

17 Andrew K. T. Yip, 2003, 'The Self as the Basis of Religious Faith: Spirituality of Gay, Lesbian and Bisexual Christians', in Davie, Heelas and Woodhead, *Predicting Religion*, pp. 135–46.

18 James A. Beckford, 1989, *Religion and Advanced Industrial Society*, London: Unwin Hyman.

19 Edward R. Wickham, 1957, *Church and People in an Industrial City*, London: Lutterworth Press, p. 268.

20 David Harvey, 'Cell Church: Its Situation in British Evangelical Culture', *Journal of Contemporary Religion*, 18(1) (2003), 95–109.

21 For example, in Christian Schwarz, 1996, *Natural Church Development*, Churchsmart Resources.

22 Nancy A. Schaefer, 2002, 'Morris Cerullo's London Revivals as "Glocal" (neo-) Pentecostal Movement Events', *Culture and Religion*, 3(1) (2002), p. 114.

23 Stewart Hoover, 1988, *Mass Media Religion: The Social Sources of the Mass Media Church*, Newbury Park, California: Sage.

24 Manuel Castells, 1998, *The Information Age: Economy, Society And Culture, Vol. III End of Millennium*, Malden, Massachusetts and Oxford, UK: Blackwell.

25 Vurch website – http://www.vurch.com/l1prayer.htm – accessed 17.02.06.

2

Performance

In 1974 Alan Kennedy published *The Protean Self*. An analysis of post-war – or, as he put it, postmodern – literature, it identified an important trend in recent writing. Put simply, Kennedy argued that dramatic metaphors pervaded the work of such disparate figures as Joyce Cary, Muriel Spark, John Fowles, and Anthony Burgess. This he linked to a new understanding of the self. 'The inherent solipsism of the inner Ideal self', he wrote:

> is countered by the re-emergence in the novel of the twentieth century of the protean self. The protean self is capable of externalisation, of playing numerous roles . . . without being guilty of living 'in bad faith' or 'inauthentically.' The centre holds after all. The protean self is not primarily concerned, though, with playing the set roles of society . . . but with the more vital task of creating free and unique, ordered ways of living out individual subjectivity.[1]

Kennedy's insight was an important one. Without denying the constructedness of modern notions of selfhood and identity, he was able to show how recent writers had reconciled the search for authenticity with the multiplicity of roles that individuals were now required to enact. In emphasizing the importance of authenticity, Kennedy was of course following Lionel Trilling, whose *Sincerity and Authenticity* had come out a few years earlier.[2] In stressing the significance of ideas about performance, he was, as he recognized, echoing Erwin Goffman, whose *Relations in Public* was equally new.[3] But, above all, what he was doing was showing the importance of metaphors taken from drama in modern literature and modern life. That insight – and his emphasis on the paradox of authentic role-playing – is of enormous importance.

Building on this insight, one category that we consider helpful in conceptualizing the place of Christianity in British society is that of performance. Naturally, we are not suggesting that performance provides an all-purpose explanation or analogy for (post)modern life. As Zygmunt Bauman acknowledges, 'No single-factor model is likely ever to account for the complexity of the "lived world" and embrace the totality of human experience.'[4] Nor do we claim to be unique in adopting an image taken from theatre.

Indeed, as Kennedy has shown, it is one that permeates post-war British fiction. But it seems to us a far more creative way forward than the biological analogy adopted by many previous writers, which postulates the birth, growth, maturity, and death of Christianity as though it were an organism rather than a religion. It seems, too, to be a more fertile metaphor than that of the market, which has been so prevalent in the recent literature, and which reduces religious identity to the status of a purchase and religious belief to a form of consumption. As the introduction to this book suggested, we find this particular master metaphor especially unhelpful. Instead, it is hoped that the notion of performance provides a more nuanced, multifaceted, and many-layered approach. In particular, the tensions at the heart of perform-ance seem pertinent to our needs. Performance may be theatrical; it may be liturgical; it may be highly planned or entirely spontaneous; it may be highly elaborate or wholly functional. One can perform a duty and perform a role. Indeed, performance carries with it the possibility of performing many different roles. And because of that it implies a dilemma: the problem of dis-tinguishing between authentic and inauthentic performance. This dilemma is central to our analysis.

Literary theorists and anthropologists have frequently deployed the metaphor of performance, and since the mid-1980s, a series of theologians including Nicholas Lash, Frances Young, and – most recently – Stanley Hauerwas have explored the performative aspects of Christianity.[5] For Hauerwas,

> Religious belief is not just some kind of primitive metaphysics, but in fact it is a performance just like you'd perform *Lear*. What people think Christianity is, is that it's like the text of *Lear*, rather than the actual pro-duction of *Lear*. It has to be performed for you to understand what *Lear* is – a drama. You can read it, but unfortunately Christians so often want to make Christianity a text rather than a performance.[6]

It must be acknowledged that this turn has not been welcomed by all: David Fergusson, for one, deprecates what he sees as the reduction of theological truth to the status of performance. The danger is, he argues, that such a slippage allows Christians to domesticate the Bible, and to abandon a Christological perspective in favour of an ecclesiological one. Instead of being challenged by Scripture, they simply play at being a church.[7] Addition-ally, it should also be admitted that even those who do equate Christianity with performativity recognize some of the dangers inherent in the metaphor. 'The Christian faith', Hauerwas has written, 'is far too rich and complex to be captured by a single analogy.' Nevertheless, he goes on, 'analogies derived from the performing arts prove wonderfully insightful and instructive.'[8] Both Hauerwas's caution and his enthusiasm seem well-directed. The metaphor of performance – whatever its limitations, and whatever its hazards, does seem to be a strikingly rich one.

For precisely that reason, indeed, the idea of 'performativity' has in recent years taken on increasing importance in studies of selfhood and of identity.[9] The work of Judith Butler in particular has been of immense importance in promoting performativity as a critical concept. For her, gender – like much of life – is 'an act', it is 'performance'.[10] 'As in other ritual social drama,' she writes, 'the action of gender requires a performance that is *repeated*. This repetition is at once a reenactment and experiencing of a set of meanings already socially established; and it is the mundane and ritualised form of their legitimation.'[11] Put simply, what this means is that even in apparently stable categories like sex, sexuality, or gender, there is an element not just of instability, but also of role-playing, of performance. More than that, each performance – each act of performativity – reinforces and relegitimates the role that we are playing. Performance, then, is a central part of human existence: fundamental to our identity and not reducible to models of consumption or of the market.

Although this work is suggestive and significant, our use of the metaphor of performance is somewhat different.[12] Judith Butler is clear that there is a distinction between performance and performativity. Whilst the first is chosen, she maintains, the latter is a reproduction of norms which precede, constrain, and exceed the performer.[13] This reveals a divergent understanding of performance from the one that this study seeks to present. In the first place, as Andrew Parker and Eve Kosofsky Sedgwick have suggested, the distinction between performance and performativity remains an open question.[14] Second, as some critics of Butler have argued, her notion of performativity is almost exclusively linguistic and highly individualistic. It takes little account of embodiment or of collective action and social context.[15] Although in her later work Butler has attempted to engage with these challenges,[16] some of the initial criticisms of her work must still stand.[17] By positing what is arguably a textual rather than a material body, Butler's performativity fails to represent the lived experience of embodied individuals.[18] By emphasizing the transgressive potential of individual performativity, she ignores the possibility of collective action and downplays the importance of the environment in which that action occurs. Our notion of performance, by contrast, takes into account actions as well as words, bodies as well as minds. How could we do otherwise? Religion and religious practice is frequently highly ritualized. Indeed, ritual performance is arguably constitutive of religion itself.[19] Much of this ritual and thus much of religion is evidently – and importantly – both embodied and corporate. The movements of a formal liturgy; the wearing of particular clothes or ornaments, from a crucifix to a 'What Would Jesus Do?' bracelet; the collective involvement of a family in a funeral, a wedding, or a baptism: all of these are better encompassed by performance rather than performativity as defined by Butler.

More importantly still, as we have already suggested, our account of performance rests on the revelation of tensions within the term itself, tensions which make performance rather than performativity a rather more creative concept for us to use. Performance and its cognates are words of extraordinary versatility. In their oldest form, they denote the carrying out of something commanded. The Book of Common Prayer and its 1928 revision both, for example, include in the wedding service the prayer that the couple 'may surely perform and keep the vow and covenant betwixt them made'. Set against this sense of performance as duty is a countervailing definition: that of performance as play-acting.[20] Thus, while priests are required to 'perform the mass', worship leaders may be advised to 'avoid the temptation of performance'.[21] What distinguishes 'good' and 'bad' performance is authenticity. Even the carrying out of a duty may be considered inauthentic. Likewise, as Kennedy observed in 1976, forms of role-playing were not seen as inevitably fraudulent or inauthentic. Indeed, the reverse might well be true. 'Dramatic self-presentation', he concluded, 'is something that is part of authentic individuality.'[22] The point is that in a world of performances, there will always be a tension between performing a duty and performing a role; between authenticity and duplicity. Indeed, individuals may have to perform many more roles and undertake many more duties than one. At the same time, it should be noted, performances vary in type: some are improvised; some follow a script. Both may be experienced as authentic or inauthentic. As the section on Experience shows, performing the formal liturgy of a Tridentine mass may – for example – be seen as legitimate because it provides a clear script to follow and a set of coherent roles to enact. Or, it could be seen as illegitimate because it does not provide the spontaneous performance the worshippers are seeking. For some there is freedom in following a script; for others only improvisation will do.

Arguably, at the start of this period, for many people church attendance was a duty: a duty that was performed each week.[23] People, as Grace Davie has noted, felt an obligation to attend. By the end of this period, far fewer shared this sense. What changed, though, is not that a smaller number of people wanted to consume religion. Rather, people were less and less likely to attend if they saw that attendance as inauthentic; if instead of seeing it as a duty it was nothing more than play-acting, nothing more than performing a role. This could not be described as simple secularization, but rather the consequence of a search for authentic experience. As Philip Richter and Leslie Francis have observed, 'One suspects that, were it not for their strong desire for personal authenticity, some church leavers would have found it easier to remain and continue "going through the motions".'[24] Certainly, as William Whyte argues in the next essay, the desire to perform an authentic role may well drive some ministers out of their churches, where they feel that they are unable to be authentic and have come to impersonate rather than embody priesthood. Likewise, as Mark Chapman shows, the 1960s saw a series of attempts to escape the perceived play-acting of much conventional religion. Churches and churchmen were perceived as barriers to the authentic experience of religion as 'South Bank Theology' sought to revitalize the performance of faith.

For other people, however, throughout our period, attendance at church remained – indeed, became more – authentic. This was a duty they were willing to do. Changes in liturgy reflect this 'expressive revolution'; as religious services became ever more informal and emotional performances.[25] The charismatic revival is a particularly good example of this, with the rediscovery of *glossolalia* marking a self-conscious break with the supposedly inauthentic performance of conventional speech.[26] Arguably, too, for many people, the notion of multiple roles became increasingly significant. Perhaps this explains the persistent involvement of churchgoers in wider community activities. Almost certainly, it underpins the relationship between Christians and the peace movement, anti-Apartheid agitation, and the Make Poverty History campaign. For these people, multiple roles – some focused on the church and others not – meant a more authentic life.[27] In that sense the tensions at the heart of performance could be both challenging and fruitful for institutional religion.

With this in mind, we might pursue our model in a number of different directions. We might, for example, engage with Callum Brown's assertion that the 1960s saw a radical shift in female piety as working women abandoned the church. There seems no reason to believe that these people were any less likely to seek an authentic life, or any less able to do so by performing multiple roles. It seems highly plausible that for many, this pursuit of authenticity led to religion rather than away from it – although the roles they performed may have been very different from those traditionally taken on by women. Likewise, we might interrogate Paul Heelas's and Linda Woodhead's contention that the post-war period witnessed a 'subjective turn' in which individuals rejected a life lived primarily as 'a dutiful wife, father, husband, strong leader, self-made man etc.' in favour of a 'subjective life', characterized by solipsistic search for individual meaning.[28] Not only does this imply a potentially rather crude binary between what they term 'life-as' and the 'subjective life' – between the ordered life of modernity and the freer lifestyle of postmodernity – but it also ignores the contexts in which modern Britons operate. Self-evidently, they are capable of performing multiple roles and have to share the stage on which they perform with other actors who also have an influence on their performance.

This much is clear from the short case studies in this section. In the first one, William Whyte uses our analogy with performance to explore two of the key problems facing institutional religion in the present day: the division over sexuality and the decline in vocations to ordained ministry. In both cases, he suggests, the debate is framed by battles over the authenticity (or inauthenticity) of particular performances. Like everyone else, both priests and gay Christians are called upon to perform a number of different roles. These can be mutually sustaining – but they can also create tensions. How can a priest reconcile the demands placed upon her to perform as a public figure with her own private search for spiritual fulfilment? Is it possible to live an authentic life as a member of the church and as a sexually active gay man or woman? Or is there such a conflict between the performances of these two roles that a choice has to be made between them?

In the next case study Mark Chapman wrestles with similar dilemmas. The rise of 'South Bank Theology' in the 1960s, with its emphasis on finding God outside the structures of organized religion, grew out of a debate on how priests and people could perform religion more authentically. Although he argues that the experiment was a failure, nonetheless it is an important illustration of our point. Born of immense optimism, the movement Chapman characterizes as 'English Bonhoefferism' repudiated the way in which the church had traditionally performed. Real religion, it was argued, was the product of the everyday performances of everyday people. The church and the church's worship were not seen as vehicles for God's performance, but as a barrier to it. What the church needed to do was abandon the comfortable, conventional, and essentially inauthentic systems of belief and worship which were standing between the people and God. But this raises an obvious question: if the worship and work of the church is inauthentic, where is a more authentic performance to be found? And – more importantly still – who is to enact it? Pursuing the spontaneous over and above the scripted, and defining the worshipping church as inherently inauthentic, 'South Bank' theologians turned to what they saw as a secular yet nonetheless implicitly Christian world for inspiration. This was, Mark Chapman shows, a bold and ultimately mistaken move. Rejecting the institution of the church, they neglected the need to pass on religious knowledge and foster Christian experience. The result could be seen as a case of people who stopped believing because they stopped belonging. The liturgy – the work of the church – ceased to be performed and to be seen as a performance both apart from and beyond the world.

Both Mark Chapman's and William Whyte's case studies focus on individuals and the subjective search for authentic performance. In the final case study, by contrast, Grace Davie looks towards the collective and to the response of the British population as a whole to two iconic and ironically simultaneous events: the second marriage of Prince Charles and the funeral of Pope John Paul II. Setting them within their European and, indeed, global contexts, Davie uncovers a number of apparent paradoxes about the public performance of religion within a rapidly changing nation. On the one hand, she notes, Britain in the early twenty-first century has few regular church-goers and thus few people who see the weekly performance of a religious service as a central part of their life. On the other, though, it is clear that at moments of crisis or celebration it is expected that the church – and particularly the Church of England – will perform a unifying and mediating role. It has a script that all can follow and enacts a performance on behalf of the nation as a whole. In that sense, and in those circumstances, the very formality of the church's performance serves to make it authentic and meaningful even for those who have little experience of it in everyday life. Yet there still remains a tension between the authentic and inauthentic, the spontaneous and the scripted performance.

After the death of Diana, the Royal Family was widely criticized for following protocol and initially refusing to participate in the improvised scenes of grief in the streets of London. Sticking to the script was seen as inauthentic. Such spontaneity would, however, have been regarded as entirely inappropriate for the funeral of Pope John Paul II – or indeed, Queen Elizabeth the Queen Mother. Their formal funeral services were seen to be entirely fitting, an appropriately ordered performance for people whose lives had been devoted to duty. And even so, it should be remembered that the Papal funeral was interrupted by spontaneous applause and chants of 'Santo Subito (Sainthood immediately)' by the crowds in St Peter's Square. Given the fluidity of people's notions of authentic performance, there is little wonder that it can go wrong – nor that Prince Charles' second wedding caused so many headaches for those who organized it. Deciding to have a civil wedding – partly, no doubt, because a re-enactment of his religious marriage to Diana would have seemed inauthentic given the circumstances of his divorce – Charles had to write a new script. Given the concurrence of a Royal wedding and a Papal funeral, so did the British state. There was no precedent for all the party leaders and the heir to the throne going to Rome for such an event, but that is what everyone agreed must happen. The actors thus had to find new parts to play, with the Archbishop of Canterbury joining in the obsequies for the Pope, and the Queen refusing to participate in her son's civil wedding service and instead taking up a role in what was for her the authentic performance of a Christian blessing. As this suggests, within the public space of a plural society, there are many competing and co-existing performances. Each must be taken on its own terms.

Consequently, we would want to assert that neither the master metaphor of the market nor the biological analogy which sees religion as a sort of organism can explain these phenomena. Instead, any useful model of social change will take into account an apparent paradox: first, that post-1945 Britain can be characterized as a period in which authenticity was at a premium; second, that at the same time, role-playing became a well-understood analogy for modern life. We would suggest that these contradictions make the notion of performance a central one for the study of modern religion. Performance can be bad – it can imply inauthenticity, dishonesty, and (in the sense of performing a duty) even compulsion. Performance can also be good – it can imply authenticity, dutifulness, and (in the sense of performing a multiplicity of roles) it can be equated to freedom. Above all, it can be argued, performance is an important category of analysis, and one which is both more creative and more resonant than many other analogies.

Notes

1 Alan Kennedy, 1974, *The Protean Self: Dramatic Action in Contemporary Fiction*, London: Macmillan, p. 9.

2 Lionel Trilling, 1972, *Sincerity and Authenticity*, Oxford: Oxford University Press.

3 Erwin Goffman, 1971, *Relations in Public: Microstudies of the Public Order*, Harmondsworth: Penguin.

4 Zygmunt Bauman, 2004, *Identity: Conversations with Benedetto Vecchi*, Cambridge: Polity Press, p. 33.

5 Nicholas Lash, 1986, 'Performing the Scriptures', in his *Theology on the Way to Emmaus*, London: SCM Press, pp. 37–46; Frances Young, 1990, *The Art of a Performance: Towards a Theology of Holy Scripture*, London: Darton, Longman & Todd.

6 http://www.homileticsonline.com/subscriber/interviews/hauerwas.asp – accessed 03.10.06.

7 David Fergusson, 1998, *Community, Liberalism, and Christian Ethics*, Cambridge: Cambridge University Press, p. 70.

8 Stanley Hauerwas, 2004, *Performing the Faith: Bonhoeffer and the Practice of Non-Violence*, London: SPCK, p. 106.

9 For example, see the sceptical survey of its impact on anthropology in Rosalind C. Morris, 'All Made Up: performance theory and the new anthropology of sex and gender', *Annual Review of Anthropology*, 24 (1995), 567–92.

10 Peter Osborne and Lynne Segal, 'Gender as Performance: an interview with Judith Butler', *Radical Philosophy*, 67 (1994), 32–39.

11 Judith Butler, 1990, *Gender Trouble: Feminism and the Subversion of Identity*, New York and London: Routledge, p. 178.

12 Although see Elizabeth Stuart, 1997, 'Sex in Heaven: the queerness of theological discourse on sexuality', in Jon Davies and Gerard Loughlin (eds), *Sex These Days: Essays on Theology, Sexuality, and Society*, Sheffield: Sheffield Academic Press, pp. 184–204, pp. 190–91.

13 Judith Butler, 1993, *Bodies that Matter: On the Discursive Limits of 'Sex'*, New York and London: Routledge, p. 234.

14 Andrew Parker and Eve Kosofsky Sedgwick, 1995, 'Introduction', in Parker and Sedgwick (eds), *Performativity and Performance*, New York and London: Routledge, pp. 1–18.

15 Amy Hollywood, 'Performativity, Citationality, Ritualization', *History of Religions*, 42(2) (2002), 93–115, p. 94.

16 See especially Butler, *Bodies that Matter*.

17 Susan Bordo, 2003, *Unbearable Weight: Feminism, Western Culture and the Body*, Berkeley: University of California Press, pp. 290–93.

18 See also Jeremy R. Carrette, 2000, *Foucault and Religion: Spiritual Corporeality and Political Spirituality*, London and New York: Routledge, pp. 143–6.

19 Stanley Jeraraja Tambiah, 1985, *Culture, Thought and Social Action: An Anthropological Perspective*, Cambridge, Mass.: Harvard University Press, pp. 123–66.

20 See also Peter Iver Kaufman, 1999, 'The "confessing animal" on stage: authenticity, asceticism, and the constant "inconstancie" of Elizabethan character', in Salim Kemal and Ivan Craskell (eds), *Performance and Authenticity in the Arts*, Cambridge: Cambridge University Press, pp. 49–65, at p. 52.

21 Pete Ward, 2005, *Selling Worship: How What We Sing Has Changed the Church*, Carlisle: Paternoster Press, pp. 171–2, 176–7.

22 Kennedy, *The Protean Self*, p. 19.

23 Ross McKibbin, 1998, *Classes and Cultures: England, 1918–51*, Oxford: Oxford University Press, Ch. 7.

24 Philip Richter and Leslie J. Francis, 1998, *Gone But Not Forgotten: Church Leaving and Returning*, London: Darton, Longman & Todd, p. 42.

25 Bernice Martin, 1981, *A Sociology of Contemporary Cultural Change*, Oxford: Basil Blackwell, Ch. 2.

26 Thomas J. Csordas, 2001, *Language, Charisma, and Creativity: Ritual Life in the Catholic Charismatic Renewal*, New York: Palgrave, p. 55.

27 See also Roof, *Spiritual Marketplace*, p. 158 for an interesting transatlantic comparison.

28 Heelas and Woodhead, *Spiritual Revolution*, p. 3.

Case Studies

Performance, Priesthood, and Homosexuality
  William Whyte

Theology in the Public Arena: The case of South Bank Religion
  Mark D. Chapman

A Papal Funeral and a Royal Wedding: Reconfiguring Religion
in the Twenty-first Century
  Grace Davie

CASE STUDY

Performance, Priesthood, and Homosexuality

WILLIAM WHYTE

I'm a man, God created me a man,
and I'm going to learn how to act like a man
('Justin', an 'ex-gay' Christian).[1]

Several of the fiercest religious struggles that took place in Britain after 1945 can be understood as debates about performance. This short essay will explore two of them: the contemporary crisis within the churches over homosexuality; and the longer-term decline in vocations to ordained ministry, a decline which began in the 1960s. Both have been explained as a product of simple secularization. The conflict over homosexuality has, indeed, been seen as an eruption of the secular into the church itself, as certain Christians have adopted new categories of identity and abandoned older, more orthodox traditions.[2] A decline in vocations has similarly been understood as a secular phenomenon: underwritten by a secular society that challenges the church, makes priesthood irrelevant, and renders priests themselves redundant.[3] No doubt there is something in both these accounts. But an exclusive emphasis on secularization begs too many questions and leaves too many answers unexamined. By contrast, I will argue, the idea of performance allows us to dig deeper into the issues. Arguments about homosexuality are not reducible to a crude binary: a struggle between tradition and innovation. Nor can falling numbers of vocations to ordained ministry be reduced to a simple narrative of professional failure. Instead, I shall suggest, what contemporary Christians confront is a dilemma about the authenticity of their performances.

Homosexuality, Christianity, and Performance

The issue of homosexuality is undeniably the most significant dividing line in contemporary church politics.[4] Yet models of identity and behaviour drawn from the master metaphor of the market seem hard pressed to explain why this should be so. To be sure, writers like Michael Delashmutt have argued

that 'human sexual experience has become a commodity, a privately consumed good, which is alienated from either the human body or social community'.[5] Likewise, Jon Davies maintains that debates about sexuality
represent 'the irruption of the sexual market into the church'; 'the ruthless,
ceaseless radicality of the market in which sex, like everything else is merely
a wallet'.[6] This does not, however, convince. Even if one accepts their contention that heterosexual sex has become commodified (and there are good
reasons for doubting this), the debate on homosexuality has been conducted
in very different terms. In an important sense, indeed, this has been a debate
about performance rather than consumption.

In his *20 Hot Potatoes Christians Are Afraid to Touch* the influential
American evangelist Tony Campolo condemns homosexuality but defends
homosexuals. 'It is *very* important', he writes, 'that all of us distinguish
between homosexual *orientation* and homosexual *behaviour* . . . the first is
desire. The second is action. The first is temptation. The second is yielding to
temptation.'[7] It is a theme picked up in Nicky Gumbel's *Searching Issues*,
published as part of the Alpha empire. 'Nowhere does the Bible condemn
homosexual orientation, homosexual feelings, or homosexual temptation',
he writes. It is only 'homosexual practice' that is forbidden.[8] And this pro-
hibition is a lived experience for many. Martin Hallett, founder of the True
Freedom Trust, counsels homosexuals to live entirely celibate lives.[9] 'If I
were not a Christian,' he writes, 'I would be happily involved in gay relationships.'[10] At a more exalted theological level, the St Andrew's Day
Statement of 1995, which was promulgated by the Church of England
Evangelical Council, similarly sought to differentiate practice from personality; real identity from assumed or constructed one.[11] Oliver O'Donovan is
a case in point. A signatory to the statement, he broadened its condemnation
of homosexual practice by attacking all homosexual behaviour – whether
sexual or not – and by distinguishing between homosexuality and a cultural
movement he termed 'gay'. '"Homosexual"', he wrote, 'refers simply to the
psychosexual patterns of emotion. To be "gay" one must have a prevailing
interest in homosexuality, an identification with homosexual people, and
an assertive programme.'[12] None of this, it is clear from his comments, is
acceptable within the church.[13]

By contrast, those who seek to promote the acceptance of homosexuality
within the churches adopt a very different register. They make no distinction
between orientation and practice.[14] Indeed, such a distinction is anathema.
As Roy Clements, a Baptist pastor sacked for his homosexuality, puts it, his
opponents 'have not absorbed the idea that homosexuality is an identity, not
a practice. They believe it is a sin, just like murder.'[15] For Clements, and for
others, by contrast, homosexual identity is the critical point – and homosexual practice follows from it.[16] Moreover, in this model Christianity is by
no means in conflict with homosexuality, nor homosexuality inimical to
Christian identity. To be sure, some gay Christians may very well reject

institutional religion,[17] but as Andrew Yip has shown, it is also possible for them to do so without abandoning their faith.[18] And for others, indeed, sexuality and spirituality may sit very comfortably together.[19] A connection between Anglo-Catholicism and homosexuality, for example, was postulated by Gordon Westwood in 1960.[20] Similarly, the American Presbyterian Chris Glaser recalls a powerful link between his sexuality and his faith. As an adolescent, he writes,

> The only friend on whom I could depend, the only friend who knew my terrible secret and yet had not deserted me, was God. This resulted in a heightened awareness of God's presence in my life and a deepening spirituality. At the same time, it lead to my desire to convert my sadness into joy, something I intuited as God's wish for me.[21]

An equivalent impulse underpinned the Anglican theologian Harry Williams's move from celibate homosexuality to one that gave full physical expression of his identity.[22] Like others, Williams felt that far from his sexuality challenging his faith (or vice versa), he would never have become a Christian but for his homosexuality.[23]

What can we conclude from this comparison? In one sense, all it shows is that the two sides of the debate are conducting it in very different terms.[24] For one group practice and person are distinct. For the other, there is no such distinction. Although the debate is conducted in diverging terms, with divergent assumptions from both perspectives, it is one that can be understood as concerned with the notion of performance. For those who distinguish between orientation and action, homosexuality is essentially inauthentic: it is playing a role.[25] For those who see no distinction, homosexuality is intrinsic to one's identity and identifying oneself as gay is a duty. James Alison is not alone in suggesting the way in which 'coming out' can be like an evangelical conversion experience.[26] 'The sacrament of "coming out" is a kind of letting go', observed one gay Catholic priest; 'letting go . . . in favour of trusting oneself enough to let oneself be oneself.'[27] And if this is true of homosexual identity then it is no less true of homosexual practice. For one side of the argument, this is by definition not just morally wrong, but also the result of a misapprehension. As Benedict XVI put it, 'when [homosexuals] engage in homosexual activity they confirm within themselves a disordered sexual inclination which is essentially self-indulgent.'[28] For the other side, however, sexual practice is a part of human identity: not to have sex – not to be sexual – is not to be human.[29] Fundamentally, then, these are not arguments about consumption but about identity, and – by extension – about performance.

Priesthood, Professionalization, and Performance

Without a doubt, the role and the place of the priest have changed since 1945. The number of ministers, and their relationship to the various denominations, have also changed: with fewer and fewer men pursuing a vocation, and even the ordination of women within a number of Protestant denominations failing to make up for this decline. This much is clear enough. But explaining these changes is far harder. In the older, secularizing model of social change, these changes reflected nothing but a simple decline in priestly status, moral authority, and effectiveness.[30] And indeed, Richard Harries, Anglican Bishop of Oxford between 1987 and 2006, is among many who have complained at the 'lack of validation by society as a whole'. Rather than consulting a priest, he argues, 'People will go instead to see their psychiatrist or their GP or their social worker.'[31] Closely allied to this critique is the assumption that Christian ministry somehow failed to professionalize.[32] As Towler and Coxon put it in their *Fate of the Anglican Clergy*,

> the clergyman is a jack of all trades . . . there is nothing which he does that could not be done equally well by a lawyer or bricklayer in the congregation . . . He does not have a job at all in any sense which is readily understandable today, and today, more than ever before, a person must have a job in order to fit into society.[33]

For them, the collapse in ordinations could be linked to this failure, this sense of marginality. For Towler, for Coxon, for Wilson, and for others, secularization and professionalization together undermined the ministry in Christian Britain.

Heuristically, however neither professionalization nor secularization seems sufficiently secure to function effectively as over-arching explanation. More particularly, the question of whether the clergy professionalized in this period remains an open one.[34] Above all, I would contend that instead of focusing on these abstractions, the lived experience of priests in post-1945 Britain should be taken account of. This experience suggests a very different picture: one in which performance is more important than professionalization, and in which authenticity is more fundamental than fears of secularization. Frank Musgrove's short study of late entrants to the Anglican ministry is highly suggestive in this respect. The 12 parsons he interviewed had each abandoned successful secular careers for life within the Church. They were not, he said, 'entrapped in a highly specialized division of labour: they were escaping from one, and very aware that this was the case . . . Erstwhile plumbers, architects and engineers had left fragmented lives for a new wholeness and totality, which had no margins to hide.'[35] In other words, far from feeling marginalized, the multiplicity of roles they performed as priests left them feeling more fulfilled; far from regretting the loss of professional identity, they rejoiced in the freedom that performing priesthood gave them. And the same seems true of other people who have entered the ministry. As one female priest observed in the late 1990s, 'I think there was also at one point . . . that I had all these different strands to my life and I wanted to bring [them] together.'[36] For her at least, ordination meant more than entrance to a profession.

At one level, this might be perceived as good for the church. If priesthood is bound up less with professionalization than with an authentic sense of self, then a 'failure' to professionalize should not contribute to a decline in vocations. At another level, however, this focus on authenticity may present serious difficulties – certainly, it may lead priests out of orders and discourage others from seeking them. Once again, the problem may best be understood as one of performance. Priests, as the Second Vatican Council declared, are variously called to 'prayer and adoration, in preaching the gospel message, in offering the eucharistic sacrifice and administering the other sacraments, and in performing other services for people'.[37] As we have already noted, performing this variety of roles may sustain a more authentic sense of selfhood in many ministers. Nonetheless, for others precisely the reverse may be true.[38] The performance of priesthood may become synonymous with inauthenticity, with simply playing a role and disguising one's own true self. Responding to lay expectations to be a model of unwavering faith and fulfilled optimism, this may require masking doubts and frailties. As one Anglican priest, angry at his church's unwillingness to accept his sexuality, acknowledge his partner, or deal with his HIV, complained in the mid-1990s: 'You've spent all these years building up the body of Christ and organizing the festivals and then, God, you're not allowed to feel bad. Not allowed to be real. Not allowed to be honest. Not allowed to be free.'[39] For him, as for others, performing priesthood made him less authentic rather than more: instead of finding unity in a variety of roles, he had come to believe that he was acting rather than being true to himself. Similar qualms, although over rather different issues, appear to have propelled Anthony Kenny from the Catholic Church in 1963 – and he was, of course, soon followed by others.[40] Priesthood, then, may not be a profession but it is an exemplification of the tensions implied by the notion of performance: tensions that may work equally to the benefit or detriment of organized religion. A search for authenticity may lead people into ministry. A lack of authentic experience may lead them out of it.

Conclusion

Performance, then, is not a neutral concept. It can be inauthentic (or regarded as such) just as easily as it is authentic (or regarded as such). Indeed, the question of whether a performance is authentic or not lies at the heart of many important debates. Arguably, the current crisis within the churches about homosexuality is driven by this distinction – a battle between one group that denies the authenticity of gay life and another that affirms it. Likewise, arguments about ordained ministry concern what it means to perform priesthood. Is it just play-acting, just enacting a role? Or is it about performing a duty, enacting an authentic expression of self? As the case of 'Justin', the 'ex-gay' evangelical Christian quoted at the start of this essay, suggests, this is not an easy distinction to make. 'I'm a man, God created me a man,' he declared, 'and I'm going to learn how to act like a man.'[41] For him, his true nature had been concealed by his homosexuality. Yet paradoxically it was only when he could learn to perform a masculine role that his authentic self would be revealed. Likewise, for many priests ordination brings with it a dilemma. As Rowan Williams has written, many people have a sense of 'vocation as casting', 'vocation as God finding us a *part to play*'. 'The nuisance is that [God] draws up the cast-list before doing any auditions. We find ourselves called to fulfil a definite role, but we haven't actually seen the script, and as time goes on we may suspect we would do better in another part.'[42] This is to see performance as inauthentic. For others, performing the role of a priest is in fact, a way to find fulfilment; a way to be wholly authentic, wholly oneself. The challenge – whether gay or straight, ordained or lay – is to learn to distinguish between the two.

Notes

1 Quoted in Amy Peebles, 2005, '"Restoring the broken image": the language of gender and sexuality in an ex-gay ministry', in Allyson Jule (ed.), *Gender and the Language of Religion*, Basingstoke: Palgrave, p. 197.

2 See, for example, Jon Davies, 1997, 'Sex These Days, Sex Those Days: will it ever end?', in Jon Davies and Gerald Loughlin, 1957, *Sex These Days: Essays on Theology, Sexuality and Society*, Sheffield: Sheffield Academic Press, pp. 18–34

3 An argument influentially articulated in Wilson, *Religion in a Secular Society*.

4 For the Anglican Church in particular, see Andrew K. T. Yip and Michael Keenan, 'By Name United, By Sex Divided: a brief analysis of the current crisis facing the Anglican Communion', *Sociological Research Online* 9(1) (2004) – http://www.socresonline.org.uk/9/1/yip.html – accessed 27.08.06. For a good narrative account, see Stephen Bates, 2004, *A Church at War: Anglicans and Homosexuality*, London: I.B. Tauris.

5 Michael Delashmutt, 2006, 'The Sexualisation of Popular Culture: Towards a Christian Sexual Aesthetic', *Crucible*, July–September (2006), p. 34.

6 Davies, 'Sex These Days', pp. 27–8.

7 Tony Campolo, 1988, *20 Hot Potatoes that Christians are Afraid to Touch*, Milton Keynes: Word, p. 110.

8 Nicky Gumbel, 1994, *Searching Issues*, Eastbourne: Kingsway, pp. 79–84.

9 http://www.truefreedomtrust.co.uk/ – accessed 27.08.06.

10 Martin Hallett, 1996, *Out of the Blue: Homosexuality and the Family*, London: Hodder & Stoughton, p. 29.

11 Timothy Bradshaw (ed.), 2003, *The Way Forward? Christian Voices in Homosexuality and the Church*, 2nd edn, London: SCM Press, pp. 5–11.

12 Oliver O'Donovan, 'Homosexuality in the Church: Can there be Fruitful Theological Debate?', in Bradshaw, *The Way Forward*, p. 26.

13 Ironically, as Sedgwick and Parker note in their discussion of gays in the military, this distinction is one that many queer theorists also make – see 'Introduction', in Andrew Parker and Eve Kosofsky Sedgwick, *Performativity and Performance*, New York and London: Routledge, p. 6.

14 Generally, see Yip, 'The Self', in Davie, Heelas and Woodhead, *Predicting Religion*, pp. 135–46.

15 Quoted in Bates, *A Church at War*, p. 33.

16 See Jeffrey John, 'Christian Same-Sex Partnerships', in Bradshaw, *The Way Forward*, pp. 44–59.

17 See, for example, the life stories in Tony Green, Brenda Harrison, Jeremy Innes, 1996, *Not For Turning: An Enquiry into the Ex-gay Movement*, Camberley: the authors, pp. 73–81.

18 Andrew K. T. Yip, 2000, 'Leaving the Church to Keep My Faith: the Lived Experiences of Non-heterosexual Christians', in Leslie J. Francis and Yaacov J. Katz (eds), *Joining and Leaving Religion: Research Perspectives*, Leominster: Gracewing, pp. 129–46.

19 For Lesbian, Gay, Bisexual and Transgender churches, see Melissa M. Wilcox, 2002, *Coming Out in Christianity: Religion, Identity, and Community*, Bloomington and Indianapolis: Indiana University Press.

20 David Hilliard, 'UnEnglish and Unmanly: Anglo-Catholicism and Homosexuality', *Victorian Studies*, 25(2), (1982), 181–210, p. 181.

21 Chris Glaser, 1988, *Uncommon Calling: A Gay Christian's Struggle to Serve the Church*, Louisville, Kentucky: Westminster John Knox, pp. 10–11.

22 H. A. Williams, 1982, *Some Day I'll Find You: An Autobiography*, London: M. Beazley, pp. 131, 248.

23 See *Some Issues in Human Sexuality: A Guide to the Debate*, 2003, London: Church House Publishing, p. 118–9.

24 Judith Butler, 1997, *Excitable Speech: A Politics of the Performative*, New York and London: Routledge, Ch. 3 provides a nice comparison with the debate over gays in the military.

25 Michael Vaisey, 'Travelling Together', in Bradshaw, *The Way Forward*, pp. 60–70.

26 James Alison, 2001, *Faith Beyond Resentment: Fragments Catholic and Gay*, London: 2001, p. 199.

27 Quoted in Elizabeth Stuart, 1993, *Chosen: Gay Catholic Priests Tell their Stories*, London: Geoffrey Chapman, p. 3.

28 Congregation of the Doctrine of the Faith, 1986, *Letter to the Bishops of the Catholic Church on the Pastoral Care of Homosexual Persons*, section 7 – http://www.vatican.va/roman_curia/congregations/cfaith/documents/rc_con_cfaith_doc_19861001_homosexual-persons_en.html – accessed 27.08.06.

29 For discussions of this, see Elizabeth Stuart (ed.), 1997, *Religion is a Queer Thing: a Guide to the Christian Faith for Lesbian, Gay, Bisexual and Transgendered people*, London and Washington: Cassell.

30 Wilson, *Religion*, 159–67.

31 Quoted in Mary Loudon, 1995, *Revelations: The Clergy Questioned*, London: Penguin, p. 372.

32 Bryan Wilson, 'The Paul Report Examined', *Theology* 68 (1965), pp. 89–103.

33 Robert Towler and A. P. M. Coxon, 1979, *The Fate of the Anglican Clergy: A Sociological Survey*, London and Basingstoke: Macmillan, p. 53.

34 See, for example, Alan Bryman, 'Professionalization and the Clergy: A Research Note', *Review of Religious Research*, 26(3) (1985), pp. 253–60; G. R. Dunstan, 1967, 'The Sacred Ministry as a Learned Profession', *Theology*, 70 (1967), pp. 433–42; Peter Jarvis, 1975, 'The Parish Ministry as a Semi-Profession', *Sociological Review*, 23 (1975), pp. 911–22; Martin. D. Stringer, 2004, 'Identity and the Anglican Priesthood: Debates on the Ordination of Women and Homosexuals in Sociological Perspective', in Coleman and Collins, *Religion, Identity and Change*, pp. 57–68.

35 Frank Musgrove, 'Late-Entrants to the Anglican Ministry: A Move into Marginality?', *Sociological Review*, 23 (1975), pp. 849–50.

36 Quoted in Helen Thorne, 2000, *Journey to Priesthood: An In-depth Study of the First Women Priests in the Church of England*, Bristol: CCSRG Monograph 5, p. 5.

37 Second Vatican Council, 1965, *Presbyterorum Ordinis (Decree on the Ministry and Life of Priests)*, Chapter 1, 2 – Norman P. Tanner (ed.), 1990, *Decrees of the Ecumenical Councils: Vol II Trent to Vatican II*. London: Sheed and Ward, p. 1044.

38 Robert Bogan, 1973, 'Priests, Alienation, and Hope', *The Month*, 6 (1973), pp. 195–201.

39 Quoted in Loudon, *Revelations*, p. 207.

40 Anthony Kenny, 1986, *A Path From Rome: An Autobiography*, Oxford: Oxford University Press, ch. 14.

41 Peebles, '"Restoring the Broken Image"', p. 197.

42 Rowan Williams, 1994, *Open to Judgement: Sermons and Addresses*, London, Darton, Longman & Todd, p. 171.

Theology in the Public Arena:
The case of South Bank Religion

MARK D. CHAPMAN

We met you, Lord, one evening in the way
(The quota filled, tomorrow's contract planned);
We met where cranes cross-hatched a common sky
And medieval stones remarked their lost
   Monopoly of height.
We met when we looked not up but in,
And heard the question, the insistency:
"I am the depth of all things, I am that
Young child, you snubbed, the enemy you shot,
   The case left on your file."
We meet you now in this appointed house,
Which reunites a scattered company.
Here breaking bread we know you and are known
As yours, as servants of a world you chose
   To penetrate, not rule.
It is in meeting that we put our trust
(Shall those who ask for bread receive a stone?).
Dying, we live; through doubt, we understand;
And finding freedom in our slavery
   Learn Love, exhibit truth.[1]

'English Bonhoefferism'

Christopher Driver's hymn, with an accompanying unsingable tune by Erik Routley, appeared in the self-consciously radical Christian magazine *Prism* shortly after the publication of John Robinson's *Honest to God* in 1963. It concisely summarizes the book's thrust, expressing something of the assumptions of what can be called 'English Bonhoefferism'. Every few years there have been re-assessments of *Honest to God*, which became one of the biggest selling theological books of all time.[2] It is in many ways a derivative and unoriginal little book with a great deal of extended quotation, amounting to what James Packer called disparagingly but accurately a 'plateful of mashed-up Tillich fried in Bultmann and garnished with Bonhoeffer'.[3] Whatever its strengths and weaknesses,[4] however, the assertion that 'God is not a big daddy in the sky', as the *Daily Herald's* headline put it,[5] created a stir in the media and throughout the churches, helping to set the tone for theological discussion throughout the decade. The importance of the time of its publication – 1963 was, after all, the year when Philip Larkin famously noted that sexual intercourse began – has not gone unnoticed.[6] For some the book indicated a sign of renewal. The judicious Roger Lloyd wrote with an optimism typical of the period:

> What is so remarkable, what underlines the belief that God himself is at the back of all this stirring ferment, is that the awakening occurs at a moment when Christian people have quite good reasons for a greater optimism than has been possible for many years. At the moment, the Church is doing much better.[7]

Others, however, were more hostile, seeing the book as part of the general accommodation to modern thought.[8]

What has gone largely unnoticed, however, is the broader context of *Honest to God* in 'English Bonhoefferism': whatever Bonhoeffer might have meant by 'religionless Christianity'[9] in 1944, the vague and embryonic ideas presented in a few pages of his *Letters and Papers from Prison*[10] were taken up with a vengeance by a number of writers and churchmen, of whom Robinson was merely one example. A country in which the context of Bonhoeffer's thought, particularly his Lutheranism, was scarcely understood, nevertheless proved remarkably receptive to some very radical ideas. All religion, the English Bonhoefferians held (admittedly to varying degrees), had to go, and something else was needed to replace it. For many, this required a new form of Christianity predicated on seeing Christ in the secular, especially in a place called the 'Secular City'[11] with its resonances of the 'death of God' theology.[12] This city, it seemed, looked a bit like South London where many of the advocates of the abolition of religion worked, some in the cathedral at Southwark: Christ, they held, was to be seen in the suffering and meaninglessness of the world rather than in church.

This essay attempts a preliminary interpretation of English Bonhoefferism, particularly as it related to practice in the Church of England. This form of theology contains three related features. First, and most important, is the assumption that Christianity needed to be freed from 'religion' in a radical and complete way. Christ was not present in the churches, in so far as their liturgies and languages focused on a God 'out-there'. For this reason the churches were not worth keeping, at least in their present form. For one of the first times in English history, anti-clericalism was rife; the irony was that it originated from people receiving their incomes from the church. Second, the flip-side of this understanding was that the church and Christ were already present in the world and in ordinary people (whether they liked it or not),[13] and that all that was needed for the future of Christianity was to give voice to this latent Christian tendency present in all people. What was taken for granted was that Christianity would somehow be discovered in all people when freed from the traditions and language of the church. This would happen if only people could be persuaded to love one another. Finally, English Bonhoefferism was accompanied by a struggle to redirect the histori-cal assets of the Church of England away from religion (and particularly small rural churches with freehold incumbents) towards new forms of ministry in the unchurched areas of the inner city where there were few reli-gious people. In April 1965 the editor of *Prism* noted that the 'word radical in a church context is loosely used to cover those who approve of Leslie Paul [who had produced a report on the redeployment of the clergy] in the same breath as they approve of the Bishop of Woolwich'.[14] There were frequent calls for teams of clergy, some of whom would earn their living in 'the world', working in partnership with the laity, and freed from historical burdens like medieval buildings and job security.

Without wishing to belittle the achievement or question the missionary intentions of those associated with English Bonhoefferism, looking back after forty years or so it is all too obvious that the fatal flaw in such a theology was its neglect of those responsible for preserving and cherishing what Grace Davie has called the religious memory.[15] Indeed it might be suggested that without the care and nurture of existing congregations, and without explicit education in religious traditions and language, religious memory can easily be extinguished.[16] A form of theology predicated on the conscious and explicit elimination of religious language and cultic practice was hardly likely to succeed in perpetuating the survival of churches in an often hostile environment.

Freedom from religion

The first assumption of English Bonhoefferism was that there was not much point in being religious, if that implied supernaturalism of any kind, since religion had been superseded in a world 'come of age'.[17] This was clearly expressed in *Honest to God*: religion was no longer 'a pre-condition of faith'.[18] Furthermore, the sort of people who went to church did so because they wanted the kind of supernatural props that had become meaningless: '"God" as a working hypothesis, as a stop-gap for our embarrassments, has become superfluous.'[19] Consequently they were not the sort of people who really mattered but were deluded and immature. Something different was required. Quoting Bonhoeffer directly, Robinson asked:

In what way are we 'religionless-secular' Christians, in what way are we the *ek-klesia*, those who are called forth, not regarding ourselves from a religious point of view as specially favoured, but rather as belonging wholly to the world? In that case Christ is no longer an object of religion, but something quite different, really the Lord of the world.[20]

Religionless Christianity must have been a hot topic of conversation in the Bishop's house. His wife, Ruth Robinson, produced a lengthy article for *Prism* on 'Religionless Christianity for Children', which displays more of a debt to Rudolf Bultmann than Bonhoeffer, but which ends with an understanding of the essence of Christianity not in dogma but in love. Writing about the Christmas story, she noted that her own children did 'not seem bothered by the suggestion that it may not have happened exactly like that'. The child sees it as 'a way in which *history* can be recorded so as to reveal its significance in depth as well as in space and time'.[21] Through education, the child was gradually to grow in the ability to separate out the levels of myth and to experience the underlying reality of love: 'Let the child then be allowed to apprehend the reality of love for himself *first*, without having a premature definition thrust upon him. Similarly, let him understand *for himself* what forgiveness, repentance, reconciliation, atonement mean without religious overtones.'[22]

At times religionless Christianity could become boldly anticlerical. In the editorial of the edition of *Prism* following the publication of what it called 'H*n*st T* G*d', presumably to avoid voicing the holy name, Nicholas Mosley wrote unguardedly: 'The main reason why the millions stay outside the Church is because they can't stick the thousands inside the church; or rather, they can't stick the domestic carry-on between the domestic pastor and his flock.'[23] A few months later he continued in a similar vein in a review of Michael Ramsey's *Image Old and New*, suggesting that the real issues were less over the questions of belief, and more to do with practice, as had been suggested by Harry Williams and Donald Mackinnon in *Objections to Christian Belief*.[24] The problem was whether the 'traditionally pious are in fact doing evil'. Clergy (including even bishops and Cambridge deans) who on Sundays 'bob up and down' and 'make their peculiar statements' have 'allowed themselves to become aligned in function on the side of the devil'.[25] There is some truth in Donald Hughes' satirical blessing:

Go forth into the world, to proclaim that the only obstacles to truth are Religion and the Church; and may the Depth of all Being grant you a modern outlook and a muddled mind, and keep you from coming here again to expose yourselves to this retarded and probably hypocritical congregation. Amen.[26]

On this model, the church's focus should therefore not be so much about nurturing congregations and passing on its seemingly irrelevant traditions with their strange choreography and language as about getting in touch with 'real' Christianity which was not religious at all and which was to be found beyond the church doors in the world.[27] This was despite the fact that it had been remarkably successful, at least in numerical terms, through the 1950s.[28] There was a widespread belief that very many people outside the churches found religious forms of Christianity simply meaningless.[29] Consequently, the church was charged with the duty of becoming non-religious. According to Robinson, instead of seeing itself as a preserver of religious truth and tradition, the church was to become an agency of service and 'self-effacing secrecy' which, 'so far from requiring the stepping up of the Church as a religious organization, points rather in the direction of its *dépouillement* or stripping down which Bonhoeffer believed it must undergo'.[30] The church had a duty to reform itself in order to present a version of Christianity which was not so much a religion or a set of cultic practices, as the search for God or 'the "beyond" in the midst of our life'.[31] To do this it had to adopt a new life modelled on the self-giving love of Jesus, the 'man for others'.[32] In an early assessment of this approach Roger Lloyd commented on the difficulty of the task:

> The church has to persuade [the secular man] to want what he does not want now, to trust him whom he does not know and whom, on the hypothesis, he sees no reason to trust, and to see that, without God, whether defined as the wholly other or as the ground of our being, he cannot make any sense of life, or even wish to have it abundantly. It is a tall order. At present very few of us know more than a little of how his mind works, nor yet of how to present a re-interpreted Gospel to him.[33]

Reforming the Ministry

The Robinsons were saying little that was new. The pages of *Prism*, which in many ways was the unofficial magazine of 'South Bank Theology',[34] were full of ideas for practical expressions of religionless Christianity. For instance, even before *Honest to God* was published, the lay theologian and ICI Executive, John Wren-Lewis, wrote an article with the bold title, 'On Not Going to Church'.[35] God was known, he wrote, 'in day-to-day encounters of personal life' and not through compulsive ritualism. Liberty of the gospel 'seemed like a frightening irreverence towards holy things'. While it was important for people to acknowledge God, it was also crucial that 'in our zeal to get them to do this, we should on no account run the risk of re-introducing idolatrous, ritualistic attitudes – and we run that risk if we concentrate overmuch on the business of churchgoing'. A large amount of traditional theology, he suggested emphatically, was *'totally mistaken'*, and reflected 'a church life which was the very opposite of the free community of those who have the liberty of the Gospel'.[36]

There were many experiments with forms of 'non-religious' Christianity and work among those isolated from the churches. Most famous of all these experiments was Nicolas Stacey's work as Rector of Woolwich. He transformed his church into a centre of non-religious social activity, with coffee bars, advice bureaux and youth clubs. His innovations were met by much criticism, with one Southwark vicar threatening: 'If Stacey thinks he can build the Kingdom of God by frying eggs on the altar and percolating coffee in the organ pipes he should think again.'[37] In a similarly unconventional form of ministry, Kenneth Leech wrote in January 1964 of his work, while still an ordinand, among prostitutes, homosexuals and 'beatniks'.[38] A few months later the young Richard Holloway wrote of 'The Gorbals Group' in Glasgow, making the Bonhoefferian claim that the 'church which should exist for others, for the world, now exists for itself'.[39] The philosophy of these approaches was encapsulated in a straightforward piece of practical Bonhoefferism by Christopher Byers, at the time a curate in Bermondsey:

> In the world of the secular it is easy to see what are the units of our community which really matter. They are the family, the factory and the school. It is here that Christ has to be made flesh for modern man. It is here that the needs of man 'come of age' are most apparent. They are grown-up needs which the Church cannot meet while struggling to keep her own 'life' going. But the Church is called to meet those needs from the resources of Christ, and could do so if there was a willingness to serve the world for which Christ was content to die.[40]

How the church would retain identity through its service was left unsaid.

Similarly, in a retrospective contributed to the final edition of *Prism*, John Robinson summarized his understanding of what he had done for the church: 'I would like to think that it is the Kingdom cracking open the church, God showing us the suffocating character of the religious organisation which his church has become by breaking it down and remaking it.' His fear was that resources would be diverted from the real business of the church in service (in support of such organizations as Christian Action and the Notting Hill Housing Association) to keeping the show on the road.[41] Again there was little said about the nurturing and care of the distinctively religious: presumably Christianity would survive simply through the ministrations of the well-educated elite leadership who were entrusted with putting these reforms into practice, rather than through the devotions of the people of the suburbs. In a December 1964 *Observer* article entitled 'A Mission's Failure', Stacey chronicled his disillusionment with these alternative forms of ministry, and in 1969 resigned his living and went to work for Oxfam. His concerns posed important questions for the Southbank radicals, with Mervyn Stockwood responding to this piece with the rhetorical question: 'Why do men appear to respond more readily in Reigate, Purley and Coulsdon than in Woolworth, Woolwich and Battersea?'[42]

Removing the holy

Given this clamour for a new version of 'religionless' Christianity, it comes as little surprise that much of *Honest to God* (and much else from the same period) amounts to a proposal for a worldly spirituality rather than a constructive theology. It is interesting to note that in one of the early reviews, Christopher Evans felt that the book fitted most appropriately among books of devotion rather than theology.[43] Similarly, in articles for the *New Yorker*, Ved Mehta noted (accurately) that the 'style of the book, like that of a schoolboy's composition, was showy – bulging and straining at almost every point with far-fetched analogies constructed for purposes of polemics'. It was, he went on, 'a prayer, a *cri de coeur*'.[44] Much of the book, particularly Chapter 5 ('Worldly Holiness'), is concerned with attempts to take liturgy, prayer and the other trappings of Christianity out of church and into the 'common'. Much involves the re-orientation of Christianity away from 'the Holy' towards the realm of the ordinary (where the laity were presumed to dwell).[45] A worldly spirituality required a reform of the liturgy, so that it should take place not in the 'glass case' of the sanctuary with its projection of a God 'out there', but in the midst of the people. The worst that could possibly happen was that 'churchiness will keep on reasserting itself'.[46]

Even before *Honest to God* Robinson had been known as a liturgical reformer,[47] something he shared with many of his Southwark colleagues after his appointment to Woolwich. The cathedral and prominent parish churches through the diocese were in the vanguard of liturgical change.[48] The chapel of the diocesan conference centre was dedicated to the 'people of God'. Architects set about redesigning buildings, and musicians created new sounds for the liturgy. In 1964 Ian Henderson described a service in Southwark Cathedral with congregational participation, con-celebration (which he did not perceive as a clericalization of worship), and catchy tunes: 'I am ready to believe that spirits were raised a little nearer heaven by this latest Southwark experiment. I repeat did they like it? Yeah, yeah, yeah – or words to that effect.'[49] Under the influence of Parish and People and the Keble Conference Group for Liturgical Renewal, liturgical reform spread through the Church of England. Even that bastion of Oxford Anglo-Catholicism, Pusey House had a 'folk' mass.

Other attempts to express the ultimate and the beyond in everyday life quickly emerged. Mervyn Stockwood wrote of a new window depicting 'engineers, office cleaners, lightermen, printers, distillers and housewives' he had dedicated at Christ Church, Blackfriars. 'It's true,' he wrote, that they're not like the usual stained-glass window, but they're none the worse for that. In fact, it's possible that the conventional church window, like many a hymn, has done much to give people a false idea of Christ and has encouraged them to think that religion is divorced from reality . . . Christianity is not an escape into a realm of make-believe, but a way of life that relates God to human experience.[50]

Reforming the structures

Since clergy had traditionally been educated in theology and religion and spent their time doing religious things, professional ministers in the traditional mould were under threat from English Bonhoefferism. Worldly spirituality required ministers who were active in the world rather than liturgical functionaries located in a separate ecclesiastical sphere. Robinson predicted as early as 1952 that 'the coming pattern of [the Church of England's] ministry is bound to be largely non-professional, in the sense that its priesthood will consist in great proportion of men working at secular jobs at every level'. This had implications for the ways in which the clergy were to be trained: 'It is essential that it must be done *without* taking men out of the jobs and milieu in which they are.'[51] This desire soon led to new patterns of training with the setting up of the Southwark Ordination Course under Stanley Evans, and the gradual increase in the number of non-stipendiary clergy and worker priests.[52] Sometimes there was extraordinary optimism about the possible effects of redirecting ministry towards the inner city. Indeed this proved one of the major faults of the Paul Report, which predicted the numbers of clergy doubling within a few years. Properly directed these new clergy would create a (non-) religious revival. At the end of 1963, John Robinson suggested that releasing 1000 clergy for work in urban parishes would lead to an increase of 100,000 communicants.[53] Others were less sanguine, reading the statistics differently. Trevor Beeson, for instance, contemplated strategic withdrawal from certain areas where the church seemed ineffective.[54]

Prism was full to the brim with articles calling for a reform of the ministry and the parochial system. Most popular was the idea of clergy teams (and an abolition of the antiquated system of patronage and remuneration) which would allow clergy the time and energy to engage with people in the world including in their workplaces. One writer, Robert Jeffery, explicitly linked these pastoral reforms which emerged from the Parish and People Movement and the Paul Report with English Bonhoefferism:

It cannot be denied that most parishes fail to make any real contact with the majority of people. Most parish priests, deep down, know that they are failing, lacking real integrity, and becoming introverted. There are a few exceptions, but we can't all be exceptional men. Perhaps this fleeing from the parishes, which seems to be increasing, will compel the Church to look at this problem and see that Bonhoeffer's call for 'religionless Christianity' means a lot in terms of practical pastoralia.[55]

Others, including Christopher Byers, held that the whole parochial system needed simplifying and rationalizing; and along with this the church needed to embrace the secular. The main problem was being 'lumbered with the machinery of the past – which resists the secular instead of embracing it'. There was little need for new churches but a great need for specialist clergy working in a practice like groups of doctors. Although weekends would be left for recreation, people would be encouraged to meet in small house groups, with schools being booked for big occasions. In this way, he held, society might become 'less religious and more Christian'.[56]

English Bonhoefferism and 'secular Anglicanism'

This survey of English Bonhoefferism has necessarily been selective. It has focused on the practical expressions of religionless Christianity. This has been understood as a kind of clergy-led anticlericalism. The idealization of the 'secular city' and non-churched laity as the place where Christ was to be met led to the neglect of churchgoers, many of whom were understood as immature and as somehow clinging on to an outmoded supernaturalism and religious world-view. While there might have been an emphasis on ultimacy and depth in English Bonhoefferism, there was little sense in which Christianity was seen as needing the mythological, symbolic and traditional. God-language could be restated in human terms; the whole tradition was to be glimpsed in a religionless and very human way – and was to be found solely in and among the secular. There is consequently something in Alasdair MacIntyre's charge that the striking thing about John Robinson was that he was an atheist.[57] However, as I have suggested, removing religion from Christianity and disposing of the traditional was a highly risky strategy for the church. It required that people would somehow discover for themselves the 'ultimate' truths that lay beneath religious language. And this would happen if the church refocused its energies on practical expressions of love and service.

There is some sense in which the English Bonhoefferians were nostalgic for a kind of universal, culturally relevant Christianity divested of the Victorian trimmings of religion. It is interesting that the 'first intimations of the electrifying challenges implicit in the concept of the entire west as a collection of multicultural societies'[58] were scarcely mentioned by these theologians of the 1960s. Instead the 'secular Anglicanism'[59] which had sustained English society through the twentieth century was adopted in its most radicalized form, so much so that its cultic underpinning was cleared away. The ever-present threat in secular Anglicanism of the transformation of Christianity into a vague religion of love and service was finally put into practice by the English Bonhoefferians. From both within and outside Christianity, how-ever, others were challenging this understanding. As Matthew Grimley writes: 'The belief that society could, or should, pursue a single, broadly agreed version of virtue, or the good life, was abandoned' from the 1960s onwards. Indeed it was little surprise that the church ceased to be the major voice in the state after the idea of a 'national character' on which that state was built began to disintegrate.[60] It was almost as if the English Bonhoefferians transformed a highly radical theology based on some late prison writings of a German Lutheran who did not regard Barth as going far enough in his critique of religion,[61] into a justification for the state religion of liberal Anglicanism with its universal claims and vision of a unified church and state. Religionless Christianity was perhaps a last ditch and somewhat idiosyncratic attempt at supporting a dying ideology.[62]

At the same time, the radical theology of the 1960s might well be included among what Arthur Marwick calls the 'original and striking (and sometimes absurd) developments in elite thought' that characterized so much of the 1960s avant-garde. A theology seeking to abolish the very religion required to sustain it might well be one of the most absurd developments of all.[63] Its approach was, of course, based on a number of delusions: first, there was the assumption that the non-churched and the working classes could somehow be won over to Christianity. Second, it assumed that Christianity could survive without the body of Christians prepared to go to church and pay their way (often the suburban middle-classes). In a country with the lowest churchgoing rates in Western Europe, it was a fatal error to criticize the faithful few in the hope of finding Christ among the faithless many, who had on the whole always been content to let others take care of their religion, provided the church was there when they needed it.[64]

From within the *Prism* circle the most outspoken dissident was Valerie Pitt, who claimed in the final issue of the magazine that 'we suffer delusions of a past grandeur'. This was particularly true of Leslie Paul:

> His kind of nostalgia is the sad surprising thing about all our reformers who see clearly enough that there is a ruin but hope against hope, some-how, to restore it, to see the kingdom realised and alienation of the people removed. *Prism* itself has followed hard in this grail quest, for somewhere it thinks there must be a magical vessel, a charm which will restore the wasteland and undo what is done.[65]

Instead, she understood the Church of England as a 'minority body which has to suffer a deserved isolation and needs to withdraw to learn to live as a body. Withdraw? From the nightmare of this shaken clergymen shrink appalled in convocation and the columns of *The Times*: "We shall become", they say, "a ghetto".' A greater risk, however, was that the church might be 'caught forever in the Parish Communion Culture of the twentieth century'.[66] She ended her contribution by challenging the South Bank orthodoxy:

> It is worth perhaps enquiring whether the withdrawal of our talents, of our love, from all the disturbing, irritating misguided pew fodder isn't one of the reasons why it is so provincial, so closed in a sub-Christian world.
>
> To undo the terrifying effects of the Anglican synthesis, all of us have, really, to withdraw into the Church's society, into the cosy circle of the household of faith – which is not in the least like the High Table at King's. Indeed, I daresay for a while it will be dreadfully provincial – like the Lord's life in Galilee.[67]

Pitt's alternative suggestion amounts to a traditional Anglo-Catholic defence of Christianity as composed of highly committed groups living in small sacramental communities which, sociologically at least, look rather like sects. It can be argued that such groups might well have been better able to articulate this sort of 'provincial' and religious Christianity and to weather the 1960s' storm. They might have been better prepared for multi-culturalism and the loss of Anglican hegemony. In the 1960s, however, few were prepared to sacrifice what Donald Mackinnon called the 'status of invulnerability' and to flirt with the obscurity of the ghetto.[68] However radical it might have appeared, English Bonhoefferism was the last stand of a collapsing national ideology.

Notes

* I am grateful to the Very Revd Robert Jeffery and the Revd Michael Brierley for their thoughtful comments on an earlier draft of this chapter.

1 Hymn by Christopher Driver (a free church journalist who became a distinguished food historian) in *Prism* 73 (May 1963), p. 22.

2 Eric James (ed.), 1988, *God's Truth Essays to Celebrate the Twenty-fifth Anniversary of* Honest to God, London: SCM Press; Henriette T. Donner, '25 Years On!: Looking Back to Radical Theology and Radical Ministry in Britain' in *The Modern Churchman*, 31 (1989), pp. 30–5, 16–28; John Bowden (ed.), 1993, *Thirty Years of Honesty: Honest to God Then and Now*, London: SCM Press; Henriette T. Donner, 'Where were you when *Honest to God* appeared', *Theology* 99 (1995), 276–84; Colin Slee (ed.), 2004, *Honest to God: 40 Years On*, London: SCM Press. On Robinson, see Eric James's excellent biography, 1987, *A Life of Bishop John A. T. Robinson*, London: Collins, esp. Ch. 6.

3 J. I. Packer, 1963, *Keep Yourselves from Idols*, London: Church Book Room Press, p. 5.

4 These have been discussed at length elsewhere. See esp. Alastair Kee, 1988, *The Roots of Christian Freedom: The Theology of John A. T. Robinson*, London: SPCK.

5 19 March 1963.

6 Keith W. Clements, 1988, *Lovers of Discord*, London: SPCK, p. 184; Paul A. Welsby, *A History of the Church of England*, Oxford: Oxford University Press, p. 111. For the context see Gerald Parsons (ed.), *The Growth of Religious Diversity: Volume I: Traditions*, London: Routledge, 1993, pp. 23–94, esp. pp. 56–60; and more generally, Arthur Marwick, *The Sixties: Cultural Revolution in Britain, France, Italy and the United States, c. 1958–1974*, Oxford: Oxford University Press, 1998, Ch. 2.

7 Roger Lloyd, 1964, *The Ferment in the Church*, London: SCM Press, p. 13.

8 See Clements, *Lovers*, Ch. 7 and Welsby, *History*, Chs 5–8 for useful surveys. A selection of reviews was published in David L. Edwards (ed.), 1963, *The Honest to God Debate*, London: SCM Press. For a survey of most of the later material, see also Hermann Bendl, 'Bischof John A. T. Robinsons Buch Honest to God (Gott ist Anders) im Spiegel Anglikanischer Kritik, Dokumentation und Analyse' (Munich, diss, 1980). There was a flood of pamphlets. Typical conservative evangelical reactions came from Packer, *Keep Yourselves from Idols* and Leon Morris, 1964, *The Abolition of Religion*, London: IVP. A thoughtful Anglo-Catholic reaction came from Eric Mascall, 'Reflections on the "Honest to God" Debate', *Thought*, 41 (1966), 183–97. More sympathetic are O. Fielding Clarke, 1963, *For Christ's Sake: A Reply to Honest to God*, London: Religious Education Press and John M. Morrison, 1966, *Honesty and God*. The best pamphlet of all was Michael Ramsey, 1963, *Image Old and New*, London: SPCK. George Carey reviewed Ramsey's reaction in 'Michael Ramsey's Response to *Honest to God*' in Robin Gill and Lorna Kendall (eds), 1995, *Michael Ramsey as Theologian*, London: Darton, Longman & Todd, pp. 159–75. The book even made a mark on the Continent. It was reviewed by Eduard Schillebeeckx, 1964, *Personale Begegnung mit Gott: Eine Antwort an J. A. T. Robinsons "Honest to God"*, Mainz: Grünewald.

9 1971, *Letters and Papers from Prison*, London: SCM Press, pp. 280, 285. The collection was first translated in 1953. Robinson cites 'religionless Christianity' with approval in *Honest to God*, p. 35.

10 *Honest to God*, pp. 22–3. See also Werner and Lotte Pelz, 1963, *God Is No More*, London: Victor Gollancz. This virtually unreadable book by German refugees contains one of the strongest attacks on religion, as something that 'enables us to withdraw from the mysterious insecurity of life into pseudo-mysteriousness' (p. 107). An earlier Bonhoefferian approach was made by R. Gregor Smith, 1956, *The New Man: Christianity and Man's Coming of Age*, London: SCM Press. A useful survey is offered in Robert J. Page, 1965, *New Directions in Anglican Theology*, New York: Seabury, pp. 115–38.

11 See, for example, Douglas Rhymes, 1967, *Prayer in the Secular City*, London: Lutterworth which begins with a question from Bonhoeffer: 'What is the place of prayer and worship in the entire absence of religion?' (p. 9); see also, Harvey Cox, 1965, *The Secular City: Secularization and Urbanization in Theological Perspective*, New York: Macmillan.

12 See, for example, Paul van Buren, 1963, *The Secular Meaning of the Gospel, Based on an Analysis of its Language*, London: SCM Press.

13 See, for example, J. A. T. Robinson, 1960, *Christ Comes In*, London: Mowbray.

14 *Prism* 96 (April 1965), p. 3.

15 Davie, *Religion in Modern Europe*, pp. 59–60, 81. She builds on the work of Danièle Hervieu-Léger, 1993, *Religion pour Mémoire*, Paris: Cerf and 2000, Danièle Hervieu-Léger, 2000, *Religion as a Chain of Memory*, trans. Simon Lee, Cambridge: Polity Press, Part III.

16 Davie, *Religion in Europe*, p. 182.

17 Bonhoeffer, *Letters*, pp. 326–9.

18 Robinson, *Honest to God*, pp. 36–7, 129.

19 Bonhoeffer, *Letters*, p. 381.

20 Bonhoeffer, *Letters*, pp. 280–1; cited in Robinson, *Honest to God*, p. 122. See also pp. 61, 7.

21 Ruth Robinson, 'Religionless Christianity for Children', *Prism* 72 (April 1963), p. 31.

22 Robinson, 'Religionless' pp. 33, 35.

23 'H*n*st T* G*d', *Prism* 73 (May 1963), p. 4.

24 D. M. MacKinnon (et. Al.), 1963, *Objections to Christian Belief*, London: Constable. See Clements, *Lovers*, pp. 168–76

25 *Prism* 74 (June 63), pp. 59–60.

26 'Neo-Matins', *Prism* 85 (May 1964), p. 68.

27 Robinson, *Honest to God*, p. 85. In a number of places Robinson criticizes religious revival and any attempt to 'withdraw' from the world into a religious clique. See esp. pp. 85–6.

28 The 'return to piety' in the 1950s has been noted by many authors. See Hastings, *A History*, pp. 444–72; Brown, *Death*, pp. 170–5; Davie, *Believing without Belonging*, pp. 30–33.

29 Robinson, *Honest to God*, p. 141.

30 Robinson, *Honest to God*, p. 137.

31 Robinson, *Honest to God*, p. 121.

32 Robinson, *Honest to God*, Ch. 2, esp. pp. 75–76; Bonhoeffer, *Letters*, p. 381.

33 Lloyd, *Ferment*, pp. 117–18.

34 The term seems to have been coined by Mervyn Stockwood in an article for the *Evening Standard*: 'South Bank Religion – what I'm trying to do' in Mervyn Stockwood, 1964, *Bishop's Journal*, London: Mowbray, pp. 65–8.

35 John Wren-Lewis, 'On Not Going to Church', *Prism* 6 (February 1962), pp. 25–9.

36 Wren-Lewis, 'On Not Going to Church', pp. 27, 28, 29.

37 Nicolas Stacey, 1971, *Who Cares?*, London: Anthony Blond, p. 114.

38 Kenneth Leech, 'The Church and the Social Outcast', *Prism* 81 (January 1964), pp. 9–14, at pp. 13–14.

39 Richard Holloway, 'The Gorbals Group', *Prism* 86 (June 1964), p. 21.

40 Christopher Byers, 'Secularisation and the Parochial Machine', *Prism* 82 (February 64), pp. 18–21.

41 John Robinson, *Prism* 99 (July 1965), p. 15.

42 *The Bridge* (Southwark Diocesan Magazine) cited in James Bogle, *South Bank Religion: the Diocese of Southwark: 1959–1969*, London: Hatcham Press, p. 22.

43 Broadcast review in Edwards, *Honest to God Debate*, pp. 110–13, p. 111.

44 Ved Mehta, 1966, *The New Theologian*, London: Weidenfeld and Nicolson, pp. 9, 11.

45 Robinson, *Honest to God*, p. 85. See Timothy Beaumont (ed.), 1963, *The Layman's Church*, London: Lutterworth.

46 Robinson, *Honest to God*, p. 89.

47 John A. T. Robinson, 1960, *Liturgy Coming to Life*, London: Mowbray.

48 See Bogle, *South Bank Religion*, Ch. 4.

49 'The Southwark Sound', *Prism* 84 (April 1964), pp. 19–21, here p. 21.

50 Stockwood, *Bishop's Journal*, p. 36.

51 *Theology* (June 1952), pp. 203–4. See also John A. T. Robinson, 1960, *On Being the Church in the World*, London: SCM Press.

52 See Bogle, *South Bank Religion*, Ch. 5.

53 John Robinson, 'Manpower and the Ministry', *Prism* 80 (December 1963), p. 18.

54 'Statistical Theology and Mission', *Prism* 84 (February 1964), pp. 13–15.

55 Robert Jeffery, *Prism* 75 (July 1963), p. 16.

56 Byers, 'Secularisation and the Parochial Machine', p. 19.

57 Edwards, *Honest to God Debate*, p. 215. His assessment admittedly lacks subtlety and fails to grasp Robinson's panentheism. See also Rowan Williams, 2004, '*Honest to God* and the 1960s' in *Anglican Identities*, London: Darton, Longman & Todd, pp. 103–20.

58 Marwick, *Sixties*, pp. 19–20.

59 Marwick, *Sixties*, p. 35.

60 Grimley, *Citizenship*, pp. 210, 221, 225.

61 Bonhoeffer, *Letters*, p. 280.

62 In Brown, *Death*, pp. 190–91 a different interpretation is offered.

63 Marwick, *Sixties*, p. 19.

64 Marwick, *Sixties*, p. 35. This may be why Marwick has so little to say about religion.

65 *Prism* 99 (July 1965), pp. 18–19.

66 *Prism* 99 (July 1965), p. 20.

67 *Prism* 99 (July 1965), p. 21. Here there are resonances of Donald MacKinnon, 1969, 'Kenosis and establishment' in *The Stripping of the Altars*, London: Fontana, p. 34.

68 Mackinnon, 'Kenosis', p. 33. See also Mark D. Chapman, 'Charles Gore, Kenosis and the Crisis of Power', *Journal of Anglican Studies* 3 (2005), 197–218.

A Papal Funeral and a Royal Wedding: Reconfiguring Religion in the Twenty-first Century

GRACE DAVIE

At the beginning of April 2005 Pope John Paul II died, bringing to an end an unusually long papacy. His death came after several years of illness in which his physical strength was clearly diminished, but not his mental or spiritual stature. The moment had been anticipated – the obituaries were ready, so too the commemorative programmes to which suitable concluding statements were added before they were broadcast. They received maximum coverage in the week that followed.[1]

The tone of these tributes was revealing. John Paul II was universally acclaimed for his resistance to communism in East Europe. Both his presence, and his frequent visits to Poland in the 1980s, were recognized as a powerful catalyst in the chain of events that led, extraordinarily fast, to the collapse of communism as a political system. Rather more nuanced were the reactions to his thinking on moral issues – more precisely to his statements regarding the absolute sanctity of the human person, including the human embryo. Here respect was tempered by criticism, particularly with regard to John Paul II's uncompromising views on birth control, a 'problem' inextricably (though not always correctly) connected in many people's minds to the AIDS epidemic in Africa.

One point stands out, however. The Pope was a global figure in every sense of the term: probably the best-known individual in the modern world, instantly recognized wherever he went, totally in command of the world's media, and strikingly adept in using the latter to drive a truly global agenda. No one was surprised therefore when the world turned towards Rome as it became clear that the Pope was dying. Few people, however, anticipated the *scale* of the reaction that followed, as almost every country suspended 'normal' activities in order to mark the event. Rome became the centre of attention for heads of state, for religious leaders, for journalists of all kinds, and for hundreds of thousands of individuals (Catholic and other), many of whom converged on the city in the week preceding the funeral. Here there is overwhelming evidence of the continuing presence of religion in the modern world and of the relationship between religion and globalization. The influence of the Pope transcended every imaginable boundary, political as well as religious. Not everyone liked what they saw, but few could deny the global impact of this remarkable man.

The strange juxtaposition of events in Britain in the first week of April 2005 is instructive in this respect, not least for the paradoxes that it reveals. Here, a second, and as it happens secular, marriage of the heir to the throne was postponed in order that Prince Charles himself, Tony Blair (as Prime Minister) and Rowan Williams (as Archbishop of Canterbury) should attend the funeral of the Pope in Rome. But no Prime Minister or Archbishop of Canterbury or heir to the throne had ever been to such a funeral before, never mind prioritizing this over a royal wedding – a gesture that symbolizes the wholly different configurations that are emerging in the twenty-first century. Increasingly the links, tensions and antagonisms between faiths and peoples of faith become the dominant factor; domestic agendas (royal weddings, the calling of a general election and even the Grand National) were simply rearranged. How is it possible to explain this very different state of affairs and why has it come about? That is the purpose of this contribution. It will be divided into three sections: the domestic agenda, the European framework and the global context. Each is significant in understanding not only the events themselves but the current state of religion in Britain, Europe and the world.

The domestic agenda

In September 1997, the Royal Family was present at a very different occasion – the funeral of Prince Charles' ex-wife, an event that marked the end of an extraordinary week in the life of this country. Princess Diana and her then boyfriend (Dodi al-Fayed) had been killed in a car accident in Paris, an incident that provoked an outpouring of grief that had not been anticipated, but from which can be learnt a great deal about the religious life of this country.[2]

Diana, in fact, was quintessentially English in her religious life. Like many people of her age, class and upbringing, she was baptized in the Church of England and in the fullness of time was both confirmed and married in the same church. As things began to go wrong in her personal life, she drifted away from these moorings. More precisely, we know that she visited gurus on different occasions, that she flirted with Catholicism (her mother had by this time become a Catholic) and at the end of her life was keeping company with the son of a prominent Muslim. It was, however, the Church of England that buried her, and any suggestion that this 'service' might have been withdrawn would, quite clearly, have caused outrage. The fact that Princess

Diana had not led an unequivocally Christian life was immaterial – she, like the rest of us, had a right to the services of the church at the end of her life. It follows that the churches should be there to meet such needs even if most of us choose not to attend them on a regular basis.

The reaction to Diana's death was neither secular nor rational in the conventional understandings of these terms. But what was it? The answer is complex, but one point is clear: significant numbers of British people were instinctively drawn to their churches in this very unusual week. This happened in two ways. First the churches became an important, though not the only, gathering point for a whole range of individual gestures of mourning in which Christian and less Christian symbols became inextricably mixed, both materially (candles, playing cards and madonnas) and theologically (life after death was strongly affirmed, but with no notion of final judgement). More significant, however, was the awareness in the population as a whole that multiple and well-intentioned gestures of individual mourning were inadequate in themselves to mark the end of this particular life, as indeed of any other. Hence, the need for public ritual or public liturgy (in other words a funeral) and where else but in the established church? [3]

Other royal occasions tell us similar things. The power of tradition and the place of liturgy within this played a central role in the Queen Mother's funeral in April 2002. There was no need to improvise on this occasion. The ceremonial surrounding her death had been planned to the finest detail, with the full co-operation of the Queen Mother herself. The same was true some two months later at a rather happier occasion: the Queen's Golden Jubilee.[4] A service in St Paul's – hosted and led by Anglicans, but incorporating contributions from both the Catholic Archbishop of Westminster and representatives of the free churches – combined thankfulness for the past with hope for the future. The participation of a wide range of Christian denominations was, moreover, an expected part of this occasion, reflecting the fact that an ecumenical presence is now commonplace (almost obligatory) in any public ritual. More significant perhaps, was the presence – though not the participation – of eight leaders from other world faiths, all of which are now present in Britain, though in varying numbers.

Diversity, both ethnic and religious, was even more present in the parade that followed the same afternoon. For the first time ever, acts from the Notting Hill Carnival were seen outside the annual festival in West London, an event dominated by Afro-Caribbean culture, music and dance. Even more significant from the point of view of religion, were the 5000 gospel singers who took part in this event, illustrating newer dimensions in the religious life of Britain. Part of this can be explained by the growing presence of Afro-Caribbean communities in London and other urban areas. The presence of white singers as well as black is, however, interesting. So too the contrast between the formal service at St Paul's in the morning with the images of modern Britain (including the religious elements) presented in the afternoon, offering contrasting styles of Britishness. Both were enjoyed by a crowds of a million or more and broadcast live on television.

The gradual acceptance of Prince Charles's second marriage should be seen in this context. Quite clearly, the position of the monarchy has changed in British society but it is not yet a thing of the past. Royal occasions, moreover, not only remain significant events in the life of the nation, but become revealing barometers of social change – not least with respect to religion. Hence the need to pay attention both to the marriage of Prince Charles and Camilla Parker-Bowles and to the way in which this was celebrated. Essentially the marriage itself, a civil ceremony followed by a blessing in St George's Chapel in Windsor, is evidence of the mixed economy that is pervasive in the religious life of this country. The historic churches of Europe are no longer able to discipline the beliefs and behaviour of European populations. They remain nonetheless significant players in the lives of European people – willing, among other things, to bless a second marriage even if the circumstances that preceded this proscribe the possibility that the marriage service itself should take place in church. And as second (or even third) marriages become increasingly common, this situation is likely to increase.[5] The unexpected on this occasion lies not in the nature of the wedding, but in the juxtaposition of the royal marriage with an event which a generation earlier would have gone largely unnoticed at least by the wider British public.

The European framework

Before turning to Pope's funeral as such, it is important to put the British material into its European context. In this respect, if not always in others, Britain fits well within a European framework. Parallels to the Diana incident can, for example, be found in other European societies. One such can be found in the reaction of Swedish people to the sinking of the Estonia with the loss of some 900 lives in 1994.[6] The shock for Swedish people, a safety-conscious and peace-loving nation if ever there was one, was immense; with no exaggeration the unthinkable had happened. And almost without hesitation, Swedish people went to their churches not only to gather, to light candles and to mourn privately; but also in the correct anticipation that someone (the Archbishop) would articulate on their behalf both the sentiments of the people and the meaning of the tragedy for human living. This, for Swedish people, is precisely what the churches are for and why they remain an important element in a supposedly secular Swedish society.

The death of President Mitterand is more equivocal. Here a life-long agnostic (admittedly with mystical tendencies) left an ambiguous note at the time of his death, which read *'une messe est possible'*. But what did this mean – that a Mass was possible, but not strictly speaking necessary? Or was this

effectively a plea for some sort of Christian ritual at the end of a life dominated throughout by the markedly secular politics of the French left? The
answer came in not one Mass, but two – a public Mass in Notre Dame in
Paris and a private Mass in Jarnac in South West France. They were held
simultaneously and shown on a split screen on French television.[7]

For the great majority of Europe's citizens, a Christian heritage still counts
at the time of a death. Life-styles, however, are very different and increasingly are lived outside the framework of the churches. The life course, moreover, has changed as people live longer (a fact epitomized by the Queen
Mother) and as marriage to one person for 40, 50 or even 60 years is increasingly seen for what it is: not a golden age, but the norm for a relatively short
period of European history which peaked in the early post-war decades. In
this respect, the prevalence of divorce among the younger royals is entirely in
line with many others in their generation. To what extent this is indicative of
the process known as secularization is a much more difficult question. It is
more accurate, I think, to see these changes as part and parcel of the complex
evolutions of late modern societies within which demographic pressures are
as significant as shifts in public attitudes to marriage.

It is in this context that the seemingly uncompromising views of the late
Pope are so striking. They can be seen first in the unchanging nature of
Catholic teaching concerning the sacrament of marriage. Much more controversial, however, were the Pope's views on the absolute sanctity of life and
on the vexed question of contraception. Yet it was the Pope's funeral that
took precedence over a royal wedding in April 2005 and it was the funeral,
rather than the marriage, that was attended by heads of state from all over
the world.

The global context

Reactions to the Pope's death – and even more the decisions that followed
from this – reveal very sharply the growing tension between North and
South in global terms in the articulation of religious priorities. It is becoming
increasingly clear, for example, that the great majority of the world's
believers now live in the Global South, forming not only a considerable mass
of people but a significant source of power.[8] This huge and growing population has, moreover, an entirely different agenda from that which exists in the
North, both inside and outside the churches. Or to put the same point more
forcibly, the liberals of northern Europe, religious as well as secular, are
increasingly discomfited as, one by one, their expectations of the future,
premised on the principles of the European Enlightenment, are called into
question.

So constructed, the points of tension lie between a religious and populous
South and a rather more secular North. There is certainly truth in this state-

ment. Looked at more closely, however, such tensions exist as much *within* the churches as they do between different global regions. Hence the speculation surrounding the appointment of a successor to John Paul II: should the new Pope be a European or someone from the developing world, a liberal (in terms of sexual ethics) or a conservative? And how, precisely, do these attributes align themselves? The answer came quickly: the College of Cardinals elected Cardinal Ratzinger as Pope to follow John Paul II. Benedict XVI is a European and a respected scholar, but known above all for his rigorously conservative views – able therefore to win more easily than most the support of Catholics in the Southern hemisphere.

The tensions between North and South can be seen equally in the Anglican Communion, more especially in the heated debate relating to homosexuality within this world-wide grouping of churches with its centre in Canterbury. In 2003, two events raised the temperature of this discussion: a controversial appointment in the Church of England, and the decision in the Episcopalian Church (in the United States) to appoint as bishop an openly gay priest. Much of the notably acrimonious exchanges which ensued lie beyond the scope of this contribution, but not the central theme: that is the desire of the more conservative churches in the South to resist the more 'advanced' positions of the North in terms of their acceptance of homosexuality. For those in the South, homosexuality remains a sin; for those in the North, there has been a gradual – if somewhat uneven – acceptance of different forms of sexuality, though a marked reluctance until very recently to test the application of such freedoms in senior church appointments. The result has been painful to say the least. An offer of a senior post in the Church of England was withdrawn, and those responsible for the appointment of an openly gay bishop in the United States were asked to repent. The Anglican Communion as such has come under severe strain.

There is a further twist in the story: that is the readiness with which some, though by no means all, representatives of conservative opinion in the North will make use of the North/South tension to advance their own cause. Observers of the controversy are of one mind in this respect: that is, that minority sections of the Anglican churches in the North – minorities, however, which are growing both in size and confidence – have worked with (some would say exploited) their colleagues in the South to challenge the dominance of a liberal elite. Hence the significance of the issue, which is ultimately about power. For centuries, power has resided in the North; indeed to a considerable extent it still does – in terms of tradition, precedent, knowledge or, more immediately, of money. The current challenge reflects a new source of power. It comes from numbers, more precisely from the growing mass of believers in the South – aided and abetted by a minority in the North – who feel that their more conservative views have been marginalized for too long.

The outcome of these complex and painful debates is far from clear despite the evident flexibilities of Anglicanism if these are compared with the Catholic Church. One thing, however, is certain. The Church of England can no longer ignore what is happening elsewhere; nor can the churches in the North dominate the agenda. Interestingly the secular press is beginning to grasp this point. It is as ready to pay attention to these discussions as its religious equivalents. One reason for this lies in the issue itself: homosexuality attracts attention both inside and outside the churches. Another can be found in a growing, if gradual, awareness of the religious factor in the modern world order and its capacity to influence domestic as well as global priorities. It was this that Pope John Paul II understood so completely. So too, possibly, did the heads of state and their ecclesiastical equivalents who chose to attend his funeral. The British were not the only ones to rearrange their schedules.

Notes

1 Little has been published on the funeral of John Paul II, despite maximum coverage in the world's media. There are two recent biographies of the Pope: George Weigel, 2003, *Witness to Hope: The Biography of John Paul II*, London: HarperCollins (later, post-funeral editions are also available) and Edward Stourton, 2006, *John Paul II: Man of History*, London: Hodder & Stoughton.

2 See Tony Walter (ed.), 1999, *The Mourning for Diana*, Oxford: Berg Publishers for a comprehensive and balanced account of this occasion.

3 On the liturgy itself, see Grace Davie and David Martin, 1999, 'Liturgy and Music', in Walter (ed.), *Mourning for Diana*, pp.187–98.

4 On both these events, see the extensive media coverage at the time and Grace Davie, 2004, 'Rituels royaux en Angleterre: deux enterrements et un jubilé', in Erwan Dianteill, Danièle Hervieu-Léger and Isabelle Lautman Saint-Martin (eds), *La modernité rituelle: Rites politiques et religieux des sociétés modernes*, Paris: L'Harmattan, pp. 23–38. This chapter also covers Princess Diana's funeral. Ian Bradley, 2002, *God Save the Queen: The Spiritual Dimension of Monarchy*, London: Darton, Longman & Todd, is a useful background text.

5 Davie, *Believing without Belonging*, and *Religion in Modern Europe*, for a more detailed discussion of these changes and their implications for the British (and European) churches.

6 Grace Davie, 'From Obligation to Consumption: A Framework for Reflection in Northern Europe', *Political Theology*, 6(3) (2005), 281–301 and Grace Davie, 2006, 'Vicarious Religion: A Methodological Challenge', in Nancy Ammerman (ed.), *Everyday Religion: Observing Modern Religious Lives*, New York, Oxford: Oxford University Press.

7 See Danièle Hervieu-Léger, 1999, '"Une messe est possible". Les doubles funérailles du Président', in J. Julliard (ed.), *La Mort du Roi: Autour du François Mitterrand*, Paris: Gallimard, pp. 89–109.

8 See Philip Jenkins, 2002, *The Next Christendom: The Coming of Global Christianity*, New York, Oxford: Oxford University Press and Davie, *Religion in Modern Europe*.

Part II

Generation

3

Transmission and Transformation

Age is among the most fundamental determinants of human life and identity. In the late twentieth century, when Western society was given the gift of an extended life expectancy of at least 20 years, age became an absorbing cultural preoccupation, a major focus of policy and a foundational principle of consumer marketing. The sheer size and strategic positioning of the post-war generation has made this issue impossible to ignore. In political and cultural terms the Baby Boomers are highly visible and much debated.[1] There is agreement among scholars that this generation, reaching maturity in the 1970s, played a key role in transforming the social, cultural, economic and political milieu of the closing years of the twentieth century.[2] The ageing population is now regarded as a central aspect not only of the social structure but also of political debate surrounding economic growth, social welfare and military capability.[3] The policy implications of such major demographic change are haunting governments and forcing their way to the top of political agendas. For many economic analysts too, generation is a far more important economic driving force than class membership[4] and in practical terms the most common application of the idea of generations is their function as consumer groups targeted by advertisers seeking to sell age-appropriate products and lifestyles.[5] Given this preoccupation, it is not surprising that age has also assumed a key role in explanations of religious change. This section of the book explores and challenges some of these explanations, and in particular scrutinizes the claims made by historians and sociologists for the 1960s generation as agents of change, and their assumptions about inter-generational transmission of religious beliefs.

In his influential book, *From Generation to Generation* (2003), Shmuel Eisenstadt has argued that among the most important aspects of the cultural programme of modernity has been the strong tendency to construct clear demarcations between different life-spans. He correlates the emergence of relatively autonomous youth groups and youth cultures within societies in which the main integrative principles are different from the particularistic values governing family and kinship groups. The late twentieth century, then, with its high statistics of family breakdown and the geographical diffusion of kinship groups, is seen to have exhibited a growing discontinuity between the generations and a weakening of authoritative guidance by parents and teachers.[6] In Danièle Hervieu-Léger's terms, the 'chain of memory' which once linked one generation to another has been broken.[7] While we want to qualify this analysis, it is nonetheless worth noting its power, popularity, and pervasiveness.[8] In particular, we point to the extent to which contemporary writers on religion have framed their accounts in terms of the failure of the churches to reach out to particular age cohorts – be they Generation X, Generation Y, the Baby Boomers or the Baby Busters.[9] In most cases, the emphasis has been on stark differences between generations – the so-called generation gap – and on the problem of communication between different age groups.[10]

A particular emphasis has been placed on the 1960s generation – the so-called Baby Boomers. Hugh McLeod sees this generation as formative in a crisis of popular religiosity and in the diminishing social role of Christianity in the late twentieth century.[11] Likewise, Charles Taylor locates the growth of a distinctive kind of 1960s consciousness in which expressive individualism became a mass phenomenon and within which new patterns of religious self-identity were negotiated. This generation, he argues, witnessed a 'quite new predicament'.[12] Generational change has also been interpreted in a semi-apocalyptic manner in Callum Brown's bold heralding of the final demise of Christian Britain.

Brown's account of generational change is, in many respects, simple to state. The sudden and terminal decline into which British Christianity plummeted in the early 1960s after a long and prosperous nineteenth century (which lasted from 1800 to 1963, according to Brown) was the result of a catastrophic and abrupt social revolution in which the abandonment by women of ascendant puritan evangelicalism was the key feature. The contraceptive pill is argued to have done more for women than merely lowering fertility rates. It weaned women off the cycle of intergenerational renewal of Christian affiliation which tied people to the church and to Christian moral benchmarks, and in so doing relentlessly and irreversibly destroyed the 'core religious and moral identity of the nation'. Brown's revisionist analysis rests on the idea of a hegemonic religious core which dominated Britain throughout the long nineteenth century. This core was defined primarily by a puritan discourse which delineated the protocols of personal belief and behaviour in terms of evangelical Christianity. This discursivity, in Brown's view, was constructed along the lines of gender. During the long nineteenth century, women were regarded as innately pious and men as naturally irreligious. While men were inclined naturally to drunkenness, women were given to modesty, chastity, temperance, sobriety and thrift. Brown argues that in the era before 1960, this discourse was dominant beyond the boundaries of churchgoing. It lay at the very heart of popular culture itself as a hegemonic idea that cannot simply be reduced to statistics but existed in the form of a more intangible ethos and atmosphere. It was this atmosphere that was the sudden victim of transformations in the mores of women which, to use

Brown's language, ushered in 'the sudden plunge to a truly secular condition'. Women, being the bulwark of popular support for organized Christianity were, of course, by definition responsible for the subsequent dislocation of the nation from Christian piety. In Brown's view 'piety and femininity were mutually enslaved discursive constructions'and 'each would endure for as long as the other did'.

Brown's use of generation as an idea is problematic in a number of key respects. Overridingly, he assumes that Christianity is a coherent treasure trove of affiliations, identities and values which in order to survive must be passed down more or less intact from one generation to the next. Thus when women cancelled their subscription to *the* discursive domain of Christianity they were metaphorically dropping *the* hegemonic cultural inheritance, causing the nation's family silver to fall to the ground in the loud clatter of a 'short sharp cultural revolution'.[13] The idea that Christianity might be reinterpreted within and between generations, and passed on in several and less tightly defined discursive patterns, does not sit comfortably with the implicit definition of generational transmission which Brown adopts. He uses generation to imply a coherent and largely static collectivity which is interrogated as a monolithic whole. The term operates as a reductive image in his analysis, which moulds post-war women into a unified group who function as the bearers, and recipients, of cultural discourse with a remarkable degree of hegemony.

In recent years, however, the idea of generational coherence has been much challenged, particularly in the work of feminist scholars and narrative theorists. Astrid Henry, for example, in her study of three post-war generations of feminists in the US, has asked whether it is in fact legitimate to understand generations as monolithic and coherent cultural communities.[14] Henry accepts the traditional idea that generations do constitute what Mannheim has called an 'identity location';[15] that is, they are made up of those who share a common generational identity by virtue of their shared experience of, and active involvement in, historical events which transform a random group of people of roughly the same age into a coherent generation. But she pushes this symbolic definition of generational communality one step further by separating out generational identity from the strict application of date of birth. She points to the ways in which people of a certain age do not naturally or necessarily share a single generational identity. Her approach highlights the ways in which women of the same age opt in or out of the symbolic associations of particular generational feminist discourse. Women can and do adopt and reject particular generational styles or identities in different ways and at different stages across the life span. To be sure, the result of this process is far from clear, and is evidently understudied.[16] But we can conclude that the monolithic image of a generation may in fact be an unhelpful and constraining fiction. It has the potential to create an idea of the first generation as the 'mothers' and the second and third generations as daughters – that is the passive recipients of a set of cultural values and ideals which are already formed and bequeathed by older generations. Recent debates about the nature of post-feminism, and the question of whether it should be seen as a betrayal or a development of the women's movement, seem to bear out this interpretative emphasis.[17] Yet what such an analysis neglects is the ways in which the meaning, character and form of feminist identities are negotiated in and between women of different age groupings using a symbolic language of generation to mediate change over time. 'The insistence on speaking of feminism in terms of distinct and discrete generations obscures the ways in which continuity exists across feminisms and prevents us from recognising other forms of difference among feminists of different ages.'[18]

This critique has much to suggest when it comes to considering the transformation of Christianity in Britain in the late twentieth century. To see the post-war generation of women as the last of a long line of coherent culture bearers is to neglect the complex way in which the cultural identity of each generational cohort is renegotiated over time by a series of interlocking, and at times contradictory, subgroups. First of all, this model neglects those subgroups who persist in the religious pattern of previous generations, whether through active identification with the churches and with Christian doctrine or through a more subtle layer of folk tradition in which partial and selective association with Christian practices, beliefs and values is the norm. There is evidence to suggest far greater generational continuity in both these areas than Brown is willing to concede in his hegemonic description of intergenerational transmission. Gerald Parsons, for example, has recently collected together evidence of various studies of belief in the period after 1960 which when amassed suggests a 'penumbra of residual and peripheral Christian belief in Britain in the latter decades of the twentieth century'.[19] Diffusive or, in Brown's terminology, 'discursive Christianity' may have been more persistent within some family and communal structures than is often supposed. Parsons points to the work of Ahern on the inner city,[20] Foster's case study of Hull,[21] and Bailey's work on diffusive Christian belief;[22] all of which suggest continuities with the pattern of implicit or folk religion which Williams identified in her study of popular religion in the period prior to World War Two. The second half of the twentieth century, like the first, may also have seen communities in which 'there existed a personal familial and corporate familiarity with a series of religious images, teaching and symbols which remained a vital part of popular heritage' and in which 'Church based symbols were passed down from one generation to another as part of the fabric of family and communal life'.[23]

Even among those who do not fit within this pattern, the reality might well be rather different from the collapse in discursive Christianity postulated by Brown. We should not, of course, downplay those who very deliberately chose not to identify themselves with their parents' faith. Nonetheless we must recognize that this lack of identification is not always permanent and that, being relational, it can be renegotiated. Evidence from America suggests that family formation can have a dramatic effect on religious identity, as previously 'secular' people take their children to church. To be sure, this may not be the case in Britain – though it is an important issue that needs further investigation, particularly with regard to the effects of demand for church schools.[24] But in any event, the extent to which generations remain dynamic does need to be acknowledged. In Hervieu-Léger's terms, the chain of memory can be remade.[25] Indeed, an uncritical approach to generational transmission not only overlooks the possibilities of diversity and persistence but it underplays the specific quality of renegotiation whereby the discourse which develops *between* generations is equally formative in changing religious values. Brown's model tends to lose sight of the fact that Christianity is not just passed on, it is also actively chosen. This choice is not only made and remade again in every generation, but it can also be highly selective. In late twentieth-century Britain the refusal of younger generations to identify with particular discursive constructions of Christianity – a process which Henry calls 'disidentification' – can constitute a selective disavowal of earlier generational versions of Christian obligation and affinity. This should not necessarily be seen as a rejection of Christianity *per se*, nor should it be automatically dismissed as evidence of decline, when it can in fact be explored as quite the opposite. To reject some elements or indeed much of a 'puritan evangelical discourse' may be the means through which younger generations establish their own religious identities over and against those of their parents and grandparents.

If we are solely concerned with a model in which the crucial determinant is the extent to which the parents pass on their faith to their children, we may miss, for example, the more subtle ways in which many members of Generation X – that is those born between 1961 and 1981 – actively reject the patriarchal overtones of the intergenerational transmission of religious values. This rejection is integral to the ways in which the second and third post-war generations established the basis of their own religious authenticity. Authenticity is valued among them as a currency which holds genuine authority over and against the debased regurgitation of second-hand faith. As Charles Taylor points out, these generations were animated by the belief that 'each of us has his or her own way of realising one's own humanity and that it is important to find and live out one's own as against surrendering to conformity with a model imposed from outside by society or the previous generation or religious or political authority.'[26] In particular, disindentification among women with their traditional roles as teachers of prayers, organizers of Sunday schools and guardians of the rites of passage may best be considered as a discursive dialogue with many aspects of the parents' faith, rather than a straightforward rejection.

Taylor suggests that contemporary religious life and practice must above all be a feature of individual choice that 'must speak to me; it must make sense in terms of my spiritual development as I understand this'.[27] The Baby Boomers' concession to the active choice of their offspring when it comes to their own spiritual direction should not therefore be interpreted automatically as an overt rejection of Christian ethics in its entirety. Perhaps to bring faith alive, and to distinguish the contours between real and merely imbibed or inauthentic religious performance, this generation had to picture themselves as 'motherless' – disconnecting their notion of authentic faith from the connotations of past generations. Just as Henry concludes that there may be something politically empowering about the cultural matricide of third-generation feminists,[28] so too there may be spiritual renewal in the rejection of protocols which prohibited sons and daughters from stepping onto the religious stage without the necessary credentials of an earlier period – credentials which they no longer choose to acknowledge as authoritative. Moreover, if as Roof suggests, there may have been a basic transition from 'religious belonging to personal meaning', people may go to church in order to see themselves and not their church leaders as the architects of their religious identity.[29] That must transform their understanding of institutional religion – and their relationship to it.

This has important implications for the study of more recent generations. Certainly, the work of Richard Flory and Donald Miller suggests that Generation X has not lived up to the cynical and apathetic image with which it was labelled by the media.[30] In fact, it can be argued that the Generation Xers share important constructive characteristics, developed in relation to their parents' attitudes. While the Baby Boomers who came of age in the 1960s were more individualistic, their children tend to show more interest in community and structure rather than in a purely personal spiritual journey. 'GenXers', Flory and Miller write, 'are not simply religious consumers, although they are that, but also producers'; people who are more than individualistic seekers, and want to create community as well as seek personal fulfilment.[31] An analysis of American data does not necessarily translate easily to a British context; and we might also challenge the authors' use of a market metaphor. But their conclusion should provoke a reconsideration of conventional ideas about generation. In particular, it should lead us to ask whether it is right to assume that the notion of authoritative figures passing on fixed sets of religious ideas is likely still to hold sway among any generation in our period.

The multigenerational interviewing upon which Brown rests his analysis of generational transmission is also problematic because it tends to see Christian language as fixed and unchanging and to measure only the extent to which this pattern of language remains as a kind of residue across generations.[32] He leaves little scope for complex changes in linguistic and symbolic associations over time. It is our belief that generational transformation is as important a paradigm as intergenerational transmission – especially when engaging with more recent generational changes. In this regard transmission itself is a word which is worthy of brief consideration. It has received a considerable amount of attention from sociologists and narrative theorists all of whom have challenged the idea that the shift from age heterogeneity toward age-homogeneous groups necessarily means a decline in the transmission of ideas. New ideas and cultural norms can move within peer groups as well as between them. During the late twentieth century the mainstream churches, based as they are on age heterogeneity, have become strikingly adept at cultivating and appealing to subsidiary age-homogenous groups within it.[33] In these cases, asymmetrical interaction between age groups is still present but same-age groups form various subgroups within church organizations. These age groups may and often do perform the same functions that are frequently postulated for the interaction of age-heterogeneous elements or agencies of socialization. Peer groups can themselves become interesting conduits for continuity as well as change within a social system. This has been underlined by the report of the 'God and the Generations' Working Group sponsored by the Evangelical Alliance in 2000–2001, which critiqued over-schematic models of generational change and also addressed the pressing issue for the churches of leadership transition.[34] In other words, transmission and transformation should not be separated from each other.

The growth of specific generational consciousness may in itself lead to a greater awareness of an individual's location and hence be a means of bonding with preceding and succeeding generations. In her work on generational consciousness and political engagement, Molly Andrews argues this case.[35] As Henry does, she further develops Mannheim's definition of generation by suggesting that the kind of consciousness which Mannheim sees as integral to the formation of self-conscious generational communities also requires an awareness of generational distinction between different age groups and reliance upon connections between generations. Andrews argues for the centrality of story-telling as the medium through which ideas, values, customs and norms are passed between generations. In her analysis, individuals construct the stories that they tell about their lives as members of a particular generation but they do so largely for members of other generations. An individual's age suggests certain definite expectations of future activities and of relationships with other people at the same or at different stages of life. These frequently involve the interpretation and mediation of existential questions. People map out their own expectations and possibilities in terms of these definitions, and ascribe to themselves and others places within these contours. The expectations of one age group never stand alone and historical consciousness is in this way necessary to the act of story-telling. Michael Pratt and Barbara Fiese argue a similar position in their book *Family Stories and the Life Course Across Time and Generations* (2004). They add a further dimension to their analysis by considering the ways in which individual and group story-telling alters as people move from one age stage to the next. They are always a series and they are by definition constantly in flux. Individuals at every stage of life perform given roles by virtue of age, and they are obligated to ensure some degree of continuity of the social system through this performance. The role performed by the individual at a given stage of the life span must be defined in such a way as to sharpen and emphasize relations with people at different points on the age scale.

This is a salutary and important reminder that to understand religious belief one cannot afford to take a snapshot of a single age stage. It is necessary to look at the unfolding stages of a person's life. There is agreement across the board that membership of the Christian churches is disproportionately higher among the elderly, and that the patterns of disidentification highlighted earlier are more frequently associated with youth. It is, however, false to assume that generational identity is fixed when young. Both Callum Brown and Steve Bruce place considerable emphasis on the decline of the institution of Sunday school as a disseminator of Christian culture in Britain.[36] But the failure of a mother to teach her children to pray, and to insist that they attend Sunday school does not necessarily condemn them to a prayerless and dechristianized life.

In reality, religious identities are renegotionated across the life span. In their work Angela Williams and Jon Nussbaum argue that people develop and transform their individual and social identities across their life, through young adulthood and middle age to old age. A person's place in the continuum becomes the crucial definition of his or her roles as regards the expectation of others.[37] This has vital implications for religious identities. The old tend to operate in the role of 'keepers of meaning' who seek to pass on the most valued tradition of a culture, to teach the most valued skills and outlooks, and to impart wisdom and foster the realization of human potential in future generations. It is at this stage of life that religious narratives can take on fresh meaning by virtue of a person's relationship with younger people. In the later twentieth century grandparents have tended to live longer, and so more extended periods of intergenerational exchange have been available. Churches have responded to this by focusing on interrelationships between the old and the young, and on cultivating 'All-Age' Worship, rather than (as was the case in the 1950s and 1960s) simply targeting youth groups in isolation.[38]

If generations are in series, then they will modify one another at different points. What is necessary, if we are to take generational transformation seriously, is not only an account of individual longevity but also a consideration of how generational transformation operates within and between a number of different generations. Much of the work done on generations by sociologists points to an oscillation, which develops between (and within) generations even over a relatively short period of time. Contrast has been made, for example, between passive generations and active generations who move backwards and forwards between identities. The disidentification of one generation does not imply the same for the next. Indeed the disidentification of one can itself facilitate the reidentification of the next. If generation is understood as a set of cultural styles or generational identities, then it is possible that the third generation can again identify with the first or those before it. Again, Astrid Henry's analysis of three waves of feminism is helpful here. She looks at the swing back in Third Wave feminism towards models which re-imagine mother–daughter relationships precisely in order to give young women a platform from which to speak – as daughters rather than sisters. She examines the ways in which young women are claiming back the language of motherhood in order to establish the authority of historical connection and continuity. Using the language of the past, and the authority of their grandparents, they are able to critique their parents' generation. In terms of religious history, a longer-term time horizon may well challenge the picture of inevitable religious decline. Taylor's analysis of the role of collective connections may be a helpful example of this. He looks at how many people find themselves joining extremely powerful religious communities. They do so not only as an antidote to individualism but also, ironically, as an expression of their own spiritual autonomy by claiming a link with tradition. What that emphasis on tradition may do to religion remains to be seen: though the Roman Catholic Church's increasing focus on a return to the Latin Mass seems suggestive. In that sense, intergenerational tensions can be as much a part of religious transformation as religious decline *per se*, and religious birth may well be as important a metaphor as death.

The three case studies which follow pick up on a number of key themes about generational transformation and intergenerational transmission. In the first, William Whyte explores the critical generation for Callum Brown's thesis: the women who came of age in the 1960s. He challenges Brown's contention that these people abandoned conventional gender roles, arguing instead for greater continuity. True enough, something changed; but the 1960s 'expressive revolution' identified by Bernice Martin did not mean that 1963 became a sort of year zero. Rather, ideas about identity, about gender and sexuality, and – by implication – about belief, slowly mutated. What he concludes is that the 1960s saw a resurgence of Romanticism: a resurgence that shook the institutions of church and state but which only very gradually challenged conventions of gender. This suggests that the distinctions between generations have been somewhat too starkly drawn. It also suggests that we must take a longer-term perspective if we are to understand how attitudes to gender and to generation change. Generation X, Whyte concludes, looks much more like the liberated group of women that Brown was seeking. Yet they too present challenges for analysts of religious identity: problems which a simplistic account of generational change cannot explain.

A parallel point is made by Holger Nehring in his case study on the Peace

Movement. Against accounts which see such manifestations of youth culture as implicitly secularizing, he shows the ways in which the Campaign for Nuclear Disarmament was seen by its members as a genuinely religious – and more specifically Christian – act. Yet, importantly, this was a crusade which was highly critical of the institutional church: seeing it as incapable of responding to the modern challenges of nuclear war. Nehring also notes contemporary critics of CND, who were all too willing to see the organization as an expression of the rootless, secular, Baby Boomer generation. This was arguably a misinterpretation, but it is one that has been repeated by subsequent writers. The case study ends with a call to problematize our notions of what 'religion' is. Challenging much writing on the subject, Nehring argues that a more rewarding avenue of research might instead analyze the ways in which contemporaries defined their 'religion' and how precisely they encoded transcendence as the key parameter of religious thinking and practice.

In our final case study, Jane Garnett questions the extent to which categories like generation, denomination, and faith have been unsettled by the advent of digital technology. Specifically, she explores the impact of the Internet on Generation Y – that is, on the generation born from the early 1980s onwards. These are the people who have grown up familiar with computer technology, and who are – according to some commentators – as happy in a virtual as in the real world. Does this mark a revolution? Is Generation Y unreachable or unteachable by the institutional church? Garnett would suggest not. To be sure, she notes, the Internet does open up possibilities for transglobal and transgenerational communication that simply did not exist two decades ago. It permits the creation of new kinds of community, and provides a bewildering variety of alternative sources of information, guidance and authority. But if this presents challenges to the institutional church, then it also offers opportunities – opportunities that have been eagerly seized by some. More than this, and more intriguingly still, by allowing individuals and groups to create their own virtual institutions, the Internet potentially permits the possibility of imagining still more authentic expressions of people's beliefs. As this suggests, the essay concludes by challenging those commentators who see the Internet as a wholly separate space or as an ineffably alternative world. Like sailors on the sea, Garnett writes, those surfing the Internet always bring their own culture with them, and however much they are changed by the experience, they do not spend all their lives afloat. The Internet is important, then, but it is not the great break in history that enthusiasts or critics perceive.

The study of intergenerational transmission and generational transformation, then, involves more than just the tracing how cohorts hand on an unchanging and stable tradition. First of all, it necessitates an exploration of what a generation is and how it may be defined. Second, it requires a far more dynamic understanding of how generations inter-relate and how they contain multiple voices and an extraordinarily wide range of experiences.

Still further, it demands a far more subtle and nuanced account of religion itself. If religion is a chain of memory then it is one that is constantly being remade. If it is a discourse, then it is one that is frequently rewritten. If it is a possession, then it is not one that is owned by any particular group or generation. To return to an aquatic analogy, we might argue – with Jackson Carroll and Wade Clark Roof – that generations should be seen as waves.[39] Yet generational transmission means more than just the study of waves crashing against the shore. It means studying the ebb and flow of tides; the eddies and whirlpools that disturb the water as well as the calm deep, where the action is all below the surface. Generational transmission is, we would argue, a key concept for the study of religion. But it is – like the sea – still uncharted in many respects.

Notes

1 See, for example, Allan Bloom, 1987, *The Closing of the American Mind*, New York: Simon and Schuster; Wade Clark Roof, 1993, *A Generation of Seekers: The Spiritual Journeys of the Baby Boom Generation*, San Francisco: HarperSanFrancisco.

2 E. Wattenberg, 'The Fate of the Baby-Boomers and Their Children', *Social Work*, 31 (1986), 20–8; B. S. Turner, 'Ageing and Generational Conflicts', *The British Journal of Sociology*, 49(2) (1998), 299–304 and Hans Mol, 1985, *The Faith of Australians*, Sydney: Allen & Unwin.

3 P. Peterson, 'Gray Dawn; The Global Ageing Crisis', *Foreign Affairs*, 78(1) (1999), 42–55; June Edmunds and Brian Turner (eds), 2002, *Generational Consciousness, Narrative and Politics*, Lanham: Rowman and Littlefield.

4 Pierre Bourdieu, 1993, *The Field of Cultural Production: Essays in Art and Literature*, Cambridge: Polity Press.

5 Dana Heller, 2000, 'The Anxiety of affluence', in Devoney Looser and E. Ann Kaplan (eds), *Generational: Academic Feminists in Conversation*, London: University of Minnesota Press, pp. 309–26.

6 S. N. Eisenstadt, 2003, *From Generation to Generation*, 3rd edn, New Brunswick: Transaction, pp. xlii, xxvii.

7 Hervieu-Léger, *Religion*, pp. 124–7.

8 For a definition of the concept of generativity see Ed de St Aubin, Dan P. McAdams and Tae-Chang Kim (eds), 2003, *The Generative Society: Caring for Future Generations*, Washington: American Psychological Association.

9 Most recently in Sara Savage, Sylvia Collins-Mayo, Bob Mayo (eds), 2006, *Making Sense of Generation Y: The World View of 15– to 25–year-olds*, London: Church House Publishing.

10 This is a particularly pronounced tendency in North America. See, for example, George Barna, 1994, *Baby Busters: the Disillusioned Generation*, Chicago: Northfield; Wendy Murray Zoba, *Generation 2K: What Parents and Others Need to Know about the Millenials*, Downers Grove, IL: Intervarsity Press; and Dawson McAllister and Pat Springle, 1999, *Saving the Millennial Generation*, Nashville: Thomas Nelson.

11 Hugh McLeod, 'The religious crisis of the 1960s', *Journal of Modern European History*, 3(2) (2005), 205–30. See also his *Religious Crisis of the 1960s*; forthcoming, Oxford University Press, which will develop this thesis.

12 Taylor, *Varieties*, p.107.

13 Brown, *Death*, pp. 1, 59, 68

14 Astrid Henry, 2004, *Not My Mother's Sister: Generational Conflict and Third Wave Feminism*, Indiana: Indiana University Press.

15 Karl Mannheim, 'The Problem of Generations', in Paul Kecskemet (ed.), 1952, *Essays on the Sociology of Knowledge*, London: Routledge and Keegan Paul, p. 292.

16 James R. Tilley, 'Secularization and Aging in Britain: does family formation cause greater religiosity?', *Journal for the Scientific Study of Religion*, 42(2) (2003), 269–78.

17 See Anita Harris (ed.), 2004, *All About the Girl: Culture, Power, and Identity*, London and New York: Routledge; esp. pp. 3–14, 59–67.

18 Henry, *Not My Mother's Sister*, p. 45.

19 Gerald Parsons, 2004, 'How the Times they were A-changing' in Wolffe, John (ed.), 2004, *Religion in History: Conflict, Conversion and Coexistence*, Manchester: Manchester University Press, pp. 161–89, at p.174.

20 Geoffrey Ahern, '"I do believe in Christmas": White Working-Class people and the Anglican Clergy in the inner-city London', in Geoffrey Ahern and Grace Davie, 1987, *Inner City God: the Nature of Belief in the Inner City*, London: Hodder & Stoughton, pp. 75–133.

21 Peter Foster, 1989, *Church and People on Longhill Estate*, Hull: University of Hull.

22 Edward Bailey, 'The Folk Religion of the English People', in Paul Badham (ed.), *Religion, State and Society in Modern Britain*, Lewiston: Edwin Mellen Press, pp. 145–58.

23 Williams, *Religious Belief*, p.147.

24 See Vern Bengtson, Timothy Biblarz and Robert Roberts, 2002, *How Families Still Matter: A Longitudinal Study of Youth in Two Generations*, New York: Cambridge University Press, p. 153 and Tilley, 'Secularization and Aging', pp. 269 and 277.

25 Hervieu-Léger, *Religion*, Ch. 8.

26 Taylor, *Varieties*, p. 83.

27 Taylor, *Varieties*, p. 95.

28 Henry, *Not My Mother's Sister*, p. 101.

29 Roof, *Generation of Seekers*.

30 Richard W. Flory and Donald E. Miller, 2000, *GenX Religion*, London: Routledge – see especially, Flory, 'Conclusion: towards a theory of GenX Religion', pp. 231–49.

31 Flory and Miller, *GenX Religion*, p. 244.

32 Brown, *Death*, pp. 181–6.

33 The growing success of Godly Play – a programme designed to teach children biblical narratives – might be an example of this. Jerome Berryman, 1991, *Godly Play: A Way of Religious Education*, San Francisco: HarperSanFrancisco. On one (Anglican) diocese's experience of this, see http://www.oxford.anglican.org/page/1076 – accessed 29.10.06.

34 David Hilborn and Matt Bird (eds), 2002, *God and the Generations. Youth, Age and the Church Today*, Carlisle: Paternoster Press.

35 M. Andrews, 'Generational Consciousness, Dialogue and Political Engagement', in Edmunds and Turner, *Generational Consciousness*, pp. 75–89.

36 Bruce, *God is Dead*, pp. 68–9; Brown, *Death*, p. 188.

37 Angela Williams and Jon F. Nussbaum, 2001, *Intergenerational Communication Across the Life Span*, Mahwah, NJ: Lawrence Erlbaum.

38 See Anne Barton, 1993, *All-Age Worship*, Bramcote: Grove; Tony Castle, 1994, *All-Age Events and Worship*, London: Marshall Pickering; David Gamble, 1991, *One: Young and Old United*, London: Methodist Publishing House. See also Albert Jewell, 2001, *Old People and the Church*, Peterborough: Methodist Publishing House.

39 Carroll and Roof, *Bridging Divided Worlds*, Ch. 1.

Case Studies

The *Jackie* Generation: Girls' Magazines, Pop Music, and the
Discourse Revolution
  William Whyte

'The Long, Long Night Is Over.' The Campaign for Nuclear
Disarmament, 'Generation' and the Politics of Religion
(1957–1964)
  Holger Nehring

Internet Generation: Computer-Mediated Communication and
Christianity
  Jane Garnett

CASE STUDY

The *Jackie* Generation: Girls' Magazines, Pop Music, and the Discourse Revolution

WILLIAM WHYTE

Jackie was founded in 1964.[1] It was an immediate and extraordinary success, selling 650,000 copies a week and becoming much the biggest girls' magazine in the business. Although sales were to decline as the 1960s went on, a decade later it was still a phenomenon.[2] Subsequently it has been the subject of a number of fascinating studies.[3] And, of course, *Jackie* features centrally in the core thesis of Callum Brown's *Death of Christian Britain*. It reflected – or helped create (the distinction is not clearly made) – the 'discourse revolution' that Brown identifies in the 1960s. 'Rooted in swinging London, *Jackie* persisted in asserting the separation of sex roles, but acknowledged that women worried over men and accepted that love was not necessarily for ever', he writes. What is more, and what was novel about *Jackie*, 'was the disappearance of discourses on domesticity, separate spheres, and women's limited career aspirations . . . Discourses on feminine identity was [*sic*] now conveyed by everything other than family, domestic routine, virtue, religion, or "respectability".'[4] This discourse revolution is, Brown suggests, the real cause of secularization within Britain. This was a generation of women that replaced Jesus with *Jackie*. Or, more fairly, the *Jackie* generation was one that looked to popular culture rather than to the church when it wanted to make sense of the world, and which consequently abandoned conventional piety, femininity, and Christian belief. If true, this is a striking and important piece of analysis. But is it actually accurate? This short case study will suggest not.

For one thing, it might be objected that Brown's characterization of the role of women is inadequate. His contention that religion was feminized in the nineteenth century – that in the Victorian era men abandoned the church, leaving piety the preserve of women – is highly problematic. After all, the belief that women were more susceptible to religion than men is not a new one. It was a commonplace of classical thought, with Plato arguing that visions of the gods were an especially female delusion.[5] In more recent writing Brown himself concedes that a preponderance of women attending church 'has been a widespread characteristic of Christianity over many centuries'.[6] And even if it could be shown that more women attended church in previous eras, this would still not prove that religion had been feminized. Throughout the nineteenth and twentieth centuries the churches were, of course, run by men. More than this, their discourse was characterized by masculine language, by references to God and to humanity as exclusively male. If feminization was to occur, one might argue, then it could not have done so until after the 1960s with the ordination of women in the Methodist (1974) and Anglican (1992) churches, and the adoption of inclusive language by a wide variety of denominations. This would, of course, run counter to Brown's contention of a defeminized religious sphere in the same period.[7]

Brown's contentions about the role of men are also open to question. Presupposing an unproblematic and, indeed, apparently unchanging masculinity, he does not take account of the ways in which male identity and performance may have shifted in this period. Angela McRobbie and Jenny Garber, for instance, have contended that the emergence of the 'Mods' in the 1960s reflected the creation of a '"softer" working-class subculture', one that allowed both men and women to redefine their roles.[8] This softening was reflected in popular music, with a blurring of the boundaries between the 'soft ballads' which had characterized 'girls' music' and the 'hard rock 'n' roll' that had previously been a male preserve.[9] To be sure, much of this simply perpetuated male hegemony.[10] But the ways in which this softening might affect men was made clear in the 1970s, with the emergence in popular music of alternative forms of masculinity. The 'camp, gay exterior' of many male pop stars, the success of the avowedly bisexual David Bowie, and even the growth of punk: all these reflected new models of maleness, models which contended with 'harder' ones, naturally, but which were the product of a changing masculinity; one that was not fixed or static as Brown seems to imply.[11]

Above all, it might be argued that Brown's analysis of popular culture is misleading in many respects. Although he is no doubt quite right to take pop music and magazines quite seriously, it may be objected that he has not taken them seriously enough. Not least, he has ignored the wider context in which the *Jackie* generation grew up. In *Bomb Culture*, the artist and activist Jeff Nuttall argued that the 1960s were characterized by a sort of Romantic pantheism.[12] It was an insight taken up nearly 20 years later by Robert Pattison in his study of modern American music, *The Triumph of Vulgarity*. Pop, he said, had expropriated Romanticism's 'refined traditions of self, sex, science, and social organization' and coupled this with 'a central pantheist identification of self and the universe realized in the vulgar mode of feeling'.[13] In other words, modern pop music marks the triumph of emotion over reason, of instinct over reflection, of the spontaneous over the planned, of freedom over control. Arguably, these are the defining aims of the *Jackie* generation: people who bought into Paul McCartney's pantheism, and his

1967 declaration that 'God is in everything'; people who welcomed John Lennon's Romanticism, with his 1971 dream of a world living as one.[14] It is this 'expressive revolution' – to use the phrase Bernice Martin so influentially borrowed from Talcott Parsons – that reshaped youth culture, and the social thought of post-war Britain more generally. And it is this Romantic pantheism that can, more than anything else, be found in the pop music, magazines, and advice columns that Brown has studied.[15]

One question, of course, remains: whether this Romantic pantheism was necessarily inimical to Christianity. The answers are not entirely clear. Pantheism surely should be problematic for the churches. Indeed, Nuttall called for the creation of a new religion, one that would abolish 'the corny authoritarian God of the churches'.[16] But as Pattison put it, in America at least, 'the rocker is capable of adoring Dionysus in the disco by night and Christ in the cathedral by day'.[17] This may, as he goes on to suggest, ultimately threaten transcendent religion. It has not yet done so.[18] Even the Sex Pistols, in many ways the archetypal expression of this form of Romanticism, could not escape the legacy of Christianity; as Glen Matlock, their original bassist, recalled of Johnny Rotten: 'John's a fucked-up Roman Catholic and that came out in the lyrics. One of the songs we never used was about waiting for the Archangel Gabriel.'[19] The same was surely true of the Beatles, used by Brown to illustrate the discourse revolution, yet also often highly religious in their sensibility.[20] Although the genesis of Paul McCartney's 'Let it Be' (1969) is contested, its debt to traditional Catholic teaching is both obvious and clear. In that sense, perhaps what we are studying is the mutation of language, rather than death by discursive decay.[21]

More specifically, it is worth enquiring whether such an expressive revolution changed gender roles or the ways in which gender was articulated. Once again, Callum Brown's instincts are surely right. Girls' and women's magazines do provide a uniquely helpful way into this issue. Although the 1960s actually witnessed a decline in the market, there remained a quite bewildering range of periodicals.[22] Moreover, as Brown suggests, there were some important changes to the content of these journals. There is a world of difference between Monica Dickens regularly condemning married women who worked, as she did in the *Woman's Own* of the early 1960s, and the first editorial in *Cosmopolitan* written a decade later which hymned the *Cosmopolitan* girl.[23] 'You're very interested in men, naturally,' it declared:

> But you think too much of yourself to live your life entirely through *him*. That means you're going to make the most of yourself – your body, your face, your clothes, your hair, your job and your mind. How can you fail to be more interesting after that?[24]

Nevertheless, it is important not to get too carried away with all this. Despite these developments there are still some important reasons for doubting the narrative that Brown suggests.

There is, for example, more than a whiff of Whiggery about Brown's account. As well as noting the development of new journals, we should also acknowledge those women's magazines which did not adopt a permissive or conventionally feminist agenda in the 1960s and 1970s. The failure of *Nova* – founded in 1965 for a new type of working woman – contrasts powerfully with the continued success of *Mother, The Lady*, and *Homes and Gardens*, which, strikingly and unusually, experienced no real decline in sales during the 1960s.[25] As late as 1978 *Woman and Home* was IPC's biggest selling magazine.[26] More than this, it would be wrong to assume that an acceptance of working women, or a desire to maximize women's sexual fulfilment, was confined to the 1960s. Arguably, the advice offered by Monica Dickens in the 1950s represented nothing more than reaction.[27] Her pre-war predecessors had been far keener on women's work, and more willing to countenance a life beyond the kitchen.[28] Similarly, when in 1987 *Woman's* agony aunt, Virginia Ironside, decided to celebrate the fiftieth anniversary of the problem page, she returned to Peggy Makin's 'Evelyn Home' column of the 1930s in search of copy. 'I expected her advice would be rather mealy mouthed and inappropriate, and require me to give very different answers in 1987' she wrote. 'But I found I largely agreed with her replies; so it wasn't worth doing a "then" and "now" comparison.'[29] By contrast, perhaps the single most influential and innovative agony aunt of the 1960s, Marje Proops, eschewed feminism.[30] Most women, she maintained, simply wanted to get married. Her controversial suggestion that pre-marital sex might not be wrong was also less radical than might at first appear. It was prompted by a BBC programme on a group of Quakers who had concluded that 'sex experience before marriage tends to make people better-adjusted partners'.[31] This was less discourse revolution than gentle reform.

It is also the case that the content of women's magazines was considerably more diverse and often more contradictory than might be expected. Even *Cosmopolitan*, which pioneered the first male pin-up (albeit for only two years), and which was self-consciously designed for the self-confident working woman, nonetheless remained remarkably conventional in many of its attitudes. At times, it could even be rather conservative. A quiz in 1972 included the following enquiry:

> What this country needs is a good strong Christian statesman who can really lead us. Do you:
> a. feel is he long overdue?
> b. agree because democracy is desirable but inefficient?
> c. see this attitude as dangerous?
> d. feel that such a man does not exist?
> e. agree with some reluctance?[32]

While the answers included the possibility of expressing some doubt – and even outright rejection – the burden of this exercise obviously presupposed a common set of conventionally Christian assumptions amongst the *Cosmo* girls. Likewise, an article of 1973 entitled 'Why I Became a Nun' presented a remarkably positive account of the religious life, concluding: 'To those who believe in living life to the full they [the nuns] appear to be very incomplete people, but then it is not this life that is their main concern. For them it is no more than a preparation for the real life that lies ahead.'[33] Admittedly, these articles were irregular, and framed by others advocating abortion, discussing lesbianism, or rejecting the stigma of 'living in sin'.[34] Nonetheless, the variety of voices heard in this magazine makes it hard to conclude that a single discourse had established itself even in the most advanced journals.

We need also to be sensitive to the ways in which these magazines were read as well as written. Not only was the readership highly diverse, with men and boys making up no less than a third of all *Cosmopolitan* and nearly a quarter of *Jackie* readers.[35] What was read and in what ways it was read really matter. Elizabeth Frazer has shown in her analysis of 'Teenage girls reading *Jackie*' that even inexperienced readers are highly reflexive about the texts they encounter: well able to reflect on the gap between reality and descriptions of reality; capable of being ironic as well as accepting.[36] It is a point picked up by other writers, and most notably by Angela McRobbie, who has revised her initial analysis of *Jackie* to take account of the strategies that readers use to interpret the message of any given text.[37] This may mean – as some have argued – that no matter what girls' magazines actually contain, no matter what ideology informs them, they nonetheless serve as a sort of liberation for their readers. Certainly, the suggestion that they were used as an alternative to the officially sanctioned and highly gender-biased schoolbooks of the period is attractive.[38] But it is also important to recognize that the experience of everyday life might run counter to any message of emancipation contained within these publications. As Simon Frith pointed out at the time, very few girls were being educated for long-term careers. Indeed, the percentage of girls entering work which involved no further training had barely changed between 1964 and 1974. It was still well over 70%. 'Marriage', he wrote in 1978, 'is girls' primary occupational role.'[39] While that remained true, whatever they read would be mediated by expectations that were focused on domesticity, femininity, and – it might be maintained – precisely the conventional pieties that Brown believes had vanished more than a decade before.[40]

Which brings us to *Jackie*. What exactly were the girls of the *Jackie* generation reading – and what did they make of it? Callum Brown relies in his account on Angela McRobbie's 1977 paper on the magazine. Much republished and revised, it does indeed remain the standard work on *Jackie*. But Brown's version of this paper is highly contentious, not to say misleading. Far from arguing that *Jackie* represented women's liberation, McRobbie maintained that it perpetuated existing stereotypes of femininity, driven by an ideology which conceived of girls only as future wives and mothers.

'*Jackie* asserts', she concluded, 'the absolute and natural separation of sex roles . . . .Boys can *be* footballers, pop stars, even juvenile delinquents, but girls can only be feminine.'[41] And, in other work, she went still further, attacking *Jackie's* exclusive emphasis on romance, its preoccupation with female passivity, its celebration of male achievement:

> The possibility of enjoying oneself out there in the real world or of struggling to make it more enjoyable; the possibility of working with men and women in a satisfying way and one which does not always depend on romance for its thrills; – all of this is ruled out.[42]

In that sense, she argues, *Jackie* was not a way out of convention, but a way back in; not a new sort of freedom, but a prison. Rather than heralding the disappearance of 'discourses on domesticity, separate spheres, and a woman's limited career ambitions', as Brown suggests,[43] *Jackie* merely 'produced a more neurotic femininity'.[44]

In that respect, *Jackie* was in good company. It is very hard to find evidence of the discourse revolution that Brown proposes. Little in the magazines or music of the 1960s and 1970s seriously challenged prevailing gender norms. Even in the mid-1970s, more than 80% of popular music was about romantic and sexual relationships, music, dancing, or humour.[45] Similar figures can be obtained in the music of the 1930s.[46] More than this, the messages propounded by popular music, and the ways in which music was appreciated, remained strikingly gendered. Girls, even in the 1970s, were always intended to listen to music rather than to make it; and to listen to music at home rather than in public. Pop songs aimed at the female audience in the 1960s and 1970s tended to 'deny or repress sexuality'.[47] Frequently, those that challenged this, like the Rolling Stones' 'Under My Thumb' (1966), reinforced a sense of male superiority and female submission.[48] Even women performers often found their gender role problematic.[49] As the singer Kate Bush observed in 1978, 'I just think I identify more with male musicians than female musicians because I tend to think of female musicians as . . . ah . . . females.'[50] In that sense, pop music, like girls' magazines failed to provide an alternative form of femininity for the *Jackie* generation. Naturally, we need to recognize that pop, like periodicals, has a history of reception as well as of creation, and that the women who grew up after 1964 could interpret these messages in very different ways.[51] But it is hard not to conclude with Simon Frith that in the late 1970s girls' leisure was 'not really a break from work, at all, but is, rather, an integral part of their careers as domestic labourers'.[52]

Even as Frith wrote, of course, the music world was changing. While the female singers of the 1960s had, in Sheila Whitely's terms, 'occupied a "second division" pop status', the 1970s saw a few individual women break through.[53] In the late 1970s, Punk forced open the closed musical market, providing access to a new breed of assertive and sexually provocative women artists like Siouxsie Sioux and Poly Styrene.[54] It must be stressed, though, that most British female punk bands remained, as Lucy O'Brien puts it, 'of cult-level status', and even high-profile acts were far outsold by more mainstream groups.[55] By way of comparison, while the Slits' only top 100 single 'Typical Girls' charted at 60 and remained there for only three weeks, the exceptionally conventional Nolan Sisters consistently outperformed them, staying in the charts with various records for 90 weeks in total. The success of such equally unchallenging groups as Abba or the Three Degrees – neither of which made any effort to subvert traditional ideas about gender – only makes the point more plain.[56] The plates were shifting, but only slowly.

Indeed, were one looking for a discourse revolution, then it might best be found in the late 1980s and 1990s, rather than in the 1960s or 1970s.[57] The girls' magazines of the post-Thatcher era – publications like *Just Seventeen*, *More*, and *Sugar* – were a world away from the pious domesticity of *Jackie*, *Petticoat*, or even *Cosmopolitan*. To be sure, their messages were mixed; their ideals were often contradictory; they remained resolutely heterosexual in focus; and their concept of equality, as Stevi Jackson has complained, seemed to mean little more than women 'behaving like men'.[58] But with their in-built irony, their emphasis on female empowerment, and their cheerful hedonism they do mark a break with the past.[59] As McRobbie put it, by the end of the 1980s, a new climate prevailed 'where dependency on boys and on romance' gave way 'to a new, more confident, focus on the self'.[60] The same was surely true of pop.[61] New female artists like Madonna carved out a place for assertive women within popular music – a place that would be filled in the mid-1990s by the Spice Girls and their much-repeated call for 'Girl Power'.[62] However rhetorical and however cynical this was, it did reflect a new self-confidence; one that was echoed in Beyoncé's declaration in 2000 that the key theme of her band was 'for women to be independent, strong women, and for women to demand respect'.[63] As the lead singer of Destiny's Child – at that point the best-selling all-female group of all time – her views did perhaps possess some salience. Certainly Destiny's Child's 'Independent Woman Part One' (2000) offered a very different picture of femininity from that of the girl groups of the 1960s or 1970s. 'Try to control me, boy,' they sang, 'and you'll get dismissed.' And this shift in popular discourse was apparently accompanied by a change in women's attitudes. While 82% of white girls interviewed in 1972 wanted to marry – one third of them before they were 20 – only 45% of a similar group had the same ambition in 1994; a further 46% were simply not sure.[64]

This may not, of course, amount to a discourse revolution. Without further and fuller research, it remains merely a conjecture. Nonetheless, the music of the 1990s, with its emphasis on freedom, on women's independence, and on individual fulfilment, does seem to be rather different from that of the 1960s. Arguably, what it represents is a playing out of the

Romanticism that first recurred in the 1960s – but a Romanticism that now has a place for women too. Strikingly, it may also retain a role for religion. As David Gauntlett has commented, 'Of the post-Madonna stars, Britney, Destiny's Child and others have milked the paradox of their well-behaved Christian values contrasting with the raunchiness of their performances.'[65] Even at the turn of the twentieth-first century, it seems, some of the old ideas remained – if only as foils to other, newer, more provocative ones. The search for authenticity may create strange juxtapositions, but then that is what Romanticism is all about.

As this suggests, Brown's discourse revolution remains, at the very least, open to question. For a number of reasons, indeed, one might conclude that the move from female piety to women's liberation was a much slower and more piecemeal one than he suggests. The *Jackie* generation was, in many respects, more traditional in its understanding of gender than he maintains. This is not to deny that the 1960s were important, nor to undermine the contention that women's roles changed significantly in the last 40 years of the twentieth century. Yet there are also good reasons for doubting that the change was sudden, and that it amounts to the death of Christian Britain, much less the sort of death that Callum Brown predicts. Rather, what we might conclude is that the 1960s saw a resurgence of Romanticism: an expressive revolution that shook the institutions of church and state but which only very gradually challenged conventions of gender. In that sense, perhaps it was not *Jackie* but Shelley that ultimately shaped the 1960s and the decades that followed most.[66]

Notes

1 For their help and advice on this essay, I am extremely grateful to Dr Daniel Butt and the Revd Paul Willis.

2 Angela McRobbie, 2000, '*Jackie* Magazine: Romantic Individualism and the Teenage Girl', in her *Feminism and Youth Culture*, 2nd edn, Basingstoke: Macmillan, pp. 67–117.

3 See also Olive Braman, 1977, 'Comics', in Josephine King and Mary Stott (eds), *Is This Your Life? Images of Women in the Media*, London: Virago, pp. 83–92; Elizabeth Frazer, 'Teenage Girls Reading *Jackie*', *Media, Culture and Society*, 9(4) (1987), pp. 407–25; Stevi Jackson, 'Ignorance is Bliss When You're Just Seventeen', *Trouble and Strife* 33 (1996), 50–60; Angela McRobbie, 1981, 'Just Like a *Jackie* Story', in Angela McRobbie and Trisha McCabe (eds), *Feminism for Girls: An Adventure Story*, London: Routledge and Kegan Paul, pp. 113–26; Angela McRobbie, '*Jackie* and *Just Seventeen*: Girls' Comics and Magazines in the 1980s', in McRobbie, *Feminism and Youth Culture*, pp. 135–88.

4 Brown, *Death*, pp. 176–7.

5 Robin Lane-Fox, 1986, *Pagans and Christians*, London: Penguin, p. 119.

6 Callum G. Brown, 2006, *Religion and Society in Twentieth-Century Britain*, Harlow: Pearson, p. 30.

7 Brown, *Religion and Society*, pp. 30, 278.

8 Angela McRobbie and Jenny Garber, 1976, 'Girls and Subcultures: An Exploration',

in Stuart Hall and Tony Jefferson (eds), *Resistance Through Rituals: Youth Subculture in Post-war Britain*, London: Hutchinson, pp. 209–22.

9 Angela McRobbie and Simon Frith, 'Rock and Sexuality', *Screen Education* 29 (1978–9), pp. 3–19.

10 John Shepherd, 1987, 'Music and Male Hegemony', in Richard Leppert and Susan McClary (eds), *Music and Society: The Politics of Composition, Performance, and Reception*, Cambridge: Cambridge University Press, pp. 151–72.

11 The phrase is from Terri Goddard, Jan Pollock, and Marion Fudger, 1977, 'Popular Music', in King and Stott, *Is This Your Life?*, pp. 143–59, at p. 153.

12 Jeff Nuttall, 1968, *Bomb Culture*, London: MacGibbon and Kee, p. 136. See also Jeremy Seabrook, 1971, *City Close-Up*, London: Allen Lane, pp. 188–90.

13 Robert Pattison, 1987, *The Triumph of Vulgarity: Rock Music in the Mirror of Romanticism*, New York and Oxford: Oxford University Press, pp. vi, 87.

14 Sara Cohen, 1991, *Rock Culture in Liverpool: Popular Music in the Making*, Oxford: Clarendon Press, p. 157.

15 Martin, *Sociology of Contemporary Cultural Change*, pp. 15, 184.

16 Nuttall, *Bomb Culture*, p. 249.

17 Pattison, *Triumph of Vulgarity*, p. 183.

18 Pattison, *Triumph of Vulgarity*, p. 183.

19 Quoted in Jon Savage, 2001, *England's Dreaming: Sex Pistols and Punk Rock*, 2nd edn, London: Faber & Faber, p. 127.

20 Brown, *Death*, pp. 178–9.

21 David Martin, 2002, *Christian Language and Its Mutations: Essays in Sociological Understanding*, Aldershot: Ashgate.

22 Cynthia L. White, 1970, *Women's Magazines, 1693–1968*, London: Michael Joseph, pp. 170–8, 218.

23 White, *Women's Magazines*, p. 166.

24 *Cosmopolitan*, March 1972, p. 10.

25 White, *Women's Magazines*, pp. 170–85, 222–4, 236–41.

26 Carolyn Faulder, 1977, 'Women's Magazines', in King and Stott, *Is This Your Life?*, pp. 173–94.

27 Although see Stephanie Spencer, 2005, *Gender, Work, and Education in Britain in the 1950s*, Basingstoke: Palgrave Macmillan, Ch. 6.

28 For girls' magazines see also Penny Tinkler, 1995, *Constructing Girlhood: Popular Magazines for Girls Growing up in England, 1920–20*, London: Taylor and Francis.

29 Robin Kent, 1987, *Agony: Problem Pages through the Ages*, London: Star, pp. 26–7, 250.

30 Marje Proops, 1976, *Dear Marje*, London: Andre Deutsch, pp. 187–8.

31 Angela Patmore, 1993, *Marje: The Guilt and the Gingerbread*, London: Warner, pp. 187–8, 180.

32 *Cosmopolitan*, June 1972, p. 47.

33 *Cosmopolitan*, July 1973, p. 41.

34 See, for example, *Cosmopolitan*, May 1972, pp. 31–3; August 1972, p. 59; June 1973, pp. 92–5.

35 Janice Winslip, 1987, *Inside Women's Magazines*, London and New York: 1987, p. 5; White, *Women's Magazines*, p. 232.

36 Frazer, 'Teenage Girls Reading *Jackie*', p. 419.

37 Angela McRobbie, 1999, *In the Culture Society: Art, Fashion and Popular Music*, London: Routledge, p. 50.

38 Janet Batsleer, Tony Davies, Rebecca O'Rourke, Chris Weedon, 2003, *Rewriting English: Cultural Politics of Gender and Class*, London and New York: Routledge, pp. 147–51.

39 Simon Frith, 1978, *The Sociology of Rock*, London: Constable, pp. 29–30.

40 Mike Brake, 1980, *The Sociology of Youth. Culture and Youth Subculture: Sex and Drugs and Rock 'n' Roll?*, London: Routledge and Kegan Paul, Ch. 5.

41 McRobbie, '*Jackie* Magazine', pp. 78, 91.

42 McRobbie, 'Just Like a *Jackie* Story', p. 122.

43 Brown, *Death*, p. 177.

44 McRobbie, *Culture Society*, p. 46.

45 Dave Laing, 1985, *One Chord Wonders: Power and Meaning in Punk Rock*, Milton Keynes: Open University Press, pp. 27–8.

46 James Nott, 2002, *Music for the People: Popular Music and Dance in Interwar Britain*, Oxford: Oxford University Press, Ch. 8.

47 Frith and McRobbie, 'Rock and Sexuality', pp. 8, 11.

48 Neil Nehring, 1993, *Flowers in the Dustbin: Culture, Anarchy, and Postwar England*, Ann Arbor: University of Michigan Press, pp. 252–3. Although see also Margaret Geddes, 1973, 'Roll Over and Rock Me', *Spare Rib* May 1973, pp. 6–8 and Dave Laing, 1969, *The Sound of Our Time*, London and Sydney: Sheed & Ward, p. 145.

49 Cynthia Cyrus, 'Selling an Image: girl groups of the 1960s', *Popular Music*, 22(2) (2003), 173–93.

50 Simon Reynolds and Joy Press, 1995, *The Sex Revolts: Gender, Rebellion, and Rock 'n' Roll*, London: Serpent's Tail, p. 236.

51 Karen Pegley and Virginia Caputo, 1994, 'Growing Up Female(s): Retrospective Thoughts on Musical Preferences and Meanings', in Philip Brett, Elizabeth Wood, Gary C. Thomas (eds), *Queering the Pitch: The New Lesbian and Gay Musicology*, London and New York: Routledge, pp. 297–313, pp. 301–5.

52 Frith, *Sociology of Rock*, p. 68.

53 Sheila Whitely, 2000, *Women and Popular Music: Sexuality, Identity, and Subjectivity*, London and New York; Routledge, p. 10; see also Chs 1–2, 6–7.

54 Mavis Bayton, 1998, *Frock Rock: Women Performing Popular Music*, Oxford and New York: Oxford University Press, Ch. 4.

55 Lucy O'Brien, 2002, *She Bop II: The Definitive History of Women in Rock, Pop and Soul*, London and New York: Continuum, p. 149.

56 *Guinness Book of British Hit Singles and Albums*, 2005, London: Guinness.

57 Although Marjorie Ferguson sees a shift beginning after about 1974. See her 1983 *Forever Feminine: Women's Magazine's and the Cult of Femininity*, republished 1985, Aldershot: Gower, pp. 96–117.

58 Stevi Jackson, 'Ignorance is Bliss When You're Just Seventeen', *Trouble and Strife* (1996) Vol. 33, 50–60, at p. 57.

59 McRobbie, *Culture Society*, Ch. 4.

60 McRobbie, '*Jackie* and *Just Seventeen*', p. 183.

61 Diane Railton, 'The Gendered Carnival of Pop', *Popular Music* 20 (2001), pp. 321, 232, 330.

62 Eva Leach, 'Vicars of "Wannabe": Authenticity and the Spice Girls', *Popular Music* 20 (2001), pp. 143–68.

63 David Gauntlett, 2004, 'Madonna's Daughters: Girl Power and the Empowered Girl Pop Breakthrough', in Santiago Fouz-Hernàndez and Freya Jarman-Ivens (eds), *Madonna's Drowned Worlds: New Approaches to her Cultural Transformations, 1983–2003*, Aldershot: Ashgate, pp. 161–75, p. 167.

64 Sue Sharpe, 1994, *Just Like a Girl: How Girls Learn to be Women*, 2nd edn, London: Penguin, pp. 264–70.

65 Gauntlett, 'Madonna's Daughters', pp. 173–4.

66 Pattison, *Vulgarity*, pp. xi, 113.

'The long, long night is over.'[1]
The Campaign for Nuclear Disarmament, 'generation' and the politics of religion
(1957–1964)

HOLGER NEHRING

For some contemporaries critical of the Campaign for Nuclear Disarmament (CND) in the late 1950s and early 1960s, the movement appeared as a symbol for all that had gone wrong in Christian Britain since the end of the Second World War. CND's critics expressed their consternation at the entire lack of Christian values and morality among the protesters.[2] A popular Sunday newspaper even sent a journalist to one of the annual marches which took place on the Easter weekend in order to catch young female protesters in compromising positions and to paint a picture of filth and moral decay – albeit without much success.[3] The argument of the historian Callum Brown and others who have discussed the thorough 'secularization' of British society since the early 1960s has reaffirmed this position, arguing that 'much of what was troubling British Christian culture by 1960 had to do with young people'.[4]

But did CND really point to the birth of an a-religious generation of younger protesters who were oblivious to the great importance that religion – and especially Nonconformism – had for previous protest movements? This chapter offers a rather sceptical assessment of such assertions.[5] It follows Benjamin Ziemann's recent approach to changes in West German Catholicism and shifts our glance away from what had allegedly been lost towards analysing the ways in which religion was being transformed. It focuses on the ways in which transcendence and the construction of community were related. Religious arguments and forms of communication are distinct in that they interrogate transcendence and regard what happens in the real world under the aspect of its relation to transcendence. This distinction between this world and the transcendent God can, however, only be the basis for a religious community as long as it remains plausible for social actors.[6] Christians involved in CND framed and encoded the distinction between world and God in a way that contradicted the dominant approaches within the Anglican Church and Nonconformity at the time. 'Generation' was used as an argument against CND by those who disagreed with the campaign's encoding of religious community.

In order to trace this debate, the first section offers a short summary of CND's social composition, focusing particularly on the religious influences in the biographies of some of the main activists. The second section examines the ways in which CND activists framed their protests in religious terms and seeks to bring out the particular context in which this framing was able to gain such a great degree of plausibility for the protesters, regardless of whether they were old or young. The third part shows how outside observers interpreted CND. Rather than regarding the campaign as related to a different conception of religion, they interpreted it in terms of generation and class and thus wrote religion out of CND's history.

Christians on the March

The Campaign for Nuclear Disarmament was founded by a group of London-based intellectuals in early 1958 in order to agitate for Britain's unilateral nuclear disarmament after the Labour Party's 1957 Conference had failed to adopt a motion which made this policy part of the Party's programme. CND's first phase lasted until 1963 when popular support broke away in the wake of the Partial Test Ban Treaty. CND organized a number of protests, most famously the annual marches between the nuclear-weapons research establishment Aldermaston, Berkshire, and London.[7]

CND attracted a significant number of Christians. Frank Parkin's sociological research suggests that 40% of former CND supporters were practising Christians, which far exceeded the number of regular churchgoers at the time. As with previous extra-parliamentary campaigns, the peculiarity of CND was the strong representation of activists from Nonconformist backgrounds, such as Methodists, Baptists, Quakers and Unitarians, who had been closely linked to organized pacifism since the late eighteenth century. Nonconformists outweighed Anglicans significantly: 52% were Free Church members (Quakers, Methodists, Presbyterians and Baptists), 34% Anglicans, and 4% Roman Catholics.[8] In a later survey, Richard Taylor and Colin Pritchard found that 43% of their sample 'strongly agreed with the Christian belief system'.[9]

Clergymen and lay Christians played an important role in the campaign's leadership. John Collins, a Canon of St Paul's Cathedral and the founder of Christian Action, and the Methodist Donald Soper were only the two most prominent. Especially Welsh CND drew on many clergymen when advertising its activities. Kingsley Martin, the editor of the *New Statesman*, who had first come up with the idea for a campaign for nuclear disarmament in late 1957, and the historian Edward P. Thompson also came from Nonconformist backgrounds, though both had renounced their religion. Ministers frequently served as chairmen or secretaries of local CND branches.[10] Through their very active role as those who formulated the pamphlets and think pieces, and as intellectuals who represented the campaign symbolically, they had a considerable influence on the way in which CND presented itself to the general public.

From 1961 onwards, the Christian presence within the Campaign was institutionalized in a specific sub-group: Christian CND (CCND), run by Pamela Frankau, Francis Jude and Diana Collins, the wife of Canon Collins.[11] CCND ran its own journal, *Rushlight*. CCND never grew very large: only 14 people were actively involved in 1962, and the mailing list of its journal *Rushlight* contained only 750 names.[12] Yet although the institutionalization of the explicitly Christian voices might be regarded as a failure, it is remarkable how little debate there was within CND about its Christian message and how much Christian language and Christian understandings of morality and transcendence influenced the ways in which CND presented itself to the public.

CND's revivalism

Indeed, to observers today, CND might very well appear as a kind of radical revivalism. Its language was full of elements of a Christian morality – such as the importance of Christian conscience – which it sought to apply to politics. Many of its pamphlets conjured up images of the apocalypse. In order to prevent it, the protesters argued, drastic changes in British society were necessary.[13] Yet Christian CND protesters were not merely romantics. They very much regarded themselves as the sharp-eyed realists who offered a plausible interpretation of the society around them which was hardly represented in institutionalized religion and in mainstream politics. Most activists regarded their involvement in the anti-nuclear-weapons movement not as anything radical or new, however, but as an attempt to rescue what they thought had been lost in their own lifeworlds: Britain's Christian moral community and the sense of security that such a community could give them.

From an anthropological perspective, churches are one of the key providers of 'security' through providing eschatological hopes of transcending the quotidian world. Yet a minority of Christians in both Britain and West Germany increasingly felt that institutionalized religion failed to live up to these aims in an age of potential nuclear war. The protests against nuclear weapons offered them an alternative home in which they could translate their fears into demands for security. While it is difficult to capture individual beliefs with the available sources, the published and unpublished interpretations of the marches *sub specie aeternitatis* allow some glimpses into the activists' Christian-moral economies.

The general context in which Christians framed their expectations was the belief, first codified by St Augustine as a norm for individual judgements of conscience, that wars fought by Christians had to be 'just', both in terms of their causes and their military practices.[14] The arrival of mass warfare, however, in particular the bombing of cities in World War Two and the destructive power of nuclear weapons, put the doctrine under increasing strain. Protestant churches in both Britain and West Germany, as well as on the global ecumenical level, condemned nuclear weapons in the most drastic terms.[15]

Yet there was no agreement about what practical consequences should be drawn, and CND activists felt that the churches' actions lagged behind their words.[16] The majority in the churches' hierarchies believed that, given the communist threat, nuclear deterrence might be admissible.[17] Hence, while the British Council of Churches condemned nuclear weapons as 'an offence to God and a denial of His purpose for man', it called British unilateral disarmament 'impracticable and possibly disastrous'.[18] As the Anglican Church was part of the fabric of the English state, official opposition to nuclear weapons from these groups remained rather ambivalent and subdued. There were only about 12 unilateralist bishops and suffragans in England and Wales, out of over a hundred, namely those from Manchester, Birmingham, Chichester, Southwark, Llandaff, Bangor, Plymouth and Woolwich.[19] This only helped accentuate many Anglicans' disappointment with their church's stance.[20] Canon Collins expressed the feelings of many British activists when he wondered, taking up arguments against the aerial bombing of German cities during World War Two, how 'a Christian or a liberal man or woman [could] stand such a denial of the basic rule that only love can expel fear?'[21]

The historical backdrop to these expectations did not only lie in the late 1950s and early 1960s, however, but pointed back to the hopes for a re-Christianization of British society which had been common among both progressive and conservative Christians immediately after World War Two and which were connected to the debates about Christian community since the late 1920s. Many of those who participated in CND felt disappointed about the lack of success of a 're-Christianization' of British society. They thought that the churches had not been active enough in their attempts to win over the population and had given up ideals of a Christian community; their moral weakness in the face of nuclear weapons only illustrated this more general point.[22] For many Christian activists, the demonstrations and annual marches thus became Christian processions, a 'heyday of their personal evangelism of mankind and the victory of Christian morality', and into practices of Christian brotherhood and fellowship which they believed had been lost in society more generally.[23] This belief was even shared by some activists who saw themselves as secular.[24]

Behind this was the belief that 'security' could only be created through active Christian works in the world, 'not in fine sermons, but in action'.[25] This was, some ministers believed, particularly attractive for the young: 'The Campaign has given them something to live and fight for in a day when politics and the Church seem ingrained with antiquarianism, irrelevance and hopelessness.'[26] This reflected a very specific theological world-view. For many activists, the incarnation was at the very centre of the Christian belief system. The incarnate Christ had shattered the boundaries between spiritual and physical worlds. Thus, addressing humanity's physical needs and working towards preventing its destruction was a spiritual act. Christian action was, therefore, not only about religion, but it related to the world as a whole: 'Beware lest you worship the Satan of Separation and not the God who came to earth to die between two thieves to save.'[27] The movement became, in the words of a British activist, 'necessary not chiefly to save our skins but to save our souls'.[28]

The activists' religiosity was not only conditioned by official interpretations of the revelation. It also relied on people's own experiences with the world. On the one hand, Christian activists emphasized their individual experiences and moral norms against the church hierarchies and thus 'privatized' their religious beliefs. On the other hand, however, they believed that these private beliefs should be taken seriously in the politics of security and that religion should play a role in the deliberations of social justice.[29] This was not merely a transition towards 'believing without belonging', or the abandonment of the churches in an age of affluence.[30] Rather, their beliefs carried the activists into communities which did not coincide with the institutionalized churches.[31]

It was on the marches themselves that CND protesters actualized their concerns. The Easter weekend was particularly apt for a Christian interpretation, as it carried connotations of new beginnings and the resurrection. Through the marches, the protesters endowed Easter with a unique meaning. Instead of going to church or on the traditional Easter walk with their families, the protesters went on the march, thus redefining the Christian message of Easter in explicitly political terms, transcending the norms of privacy at the time and yet expressing their own private moral economies. Prayer sessions and services were held along the 50-mile march between the nuclear-weapons research establishment in Aldermaston, Berkshire, and London. It was this language of Christian brotherhood which was at the root of British extra-parliamentary protests.[32]

For Christian protesters, the marches were annual calls for repentance and renewal, both a physical act of atonement and a spiritual revival. The thousands of marchers who strolled through the countryside evoked such national Christian narratives as Chaucer's *Canterbury Tales*. One CND supporter described the march as a civilising mission, a march away from fear towards normality, towards human standards, towards the real people in the nursery rhyme whose houses are over the hill but not so far away that we will not get there by candlelight, whose hands are set to the plough and the making of things.[33]

Singing to the tune of 'Oh, when the saints . . . ', they called themselves a band of 'lonely pilgrims' who travelled 'through this world of woe'.[34] The marches were, therefore, life-changing experiences in that they not only expressed their feelings, but also made the protesters part of a new community.[35]

Fellowship and community were key for the activists: '[t]he brotherhood of man is no longer a notion, it's here.'[36] The language of 'community' and 'fellowship' was both a precondition for and a result of the social interactions between protesters from very different backgrounds. As the terms 'community' and 'fellowship' were able to speak to very different political and social groups – from Christians to pacifists to humanists – they helped bridge the gaps between the different activists. Moreover, once the movements had emerged, the concepts 'community' and 'fellowship' helped the activists to find inter-personal security. To outside observers, this rhetoric endowed the movements with a seeming homogeneity and moral immediacy.[37]

'Generation' as an argument in the politics of religion

CND's most vociferous critics were Christian as well. Yet rather than highlighting CND's moral mission, they regarded the campaign as an insidious plot to undermine British democracy and, with it, Christianity. They took up the arguments of the popular-conservative Christian revivalism of the Billy Graham type and made themselves heard through pressure groups such as Moral Re-Armament. Other Christian critics of CND were more sympathetic to the general cause of the campaign, but regarded the campaign limitation to nuclear weapons alone as rather cowardly. Conservative Quakers in particular had hoped to see a much stronger emphasis on pacifism and non-violence.[38]

While some of these specific arguments reached the public arena, the argument that found most resonance in the politics of religion in late 1950s and 1960s Britain was that of 'generation'. Debates within the Anglican Church focused on the lack of interest in churchgoing among the young and pointed out that the post-war approach to evangelism set out by Archbishop William Temple in his 'Towards the Conversion of England' (1943) had been a failure.[39] It also surfaced in the debate about *Honest to God* in which John Robinson conceptualized God as participant in human society and thus endowed Anglican religion with a radical mission of social change.[40]

Likewise, the debates about *The Secular City*, published by the American Harvey Cox, and Paul van Buren's *The Secular Meaning of the Gospel* soon came to focus on the role of the young as critics of their secular and positivist theology sought to link van Buren's and Cox's alleged acceptance of secular society to social and moral decay.[41]

Similarly, some Quakers refused to be drawn into a movement and join 'the Teddy Boys, the income tax dodgers and the Algerian "colons" in bringing the law and democratic government into contempt'.[42] And, on his return to Britain in 1966, Billy Graham saw 'psychopathic madness' in the pop culture and materialism, 'the lust for pleasure, the silver-chromed gods that have been erected since the war' and which were cherished by the young.[43]

The reason for the attraction of 'generation' as an argument by CND critics lay in the adaptability of the term as a symbol for a range of cultural, social and political developments with which CND's critics were unhappy. Although there existed a 'Youth CND' and a student section, and although there was a concurrent rising interest among activists, government officials, parties and sociological circles in analyzing and understanding problems of 'youth', most descriptions of the campaign as a youth movement came from outside and had mostly negative connotations.[44]

CND, 'generation' and the transformation of religion

CND was, therefore, not the symptom of a gradual religious decay in post-1945 Britain. The title 'youth movement' and the description of CND as a generational phenomenon were, for the most part, identifications from the outside which brushed over the contradictions between experiences and expectations which many of the protesters felt. They also neglected the pro-testers' redefinition of transcendence as politically relevant in a society which faced possible dislocations stemming from the transformation of British society, economy and culture after World War Two.

Examining CND from such a perspective thus offers important lessons for historians of religion. Historians of 'secularization' have used rather stable definitions of what 'religion' was supposed to mean and have thus merely reproduced contemporary discussions instead of analysing them. Their interpretation of an increasingly 'secular' British society, therefore, comes as little surprise. A more rewarding avenue of research might instead analyse the ways in which contemporaries defined their 'religion' and how precisely they encoded transcendence as the key parameter of religious thinking and practice.[45] For CND activists, 'religion' was no longer linked to the church as an institution, but focused on the distinction between 'political' and 'unpolitical'. Christian protesters thus sought to bring back a set of moral beliefs and community to the centre of British politics which, they felt, had become absent from more mainstream religious theories and practices. At the same time, communicating their message along religious lines offered the protestors a powerful resource in the political debates about nuclear disarmament, as it promised to endow their argument with a legitimacy which could not be matched by the worldly powers of pragmatic or scientific considerations. It is remarkable how little older and younger CND supporters disagreed on this crucial point. CND was thus not a sign of the disenchantment of the modern world, as an interpretation focused on 'secularization' implies. It instead appears as the result of CND activists' disenchantment with the ways in which the churches reacted to the political, social, economic and, not least, religious challenges of post-World War Two Britain.

Notes

1 *Peace News*, 11 April 1958, p. 8.

2 Brown, *Death*, pp. 170–192; McLeod, 'The Religious Crisis of the 1960s', pp. 205–29.

3 Christopher P. Driver, 1964, *The Disarmers: A Study in Protest*, London: Hodder & Stoughton, p. 59.

4 Brown, *Religion and Society*, p. 216.

5 For rather superficial accounts of the role of religion in CND cf. Hastings, *History*, pp. 510–11, 601, 657–8; D. W. Bebbington, 1989, *Evangelicalism in Modern Britain: A History from the 1730s to the 1980s*, London: Unwin Hyman; Meredith Veldman, 1994, *Fantasy, the Bomb, and the Greening of Britain: Romantic Protest, 1945–1980*, Cambridge: Cambridge University Press.

6 Cf. Benjamin Ziemann, 2006, 'Codierung von Transzendenz im Zeitalter der Privatisierung. Die Suche nach Vergemeinschaftung in der katholischen Kirche, 1945–1980', in Michael Geyer and Lucian Hölscher (eds), *The Presence of God in Modern Society: Transcendence and Religious Community in Germany*, Göttingen: Wallstein, pp. 380–403.

7 On CND's history cf. Richard Taylor, 1988, *Against the Bomb: The British Peace Movement, 1958–1965*, Oxford: Clarendon Press.

8 Frank Parkin, 1968, *Middle-Class Radicalism*, Manchester: Manchester University Press, pp. 27, 74–5. This contradicts the claims of a receding influence of nonconformity, especially on the peace movement, in Alan P. F. Sell and Anthony R. Cross (eds), *Protestant Nonconformity in England and Wales in the Twentieth Century*, Carlisle: Paternoster Press, 2003.

9 Richard Taylor and Colin Pritchard, 1980, *The Protest Makers: The British Nuclear Disarmament Movement of 1958–1965, Twenty Years On*, Oxford: Pergamon Press, p. 23 and tables on pp. 28, 34 and 38.

10 Hastings, *History*, pp. 510–11.

11 'Christians confer on the Bomb', *Sanity*, Nov. 1961, p. 1; CND National Executive, minutes, 30 June 1961: Modern Records Centre, University of Warwick.

12 Mailing list for *Rushlight*, n.d. (c. 1962): British Library of Political and Economic Science, London [BLPES], CND/7/17/8.

13 *Peace News*, 13 June 1958, p. 1; *Peace News*, 3 Apr. 1959, p. 2; *Peace News*, 28 Apr. 1961, p. 6.

14 Roger Ruston, 1989, *A Say in the End of the World: Morals and British Nuclear*

Weapons Policy 1941–1987, Oxford: Oxford University Press, pp. 17–20; David Ormrod, 'The Churches and the Nuclear Arms Race, 1945–1985', in Richard Taylor and Nigel Young (eds), 1987, *Campaigns for Peace: British Peace Movements in the Twentieth Century*, Manchester: Manchester University Press, pp. 189–220, at p. 190.

15 British Council of the Churches, 1946, *The Era of Atomic Power*, London: SCM Press, pp. 7 and 19; *Evanston Speaks: Reports of the Second Assembly of the World Council of Churches, August 13–15, 1954*, Geneva: World Council of Churches, 1954, p. 39; *Evanston to New Delhi 1954–1961: Report of the Central Committee to the Third Assembly of the World Council of Churches, New Delhi*, Geneva: World Council of Churches, 1961, p. 261.

16 *The Times*, 26 August 1958, p. 4; *The Church and the World: The Bulletin of the British Council of Churches*, June/July 1959, pp. 1–2; British Council of Churches, 1973, *The Search for Security: A Christian Appraisal*, London: SCM Press, pp. 9–12.

17 T. R. Milford, 1961, *The Valley of Decision: The Christian Dilemma in the Nuclear Age*, London: British Council of Churches, p. 36.

18 British Council of Churches, 1963, *The British Nuclear Deterrent*, London: SCM Press, pp. 6 and 28.

19 Driver, *The Disarmers*, pp. 199–200.

20 Cf. S. J. D. Green, 1996, 'Survival and Autonomy: On the Strange Fortunes and Peculiar Legacy of Ecclesiastical Establishment in the Modern British State c. 1820 to the Present Day', in S. J. D. Green and R. C. Whiting (eds), *The Boundaries of the State in Modern Britain*, Cambridge: Cambridge University Press, pp. 299–324; Dianne Kirby, 'The Church of England and the Cold War Nuclear Debate', *Twentieth Century British History*, 4 (1993), 250–83.

21 George Bell, Bishop of Chichester, 1955, *Nuclear War and Peace* (= Peace Aims Pamphlet, no. 60), London: National Peace Council, pp. 48–54; British Council of Churches, *Era*, pp. 53–56; 40; 53.

22 Cf. Ian Henderson (ed.), 1976, *Man of Christian Action: Canon John Collins – the Man and his Work*, Guildford: Lutterworth Press, pp. 112–5. On the background: Martin Greschat, 1990, '"Rechristianisierung" und "Säkularisierung". Anmerkungen zu einem europäischen konfessionellen Interpretationsmodell', in Jochen-Christoph Kaiser and Anselm Doering-Manteuffel (eds), *Christentum und politische Verantwortung: Kirchen im Nachkriegsdeutschland*, Stuttgart and Berlin: Kohlhammer, 1990, pp. 1–24 and Grimley, *Citizenship*.

23 Quote from *Baptist Times*, 16 November 1961, p. 10. Cf. also *The Friend*, 21 September 1962, p. 1166.

24 E. P. Thompson, 'Socialism and the Intellectuals', *Universities and Left Review*, no. 1 (1957), 31–6, p. 36; Penelope J. Corfield, 'E. P. Thompson, the Historian: An Appreciation', *New Left Review*, no. 201 (1993), 10–17, p. 16.

25 *Methodist Recorder*, 17 May 1962, p. 9; George Thomas, 1959, *The Christian Heritage in Politics*, London: Epworth Press, p. 19.

26 J. J. Vincent, *Christ in a Nuclear World*, Manchester: Crux Press, 1962, p. 133.

27 *Coracle*, 27 (November 1955), p. 15; *Coracle*, 31 (November 1957), p. 23; *Coracle*, 34 (March 1959), p. 3; *Coracle* 37 (November 1960), p. 31; L. John Collins, 1966, *Faith under Fire*, London: Frewin, pp. 129–30.

28 Revd Kenneth Rawlings, *The Junction*, April 1960, p. 5; *Christian World*, 27 March 1958, p. 8; *The Friend*, 14 September 1962, p. 1133; Canon John Collins writing in *Christian Action*, autumn 1961, p. 18.

29 Merrilyn Thomas, 2005, *Communing with the Enemy: Covert Operations, Christianity and Cold War Politics in Britain and the GDR*, Oxford: Peter Lang, pp. 124–31; Robert Banks, 'The Intellectual Encounter between Christianity and Marxism: A Contribution to the Pre-History of a Dialogue', *Journal of Contemporary*

History, 11 (1976), 309–31.

30 Davie, *Believing without Belonging*.

31 *Peace News*, 18 April 1957, p. 2; *Peace News*, 11 August 1961, p. 8.

32 *Peace News*, special issue, Easter 1958, p. 3.

33 Denis Knight, secretary of CND's film and television Committee, quoted by Driver, *The Disarmers*, p. 58; editorial, *Peace News*, 6 March 1959, p. 4.

34 *Sanity*, October 1961, p. 2.

35 CND song 'Don't you hear the H-bomb's thunder?', printed in David Widgery (ed.), 1976, *The Left in Britain, 1958–1968*, Harmondsworth: Penguin, p. 99; 'Is it any use?', n.d.: BLPES, CND/1/4.

36 Robert Bolt, 'Do you speak nuclear?', *New Statesman*, 24 December 1960.

37 Cf. on this aspect Ron Aminzade and Elizabeth J. Perry, 2001, 'The Sacred, Religious, and Secular in Contentious Politics: Blurring Boundaries', in Ron Aminzade *et al.*, *Silence and Voice in the Study of Contentious Politics*, Cambridge: Cambridge University Press, pp. 155–78

38 *Christian World*, 27 March 1958, p. 8; *Baptist Times*, 13 November 1958, p. 6.

39 *Church Times*, 11 January 1963, p. 2; *Church Times*, 15 February 1963, p. 4, *Church Times* 8 November. 1963, p. 5.

40 David L. Edwards (ed.), 1963, *The Honest to God Debate*, London: SCM Press.

41 Buren, *Secular Meaning*; Cox, 1966, *The Secular City*; *Church Times*, 8 November 1963, p. 8; *Church Times*, 22 November 1963, p. 6; *Church Times*, 6 January 1967, p. 2.

42 *The Friend*, 9 June 1961, p. 792.

43 *The Times*, 2 June 1966, p. 6.

44 Polls at the universities of Oxford and Cambridge (1961): BLPES, CND/8/2; Uwe Kitzinger in the *Listener*, 16 May 1963, p. 2; Driver, *The Disarmers*, pp. 59 and 131; Ferdynand Zweig, 1963, *The Student in the Age of Anxiety: A Survey of Oxford and Manchester Students*, London: Heinemann, p. 199; Charles Hamblett and Jane Deverson, 1964, *Generation X*, London: Tandem Books; Christopher Booker, 1969, *The Neophiliacs: A Study of the Revolution in English Life in the Fifties and Sixties*, London: Collins; Bill Osgerby, 1998, *Youth in Britain since 1945*, Oxford: Blackwell, pp. 17–29; Steven Fielding, 2003, *Labour and Cultural Change*, Manchester: Manchester University Press, pp. 168–82; Catherine Ellis, 'No Hammock for the Idle: The Conservative Party, "Youth" and the Welfare State in the 1960s', *Twentieth Century British History*, 16 (2005), 441–70.

45 Cf. Benjamin Ziemann, 2006, 'The Gospel of Psychology: Therapeutic Concepts and the Scientification of Pastoral Care in the West German Catholic Church, 1950–1980', *Central European History* 39(1) (2006), 79–106.

Internet Generation: Computer-Mediated Communication and Christianity

JANE GARNETT

The experience of the Internet has been attached with apocalyptic and other forms of deterministic language to the definition both of a generation and of an epoch. The 'Millennials' (those born since *c.*1980) or 'The Internet Generation' navigate in the vast sea of 'The Information Society' or 'The Digital Age'. How decisive a social and cultural caesura does the Internet in fact represent? How do the terms in which it has been discussed relate to wider theoretical debates about the implications of modernity and post-modernity? To what extent does it challenge or disturb existing categories of social theory – including theories of secularization? What conclusions should be drawn from the sheer quantity of sites related to religion on the Internet?

Paradoxically, the Internet was developed both out of the positivistic and totalizing aspirations of scientific modernity and out of 1960s counter-culturalism.[1] The technology itself seemed to offer ways to re-enchant a world left disenchanted by the processes of modernization. The concept of cyberspace as an ideal zone beyond space, time and the constraints of materiality led to its being likened to the New Jerusalem, or to an 'eternal present' which 'will be seen as a Fountain of Youth, where you will bathe and refresh yourself into a sparkling juvenile'.[2] The association of youth with a new dawn was beguiling and befuddling. The idea of a conceptual chasm dividing the new from the old threatened to be as programmatic and reductionist as any other form of technological determinism. The rhetoric of liberation and of free association in virtual communities which were chosen rather than given[3] could sit easily with other liberalizing rhetorics, and seem to challenge all established social and conceptual norms, including religious ones. Simplistic analogies were made with the impact of printing on the development of the Protestant Reformation. The Internet could either be conceived as a timely substitute for the community and transcendence offered by religion, or, in its democratic structure, be seen to favour non-hierarchical religious groups – new religious movements rather than long-established mainstream churches.[4] Maintaining the double heritage of its genesis, computer-mediated communication (CMC) on the one hand offered hypertext, multimedia interfaces and the potentiality to open up ways of thinking hitherto undreamt of; on the other, its processes were co-opted and directed to established commercial ends by giant operators like IBM and Microsoft. As the initial *naïveté* wore off, and the master-narrative of liberalism and consumer choice dug deeper, the Internet was figured as a metaphor of postmodernity, standing (for good or ill) for fragmentation of identity, transience, lack of authority, instant gratification and a culture of entertainment and spectacle.[5] These cultural characteristics, apparently reified in computer-mediated communication, have themselves been attributed with hegemonic power in the late twentieth and early twenty-first centuries.

Both as a medium and as a metaphor, in fact, the Internet seems to facilitate and to represent reconceptualization rather than rupture. The cultural challenges identified in postmodernity are being confronted as much as they are being mirrored by means of this evolving technology, which is itself in a constant process of reconfiguration. There is always a lag in the embedding of social theory. The grand theses of early twentieth-century sociology, developed in the context of a reaction against cultural and social norms shaped by centuries of Western Christian tradition, had achieved a dominant position by the mid-twentieth century. Much of the conceptual apparatus continues to claim normative status even in modified forms. Yet the changes in Western society over the last three decades, which have called into question not just particular meta-narratives, but also the whole concept of social theory, have also stimulated the construction of new models of communication and organization in response to some old demands – for community and for moral authority. Even in terms of the broad-brush approach of current generational theory, the attitudes of the last two generations – the so-called Generation X (those born between c.1964 and 1981) and the Millennial Generation – have been characterized in conflicting ways: as on the one hand approximating to a postmodern sensibility of scepticism, anti-institutionalism, individualism, materialism and political cynicism; and on the other showing a growing consciousness of and positive engagement with global issues that raise ethical challenges to long-standing economic and social assumptions. Mainstream Christian churches, which in many ways now benefit from being more counter-cultural than cultural, have participated in this latter trend.[6] What has been characterized by Zygmunt Bauman as 'liquid modernity' – a situation in which jobs, families, neighbourhoods are no longer stable, in which people have become consumers rather than producers, in which relationships have become ever more superficial, and in which delayed gratification no longer makes sense – presents a compelling diagnosis of a series of social challenges, but it does not represent a social end point. The very articulation of a social pathology signals a consciousness of a need to pose critical questions. Indeed Bauman calls for the cultivation of more dialogical thinking, of communication which is not just about the transfer and receipt of information.[7]

Over the last decade, Christian engagement with the Internet in this context has become increasingly sophisticated and self-reflexive. Churches and other Christian organizations have recognized the importance of the medium, and the need to confront its challenges in a serious way. The World Association for Christian Communication, an ecumenical organization dedicated to addressing the 'potential for both solidarity and threat to humanity' in modern communications, stresses that even though the Internet, by comparison with other mass media, is potentially less hierarchical in that it deals with horizontal rather than vertical flows of material, there is still far more potential for constructive interactivity and participation than has yet been attained.[8] This organization is financed in the UK by the Community Media Association (a non-profit organization set up in 1983 to develop media access for local communities), the Council for World Mission, Feed the Minds/SPCK, the Methodist Church UK and the Open Society Foundation. The European Christian Internet Conference has now held eleven annual conferences, the latest in June 2006 in London on the theme of the challenge of convergency for the church in the areas of *communio, educatio, missio*. This conference underscored the significance of media literacy as a lifelong, global and combative project – not just the acquisition of a set of technical skills, but the development of a critical understanding of the ethical, political and social implications of communication. Churches were urged to get more involved in the UN World Summit on the Information Society (WSIS), to grasp the opportunity to shape the debate on and practice of new information technologies. The opportunity for churches to develop a new profile in this area was evidenced by the compatibility of goals expressed by civil society organizations towards the affirmation of human dignity and the fundamental aspirations of Christian bodies (including NGOs).[9]

One specific issue raised was the monopolization of access to the Internet by major commercial software providers. Reference was made to ongoing Christian investigation into the ethical and theological implications of using open-source and non-proprietary formats. An article was cited which pointed to the affinity between the 2002 Pontifical Statement on 'The Church and the Internet' (which emphasized that the use of new information technology and the Internet needed to be 'informed and guided by a resolute commitment to the practice of solidarity in the service of the common good') and the principles of the free software movement. This article called on the Catholic Church to adopt the Free International Standard OpenDocument for office documents in all Catholic institutions world-wide, to avoid proprietary files and protocols, and to make sure that all official Catholic websites are viewable by any browser.[10] In the context of '*communio*', the keynote speaker drew attention to the tensions between the potential empowering of the individual brought about by the Internet, and the Christian demand for embodied community, and suggested the need for the development of an ecclesiology of the Internet. Reflection on the relationship between the cultural and the counter-cultural was encouraged: church sites could operate in ways that were counter-cultural in relation to the potential anarchy of the medium.[11] In these different ways, Christian groups, themselves networked internationally, have begun to exploit new opportunities for conversation and the establishment of a distinctive voice in global debate on communication and the development of civil society.

Initial hard research into the impact of computer-mediated communication on the concept of Christian community in Britain and elsewhere has suggested greater continuities between offline and online community than had previously been anticipated, and also a critical dialogical relationship between 'real' and 'virtual' forms of community.[12] The Internet has undoubtedly facilitated the construction of a mass of online communities, which have themselves been used creatively in many cases to amplify, develop and maintain offline community and identity, sometimes (as in the case of immigrant communities) by linking a series of local communities which have a cultural affinity but may also engage critically with each other across national boundaries.[13] While a distinction has been drawn between religion online (the presentation of traditional religious forms via CMC) and online religion (which offers alternative forms of religious experience explicitly shaped by the medium),[14] the blurring of traditional boundaries between public and private effected by the Internet has sharpened understandings of the scope and cultural significance of religious community in both contexts. It has helped constructively to complicate the binary of believing versus belonging, itself over-determined by a classic liberal model of social identity. Heidi Campbell's 2001 study of three email-based Christian online communities – a charismatic renewal group, an evangelical group of the visually impaired, and an online Anglican communion – showed on the one hand that online involvement was seen by these groups as supplementary to local church involvement; on the other that online communities served as ideal types of religious community with which to critique offline churches. Interactive discussion of faith and theology in a context in which people were judged solely for their ideas, not for their clothes or mannerisms, enhanced people's confidence and deepened their thinking in ways that were then transferred into their church communities.[15] Moreover, questions raised in online contexts are not always what clergy expect or have been confronted with before.[16] It has been suggested that consciousness of this may lead to the development of a model of ministry which is more responsive to lay demands,[17] although this in itself would hardly be a new phenomenon in the history of the Christian Church.

In its infinite variety the Internet offers scope for both interconnection and solipsism, moderated open discussion and the reinforcement of prejudice, public engagement and private reflection. It offers young people a space in the home more free from the surveillance of their parents than other media, such as the land-line telephone; a space which is open, and yet through which personal routes can be tracked and networks created.[18] A *Guardian/ICM* poll in 2005 suggested that one third of people in Britain aged between 14 and 21 had launched their own website or blog; it is now (November 2006) estimated that two new blogs are created every second.[19] Although these rapidly develop their own conventions of interaction, and the creation of a personal website or blog involves a display of identity (however playful), another aspect of the openness and scope for personalization on the Internet is the possibility of experimenting in a context in which people are (at least in theory) not subject to pressures to conform to a particular social, cultural or generational ideal. Here a distinction must be made between those sites, maybe targeting a particular age-group or constituency, that offer discussion on a range of subjects which might or might not include religion, and sites which are specifically designated as religious/Christian.

A suggestive example of the former was a Swedish site providing chat rooms and discussion groups for young people studied by Mia Lövheim in 2000. Interested in exploring the degree to which such a site could offer a sort of 'liminal' or 'transitional' space in which young people on the brink of adulthood could work out questions of religious identity, Lövheim discovered a much more complex situation. The openness and ambiguity implicit in the online context, and the absence of the full range of nuances of conversational tone or markers of cultural identity which would be present offline led those young people discussing religious identities online to feel insecure. Because of this insecurity, discussions tended to lead to the reaffirmation rather than reconstruction of stereotypes about religious identity, and to the 'construction of boundaries in order to separate "serious" religious identities from "fake" versions'. In line with other research into the situations of young people in late modern society, Lövheim's study suggests that the Internet needs to provide not just scope to reconstruct conventional models of offline identity, but also to 'reintegrate' the complexities of offline life into a coherent structure of meaning which can sustain the individual in an increasingly challenging world.[20] Again, the creation of the necessary trust may depend, to a greater extent than has yet been addressed, on the interrelationship between online experience and the everyday experience of different groups of people at different stages of their lives.

Sites that are specifically framed by their religious identity have the advantage of greater clarity and structure in this sense, although there is obviously still a wide spectrum of forms and claims to authority. Peter Scally, the Jesuit priest who manages the websites *Sacred Space* – 'Daily Prayer Online' – and *Pray as you Go* – daily prayer for downloading to an MP3 player, clearly aimed at young people – has emphasized the scope offered for exploration without feeling the need to conform to a secular view of what is cool.[21] Other Christian websites highlight their capacity to draw in those who would feel inhibited about crossing the threshold of a church or church organization, but who yet have questions to ask and needs to fulfil.[22]

It is impossible to know how many of those who use this sort of religious website or online community come from or move to 'real' church communities – or how to interpret a continuing online Christian engagement without that move to 'reality'. *Sacred Space* guides its participants through a daily prayer (available in 21 European and non-European languages), intended to give a ten-minute break from the working day at the computer – an online retreat in miniature. The Prayer Guide, which can be opted into and out of in any one of six stages, starts with a body, breathing and listening exercise to direct focused attention to physical and mental functions. The Guide then moves through a poem by Gerard Manley Hopkins, an image of crocuses, a preparatory prayer by St Ignatius, advice on how to review consciousness in the same way as one might replay what has happened during the day, how to deal with distractions, and how to figure prayer as conversation with Christ (again with reference to Ignatius and with the aid of a variety of images of Jesus). The home page makes it clear from the start that the site is produced by the Irish Jesuits, it includes a link to the monthly prayer intentions of the Pope, and its frame of reference is fundamentally within a Catholic (indeed, Jesuit) tradition.[23] Yet it is certainly intended to have a much wider reach, and there is nothing in principle to stop its working for a broader Christian constituency. It makes no explicit reference to participation in offline churches, and has no express evangelical mission to draw people from online devotional practice to offline community. *Sacred Space* maintains the vocabulary and even the grammar of a long-standing religious tradition of daily prayer in a way designed to fit with the particular rhythms of modern working life. The new medium, working with well-established cultural triggers and ritualization, focuses on the creation of an embodied religious subject: the discipline of the devotional practice is intended to enable people to develop and sustain a distinctive Christian perspective at an angle to the pressures of everyday life. The Internet, whose dominant mode of instantaneity threatens sustained reflection or meditation, is used to cut across itself and carve out space for precisely such activity – a further dimension of counter-culturality. With a staff of only two people, *Sacred Space* claims to reach 15,000 each day, who may or may not be practising members of offline church communities.[24] While the organization of the Catholic Church is profoundly hierarchical, and indeed the Vatican has shown itself to be very concerned about issues of control in relation to the Internet, this has pragmatically led to greater devolution of authority to the local level, which is the only context in which voluntary control can be exercised and effective education practised.[25] At the same time, individuals and groups within the churches can and do develop their own approaches – as they always have

done – from which the church is happy to benefit when they prove successful.

These questions of the definition of community and identity, culture and
counter-culture, come together theologically and existentially for Christian
churches in the need to address the ways in which the Internet figures the
concepts of absence and presence. Michel Kocher, a Swiss theologian and
journalist, used the story of Christ's appearing to the two disciples on the
road to Emmaus, breaking bread with them and then disappearing, to focus
the scope and limitations of spiritual communication on the Internet:

> The fundamental experience of the absence which tells of the reality of
> Christ's presence is not available in the virtual world. Why? In the virtual
> world there are never any real absences, only time-lags. In the digital
> world, what is not possible today, will be possible tomorrow.

The Internet figures absence simply as a temporary lack of information, a
lacuna which could be filled in the future, whereas absence in Christian
theology is something fundamentally numinous. Particularly in the more
sacramental forms of Christianity, such an emphasis on the meaning which
inheres in the mysterious, the real presence in the absence, challenges the
rhetoric of the World Wide Web with its apparent pretension to totality.
Moreover, as Kocher says, the Internet does make connections between real
people, but the increased chance of being present does not follow the technical logic of the communications media. Even if everyone in the world were
linked to the Internet, specific connections and deliberate personal acts of
communication would need to be made for the human presence to be given
meaning. He calls for more attention to be paid to what the Internet can
distinctively do – its multimedia and hypertextual potentiality to stimulate
and foster new forms of communication and cultural connections – and at
the same time for its limits to be made equally transparent.[26]

We are still at a very early stage in assessing the cultural impact of
computer-mediated communication. But we are already entering a phase of
its development when more nuanced distinctions are being made. In the
1980s and 1990s, the language used to analyse the Internet was too polarized, in both positive and negative terms. There is now more attention paid
to the specific ways in which the Internet can facilitate different ways of
thinking and making connections. Moving beyond thinking of the Internet
simply in terms of the transmission of information, while also resisting its
reification into a self-contained world of its own, could be the counterpart of
a more differentiated understanding of intergenerational and intercultural
communication as a whole. The narratives through which people live their
lives are not disembodied or floating, nor yet are they as culturally prescribed
as they were even 50 years ago. There is now much more social mobility,
within and between countries, and much more likelihood of occupational

and familial mobility across a person's life. In order to construct identity (itself a lifelong process, not just a project for youth), in which religious identity remains one of the possible variables, the uses made of the Internet are interwoven with personal and communal histories. The metaphor of the sea is appropriate. To navigate it effectively and not to be thrown off-course requires skill and discriminating judgement. To embark on a journey carries risks, which need to be weighed. Sailors have always carried their own culture with them, as well as being influenced by cultures with which they have come into contact. The sea has always played a powerful role in stimulating the imagination. Nobody lives their whole life on the sea, but touches down regularly on dry land.

Notes

1 John Markoff, 2005, *What the Dormouse Said: How the 60s Counterculture Shaped the Personal Computer Industry*, New York: Viking Penguin.

2 Nicole Stenger, 1991, 'Mind is a Leaking Rainbow', in Michael Benedikt (ed.), *Cyberspace: First Steps*, Cambridge MA: MIT Press, p. 56; Margaret Wertheim, 2000, *The Pearly Gates of Cyberspace: A History of Space from Dante to the Internet*, London: Virago, pp. 49–58, at p. 257.

3 A classic formulation is Howard Rheingold, 1994, *The Virtual Community: Finding Connection in a Computerised World*, London: Secker and Warburg.

4 Jean-Francois Mayer, 2003, 'Religion and the Internet: The Global Marketplace', in James A. Beckford and James T. Richardson (eds), *Challenging Religion: Essays in Honour of Eileen Barker*, London: Routledge, pp. 36–46; Jeff Zaleski, 1997, *The Soul of Cyberspace: How New Technology is Changing our Spiritual Lives*, San Francisco: HarperEdge, pp. 111–12.

5 See, e.g., Sherry Turkle, 1997, *Life on the Screen: Identity in the Age of the Internet*, London: Phoenix.

6 Flory and Miller, *Generation X Religion*, esp. pp. 231–47; David Hillborn and Matt Bird, 2002, *God and the Generations: Youth, Age and the Church Today*, Carlisle: Paternoster Press, Appendix reporting on Generation X Lifestyle Survey undertaken by the Evangelical Alliance in 2001: the questions were discussed with 515 Christian and 209 non-Christian young adults in Britain; see esp. 213–14 on the greater expressed sense of responsibility of the Christian sample towards poor countries.

7 Bauman, *Identity*; Zygmut Bauman, 2003, *City of Fears, City of Hopes*, London: Critical Urban Studies Occasional Paper; cf. Andy Hargreaves, 2003, *Teaching in the Knowledge Society: Education in the Age of Insecurity*, Maidenhead and Philadelphia: Open University Press, pp. 24–40.

8 World Association for Christian Communication, 'Christian Principles of Communication', http://www.wacc.org.uk/wacc/about_wacc/principles – accessed 17.08.06.

9 Jim McDonnell, 2006, 'The Politics of Education: The Challenge of Media Literacy in the Information Society', http://www.ecic.info/default_ecic11.asp, – accessed 31.07.06.

10 See 'Augustine's Penguin, or Open Source and the Church', – http://www.davidopderbeck.com/archives/2005/11/augustines_peng.html – accessed 31.07.06; Rick Garnett, *Mirror of Justice*, www.mirrorofjustice.com/mirrorofjustice/2005/11/free_software_a.html – accessed 18.11.05, Marco Fioretti, 'Free Software's Surprising

Sympathy with Catholic Doctrine', http://www.newsforge.com/article/pl?sid=05/11/03/16432438&from=rss – accessed 17.08.06.

11 Andy Lang, 'Is Virtual Christian Community Really Possible?', http://www.ecic.info/conference_114.asp, – accessed 31.07.06; cf. Peter A. Baan, 'Virtual Communities – A Challenge for the Church?, http://www.ecic.info/archive_ecic3.asp – accessed 31.07.06. See also Barry Hudd, Ralf Peter Reimann (eds), 2006, *European Churches on the Internet: Challenges, Experiences and Visions.* Jena: Verlag IKS Garamond.

12 Jeffrey K. Hadden, Douglas E. Cowan (eds), 2000, *Religion on the Internet: Research Prospects and Promises*, New York: JAI, Elsevier, especially essays by Lorne L. Dawson, Ken Bedell and Christopher Helland; cf. J. Slevin, 2001, *The Internet and Society*, Cambridge: Polity Press.

13 Daniel Miller and Don Slater, 2000, *The Internet: An Ethnographic Approach*, Oxford: Berg, cited by Mayer, 'Religion and the Internet', pp. 40–41; Mirca Madianou, 2006, 'ICT, reti transnazionali e vita quotidiana', in Simona Bodo, Maria Rita Cifarelli (ed.), *Quando la cultura fa la differenza*, Rome: Meltemi, pp. 187–98, with reference to Filipino culture in London and Cambridge.

14 Christopher Helland, 2000, 'Online-Religion/Religion-Online and Virtual Communitas', in Hadden and Cowan, *Religion on the Internet*, pp. 205–23.

15 Heidi Campbell, 2003, 'Approaches to Religious Research in Computer-Mediated Communication', in Jolyon Mitchell and Sophia Marriage (eds), *Mediating Religion. Conversations in Media, Religion and Culture*, London and New York: T&T Clark, pp. 213–28.

16 Mayer, 'Religion and the Internet', p. 45, referring to the first gathering of the French Christian Internet in Paris in June 2002.

17 Ken Bedell, 2000, 'Dispatches from the Electronic Frontier: Explorations of Mainline Protestant Uses of the Internet', in Hadden and Cowan, *Religion on the Internet*, 183–203, at 198–9.

18 For discussion of the role of space in the definition of youth culture, see Tracey Skelton and Gill Valentine (eds), 1998, *Cool Places: Geographies of Youth Culture*, London: Routledge.

19 Owen Gibson, 07.10.05, 'Young Blog Their Way to a Publishing Revolution', http://www.guardian.co.uk/frontpage/story/0,,1587081,00.html – accessed 18.03.06; cf John Lanchester, 'A Bigger Bang', *Guardian Weekend*, 4 November 2006, pp. 16–36 at 23.

20 Mia Lövheim, 2005, 'Young People and the Use of the Internet as Transitional Space', *Heidelberg Journal of Religions on the Internet* 1:1, http://ub.uni-heidelberg.de/archiv/5826 – accessed 18.03.06; cf. the whole volume, a Special Issue on Theory and Methodology ed. Oliver Krüger, including an essay by Heidi Campbell, 'Spiritualising the Internet: Uncovering Discourses and Narratives of Religious Internet Usage', http://www.ub.uni-heidelberg.de/archiv/5824. On the issue of identity and trust, see also Franz Foltz and Frederick Foltz, 'Religion on the Internet: Community and Virtual Existence', *Bulletin of Science, Technology and Society*, 23(4) (2003), 321–30. Ralph Schroeder, Noel Heather and Raymond M. Lee, 'The Sacred and the Virtual: Religion in Multi-User Virtual Reality', *Journal of Computer-Mediated Communication* 4(2) (1998), http://jcmc.indiana.edu/vol4/issue2/schroeder.html – accessed 18.03.06, comments on the higher level of structure and clearer sense of hierarchy in the E-Church world than in other multi-user virtual worlds.

21 'Internet Develops Prayer and Spirituality', http://www.wacc.org.uk/wacc/publications/media_action/269_jun_2006 – accessed 31.07.06. The two sites are: http://www.sacredspace.ie/ and http://www.pray-as-you-go.org (the latter produced by Jesuit Media Initiatives, based in London) – accessed 31.06.06.

22 H. C. A. Ernst, 1998, 'Are our Traditional Images of God and Christianity Being

Affected by the Internet?', http://www.ecic.info/archive_ecic3.asp; http://www.partenia. org/ – accessed 17.08.06. Partenia was set up in 1996 as an internet site, taking its name from a defunct Christian church in the highlands of Algeria. It is run as a 'virtual' diocese by its bishop, Jacques Gaillot, after he was dismissed by Rome from his see of Evreux in France for unorthodox preaching.

23 http://www/sacredspace.ie/ – accessed 31.06.06.

24 http://www.wacc.org.uk/wacc/publications/media_action/269_jun_2006 – accessed 31.06.06.

25 'The Church and the Internet', 2002, http://www.vatican.va/roman_curia/pontifical_ councils/pccs/documents/rcpc_pccs_doc_20020228_church-internet_en.html – accessed 31.06.06.

26 Michael Kocher, 2001, 'Virtual Links, Real Presence: The Internet and the Churches', http://www.ecic.info/archive/ecic6/papers01/kocher.html – accessed 17.08.06. Cf. Zaleski's interview with John Perry Barlow on the significance of metaphor: Zaleski, *The Soul of Cyberspace*, p. 35.

4

Language

What is Christian language? Both David Martin and Callum Brown – each with a different perspective and each to a different end – have suggested that the study of Christian language must be a central part of any account of modern belief.[1] But a definition of Christian language and, still more, how it might be redefined remains elusive. This section will examine different forms of religious language: looking at art, architecture, and children's literature. What unites these essays is a common search for just such a definition – a search, in Martin's words, for Christian language and its mutations. If, as Brown has argued, Christian discourse, or at least the dominant form of Christian discourse, was destroyed by the 1960s, then writers at the start of the twenty-first century are unlikely to find any Christian language worth noting. If, on the other hand, David Martin is correct to see many of the apparently secularizing discourses of the present as a working out of Christian themes, then there may be more to be said.[2] Either way, unless a more compelling definition of what we are looking for emerges, the search will surely prove fruitless.

One way of approaching the question of Christian language might be through an exploration of Christian knowledge. There is a – perfectly plausible – assumption that levels of Christian knowledge have declined throughout this period. Indeed, as Steve Bruce has cogently put it,

> At the start of the twenty-first century the vast majority of people do not go to church . . . Christian ideas are not taught in schools, are not promoted by social elites, are not reinforced by rites of passage, are not presented in a positive light in the mass media, and are no longer constantly affirmed in everyday interaction.[3]

Certainly, much traditional religious knowledge does appear to be at a discount: cultures of hymn-singing have been eroded; familiarity with the Bible or John Bunyan can no longer be assumed. Recent research suggests a remarkable distance between orthodox teaching and popular belief.[4] Nonetheless, there are good reasons for thinking that to approach this issue by focusing on evidence of Christian knowledge is a mistake – not least because it is easy to overstate the extent to which the past was populated by people possessed of extraordinary levels of that commodity. Keith Thomas, for example, has exposed widespread religious ignorance in early-modern England.[5] James Obelkevitch has unpicked the 'paganism' that characterized much Victorian religious practice.[6] Likewise, in their 1947 report *A Puzzled People*, Mass-Observation found a striking absence of Christian knowledge. As one vicar put it, 'There's no doubt that the majority of people don't know what the Christian faith is.'[7]

More than this, to assume that Christian knowledge and Christian language are the same thing is arguably unhelpful. To be sure, language is intimately related to knowledge, but it is also prior to it. It is language that shapes and organizes knowledge – and not the other way round.[8] Thus, if we are to delineate a distinctively Christian language we must look beyond the evidence of knowledge to find the strategies and grammars that make up the language itself.[9] The language of Chartism – that great nineteenth-century radical movement – was, Gareth Stedman Jones has argued, 'a complex rhetoric binding together, in a systematic way, shared premises, analytical routines, strategic options and programmatic demands'.[10] It was this complex rhetoric that enabled the Chartists to make sense of their world: to interpret their experience and to seek to change their lives. Chartist language was not, then, a form of knowledge, but an interpretative schema; a worldview. It seems likely that Christian language would share some common features with this model of radical discourse.

Taking this as a cue, it is tempting to compare accounts of religious language with depictions of working-class dialect, not least because there is also a persistent tendency among writers to outline 'an inexorable decline of dialect in the face of linguistic and cultural standardization'.[11] Moreover, this declinist model is repeated by each generation: so that commentators in World War One looked back to the mid-nineteenth century as a golden age of dialect, entirely unaware that their predecessors in the 1850s had themselves bemoaned a perceived decrease in dialect use, and portrayed the generation before them as one that had been truly in touch with traditional language. Arguably a similar process is at work in the recurring accounts of religious decline: with each successive generation imagining that its precursors possessed greater Christian knowledge than the current one. More importantly still, Patrick Joyce's work on working-class language suggests a broader comparison with Christian discourse. Communities, he argues, are held together by mythologies – by shared stories and common beliefs. 'At the centre of these mythologies', he goes on, 'was language, which in this context may be clearly understood not as the form of culture but its substance.' This worked in two ways. In the first place, the experience of everyday life created new concepts, new communities, and new linguistic formulations. In the second place, and in 'a more conscious and deliberate sense than this, working people at the time identified their language as perhaps the central aspect of their culture'.[12] The resonance with Christianity, which is also unified by language, is surely self-evident. Perhaps, then, we are in fact pursuing a sort of linguistic community rather than a language: a set of people held together both by a shared dialect and – consequently – by a common world-view?

There are a number of difficulties with such an analysis, however attractive it may at first seem. Christian language, for one thing, differs from dialect in that it claims to offer not just a distinctive vocabulary and grammar, but also a distinctive logic. It presents and represents the world in ways that differ greatly from more secular discourses.[13] In the second place, it seems unduly reductive to limit Christian language to the status of a dialect. A dialect underwrites cohesion at the risk of exclusion. Classically, Christianity has survived and grown through diversity rather than unity; being repeatedly translated from one culture into another.[14] It has, as a result, reshaped itself continually: creating patterns of language that are expansive rather than exclusive; multiplying the means by which it can reach the widest possible audience. A dialect would rather be the product of a branch of Christianity – of a church or, still more, of a sect. Specific examples of Christian language, then, may well have some of the characteristics of a dialect. But Christian language itself operates at a much more meta-dialectal level. It comprehends many dialects and transcends any one specific example.

In that sense, Christian language may be compared to what Michel Foucault called a discourse.[15] Distinguishing between language, which he termed a finite set of rules allowing an infinite number of expressions, and discourse, which he saw as a much more limited finite set of statements, Foucault sought to unpick the logic that united a discourse. On the one hand, he acknowledged the variety of voices that a discourse could comprise: voices that were sometimes so various that they became simply contradictory. On the other, he hoped to establish the underlying rationale that unified these contradictions. A discourse, he concluded, was a group of statements that belong to the same 'discursive formation'; organized not by personal choice or will, but 'a body of anonymous, historical rules'. Put simply, what this implies is that in studying Christian language, our focus is ultimately on a discourse made up of a large number of different statements organized according to particular rules. More than this, we are studying a set of statements and a group of rules sufficiently large to allow a vast range of competing and clashing concepts to co-exist. Here is no narrow dialect: but 'a space of multiple dissensions; a set of different oppositions whose levels and roles must be described.'[16] Callum Brown has, of course, outlined one of these sets of statements: the 'discursive Christianity' which found its expression in narratives of evangelical piety and strict gender differentiation.[17] This is, though, just one formulation among many. Indeed, it is the existence of alternative formulations that makes Christian language a discourse – and not just a part of another, still wider discourse.

How, though, is this language experienced by believers and non-believers alike? Religious discourse – and Christian discourse in particular – may well comprise 'a space of multiple dissensions', but it nonetheless claims a privileged status. For the believer, Christian language is simply superior to other discursive formulations: it outranks them in any linguistic hierarchy. Hence, for example, the battle between some forms of Christian discourse and science. For Creationists, the claims of science to explain the world simply do not stand up to comparison with the claims of the Bible.[18] Equally it is worth noting the resurgence of *glossolalia* in the last 30 years. As Thomas Csordas has argued, speaking in tongues is 'a phenomenon that problematizes expressive authenticity by becoming more true and more profoundly meaningful than natural language'.[19] Claiming divine authority, when an individual speaks in tongues he or she also claims access to a language that transcends and pre-dates human speech altogether. Hence too David Martin's claims for Christian language; a 'distinctive genre' he suggests, that can be translated – 'though attempts at reduction only turn it into something else'.[20]

What we are dealing with here is a very particular type of discourse. It is, in Bakhtin's terms, an 'authoritative discourse'; one that:

> demands that we acknowledge it, that we make it our own; it binds us, quite independent of any power it might have to persuade us internally; we encounter it with its authority already fused to it. The authoritative word is located in a distanced zone, organically connected with a past that is felt to be hierarchically higher. It is, so to speak, the word of the fathers. Its authority was *acknowledged* in the past. It is a *prior* discourse.[21]

Bakhtin was keen to distinguish this from 'internally-persuasive discourse', which amounts to retelling a story in one's own words – and which we might wish to insist is also an aspect of Christian language. Nevertheless, his definition is a useful one: stressing the hierarchies involved in discourse, and the claims made on behalf of these hierarchies. A comparison with the authoritative discourse of late socialism may make this point more clearly. In a recent study, Alexei Yurchak has adapted Bakhtin's analysis to explain the collapse of the Soviet Union. Socialism, he shows, was an authoritative discourse: one that shaped all other discourses within the Russian Empire; one that was accepted as 'immutable and therefore unquestionable'.[22] Ultimately, of course, the gap between this discourse and reality grew too great. But right up to the fall of the Soviet Union, the authoritative discourse of socialism was unavoidable. Arguably, Christian language serves a similar purpose and operates in a similar way: forming a set of 'generative principles' that makes it possible to construct statements possessing authority; transforming the authors of these statements into 'mediators of prior knowledge rather than creators of new knowledge'.[23]

But what has happened to that Christian language? Has it, like the discourse of late socialism, been superseded? To what extent can a language be changed, and a tradition be challenged, and yet still retain any authority? It is here that the work of Hans-Georg Gadamer may be of some use to us. For Gadamer, of course, *'a language-view is a worldview'*. Crucially, this world-view grows out of tradition. Indeed, language and tradition cannot be separated: no more than language and consciousness can. Everyone, he contends, is situated within tradition, and tradition is embodied in language. Our being and our understanding – our very selves and our views of the world – are thus fundamentally linguistic. The authority that this gives language has particular implications for the study of its specifically Christian manifestations. 'When the Greek idea of logic is penetrated by Christian theology', Gadamer goes on, 'something new is born: the medium of language', in which the mediation of the incarnation event achieves its full truth. In that way, we might say that Christian language does precede other forms of discourse; that – probably throughout the West and certainly within Britain – the tradition of Christian language has always been inescapable. 'It is literally more correct to say that language speaks us, rather than we speak it', he declares.[24] That being so, the logic, syntax, and grammar of Christian language surely still shaped communication in post-1945 Britain.

Nonetheless, Gadamer recognizes that languages change and traditions mutate. Our world-view is shaped by the encounter between tradition and the present. Indeed, 'from the way words change', he suggests, 'we can discover the way that customs and values change'.[25] One of the key problems for the student of Christian language is to see how and to what extent that discourse has changed. Have we, in Foucault's terms, witnessed one of those rare events when one discursive formation is substituted for another?[26] In his commentary on Bakhtin's analysis of language, Michael Holquist points out that when authoritative discourse is empowered it is 'privileged' and 'taboo'. 'If ever dethroned', however, 'it immediately becomes a dead thing, a relic.'[27] This is an insight that is also picked up by Alexei Yurchak. In his account of life in the Soviet Union, he shows that the authoritative discourse of late socialism became increasingly circular in its rhetoric: remorselessly repeating the same phrases and recycling the same concepts. With the advent of *perestroika*, this closed and self-replicating system was forcibly opened up. For the first time it became possible to have discussions about authoritative discourse itself, thereby 'creating a possibility of eventually questioning the whole discursive structure of socialism'.[28] The result destroyed the special authority of socialism, and thus destroyed that particular form of authoritative discourse. Is this, then, what happened to Christian Britain in this period? Did Christian discourse – either in the narrow evangelical formation identified by Brown, or the broader language outlined here – similarly collapse, challenged by new and more powerful meta-discourses?

The case studies that follow will suggest not. For although they recognize that challenges to the authoritative discourse of Christianity have been mounted in this period (as in previous periods), and that new varieties of Christian dialect have emerged (again, as has happened every generation), they do not conclude that Christian language itself has collapsed or been wholly superseded. In many respects closer to Gadamer than to Foucault or, for that matter, Habermas, they uncover dialogue and adaptation rather than what Foucault would term 'transformation' and Habermas 'sublimation'.[29] This does not mean that our authors deny important challenges to Christian language or significant alternatives to it. But they identify two crucial limitations to these challenges. First, they show the capacity of Christian language to reinvent itself. Second, as Bernice Martin in particular makes plain, they suggest that even some challenges to Christianity remain dependent upon Christian language. Following these contentions, three conclusions can be drawn. In the first place, we might contend that the 'tradition' of Christian language remains stronger than a secularizing master-narrative will allow.[30] Next, we might argue that many previous writers have confused change with collapse, ignoring the dialogue between this tradition and the present and assuming that all development is necessarily decay. Finally, we might suggest that for many – perhaps for the majority – of the population of post-1945 Britain, Christian language remained authoritative, shaping their values and constituting their worldview.

In order to sustain these conclusions, the essays that follow look well beyond the purely verbal or textual. This, of course, is a further challenge to Habermas, who famously argued that the authority of religion was grounded in 'pre-linguistic' forms that were superseded by grammatical language.[31] By contrast, this volume follows Paul Ricoeur in treating all meaningful human action as text.[32] We do not, *pace* Habermas, distinguish between linguistic and 'pre-linguistic' texts, nor do we accept that 'the linguistification of the sacred means a rationalization of the world'.[33] Nonetheless, our authors do recognize the problems that their approach presents. Perhaps most importantly, each acknowledges the need to take seriously the specific logic of each genre or medium that they are studying. As Bakhtin argued, different genres embody differing ways of understanding reality. Each genre is – as Caryl Emerson puts it – 'a category of consciousness'.[34] Thus, even before a story is written, the author, adopting the conventions of the genre, will make an assumption about the workings of time and space within that genre, about the world within which the narrative will have to operate. This will determine the perspective from which the story is told, its structure and form, and the behaviour of the characters within it. Taking a story from one genre and transposing it into another will transform the story. In a different genre, the logic will be different – sometimes radically so. As a result, the story itself will be changed. Each genre will reshape the perspective from which the story is told, the structure of the narrative, and the behaviour of the characters within it.[35] Thus, Christian language, and

Christian narratives more specifically, may be profoundly altered as they are transposed from literature, to art, to architecture, and beyond.

One of the objections which can be made about much previous analysis is that it did not take account of these transpositions. It assumed that the meanings of art or architecture, for example, could be 'read' unproblematically from the objects or buildings being studied. In fact, even before such a 'reading' could begin, a whole series of questions about the nature of the enquiry and of the evidence had to be asked.[36] It assumed too that the meanings of a pop song could be uncovered just by reading the lyrics. Yet, as Angela McRobbie and Simon Frith observed nearly 30 years ago, 'Lyrics are not a sufficient clue to rock's meanings . . . Popular music is a complex mode of expression. It involves a combination of sound, rhythm, lyric, performance, and image.'[37] Thus, an account of the Rolling Stones' 'Backstreet Girl' that only focused on the 'inexplicable callousness' of the words would be inadequate – failing as it did to engage with the contradiction between these sentiments and the gentleness of the melody.[38] Similarly, the difference between tonic classical music, harmonic pop, and the more challenging avant-garde needs to be accounted for. Is it the case, as Susan McClary suggests, that there is a gendered dimension to these distinctions?[39] Might it also be true that by their very nature, certain genres of music are better at conveying Christian language than others? Certainly, as Ian Jones and Peter Webster have already discussed, that has been an assumption for many. These are clearly areas that need further research.

The relationship between art and Christianity has also become an increasingly important issue in recent years. The success of the 'Seeing Salvation' Exhibition at the National Gallery in 2000 prompted many to reassess the tensions that placing religious art in a secular setting can produce.[40] A smaller exhibition of miracle-working images held in the Ashmolean Museum in Oxford five years later raised similar issues. On the one hand, there were those who profoundly objected to the 'promotion of superstition and bigotry' which they perceived in the collection of images taken from Roman Catholic shrines in Italy. On the other, there were those who greeted this eruption of the explicitly religious into the museum with enthusiasm.[41] A range of competing discourses was at play and in the first essay, George Pattison unpicks many of the key themes that this issue raises. To what extent, he asks, can we still talk about Christian art? Decontextualized by its display in the secular spaces of modern art galleries, and deploying a visual vocabulary that may be incomprehensible to those without a grounding in traditional religious narratives, is Christian art now nothing more than an anachronism? Has 'culture' replaced 'Christianity'? The answer, he concludes, is unclear. But it might be argued that the very success of such exhibitions suggests the continued power of Christian art. No longer hegemonic, it nonetheless still shapes and influences secular artists – while its capacity to shock and subvert remains clear.

The continued power of Christian narrative underpins Bernice Martin's sensitive rereading of Philip Pullman's *Dark Materials* trilogy. This period saw an extraordinary resurgence of religious writing – although this was a revival that bore only a passing resemblance to the heyday of popular Christian literature, in the early years of the twentieth century.[42] Some of the most popular recent books engage with religion – but only apparently to challenge conventional Christianity. Philip Pullman's work is written, in part, as an attack on organized religion, on the doctrine of the fall and original sin, and on the workings of the institutional church. Likewise, Dan Brown's *Da Vinci Code* (2003), which has sold more than 60 million copies and been translated into more than 40 languages, tells the story of clerical cover-ups, of a married Christ, and of a Catholic Church that is willing to kill. Yet, in a sense, both works are at once parasitic on Christianity and pose important questions for it. As Robin Griffith-Jones has recently observed, many of the suggestions made by the *Da Vinci Code* raise significant theological issues. They show both the demand for religious answers – and the need for the churches to take that demand seriously.[43] More than this, as Bernice Martin shows, Philip Pullman's own world-view is highly contradictory. While rejecting organized religion, he writes within a recognizably Christian tradition, finding that the logic of Christian language unwittingly leads him to reproduce conventionally Christian narratives.

Following this, William Whyte explores church buildings. The image of the empty church is a convenient shorthand for the decline of religion in modern Britain. Yet it is also misleading. Just as there were many new building projects after 1945, and many more re-orderings, conversions, and additions to existing structures, so the closure of churches should not be seen as synonymous with decline. Many – indeed, arguably, most – nineteenth-century churches were far too big. As Robin Gill observed more than a decade ago, the *Myth of the Empty Church* is as inaccurate as it is pervasive.[44] There was never a golden age in which these great barns of buildings were full. Still more importantly, many churches have closed as a result of population movement or even of ecumenical success. Above all, in the words of a 1995 report: 'what sometimes looks like a national crisis, is in fact a series of local problems'.[45] In that sense, redundancy is a more complicated issue than has been previously acknowledged. The same is true of the changes in architectural style and approaches adopted by the churches after 1945. Various denominations appropriated modern styles in the search for a truly contemporary Christian church. Thus, although the architectural vocabulary was often seen as secular, the intention was always religious. The extent to which the modern movement could be reconciled with Christianity remained an open question at the end of the century.

Which brings us back to the start of our enquiry, and to the question, what is Christian language? What we have argued is that Christian language is not reducible to a form of knowledge, measurable by testing theological literacy or the extent to which people conform to the teachings of the church. Rather, it operates both as a system of logic and as a way of interpreting the world. In that sense it can be compared to what Bakhtin termed an 'authoritative discourse', and – more precisely still – to what Gadamer (borrowing from Hegel) called a 'horizon'; the position from which, in dialogue with tradition, we perceive the world. This means that any study of Christian language must take account of the differing natures of the different texts which reveal it, and of the differing contexts within which these discourses and created and understood. Above all, it means acknowledging the capacity of this language to change, to mutate, and to renew itself, while also recognizing the ways in which it can be challenged, criticized, and superseded. To confuse change with decay, and to ignore the underlying logic of language, would be a serious mistake indeed.

Notes

1 Brown, *Death*; David Martin, 2005, 'What is Christian Language?', in Martin, *On Secularization*, pp. 171–84.

2 Martin, *Christian Language*.

3 Bruce, *God is Dead*, p. 73.

4 Michael Dalling and Raymond Francis, 1995, 'Church, Chapel, and Community in Somercotes', in Peter G. Forster (ed.), *Contemporary Mainstream Religion: Studies from Humberside and Lincolnshire*, Aldershot: Ashgate, pp. 78–107.

5 Keith Thomas, 1971, *Religion and the Decline of Magic: Studies in Popular Beliefs in Sixteenth- and Seventeenth-century England*, Harmondsworth: Penguin, pp. 179–95.

6 James Obelkevitch, 1976, *Religion and Rural Society: South Lindsey 1825–1875*, Oxford: Clarendon Press.

7 Mass-Observation, *Puzzled People*, p. 140.

8 Michel Foucault, 1989, *The Archaeology of Knowledge*, trans. A. M. Sheridan Smith, London: Routledge, pp. 31, 54, 84–5.

9 See also Sarah Williams, 'The Language of Belief: An Alternative Agenda for the Study of Working-class Religion', *Journal of Victorian Culture* 1 (1996), 303–17.

10 Gareth Stedman Jones, 1983, *The Languages of Class: Studies in English Working-Class History, 1832–1982*, Cambridge: Cambridge University Press, p. 107.

11 Patrick Joyce, 1991, 'The People's English: Language and Class in England, *c.* 1840–1920', in Peter Burke and Roy Porter (eds), *Language, Self, and Society: a Social History of Language*, Cambridge and Oxford: Polity, pp. 154–90, p. 156.

12 Joyce, 'People's English', p. 172.

13 Martin, *On Secularization*, pp. 170, 183.

14 Andrew F. Walls, 1996, *The Missionary Movement in Christian History*, New York: Orbis Books/Edinburgh: T&T Clark, pp. 27–9. See also Stanley Hauerwas, 1987, 'The Church as God's New Language', in Garrett Green (ed.), *Scriptural Authority and Narrative Interpretation*, Philadelphia: Fortress Press, pp.179–98.

15 For just such a move, see Lawrence J. Taylor, 1992, 'The Language of Belief: Nineteenth-century Religious Discourse in South-West Donegal', in Marilyn Silverman and P. H. Gulliver (eds.), *Approaching the Past: Historical Anthropology through Irish Case Studies*, New York: Columbia University Press, pp. 142–75.

16 Foucault, *Archaeology of Knowledge*, pp. 30, 168, 173, 121, 131, 173.

17 Brown, *Death*, ch. 4–5.

18 Harriet A. Harris, 1998, *Fundamentalism and Evangelicals*, Oxford: Clarendon Press.

19 Thomas J. Csordas, 2001, *Language, Charisma, and Creativity: Ritual Life in the Catholic Charismatic Renewal*, New York: Palgrave, p. 55.

20 Martin, *On Secularization*, p. 183.

21 M. M. Bakhtin, 1981, *The Dialogical Imagination: Four Essays*, Michael Holquist (ed.); trans. Caryl Emerson and Michael Holquist, Austin TX: University of Austin Press, p. 342.

22 Alexei Yurchak, 2006, *Everything Was Forever Until It Was No More: the Last Soviet Generation*, Princeton: Princeton University Press, p. 15.

23 Yurchak, *Everything Was Forever*, pp. 61, 67.

24 Hans-Georg Gadamer, 2004, *Truth and Method*, rev. edn; trans. Joel Weinsheimer and Donald G. Marshall, London and New York: Continuum, pp. 440, 391, 458–9, 470, 481, 427, 459.

25 Gadamer, *Truth and Method*, p. 446.

26 Foucault, *Archaeology*, pp. 189–90.

27 Holquist, 1981, 'Glossary', in Bakhtin, *Dialogic Imagination*, p. 424.

28 Yurchak, *Everything Was Forever*, p. 292.

29 Foucault, *Archaeology*, pp. 189–90; Jürgen Habermas, 1984–7, *Theory of Communicative Action*, trans. Thomas McCarthy; 2 vols. Cambridge and Oxford: Polity, vol. ii., p. 77.

30 Although cf. Pierre Bourdieu, 1991, *Language and Symbolic Power*, ed. John B. Thompson; trans. Gino Raymond and Matthew Adamson, Cambridge: Polity Press, pp. 115–16.

31 Habermas, *Communicative Action*, Vol. ii, pp. 77, 46.

32 Paul Ricoeur, 'The Model of the Text: meaningful action considered as text', *Social Research* 38(3) (1971), 529–62.

33 Thomas McCarthy, 1984, 'Introduction', to Habermas, *Communicative Action*, pp. v–xxxvii, p. xxiii.

34 Caryl Emerson, 1986, *Boris Godunov: Transpositions of a Russian Theme*, Bloomington: Indiana University Press, p. 5. See also Philip Ross Bullock, 'Staging Stalinism: The Search for Soviet Opera in the 1930s', *Cambridge Opera Journal* 18 (2006), 83–108

35 Bakhtin, *Dialogic Imagination*, pp. 84–254.

36 William Whyte, 'How do Buildings Mean? Some Issues of Interpretation in the History of Architecture', *History and Theory* 45 (2006), 153–77.

37 Angela McRobbie and Simon Frith, 'Rock and Sexuality', *Screen Education* 29(1978–9), p. 4.

38 Dave Laing, *The Sound of Our Time*, London and Sydney: Sheed & Ward, p. 145.

39 Susan McClary, 2002, *Feminine Endings: Music, Gender, and Sexuality*, Minneapolis and London: University of Minnesota Press, pp. 155–6. See also John Shepherd, 1987, 'Music and Male Hegemony', in Richard Leppert and Susan McClary (eds), *Music and Society: The Politics of Composition, Performance, and Reception*, Cambridge: Cambridge University Press, pp. 151–72 and Karen Pegley and Virginia Caputto, 1994, 'Growing Up Female(s): Retrospective Thoughts on Musical Preferences and Meanings', in Philip Brett, Elizabeth Wood, Gary C. Thomas (eds), *Queering the Pitch: The New Lesbian and Gay Musicology*, London and New York: Routledge, pp. 297–313.

40 On this see Grace Davie, 2003, 'Seeing Salvation: the Use of Text as Data in the Sociology of Religion', in Avis, *Public Faith?*, pp. 28–45.

41 Jane Garnett and Gervase Rosser, forthcoming 2007, 'Representing Spectacular Miracles', *Antropologicheskii forum/Forum for Anthropology and Culture*.

42 Philip Waller, 2006, *Writers, Readers, and Reputations: Literary Life in Britain, 1870–1918*, Oxford: Oxford University Press, ch. 28.

43 Robin Griffith-Jones, 2006, *The Da Vinci Code and the Secrets of the Temple*, Norwich: Canterbury Press.

44 Robin Gill, 2003, *The 'Empty' Church Revisited*, Aldershot: Ashgate.

45 Comedia, 1995, *Spirit of Place: Redundant Churches as Urban Resources*, Stroud: Comedia, p. 8.

Case Studies

Art and Religion in Contemporary Britain
  George Pattison

Dark Materials? Philip Pullman and Children's Literature
  Bernice Martin

The Architecture of Belief
  William Whyte

CASE STUDY

Art and Religion in Contemporary Britain

GEORGE PATTISON

Since the Romantic era, art and religion have lived in a conflicted yet sym-
biotic relationship. On the one hand, art has shared the general Enlightenment and post-Enlightenment striving for autonomy and has refused to be
constrained in its choice or treatment of subject-matter by the declarations of
ecclesiastical authorities. From Byron to *Jerry Springer – the Opera*, the arts
have, at every level of sophistication, been in frequent conflict with the
church. At the same time, art has also manifested a repeated striving towards
something very vaguely or even incoherently defined in terms of spirituality.
This striving has led both to art being practised and experienced as a substitute for religion, that is, as modernity's repository of 'eternal values', and as
voluntarily putting itself in the service of religion. Often it will be difficult in
any given case to see where exactly the balance lies – do we interpret
Chagall's copious use of religious symbolism as 'religious' or as a secular
artist's appropriation of more or less arbitrarily selected fragments of diverse
(both Jewish and Christian) traditions? And how and by whom might such
questions rightly be decided? Religion for its part has had an equally ambivalent attitude to art. On the one hand, it has manifested both a long-standing
suspicion of art as a vehicle of sensuality and uncontrolled imagining (as in
the predictable Christian protests about *The Last Temptation of Christ*).
Yet, on the other, it has actively sought art, both as a source for its own
renewal and as an instrument of apologetic or evangelistic outreach (as in
such diverse figures as Walter Hussey and Mel Gibson).

In this case study I do not attempt to answer or to demonstrate a method
for answering the critical and theoretical questions that this complex relationship raises. What I do hope to do is to widen the question and thereby,
to some extent, to reconfigure it. It has been typical of Christian theology, at
least, to see the whole issue in very individualistic terms: there is the *artist*,
who produces a *work* that is then *seen, heard, or read by an individual* – and,
essentially, it makes no difference if this process is multiplied a thousandfold
or whether it remains a solitary pleasure. I do not wish to challenge this
model entirely, since, in a rough and ready way, it captures the averagely

pre-reflective experience most of us have of art, whether as makers or recipients. At one level – the level at which we continue to say 'the sun rises' even when we know that it is not moving – it may even be impossible to displace. But it is certainly not the whole story, and it certainly doesn't take us very far in attempting to examine the role of art in the supposed secularization of society. That artists consciously reject or accept a religious or spiritual motivation, that works do or don't fit a recognizable canon, and that, for example, viewers do or don't feel 'edified' by the work does not provide a sufficient basis for reaching a larger view of the social role of art in society's contemporary religious profile.

I begin with three important contributions to modern thinking about culture. The first is from the early nineteenth-century German theologian Friedrich Schleiermacher, the second from the Marxist philosopher Walter Benjamin, and the third from André Malraux. Taken together they constitute an important horizon for the understanding of the relationship between art and religion in contemporary culture.

Schleiermacher, often referred to as 'the father of modern theology', was a massively influential figure in the German-speaking world throughout the nineteenth century, although in theological circles his work has been consistently under attack for much of the last 80 years. Part of the reason for this reversal of fortunes was precisely his view of the relationship between culture and religion. Here, for example, is Schleiermacher on the church: 'The highest purpose of the Church is the shaping of an artistic inheritance, through which the feelings of each individual are given shape and to which each individual in turn contributes.'[1] Note how Schleiermacher, who elsewhere describes the church as the community of those reborn through faith, here distances himself from any attempt to understand the church in dogmatic or hierarchical terms. No one was more conscious than Schleiermacher – a figure of towering intellectual abilities and achievements – of the need for teaching in the church, but, as he makes clear, the exercise of teaching, or for that matter of moral authority, is not the primary task of the church *qua* church. Reflecting his own Romantic assumptions, he is asserting that the church needed above all to be offering cultural forms that could be the vehicles by which to make manifest the inner feelings of the individual and that these feelings were, at the deepest level, universal.[2] From the perspective of much twentieth-century theology, this seemed to tie the church uncritically to the 'official' culture of the bourgeois world. Church became culture, culture served as church. Where, then, were the Christian's resources for criticizing culture?

The culture with which the mature Schleiermacher is mostly identified is what is sometimes referred to as the *Biedermeier* period, and whatever justification there may be for the negative associations of this word, it flags the fact that between Schleiermacher and ourselves lies a series of seismic shifts in the cultural fault-lines. But these shifts are not only to do with the modernist breakthrough in the arts, and such traumas as two world wars, they are also to do with what can loosely be called the technologization of modern society.

Here I turn to Walter Benjamin and specifically to his essay 'The Work of Art in the Age of its Technical Reproducibility'. Benjamin argues that, around the middle of the nineteenth century, a fundamental paradigm shift took place in the world of the visual arts, a shift that resulted from the new techniques of lithography and photography. Art became reproducible on a scale and with an accuracy that had never before been achieved. Parallel shifts followed with sound-recording and the advent of motion pictures. Benjamin's own interest is primarily in the effect this has on the contemporary making of art, art which is aimed precisely at taking advantage of this reproducibility, art which, like the record or the movie, is made precisely as reproducible or in order to be reproduced. Yet he also notes how these new discoveries change our relation to the arts of the past. Under the impact of these new technologies, art loses its special aura, its quality of once-offness. The work of art that was made to adorn a specific altar in a specific church can now be seen merely by turning a page, or (though Benjamin could not know of this) by a couple of clicks of the mouse. As he puts it, when I listen to a recording of a Mozart Mass 'The Cathedral leaves its place to be received into the apartment of the art-lover . . . '[3] This tension between the pathos of the aura and its inevitable disappearance under the conditions of art reproduction is, I suggest, pivotal to the role of the major exhibition in contemporary culture as well as to a range of other phenomena of the art-world (for example, the development of the 'Director's Cut' movie and DVD).

Malraux's concept of the 'imaginary museum' builds on Benjamin's insights, only, as the eponymous title of his book on the subject indicates, with special reference to the question of the museum. On the one hand, we have the modern museum, itself a creation of the nineteenth century, presupposing and communicating a historical reconstruction of the 'history of art' and, at the same time, constructing this history on the premise that 'the original' is the definitive work of art (although, as Malraux reminds us, the very relocation of, say, a medieval crucifix into this museum changes its nature, for it was not conceived and executed as the 'statue' it has now become). On the other hand, the rise of good quality reproduction meant that the museum was relativized in the very moment of its birth. As Malraux points out, prior to the advent of photography, even the great critics had what we would now regard as a very narrow knowledge of works of art. In the nineteenth century, he asks, 'How many artists then knew the ensemble of great works of European art? Gautier had seen Italy (without seeing Rome) at the age of thirty-nine, Edmund de Goncourt at thirty-three, Hugo as a child, Baudelaire and Verlaine – never.'[4] Photography enabled any interested amateur to become familiar with a range of art works far surpassing that known by the great critics of the past.

The development of technologies of travel and transport and the financial and managerial restructuring of the arts are also worth mentioning at this point. To a degree that is almost beyond comparison with the situation at the start of the nineteenth century, it is now possible for individuals to travel easily across continents simply to see a particular exhibition, attend a particular concert, or visit a particular archaeological site. At the same time, works of art and ancient artifacts (not to mention orchestras and theatre companies) can be safely transported round the world, stored and exhibited. These processes are further underwritten by insurance and financing developments (for example sponsorship, the *sine qua non* of any major cultural event today). As a result, to take Benjamin's example of the Mozart Mass, whilst the CD or the radio allow me to transport the cathedral into my sitting-room, I can, with almost equal ease, transport myself to Salzburg Cathedral itself for a live performance. In these terms, the whole globe has itself become, potentially, a 'museum without walls' – for those, at least, whose wealth gives access to such cultural goods.

If Benjamin had been correct in his prognostications, the advent of photography would have simply evacuated the previous desire for an encounter with the 'original'. We would be happy with the reproduction. But, typically, the reproduction, even though it may lack the aura of the original, does not free us from the passion for 'the real thing'. Progress in such technologies is not simply linear, but complex and interactive. The fact that I am familiar with the *Mona Lisa* from countless reproductions becomes a primary motive for my wanting to see the original. In this connection, it is perhaps one of the signal attractions of the major exhibition that it brings together, as a 'unique event', works that are otherwise accessible and comparable only in reproduction – yet, at the same time, the exhibition pays its way precisely by the sale of books, prints, cards and other merchandise in which the art-works are submitted to the demystifying processes of 'technical reproducibility' and popularization. In a further extension of this mediating and disseminating process, the event is publicized in newspapers, TV and radio features, so that even if I fail to see it, I can participate in the discussion around it. The major exhibition thus lives in the tension between the aura of the original work, and the conditions of contemporary society – conditions that are technological and managed. Can it then be a focus of recalling or renewing religious experience for our time? Can it, in Schleiermacher's terms, be culture as a means of expressing and communicating Christian faith?

Commenting on the 2004 El Greco exhibition at the National Gallery in London, a leading article in *The Observer* stated that

Religion – in particular Christianity – has shaped Western society in a profound way, and has left us with a cultural legacy that enriches all. A visit to the new exhibition of El Greco's vivid, spiritual works at the National

Gallery provides a glorious demonstration of the power of religious beliefs to stimulate great works.[5]

However, the writer's assumption is that, whatever inspirational power it may have had in the past, the works that religion inspired are available to us today as 'culture' without our having to buy in to their religious commitments. I am free to see El Greco's work simply as painting, as 'El Greco', and not as 'Christ'.

The tensions reflected in such an approach are very prominent in Neil MacGregor's introductory essay to the catalogue of the 2000 exhibition 'Seeing Salvation'. MacGregor starts by noting that about a third of the works in the National Gallery have an explicitly Christian content. This means that for the many who lack Christian faith, such works seem 'irrecoverably remote, now best approached in purely formal terms'. The aim of the exhibition, then, is 'to focus attention on the purpose for which the works of art were made, and to explore what they might have meant to their original viewers'.[6] Central is the representation of Jesus as 'God who became man'. This appears to flag a theological approach to the material – however, the conclusion of his essay marks the same nineteenth-century cultural understanding as that of the *Observer* leader-writer.

> In the hands of the great artists, the different moments and aspects of Christ's life become archetypes of all human experience. The Virgin nursing her son conveys the feelings every mother has for her child: they are love. Christ mocked is innocence and goodness beset by violence . . . These are pictures that explore truths not just for Christians but for everybody.[7]

Although we might note that Schleiermacher too, in a dialogue about the meaning of Christmas, could write – in true *Biedermeier* fashion – that every woman was a Madonna, every infant a Christ-child, these comments entirely beg the question. Whatever power the individual work might retain to move the individual viewer, the official gloss on what is presented is, basically, that the Church's interpretation is, at best, inadequate and, at worst, misleading.

A striking feature of the 'Seeing Salvation' exhibition was the place given to images associated with the legend of St Veronica, who supposedly received an imprint of Christ's face on the cloth with which she compassionately wiped it as he bore the cross up towards Calvary. However, this signals another aspect of 'aura' in the history of Christian art: that early Christian art was often indistinguishable from the cult of relics, a connection especially prominent in traditions of 'images not made with hands' or images directly drawn from the life and death of Christ. The point here is that such works were not created primarily as representations – under Christian theological assumptions – of their subject, but as ways in which that subject made it-(Him-)self present (a theme brilliantly explored by the art historian Hans

Belting in his work on the 'image before art').[8] In the relic, the aura is not yet associated with any aesthetic qualities – it can be a bit of rotten bone – but is the radiance of the power and presence of the holy life to which it testifies. In these terms, there is a further step beyond the kind of aura surrounding, for example, an 'original' El Greco to the aura of the relic. Yet it is just this deeper aura (if we can call so call it) that the explanatory presentation of the great exhibition must necessarily miss. In these terms such exhibitions will necessarily reinforce the whitewashing over of the original religious context in which the work was first made and made meaningful. In this perspective, even a live religious event – the King's College Festival of Nine Lessons and Carols or a papal blessing in St Peter's Square – enters into the irresistible gravitational field of the global culture industry once it is perceived as an 'event' within the cultural calendar of the time. Is this judgement on the negative effects of the culture industry on the mediation of religious art too harsh? Perhaps it would be wise to qualify it, and to do so in three ways.

First, we should be wary of sentimentalizing the past. Even in the age when the relic was imbued with supernatural powers, the cult of relics resembled that of the contemporary cultural industry in more than one respect. Mass production – or, at least, mass 'discovery' – of relics, special showings (together with privileged access for those who could pay for it), and associated commercial activities were ubiquitous in late medieval Europe. In one afternoon in Florence, I saw three right index fingers of John the Baptist, and I have seen others elsewhere: here too issues of originality and cultural mediation proved, finally, unavoidable and, arguably, played a central role in the splitting of the church in the Reformation.

Second, where faith in the power of the original is still living, even the migration of the work into the museum or onto the CD allows for a believing response. Nowhere is this more apparent than in Moscow's Tretyakov Gallery, where the visitor is likely to see groups of believers singing hymns or praying before some of the most highly treasured icons brought into the gallery at the time of Stalin's attack on the churches. 'To the pure all things are pure', and, in this sense, even the most pre-packaged work can become a resource for the believer.

Third, the exhibition (or concert or recording) can rarely lose a relation to its origin entirely – if only in the mode of provoking an awareness of the difference between the experience from which the work developed and our own experience in face of it. Jonathan Jones, writing from an avowedly secular standpoint, began an article occasioned by the blockbuster Fra Angelico exhibition at the Metropolitan Museum in New York (2005) with an anecdote about seeing a painting of the Annunciation in Florence that was completed with angelic assistance. As he commented, 'When the ceremony [of showing the painting] is over, a metal grille slides automatically into place, hiding the painting from secular eyes – from eyes like mine. My way of relating to images – my interest in "art" – suddenly has no legitimacy, is all wrong.'[9] The article goes on to contrast the ascetic ideals under which this art was produced with the kind of aesthetic experiences most of us today derive from it. However, this invites the thought that, even in the mode of the over-determined cultural event, the sacred art of the past or of other cultures can invite reflection on the limits of our own cultural horizons. If, on the one hand, such events can be seen as exemplifying the secular world absorbing all previous forms of cultural life into its global museum without walls, including those forms that were shaped by religious beliefs and aspirations, they can from the other side be seen as witnessing to the final limitations of that world – since, if the secular did not invent the past, it becomes uncertain whether it entirely governs the present or, indeed, controls the future. At the same time, and more positively, the intrinsic relation of the work to its original meaning allows for the possibility that the work – in whatever form it is transmitted – can still shape or mould our contemporary response. This may be in the manner of instruction: as countless conversations overheard in art galleries testify, many consumers of culture simply don't know even the basic outlines of the Christian story in its classical form, and the painting may well, and often clearly does, *teach*. At the same time, it may deepen what it has taught, or what is already known concerning Christian faith by unveiling possibilities of meaning that would otherwise remain covered over. That is to say, the work of art reveals dimensions of the human experience of religion that our time is ill-placed to know spontaneously. Fra Angelico and his assistants at San Marco are a case in point, for such works not only 'tell the story', they also show something of the joy, tenderness, reverence, sorrow, and even pain that belonged to the existential world of Dominican spirituality. By such means, art not only continues to sustain a cultural memory of what Christianity teaches, but also to convey something of why and how it was able to transform minds and imaginations.

Even as the culture industry incorporates and reshapes the inheritance of Christian art, uprooting it from its original religious context and meaning, it nevertheless retains a vestige of an 'ecclesiastical' function, if, that is, we are able to take seriously Schleiermacher's definition: 'The highest purpose of the Church is the shaping of an artistic inheritance, through which the feelings of each individual are given shape and to which each individual in turn contributes.'

Notes

1 F. D. E. Schleiermacher, 1990, *Ethik*, Hamburg, Felix Meiner, p. 122.

2 In the English context, of course, Schleiermacher's model is perhaps most familiar in Matthew Arnold's reworking of the Romantic vision of culture.

3 W. Benjamin, 1978, 'Das Kunstwerk im Zeitalter seiner technischen Reproduzierbarkeit', in *Gesammelte Schriften*, 1.2., Frankfurt am Main, Suhrkamp, p. 477.

4 André Malraux, 1965, *Le Musée Imaginaire*, Paris, Gallimard, p. 11.

5 *The Observer*, leading article, 15 February 2004.

6 Neil MacGregor, 2000, 'Introduction' in Gabriele Finaldi, *The Image of Christ*, London: The National Gallery, p. 6.

7 MacGregor, 'Introduction', p. 7.

8 Hans Belting, 1994, *Likeness and Presence. A History of the Image before the Era of Art*, trans. Edmund Jephcott; Chicago and London: University of Chicago Press.

9 Jonathan Jones, 'Almost a Saint', *Guardian Weekend*, 10 December 2005, p. 37.

CASE STUDY

Dark Materials? Philip Pullman and Children's Literature

BERNICE MARTIN

Fenna is Maggie's dragon.
Fenna is the one purely joyful thing in Maggie's life.
Fenna is flame and fire. Fenna moves at night.
Fenna is flame and fire and moves on the wings of the night that are dragon wings, to dance with taloned claws and mock at hopes of safety. Fenna is the dark force of the imagination as well as its golden dancing; Fenna is chaos as well as order, and brings, on fiery dragon breath, the full danger of the chasm.

Sara Maitland, Three Times Table (1990).

Philip Pullman and the Zeitgeist

Until 1995 when *Northern Lights*, the first volume of *His Dark Materials*, was published, and won the Carnegie Medal and the Children's Fiction Award, Philip Pullman was a schoolmaster who occasionally wrote modestly successful adult and teen fiction.[1] Thanks to the remarkable success of the *Dark Materials* trilogy, completed in 2000 and now translated into 30 languages, he has become a favourite guru of our time.[2] He has appeared on *Desert Island Discs*, debated with Rowan Williams, featured in innumerable cultural programmes, chat shows and literary festivals. *His Dark Materials* was turned into a play and ran for two sold-out Christmas seasons and there are plans for a three-film adaptation, while an earlier novella was used as the basis for the libretto of a children's opera.[3] In October 2005 *The Times* newspaper even ran a competition to mark the tenth anniversary of the publication of the first volume. Evidently something about *His Dark Materials* chimes with the contemporary Zeitgeist and this essay is an exploration of what that might be.

The trilogy has been denounced in some quarters as an attack on the Christian faith,[4] and Pullman has not been shy about his own atheism, though he also agrees with Rowan Williams that the 'mythic', in its profoundest sense, is a crucial part of human self-understanding.[5] Might it be, nevertheless, that the success of *His Dark Materials* reflects what the historian Callum Brown, in *The Death of Christian Britain*, claims is the end of the 'discursive Christianity' that was abruptly eliminated in the secularizing watershed of the 1960s?[6] I believe the matter is far more equivocal than Callum Brown allows, and I shall argue that Charles Taylor is a better guide to what is going on here.[7] Just like contemporary consciousness, Pullman's epic *seems* to arrive at a secular viewpoint. Yet the story, and the language in which it is told, call on the transcendent and depend fundamentally on some basic Christian values. This cannot be fully explained by Pullman's narrative device of using Milton's *Paradise Lost* as its model, though the choice is consonant with the value he places on 'myth'.

Rather than plunging directly into a discussion of the novels, I want to begin by considering the nature of the genre to which they belong. To do this I take up the quotation at the head of this piece. It may seem quixotic to begin an essay on Philip Pullman with a passage from another novelist who is, moreover, sympathetic to Christianity, but in this short extract Sara Maitland vividly conveys the essence of fantasy, the literary genre that has brought Pullman celebrity, wealth and considerable cultural clout. Pullman dislikes the term 'fantasy' because to him it signifies a trivial piling of action on fantastic action with no exploration of the human condition. For this reason he calls his own fiction 'stark realism' or 'imaginative realism' because, through the device of refashioning aspects of the world, he believes he can the better reveal what is really there.[8] Rowan Williams, too, sees this genre as a literary technique for unmasking what is hidden or taken for granted under the veneer of 'normality'.[9]

Sara Maitland's emphasis on the dark, chaotic, fierce aspects of the human imagination overlaps with the conceit at the core of Pullman's trilogy, that 'dust' is the 'dark material' that fuels the universe, and gives rise to the many dark and frightening events of his story as well as to experiences of delight. It is only in the last volume that Pullman fully reveals this as an emanation given off by sexually mature human bodies. In essence, it is what Blake meant by 'experience' by contrast with 'innocence': animals and children are 'innocent' even when their actions have cruel consequences, whereas experience, which includes everything the Judeo-Christian world has understood as 'sin', is the fruit of the self-consciousness that begins in adolescence and thereafter can never be reversed. Pullman also seems to have something like a Schopenhauerean or Nietzschean life force underlying his key idea, perhaps even a Freudian one, while the echoes of the funeral service of the *Book of Common Prayer* as well as Darwinian materialism can be heard in the metaphor of 'dust' which, in the story, is the material basis of life that somehow also transcends the material.[10]

Maitland's representation of the 'dark' forces of the human imagination perhaps comes closer to T. S. Eliot's idea of 'black material', the term he coined, in conversation with Michael Tippett, for the shapeless, chaotic, sometimes threatening substance the writer must convert into art but that tends to overflow the boundaries imposed by form.[11] The artist Thetis Blacker makes a related point in her essay 'In Praise of Darkness' where she writes: 'The blackness of nothingness is the ink of chaos from which everything that exists is drawn.'[12] Crucially, what Maitland, Eliot and Blacker conjure is a core ingredient not just of the literary or pictorial but of the *religious* (for Pullman, perhaps, the 'mythic') imagination that must always accommodate both the chasm and the glory. Furthermore, the form that both the 'dark chaos' and the 'golden dancing' – to borrow Sara Maitland's terms – assume in artistic expression is inescapably shaped by the religious language and mythic imagery built into the civilization out of which it arises. Pullman may be a strident atheist, but, as he himself accepts, he is a *Christian* atheist who takes Blake and Milton as his muses and who self-consciously re-uses the imaginative resources of Christian culture to ends that, as I hope to show, his (ambiguously) hostile intention cannot fully control.

As David Martin has argued, despite its creeds and catechisms, Christian language operates primarily as a treasury of endlessly cross-referenced images, metaphors and, above all, stories that infuse the wider culture far more powerfully than propositional theology ever can.[13] This treasury is where what Max Weber called 'enchantment' resides, in modes of speech and apprehension that already *know* there is more to human existence than meets the workaday eye.[14] It provides a code or cipher of the transcendent. Thus, a garden or landscape may be experienced as an intimation of paradise lost – or regained; a refusal of self-interested violence or a self-sacrificial act automatically resonates as a (Christ-like) redemptive gesture, even, perhaps especially, when it changes the world not one iota. The same is true when a hero armed only with love and/or integrity (and in children's literature that is often a child) faces down the full might of a corrupt or evil power. The assumption that the humblest and the greatest have equal importance in some ultimate reckoning carries echoes of the doctrine that we are all made in the image of God.

All of these items from the Christian codebook of transcendence are of the utmost structural importance in the narrative of *His Dark Materials*. Even the Lucifer figure, who in both the Milton and the Pullman version probably has something of Prometheus in his make-up, also derives some of his charisma from the Christian resonance of the hero standing alone against arbitrary authority and triumphing through his own destruction – a symbolic combination that Milton, the classical scholar and Protestant revolutionary, can hardly have been unaware of.

Taken-for-granted reference points of the religious repertoire such as these, work like prisms casting all sorts of refracted light on mundane reality. They do not disappear from the cultural vocabulary, even in a supposedly post-Christian era, but continue to provide an orientation to the world and the key to what Charles Taylor has called 'maps of meaning'. In *Sources of the Self*,

Charles Taylor showed precisely how the elements that historically made up the Master Narrative of Christianity were transmuted and embedded in the Master Narrative of the European Enlightenment. The 'modern self' and the 'modern moral structure' that underpins it, both depend on a layer of values originating in a now-buried Christian core. Taylor argues that the nature of this fundamental stratum has become 'occluded'. Although there is a widely accepted cluster of moral imperatives in the West, their ontological and epistemological bases have become invisible. Indeed, the most characteristically modern modes of consciousness reject the need for moral frameworks, those 'maps of meaning' that Taylor excavates in his work. This is particularly the case, Taylor believes, with the 'naturalist' position that denies moral ontology and transcendent reference altogether. As Taylor sums it up, the modern West has made a move unprecedented in human history by insisting on the absolute distinction between the 'natural' and the 'supernatural', defining the first as real and the second as illusory.[15] The consequence is that we live in a world that for the most part works on the assumption that the 'natural' is all there is.

Nevertheless, disaster, great joy, unexpected fear, loss, bereavement and all the other 'liminal' or 'extreme' moments of human life, tend to break open the naturalist mode, making people reach for a transcendent reference point. As Max Weber long ago remarked, in a 'disenchanted' world a sector of the cultural elite turns to the aesthetic to supply the lack, and so concert halls and art galleries become the new temples of the sacred.[16] But this does not solve the problem for the majority. This is surely why an apparently secularized population, one at least that does not abound in regular church-goers, reacts to, say, a paedophile murder with language that positively demands divine retribution and the immortality of innocent victims; or why the untimely death of a celebrity, or the disaster of terrorist bombing or a collapsed football stadium send folk flocking to the churches, and/or inventing inchoate, ad hoc rituals, or resorting to New Age prophylactics. This is what sociologists of religion mean when they refer to 'vicarious' and 'implicit' religion, the former relying on churches and their professional representatives to access the transcendent on behalf of a largely non-practising population, the latter smuggling the transcendent back into profane existence.[17] Philip Pullman's trilogy perfectly reflects this pattern where the (secular) right hand and the (religious/spiritual/mythic) left hand behave as if each has no idea what the other is doing.

If Taylor is correct about the characteristic 'naturalist' ontology that dominates Western assumptions, then any cultural activity that allows a moratorium on its remit must be worth attention. The genre of 'fantasy' literature, a vast industry today, is an obvious site where the 'naturalist' epistemology can be bracketed off and the repressed transcendent can be welcomed back as play, as 'escapism'. After all, John Locke, the father of positivist empiricism and originator of what Taylor calls 'the punctual self' (that is, one unconstrained by culture, history, language, religion or any collective assumptions, and therefore the ideal 'objective' observer), cautioned against exposing children to fairy tales. Their education should be based on first-hand discovery of the empirical world. Fairy tales are just lies, everything the modern 'naturalist' mode of consciousness Locke helped to establish has dismissed as false and therefore harmful.[18]

The stories we tell our children are usually the first place where they encounter those modalities of consciousness that the 'naturalist' perspective has seemingly purged from 'real' life. Of course, today we tell stories through a plethora of media. Even so, children's books sell in unprecedented numbers, and best sellers like J. K. Rowling's *Harry Potter* series or Philip Pullman's *His Dark Materials* become the common currency of a whole generation of children, particularly when they are also turned into films and plays and spawn ancillary products to be bought and fantasized over.[19] They mould the imagination of a generation, giving its first shape to the 'dark chaos' and the 'golden dancing'.

Fantasy literature that suspends or alters the parameters of the 'natural' has particular characteristics. Rowan Williams has pointed out that it enables children to engage in 'irresponsible talk', that is, to explore as play fantasies of autonomy, of things being other than they are, of doing and being all the things that are frowned on or never mentioned, and of seeing what kind of consequences follow.[20] The Archbishop argues that the anarchic and amoral, the frightening, and even the bad-taste fantasies that come naturally to children should be encouraged, provided it occurs under the responsible eye of parents or other adults who can guarantee the child's return to the safety of ordinariness. That, of course, is one reason why so many children's magical tales end with a return home. Fantasy literature is also, I would insist, a place where the transcendent is readmitted. Though fantasy is protean, many of its elements are derived, at one or more removes, from that 'occluded' Christian treasury. Fantasy literature that takes as its model not only an *ur*-narrative from *Genesis* but one of the most celebrated epic poems in the English language, as *His Dark Materials* daringly does, will have great difficulty transforming or reversing the myriad religious resonances embedded in those sources, even when its intention is to negate Milton's aim: 'to justify the ways of God to man'. It is time to turn to Pullman's epic itself.

His Dark Materials

The initial core of readers of Pullman's trilogy came from middle-class parents and teachers, familiar with *Paradise Lost* and brought up on C. S. Lewis, J. R. R. Tolkien, Alan Garner, Susan Cooper, Lucy Boston, Diana Wynne Jones, Joan Aiken and the like. They recognized in his tough, street-wise child heroine, Lyra, another Dido Twite (this time with *two* bad parents) or an updated Dickensian urchin with all the sentimentality excised.[21] His conceit of an externalized animal 'daemon' was an intriguing new slant on the idea of the soul and the nature of moral self-creation.[22] His elaboration of a recognizable Britain in a parallel universe was the familiar technique by which fantasy 'renders the familiar strange'.[23] His parallel universe was peopled with armoured, talking bears, witches with prophetic powers and flying broomsticks, romantic tribes of nomadic gypsies ('Gyptians'). The tally of fantastic creatures was increased with each volume. The source of evil was an all-powerful church that combined the ruthlessness of the Spanish Inquisition with the fanatical Puritanism of John Calvin and John Knox. It is recognizably the church lampooned by Blake (and every antinomian after him) as the black-clad, killjoy destroyer of the garden of love.[24]

Pullman is a consummate teller of tales. His riff and variations on Milton's great theme is both gripping and familiar. Pullman's religious villains are thrillingly bad and his heroes are pretty flawed too, but courageous, never deferential, and consistently loyal to their friends. Pullman fully exploits the celebrated ambiguity in Milton's epic that makes Lucifer, the rebel angel, a sympathetic and compelling anti-hero precisely because he is a rebel against arbitrary authority. The prime villain in Pullman's version is Lyra's mother, Mrs Coulter, adulteress and femme fatale, agent of the repressive ecclesiastical Authority, though in the nick of time she finds the redeeming altruism to save her daughter. The anti-hero is Lyra's father, Lord Asriel. He is probably closer to Nietzsche's amoral superman than to Milton's Lucifer, defying earthly and heavenly authority as wildly as Don Giovanni, and pursuing forbidden knowledge, at no matter whose cost, as tragically as Frankenstein or Faust. In *Northern Lights*, he is as keen as the church to mutilate Roger, Lyra's best friend, by slicing off his 'daemon' in order to generate the energy necessary to break through into other worlds, and happy to dupe Lyra into bringing him the boy. The forbidden knowledge Asriel is pursuing is, of course, the nature and properties of 'dust'.

The second volume introduces a teenage boy hero, Will, from the 'real' Oxford of our time, on the run because he has accidentally killed one of the men who broke into his home searching for papers belonging to his explorer father, who is missing. He meets Mary Malone, an ex-nun and Oxford scientist, also, like Asriel, studying 'dust'. They infiltrate Lyra's Oxford and travel to worlds menaced by soul-devouring spectres. Pullman develops a semi-detached sub-plot with 'green' appeal in which Mary lives among a version of Gulliver's peaceable and all-wise Houyhnhnms, the elephant-like 'mulefa', in a near-Eden. In this version they have added 'natural' technology in the form of wheels on their hooves made from the fruit of a species of tree threatened by the equivalent of environmental pollution, a sudden scarcity of 'dust'.

It took Pullman three years to arrive at the War in Heaven that the Miltonian plot required, and to draw the apparently unconnected sub-plots of Volume 2 together in the third book. The apocalyptic climax was nicely appropriate to the millennium year in which it finally appeared. As is notorious, Pullman killed off God, 'the Ancient of Days', who is not the Creator but only an angel who had once acquired supreme power in heaven but who is now in his dotage. He simply disintegrates into 'dust' with a relieved sigh when the children lift him out of his crystal box. This episode is little more than a minor tailpiece to the child heroes' rescue of the ghosts of the dead from a (distinctly Classical) Hades where they are tormented by harpies who are tamed when Lyra (Orpheus and Sheherazade combined) beguiles them with stories. The dead choose ecstatic disintegration/consummation in unity with eternal matter; it is a not-quite-materialist *auflösung*.

The other major narrative hinge made clear in the last volume is Pullman's highly equivocal reversal of the moral meaning of the Fall. The race against time that gives urgency to the story in the third volume is the pursuit of Lyra, the 'New Eve', by the fanatical emissaries of the church, desperate to kill her before she has a chance to discover sex with Will (thus entering into the realm of 'experience') and fulfil the prophecy that will destroy the power of the Authority. Lyra's parents meet a heroic end, thrown down into the eternal abyss fighting the vice-regent of heaven who is lost with them. This arch-enemy, Metatron, is revealed as a jumped-up mortal, fit prey for Lyra's mother who tricks him with promises of long-forgotten carnal pleasure. Pullman represents angels, too, as envious of the fleshly experience denied them by their ethereal substance, in spite of which they can nevertheless be killed. This gives added poignancy to the passionate loss experienced by Balthamos, an angel whose lover, Baruch, is killed defending the children. Balthamos himself dies after killing Father Gomez, the would-be assassin of Lyra and Will. Sex, or rather sexual feeling, is everywhere: the adulterous passion of Lyra's parents; Mary's rejection of her celibate vocation and her long account of her own sexual awakening to the aroused but confused Lyra; the tragic end of Will's long lost father, killed, just as Will catches up with him, by the arrow of a witch whose sexual advances he had spurned. In particular the sexual awakening of the pubescent child heroes dominates the trilogy's climax, until the damp squib of an ending returns them each to their own, now hermetically sealed worlds, to face a future of study, work and civic duty to bring about 'the republic of heaven' on earth. Will and Lyra are separated and all enchantment is banished as the soul-devouring spectres are explained as the result of the dangerous mingling of universes. The angels and other exotic creatures are repatriated to their proper habitats, chaos is subdued and we are left with a secularized Protestant work ethic in a disenchanted republic.

In a radio interview in September 2005 introducing *Paradise Lost* as the week's *Book at Bedtime*, Pullman described Milton's epic as 'a story of growing up', and this surely is what he intended in *His Dark Materials*: the end of the magical adventure and the return to everyday life, wiser and more self-knowing.[25] Yet in *The Amber Spyglass* he also seems to imply that enchantment is fine for children but adults need to face reality without it. It is true that both Milton and *Genesis* turn Adam and Eve out into the world beyond Eden to toil and suffer, but Pullman as omnipotent narrator has reversed the moral sign attached to the Fall and abolished God, so why keep the original ending – work as the wages of sin? Pullman has said that he believes the Fall was not a once-for-all cosmic phenomenon but that it happens over and over again in all our lives,[26] but that hardly explains his, or what he insists is 'the story's', need to separate the child heroes and restrict future travel between worlds to their imaginations.[27] What *was* the unique cosmic significance of Lyra's entry into the realm of experience if the transition is a mere commonplace? Perhaps Pullman's point was simply the wickedness of the church in enforcing an impossible state of innocence on grown-up humanity. But this merely displaces rather than solves the problem of evil. If the church and God are responsible for it, then abolishing them should largely eliminate evil. Instead, it simply puts an end to the story.

Rowan Williams suggests that Pullman's church is Christianity without redemption, while Hugh Rayment-Pickard argues that Pullman's ethical structure is incoherent since (even granting his consequentialist ethic) it spares his 'good' protagonists the normal uncertainty about the ethical outcomes of choice.[28] Both comments seem to me just, and underline how confused and ambivalent Pullman is about human 'sinfulness'. He is fully alive to the evil and violence that humans chronically engage in, yet he insists that '[w]hen we have a sense of who we fully are and the world we fully belong to, you tend to get things right on the whole because then you see yourself in a moral perspective, in a moral context, in a moral connection with the rest of the universe'.[29] He believes that only those who arrogantly think they are 'above all that' are responsible for what 'goes wrong', and this tends to be institutions believing they are guardians of an absolute morality. This looks very like the situational morality that is the common position of the post-1960s generations in the West.[30] We have, apparently, abandoned absolute rules, and loathe those who attempt to enforce them, trusting our own authenticity as guide, and preferring to 'play it by ear' in the ethical sphere. Yet when something shocks us morally, we still want to identify the perpetrators as unequivocally evil, just as Pullman does in his story. As Charles Taylor cogently observes, the moral basis of our lives has become 'occluded', and Pullman's fiction shows the same blind eye to the basis of its moral preferences.

Despite the celebration of sex that runs through Pullman's story, Lyra is returned to the rituals and disciplines of an all-female college in 'her' Oxford. The spin-off novella, *Lyra's Oxford*, exposes Pullman's narrative problem: a secularization closure has disallowed the very enchantment that drove the original story.[31] One wonders how he will solve the problem in his projected *Book of Dust*. In *Lyra's Oxford* he has to make do with a tail-end sub-plot out of the original narrative, yet again fuelled by the sexual jealousy of a witch. Even though Lyra is working to bring about the virtuous republic, she is still a rule breaker, sneaking out of college without permission and knowing better than the adults set to guide her, perhaps because a true heroine must always be a rebel and non-conformist, even in the 'republic of heaven'. Pullman surrounds his frail tailpiece with hints of the enchantment he has eschewed. He includes a post-card from 'our' (and Will's) Oxford, an old cruise advertisement and a preface that intimates that separated worlds mysteriously 'leak' into each other, leaving such fragments behind. It is *almost* a promise to bring back the mingled universes that hooked his readers in the first place.

Beyond the obvious echoes of 'death of God' theology, the most immediately striking thing about Pullman's story is its antinomianism, very much in the tradition of William Blake. Its double mind about the Fall as well as its most overt and insistent values echo very precisely the world-view of the counter-culture of the 1960s – down with authority and long live liberating sex! The antinomian and romantic strands of Christian culture, refracted through Enlightenment and Romantic ideas and embedded in the avant garde arts, percolated down to the population at large, initially via the youth culture of the 1960s and 70s, democratizing a 'bohemian' option that had until this point been the privilege of a small leisured elite. Sixties bohemianism was a protest against utilitarian, bureaucratic, manipulative, competitive modes of evaluation, asserting instead the primacy of experience and imagination. Its watchwords were Love, and Authenticity, and it always put the Spirit before the Letter. These are the characteristic antinomian priorities that come directly out of the Christian 'basement'. The 1960s also produced a plethora of religious seekers, exploring the mystical and the occult, with and without consciousness-altering drugs. Much of 1960s culture thus entailed a rejection of precisely that dominant 'naturalistic' modality that Taylor sees as characteristically 'modern': hence the popularity of Tolkien. It was an *anti-secularizing* cultural move. Of course, as the elements of what had been a *counter*-culture spread to the population at large, antinomian aspects were often hollowed out to become mundane consumerist markers of 'life-style' options. Nevertheless, they left a deposit in popular culture on which Pullman has been able to draw.[32] Indeed, we might even see *His Dark Materials* as the 1960s recycled for twenty-first-century children.

This cultural deposit has a double face: on the one side there is a yearning for the transcendent and enchanted (witness, say, the popularity of Neil Gaiman's graphic and other novels),[33] and on the other the rejection of religious authority as self-evidently the most damaging among the whole range of 'inauthentic' institutional authorities (hence, say, the moral panic about 'fundamentalism' or the assumption that religion is uniquely responsible for war and violence).[34] Parents (and grandparents) who sang along to John Lennon's antinomian peace hymn, 'Imagine', will know just where they are when their children encounter Pullman's moral universe. Intriguingly, Callum Brown, like Pullman, sets up the church as a straw man, easily demolished by the onslaught of the 1960s, when he argues (with very little solid evidence) that the precipitous decline of church attachment from the early 1960s must have been due to the rejection by a generation of newly sexually liberated young women of the dominant (evangelical) equation of piety and femininity. He, too, sees the New Eve bringing the destruction of sexually repressive religion, though this may well tell us more about the continuing appeal of those '60s values than about the reasons for the decline in churchgoing from 1960 onward.[35]

There has been considerable disagreement whether Pullman's condemnation of the church in *His Dark Materials* is a straightforward attack on Christianity. We never learn what the beliefs and liturgies of this fictional church are, and the Christian narrative is nowhere evident, but the villains wear crucifixes and Pullman himself admits that it is the historic Christian Church he has in his sights. As I implied above, this suggests a naïve political theory that has not grappled with the inevitable ambiguities of power and authority *as such*, whether religious or secular.[36] But under the *naïveté* of the 1960s, there is something more interesting. Like Blake and most antinomians and many secular moderns, Pullman judges *religious* authority with peculiar harshness precisely because he is employing criteria of judgement derived from Christianity itself, however much they have been repackaged as 'secular'. It is possible to identify many of the core values of Pullman's text in Christian terms. It is true there are Classical and other antecedents, as well as Christian ones, in the heroism of laying down one's life for one's friends. But we are in the Christian heartland when we come to the loyalty of chosen friendship (brotherhood and sisterhood) trumping automatic loyalty to family and tribe. The same applies to loving your neighbour as yourself – even if he is an enslaved talking bear, a 'mulefa', or a low status 'Gyptian' or street urchin. And at the very centre of *His Dark Materials* lies the supreme affirmation: love is stronger than death – and in this case also stronger than separation, or difference of species, or of universe. Affirmations don't come more distinctively Christian than that.

In the end, the 'atheism' of *His Dark Materials* may be less important than the fact that it is a bestseller that treats theological matters with the deepest seriousness in what is to all appearances a 'secular' culture. When societies like Britain and the Netherlands voraciously consume theological adventure stories like Pullman's, or Harry Mulisch's *The Discovery of Heaven*,[37] or even *The Da Vinci Code*,[38] something more subtle and intriguing is happening in popular culture than can be caught by terms like 'secular' or 'post-Christian'.

Notes

1 See the discussion of Pullman's early fiction in Hugh Rayment-Pickard, 2004, *The Devil's Account: Philip Pullman and Christianity*, London: Darton, Longman & Todd.

2 Philip Pullman, 1995, *Northern Lights*, London: Scholastic; 1997, *The Subtle Knife*, London: Scholastic; 2000, *The Amber Spyglass*, London: Scholastic.

3 The edited transcript of a series of discussions in the presence of a large audience at The National Theatre can be found in Lyn Haill (ed.), 2004, *Darkness Illuminated: Platform Discussions on 'His Dark Materials' at the National Theatre*, London: National Theatre/Oberon Books. Pullman's account of the film project occurs at pp. 83–104.

4 Rayment-Pickard, *The Devil's*, pp. 10–12.

5 Haill, *Darkness* – 'The Conversation', pp. 83–104.

6 Brown, *Death*.

7 Taylor, *Sources of the Self*.

8 Rayment-Pickard, *The Devil's*, pp. 27–32.

9 Rowan Williams, 2000, *Lost Icons: Reflections on Cultural Bereavement*, Edinburgh: T&T Clark, pp. 11–52.

10 Rayment-Pickard, *The Devil's*, pp. 61–6; Haill, 'The Conversation'.

11 'The Composer as Librettist: A conversation between Sir Michael Tippett and Patrick Carnegy', *The Times Literary Supplement*, July 1977, pp. 834–5.

12 Thetis Blacker, 'In Praise of Darkness', *Temenos*, 12 (1991), 125–8.

13 David Martin, 2002, *Christian Language in the Secular City*, Aldershot: Ashgate, 'Introduction', pp. 3–5; 'The Language of Christianity', pp. 5–16; *On Secularization*, pp. 171–84.

14 Max Weber, 1948, *From Max Weber*, ed. H. Gerth and C. Wright Mills, London: Routledge; see, 'Science as a Vocation', pp. 129–58; 'Religious Rejections of the World and their Direction', pp. 323–62.

15 Charles Taylor, 2002, 'What is Secularity?', draft paper delivered at the Symposium 'Is There an Alternative Master Narrative to Secularization?', University of Amsterdam.

16 Weber, *From Max Weber*, 'Religious Rejections'.

17 The argument is developed at greater length in Bernice Martin, 2003, 'Beyond Measurement: The Non-Quantifiable Religious Dimensions in Social Life', in Avis (ed.), *Public Faith?*, pp. 1–18.

18 Rayment-Pickard comments on the close connection Philip Pullman makes between telling stories, which Pullman sees as a defining feature of human self-consciousness, and telling lies, illustrated by his heroine Lyra's facility for both, reflected in her given name (sounding like 'liar') and in the nickname 'Silvertongue' given to her by Iorek Byrnison, the king of the armoured bears, and further underlined in the episode where Lyra enchants the tormenting harpies in Hell by telling stories.

19 It is arguable that the Rowling oeuvre is not so much 'myth-making' in Pullman's sense, as part of the genre of School Stories spiced with what Terry Pratchett calls added 'technomancy'. Michael Ostling, for example, argues that the magic in the Harry Potter books is really a form of technology rather than a re-enchantment of the world. See Michael Ostling, 2003, 'Harry Potter and the Disenchantment of the World', *Journal of Contemporary Religion*, 18(1) (2003), 3–24.

20 Williams, *Lost Icons*.

21 Dido Twite was the child heroine of a series of novels by Joan Aiken (in which the fantasy involved reversing the fortunes of the Stuarts and the Hanoverians) beginning with *Black Hearts in Battersea*, London: Jonathan Cape, 1965, and ending with *Is*, London: Jonathan Cape, 1992. Many children's stories use the device of bad, dead or absent parents to release the child protagonists into full (premature) autonomy.

22 Pullman claims that the idea of the daemon originated as a dramatic technique for

rendering interior dialogue. See Haill, *Darkness* – 'The Author', p. 49–50.

23 Williams, *Lost Icons*, p.18.

24 William Blake's poem 'The Garden of Love' was a favourite source for the 1960s counterculture. It was chosen by Brian Patten, himself a popular poet of the 1960s, as his contribution to British Poetry Day, 2005, on BBC Radio 4.

25 Pullman's introduction to *Paradise Lost* as the BBC Radio 4 'Book at Bedtime', September 2005.

26 Haill, *Darkness* – 'The Conversation', p. 89.

27 Haill, *Darkness* – 'The Author', p. 64; Rayment-Pickard, *The Devil's*, pp. 23–6.

28 Haill, *Darkness* – 'The Conversation', p. 85.

29 Haill, *Darkness* – 'The Author', p. 56.

30 Opinion poll data has consistently documented this shift since the beginning of the 1970s. See, for example, the data of the European Values Surveys or the annual survey of British Social Attitudes.

31 Philip Pullman, 2003, *Lyra's Oxford*, Oxford: David Fickling Books.

32 Martin, *Sociology of Contemporary Cultural Change*. Pullman read English at Oxford during the 1960s and his adult novels display the trademark preoccupations of late 60s taboo-breaking, particularly transgressive sex. See Rayment-Pickard, *The Devil's*.

33 For example, Neil Gaiman, 2001, *American Gods*, New York: Harper Collins, and its 2005 sequel, *Anansi Boys*, New York: Harper Collins. Terry Pratchett's best sellers are comic fantasy novels that use magic and 'alternative worlds' to reveal what is hidden. Pratchett, like Pullman, is a self-proclaimed secular humanist who nevertheless returns again and again to the theme of the human itch for self-transcendence. He has a far more sophisticated understanding of the nature of power than Pullman. The moral structure of his novels, too, depends fundamentally on the 'occluded' Christian cultural deposit.

34 Jonathan Miller's series for the BBC2 television channel, *A History of Unbelief*, 2005, is a case in point. For a critique of these views see David Martin, 1997, *Does Christianity Cause War?*, Oxford: Clarendon Press; and 'Master Narratives and the Future of Christianity', 2007 *Zeitschrift für Religions und Geistesgeschichte* 59(1), 1–13.

35 For an alternative account see Hugh McLeod, 'Religious Crisis of the 1960s'.

36 Martin, 'Master Narratives'.

37 Harry Mulisch, 1996, *The Discovery of Heaven*, trans. Paul F. Vincent; London: Viking. Mulisch, like Pullman, Pratchett and other fantasy writers exploits the principle of relativity in modern physics to make multiple realities plausible. His plot involves (another) superannuated God whose functions have been taken over by an unfeeling bureaucracy intent on rescinding God's covenant with the Chosen People. The novel contains the best fictional account of 1960s counter-culture I have come across.

38 Dan Brown, 2004, *The Da Vinci Code*, London: Corgi Books.

The Architecture of Belief

WILLIAM WHYTE

The redundant or disused church is a familiar image of secularization. It appears on the cover of Steve Bruce's *God is Dead* and has illustrated innumerable articles on the decline of Christianity in Britain. Moreover, this sense is clearly shared by some practitioners too. 'The Church needs to be incarnational, and bricks and mortar are as much a part of the incarnation as anything else,' an Anglican priest told the writer Mary Loudon in 1993. 'A closed church', he went on, 'is the incarnation of a dead God.'[1] If this is true, then there might be good reason to suspect that God died in post-war Britain. Yet, in reality, the redundant church is a very imperfect representation of belief. Simply charting the closure of churches does not go far enough. It does not explain why they were closed. It does not acknowledge the large number built to replace them. And, most importantly of all, it does not go anyway towards explaining how people in reality relate to sacred architecture. To engage with that, we need a better-grounded, more historically engaged approach; one that takes into account differences between denominations and the evolution of architecture as well as wider social and cultural changes. Only then will we get beyond the clichéd image of the abandoned church and begin to explore the architecture of belief itself.

This is not, of course, to say that redundant churches are unimportant – either in their own right or as evidence of Christian decline. For one thing, it is self-evident that the years after 1945 did indeed see a massive programme of church closure. In England, in the period between 1940 and 1980, the Methodists alone closed 5,000 churches – disposing of a quarter of their stock in a single decade. From 1969 to 1980, the Church of England made 1,434 churches redundant.[2] Nor was this process confined to England. Between 1946 and 1984, the Scottish churches between them closed 1,078 buildings; 57% of which were subsequently demolished.[3] This undoubtedly represented a major shift in the geography of Christian Britain.[4] Church buildings undoubtedly do play an important role as symbols of the wider church and as foci for the area in which they are situated.[5] Closing them, reusing them, or demolishing them has a significant impact on the congregation and on the wider community. Interviewed in the late 1980s, one Anglican priest, serving a rural parish in Cornwall, argued that 'If you've not got a church you won't get the congregation . . . they won't go anywhere else. If you've lost the visible church you've lost witness.'[6] A similar point was made by the Grubb Institute of Behavioural Studies which suggested in the mid-1970s that 'a community which is deprived of its church feels that it has been devalued, and community life is itself weakened.'[7]

Nonetheless, it would be wrong to suggest that church redundancy is the product of simple secularization or the result of a generalized process of religious decline. Doubtless, a fall in church attendance is an important factor in the process of declaring a church redundant. But in reality the relationship between redundancy and secularization is far from simple. In the first place, many churches in post-war Britain were closed because of a shift of population rather than a more specific collapse in commitment to religion. The population of Southwark dropped from 313,000 in 1961 to 196,000 in 1995. Little wonder that the Anglican diocese declared 54 churches redundant – although this, in reality, represents only 13% of the total stock.[8] Similarly, changes within the Church itself often make a building unnecessary. When the United Free Church reunited with the Church of Scotland in 1929, the number of Church of Scotland churches rose from 1,703 to 3,186. Something had to give – and so surplus buildings were simply closed.[9] Methodist reunion had a similar impact too.

Christians also have very different views about the value of church buildings. Interviewed in the 1990s, a large number of Free Church ministers rejected the concept of a redundant church altogether: if the building was not needed, they argued, then it should be disposed of.[10] At the same time, Anglican priests trained at the evangelical theological college, Oak Hill, were taught that church buildings present more problems than potential. Limited by their 'immobility', 'inflexibility', 'unfriendliness', sense of 'pride', and unfortunate 'class' connotations, churches – it was suggested – should be abandoned in favour of worship at home.[11] 'If I had my way', one Anglican priest declared in the early 1990s, 'I'd pull the lot down! All of them, from York Minster downwards . . . I'd flatten every single one.'[12] Redundancy in that sense must be understood not just as a reflection of failure – but also as a product of a series of choices made by individuals, by congregations, and by the wider church. As one report of 1995 concluded, 'what sometimes looks like a national crisis, is in fact a series of local problems'.[13]

Moreover, while church redundancy is an important issue, it should not become the sole focus of our attention. Post-war Britain witnessed the opening of many new church buildings as well as the closure of many old ones. War-damage necessitated replacement. Population changes that in one place led to redundancy, in others led to building. In the decades after 1945 the Anglican Church alone erected hundreds of new churches.[14] Even as the Methodists declared thousands of buildings redundant, they were also proudly announcing that *The Methodist Church Builds Again*.[15] By the early 1960s, over a thousand new structures had been erected, 400 of which were churches, and the remainder dual-purpose buildings or church halls.[16] Nor did the process stop there. Between 1969 and 1993 the Church of England built 400 new churches, many of which were large and architecturally important new structures. Indeed, in this period no fewer than seven new cathedrals were completed: in Brentwood (1989–91), Coventry (1956–62), Clifton (1970–3), Guildford (1932–61), Middlesbrough (1985–8), Portsmouth (completed 1991), as well as both Liverpool (1904–78) and Liverpool Metropolitan (1962–7). These were highly significant architectural statements in their own right – and they also possessed a wider cultural importance. Coventry Cathedral, as Gavin Stamp observed, was 'the last modern building in Britain *of any type* that ordinary people have queued to see inside. That was quite an achievement.'[17]

As this suggests, the architecture of these new churches served more than just a practical purpose. Buildings were meant to express ideas and to embody theological propositions.[18] Their role was 'the extension of the kingdom of God and the provision of Christian worship and fellowship where it is needed'.[19] Broadly speaking, three factors shaped the development of church architecture in this period. In the first place, architectural fashion undoubtedly had an impact. Second, liturgical reform necessitated new sorts of structure, and newly planned churches. In the third place, theological changes inspired new sorts of churches: indeed, a new idea of church. Yet although these movements are interrelated, it is important not to assume that they are interdependent.[20] While St Peter's College, Cardross (1958–66) has a modernist plan and a modernist façade, and owes much to late modernist ideas of community and to the inspiration of Le Corbusier's ultra-modern architecture, it nonetheless embodied a highly traditional idea of a seminary. As one former lecturer put it: 'the church about us was changing, but the liturgical shape of St Peter's, with its multiplicity of altars, was obsolete before it began.'[21] By contrast, Peter Hammond argued that Ninian Comper's Gothic Revival St Philip's, Cosham (1937–8), was unprecedented in its advanced understanding of liturgical planning.[22]

In general, the post-war building programmes of the Christian churches have tended to be seen as a disappointment.[23] Writing in 1991, the architectural critic Kenneth Powell argued that contemporary church buildings were 'Ugly, Mediocre and Unholy'.[24] At the end of the 1960s the liturgist Frédéric Debuyst complained that 'the overwhelming majority of the so-called "modern" churches are essentially backward-looking, unauthentic, purely formal adaptations, not creations'.[25] From very different perspectives yet in the same decade, Peter Hammond and Frank West also decried contemporary church architecture. For West, a country parson and later bishop of Truro, the problem was too much modernism. He attacked the 'fashionable ecclesiastical architect' for erecting churches which looked 'like a swimming bath from within and a shredded-wheat factory from without'.[26] For the modernist Hammond, by contrast, contemporary church buildings were not nearly contemporary enough. 'There is little that can now be done to redeem the tragic failure of the church building programmes of the last thirty years. The Church has failed to seize its opportunity – and now it is too late,' he declared in 1960.[27] Even in 1948, at the start of our period, Edward Maufe, the architect of Guildford Cathedral, expressed concern that modern churches might create 'slum spiritual conditions'.[28]

It would be a mistake, however, to conclude from these criticisms that there was a crisis of faith in church architecture, or that the churches failed in their mission to erect appropriate buildings. To be sure, there was often furious and even bitter debate. But this should neither come as a surprise, nor as an excuse to overlook the importance of this great movement of church building. Indeed the passion of these arguments reflected the importance of architecture to the modern church. Just as nineteenth-century churchmen had placed buildings at the heart of their religious reforms, so their late-twentieth century successors saw architecture as a critical means of reviving and remaking Christian Britain. Similarly, it can be seen that although the ideals of one generation were rejected by another, this does not vitiate the attempt each generation was making. A good example of this might be found at Brentwood Cathedral, where, between 1989 and 1991, a 1970s concrete extension was demolished to make way for Quinlan Terry's strictly classical treatment. This did not reflect the fundamental failure of the modernist building. Rather, it reflected a change in taste and a change in theology – an attempt to be contemporary underpinned by construction and demolition. As Paul Walker put it at the time, 'Churches that were built to meet the principles of secularity and the multi-purpose, are now being condemned for lacking any sense of the numinous, as if that had been some careless oversight.'[29] Of course it was not, but different priorities, theologies, and changing tastes had created different churches.

In the years immediately after 1945, pre-war patterns of church building remained popular: both in style and in plan.[30] As Edward Maufe put it, 'it is now generally recognized that while serving the present and looking to the future, we should yet build on tradition'.[31] His Guildford Cathedral, with its stripped down Gothicism and traditional planning, is in that respect archetypal. Increasingly, however, the churches began to look to more ostentatiously modernist architecture.[32] Coventry Cathedral represented a real break with the Gothic Revival and with interwar ideas – although its plan also remained traditional.[33] St Paul, Bow Common (1958–60), embodied the principles of the liturgical movement and expressed them in the latest architectural style.[34] SS Philip and James, Hodge Hill (1963–68), was the acme of the multi-purpose church: combining a hall and a sanctuary – the sacred and the secular – in a way firmly advocated by J. G. Davies in his *The Secular Use of Church Buildings*.[35] What unified these different buildings was the attempt to erect churches which expressed the spirit of the age, which were relevant, authentic, and modern. As the Catholic bishops of Germany had concluded in 1947, 'the church edifice today is intended for the people of our times. Hence it must be fashioned in such a way that the people of our times may recognize and feel it is addressed to them.'[36] The result was often, as Peter Hammond had hoped, *rather plain brick boxes with no tricks*. This, it was believed, best embodied the new congregational ideal of worship, best recaptured the early church concept of the house of God, and best produced a truly 'Servant Church'.[37]

Moreover, even after the collapse of the Modern Movement in architecture, the ideals that had animated the new churches of the 1960s remained seminal. Richard Giles's highly influential *Re-Pitching the Tent* echoes Hammond when it argues that 'We need today, not buildings that make grandiose or pretentious statements, but buildings that make us feel at home'.[38] Likewise, places like the Baptist Queen's Road Church in Wimbledon (1988) are designed 'not as a "Temple" full of architectural theatre and mystery, but as a "Community House" which is welcoming and easy to approach'.[39] Similarly, the builders of the Emmanuel Christian Centre in Walthamstow (1989) declared that 'we are not a stained glass window type of church'.[40] Equally, though, churches which were of the stained-glass type also deployed devices which were inspired by the reforms of the 1950s and 1960s. Christ the Cornerstone, Milton Keynes (1990–91), was self-consciously intended to 'look like a church' – and with its dome it does.[41] Yet it was also, in the words of the architect, 'an essentially modern building – albeit with Classical roots – which reflects the modern Church'.[42] The move to refit and reorder churches – thousands of which have been altered in the last twenty years – expresses a similar desire. Often incorporating carpeting, soft furnishings, and the ubiquitous coffee area, remodelled churches have sought to domesticate the sacred just as the reformers of the 1960s hoped.[43]

Far from expressing a crisis of faith, post-war church buildings exemplify the ambition and creativity of the post-war churches. Just as redundancy cannot be simplistically linked to decline, so debate about architecture should not be unproblematically coupled with crisis. Arguably, indeed, the reverse is true. The very vibrancy of these debates – which included a number of highly influential architects and theologians – reveals that.[44] Of course, redundancy could be traumatic and some new churches simply failed in their purpose. But to assume, as some writers do, that adopting or, indeed, abandoning a modernist style represented an admission of defeat is simply wrong. 'It may seem strange to those who insist that everything is becoming secularised to see so many churches being built today and to see them taking on proud, new forms', wrote Joseph Pichard. 'They are misled because their idea of the sacred is too limited.'[45] Modern church builders believed that they were stripping away the corruptions of the past and creating a new and better church. For Roman Catholics, this was as a 'rejuvenated Church . . . which expresses in Her substance all the signs of a rediscovered youth'.[46] For Protestants, this was a 'Twentieth Century Reformation'.[47] For both, buildings were a means by which to express ideals and identities. In that sense, the architecture of belief remained strikingly strong throughout the post-war period.

Notes

1 The Revd David Randall in Mary Loudon, 1994, *Revelations: The Clergy Questioned*, London: H. Hamilton, p. 192.

2 Comedia, 1995, *Spirit of Place: Redundant Churches as Urban Resources*, Stroud: Comedia, p. 17.

3 Kirsty A. Campbell, 1988, *Redundant Church Buildings in Scotland*, Research Paper 28, Edinburgh: Edinburgh College of Art/Herriot-Watt University Department of Town and Country Planning, pp. 3, 5, 19.

4 John Lowerson, 1992, 'The Mystical Geography of the English', in Brian Short (ed.), *The English Rural Community: Image and Analysis*, Cambridge: Cambridge University Press, pp. 152–74, esp. 156.

5 Susanne Seymour and Charles Watkins, 'Church, Landscape and Community: Rural Life and the Church of England', *Landscape Research* 20(1) (1995), pp. 30–44.

6 Quoted in Douglas Davies, 1990, *A Study of the Development and Work of the Rural Clergy in Five English Dioceses, Volume 1, The Rural Church: Staff and Buildings*, Cirencester: Centre for Rural Studies, Royal Agricultural College, Department of Theology University of Nottingham, p. 130.

7 Cited in Marcus Binney, 1977, 'England: Loss', in Marcus Binney and Peter Burman (eds), *Change and Decay: the Future of Our Churches*, London: Victoria and Albert Museum, pp. 27–42, at p. 37.

8 Comedia, *Spirit of Place*, pp. 21, 35. Seventeen of these churches are now used by other denominations.

9 Campbell, *Redundant Church Buildings*, p. 7.

10 Comedia, *Spirit of Place*, p. 15.

11 Ysenda Maxton Graham, 1993, *The Church Hesitant: A Portrait of the Church of England Today*, London: Hodder & Stoughton, pp. 82–3.

12 Revd David Perrett, quoted in Loudon, *Revelations*, p. 64.

13 Comedia, *Spirit of Place*, p. 8.

14 Incorporated Society for Promoting the Enlargement, Building and Repairing of Churches and Chapels, 1956, *Sixty Post-War Churches*, London: Incorporated Church Building Society.

15 E. Benson Perkins and Albert Hearn, 1946, *The Methodist Church Builds Again*, London: The Epworth Press.

16 F. W. Dillistone, 1964, 'Foreword', in William Lockett (ed.), *The Modern Architectural Setting of the Liturgy*, London: SPCK, pp. xv–xvii, at p. xv.

17 Gavin Stamp, 'Sacred Architecture in a Secular Century', *Twentieth Century Architecture* 3 (1998), p. 16.

18 Robert Maguire, 'Meaning and Understanding', in Peter Hammond (ed.), *Towards a Church Architecture*, London: Architectural Press, pp. 65–77.

19 Perkins and Hearn, *Methodist Church*, p. 46.

20 John Nelson Tarn, 'Liverpool's Two Cathedrals', *Studies in Church History* 28 (1992), 537–70, at p. 540.

21 Fr. John Fitzsimmons, quoted in Diane M. Watters, 1997, *Cardross Seminary: Gillespie, Kidd, and Coia and the Architecture of Postwar Catholicism*, Edinburgh: Royal Commission on the Ancient and Historical Monuments of Scotland, p. 62.

22 Peter Hammond, 1960, *Liturgy and Architecture*, London: Barrie & Rockliff, pp. 75–6. See also Anthony Symondson, 'Unity by Inclusion: Sir Ninian Comper and the Planning of a Modern Church', *Twentieth Century Architecture* 3 (1998), pp. 17–42.

23 For an American perspective, see Michael S. Rose, 2001, *Ugly as Sin: Why They Changed Our Churches from Sacred Spaces to Meeting Places – And How You Can Change Them Back Again*, Manchester NH: Sophia Institute Press.

24 *Sunday Telegraph*, 24 February 1991, Review Section, p. xiv.

25 Frédéric Debuyst, 1968, *Modern Architecture and Christian Celebration* (Ecumenical Studies in Worship 18), London: Lutterworth Press, p. 9.

26 Frank West, 1964, *The Country Parish To-day and To-morrow*, 2nd edn, London: SPCK, p. 101.

27 Hammond, *Liturgy and Architecture*, p. 153.

28 Edward Maufe, 1948, *Modern Church Architecture: With 50 Illustrations of Modern Foreign Churches*, London: Incorporated Church Building Society, pp. 5–6.

29 Peter Walker, 'Brentwood Cathedral: the appearance of tradition', *Church Building* 23 (1992), pp. 31–33, at 32.

30 Incorporated Society, *Sixty Post-War Churches*. Although see also Elain Harwood, 'Liturgy and Architecture: the development of the centralised Eucharistic space', *Twentieth Century Architecture* 3 (1998), 49–74.

31 Maufe, *Modern Church Architecture*, p. 3.

32 Edward D. Mills, 1956, *The Modern Church*, London: Architectural Press, p. 34.

33 Louise Campbell, 1996, *Coventry Cathedral: Art and Architecture in Post-war Britain*, Oxford: Clarendon Press.

34 Robert Maguire and Keith Murray, 1965, *Modern Churches of the World*, London: Studio Vista, pp. 90–93.

35 Nigel Melhuish, 'An Impression of Hodge Hill 1968', *Church Building* 18 (1991), pp. 4–5. John Gordon Davies, 1968, *The Secular Use of Church Buildings*, London: SCM Press, p. 243.

36 Quoted in Edward J. Sutfin and Maurice Lavanoux, 1962, 'Contemporary Catholic Architecture', in Albert Christ-Janer and Mary Mix Foley (eds.), *Modern Church Architecture: A Guide to the Form and Spirit of Twentieth-Century Religious Buildings*, New York : Dodge Book Dept, McGraw-Hill, p. 2.

37 André Biéler, 1965, *Architecture in Worship: the Christian Place of Worship*, trans. Odette and Donald Elliott, Edinburgh: Oliver and Boyd, pp. 76–7. James A. Whyte, 'The Theological Basis of Church Architecture', in Hammond, *Towards a Church Architecture*, pp. 128–90, 185–6.

38 Giles, *Re-Pitching the Tent*, p. 146.

39 Alan Brown, 'Queen's Road Church, Wimbledon', *Church Building* 13 (1989–90), p. 46.

40 Quoted in *Church Building* 14 (1990), p. 45.

41 Iain Smith, the architect of Christ the Cornerstone, quoted in Nigel Dees, 'The Shared Church of Christ the Cornerstone, Milton Keynes', *Church Building* 19 (1991), 14–16, p. 15.

42 Iain Smith, quoted in *Sunday Telegraph*, 24 February 1991, Review Section, p. xiv.

43 For a nineteenth-century example of this see Jeanne Halgren Kilde, 2002, *When Church Became Theatre: the Transformation of Evangelical Architecture and Worship in Nineteenth-Century America*, New York: Oxford University Press.

44 See, for example, Karl Barth, 'The Architectural Problem of Protestant Places of Worship', in Biéler, *Architecture in Worship*, pp. 92–3 and Paul Tillich, 'Contemporary Protestant Architecture', in Christ-Janer and Foley, *Modern Church Architecture*, pp. 122–5.

45 Joseph Pichard, 1960, *Modern Church Architecture*, trans. Ellen Callmann; New York: Orion Press, p. 167.

46 Justus Dahinden, 1967, *New Trends in Church Architecture*, trans. Cajetan J. B. Baumann; London: Studio Vista, p. 11.

47 Hammond, *Liturgy and Architecture*, Ch. 2.

Part III

Virtue

5

The Good Life

It is time to bring the idea of the good life back into the foreground of our public conversation.[1]

This was the premise of a collection of essays entitled *The Good Life* published by the think-tank Demos in 1998. The essays, from a variety of perspectives, challenged what they took to be 'the prevailing conception of the good life as an individualistic project', and reflected on the need to think harder both about definitions and about communal responsibilities. The editors affirmed that 'we cannot escape facing up to the great questions of ethics about the *content* of our lives and the *outcomes* of our strivings'.[2] This collection was one of a number of straws in the wind signalling a new public preoccupation in the 1990s with the quality of life. Questions were increasingly being asked about the reasons why economic growth seemed not to be conducing to rising contentment or social welfare.[3] From the 1950s to the 1990s, levels of affluence had risen markedly; yet over the same period it was estimated that time taken off work caused by stress-related illness had increased by 500%.[4] Moreover, commentators pointed to the widening inequalities in British society between the very rich (who were getting richer) and the poor, who were getting poorer. The relationship between objective and subjective measures of the quality of life, and the interrelationship between quality of living conditions and the quality of persons began to be systematically debated.[5] The development economist Amartya Sen raised fundamental questions about the criteria of economic judgement on a global basis.[6] He challenged utilitarian and growth-fixated models of economic well-being, and defined the goal of economic development rather as 'the promotion and expansion of valuable capabilities'.[7] Even the president of the World Bank stated in 1996 that the 'World Bank's central mission [was] to meld economic assistance with spiritual, ethical and moral development'.[8]

These debates were neither inherently nor necessarily informed by Christian thinking, but the questions of meaning and value which they confronted both revivified pre-existing Christian reflection, and opened up new scope for Christian input. Parallel and intersecting developments had been taking place in both philosophical thinking about ethics, and in moral theological responses to social and religious pluralism.[9] What all these moves had in common was a reaction against notions of value-free liberalism and utilitarianism which had significant (although never uncontested) authority in the 1960s and 1970s. Utilitarian arguments were in turn reactions against what were felt to have been stifling aspects of a previously hegemonic moral and political paternalism. Historical cycles of reaction and counter-reaction, in this context, as in others discussed in this book, influenced the development of debate about ethics and about the definition of the good life. Postmodern deconstructions of partial and monopolistic models of universal reason gave authority to plural voices (including religious ones), but it has been recognized that these voices can all too easily be relativized and silenced. Feminist theologians have pointed to the need to establish some basic criteria of human flourishing – of a good life – in order to be able to make coherent judgements about what is dehumanizing to women as well as men.[10]

The revival of virtue ethics among both secular and Christian philosophers has formed an increasingly important part of this debate, as Harriet Harris' essay in this section discusses. She sees potential in this revival for engagement with public interest in happiness, and also with societal anxieties about public morality. In arguing the latter, she suggests that virtue morality is not heavily prescriptive but does enable people to recognize and act on their responsibilities. She engages with the moral philosopher Elizabeth Anscombe's proposal that Christian emphases on law and duty undermine virtue, by arguing that through a theology of grace and an understanding of the ways in which practices shape our moral selves, notions of duty can be recast as living a life of freedom and love, which is consonant with virtue theory. She calls for more coherent and systematic dialogue between philosophers and theologians about both the definition and the practice not just of virtue as an abstract concept, but of specific virtues. Her argument identifies different late twentieth-century Christian approaches to ethics and the idea of *telos* – the construction of life goals – and points to some of the affinities of argument that might actually be found between different traditions (e.g. between virtue ethics and the revival of natural law theory). Over the last 15 to 20 years there have been increasing attempts to draw out these affinities. This seems to be part of a project on the one hand to underline the real pertinence of Christian thinking on ethics well beyond the boundaries of particular Christian communities; on the other to critique introverted ecclesial positions – 'pastoral monoculture', in Andrew Shanks' phrase – which, it is argued, can also become too individualistic (and conversion-oriented) and fail adequately to confront the sinful aspects of social and political life.[11] There have been repeated claims for the contribution of a Christian ethics drawing on Christian tradition for the sake of the wider public realm, and doing so – necessarily – in a way which is 'both particular and universal, communal and public'.[12] This more dialogic approach to Christian ethics attempts to maintain the integrity of religious traditions, while drawing out the potential for mutual understanding between them – both within

Christianity and between Christianity and other faith or non-faith-based groups.

As part of a broader reaction against welfare paternalism, Christian debate about the moral framework of capitalism had already changed register in the 1980s, when the ethical dialectic between autonomy and community became starkly polarized. Margaret Thatcher was at the forefront of the celebration in Christian language of the virtue of individual enterprise. Famously asserting that 'Economics are the method. The object is to change the soul' (1988),[13] she called evangelistically for conversion to her cause. In a speech to the General Assembly of the Church of Scotland in the same year she reconceptualized autonomy: 'man has been endowed by God with the fundamental right to choose between good and evil . . . we are expected to use all our own powers of thought and judgement in exercising that choice' – a comment which, as David Nicholls has pointed out, was radically Pelagian and called into question the Christian doctrines of sin and grace.[14] Under attack by prominent churchmen who contested what they saw as her false appropriation of Christian values, she for her part tried to de-legitimize the influence of the churches on social morality, which she argued had helped to foster a dependency culture. The stakes were raised. Still in 1988, John Paterson of the Church of Scotland held that the headlong pursuit of wealth creation was endangering any understanding of the true meaning of life; David Jenkins, the controversial Bishop of Durham, used the term 'wicked' in connection with the government's restructuring of social security.[15] In many respects the attacks on the churches' right to speak gave them new vitality in promoting principles of justice and compassion, and the capacity to develop a new moral voice. At the same time, many prominent Christian capitalists became closely associated with the Conservative government. Brian Griffiths, the evangelical head of the Prime Minister's Policy Unit from 1985 to 1990, was a key figure in the cultivation of these links, and in the campaign to promote the relationship between Christian values and enterprise culture.[16] Powerful lay Christians underpinned the radical and anti-institutional thrust of Thatcherism. In a period when on the one hand solipsistic individualism became rampant, and consumer greed ballooned out of control, and on the other (and in part in reaction) debate about ethical consumption and sustainability began to revive, Christian language on all sides of the debate about economic progress acquired a greater centrality.

The plural strands of the Christian debate revived in the 1980s have maintained momentum in a developing economic and moral climate. The Institute of Economic Affairs, founded by the Conservative Christian Lord Harris of High Cross, continues to flourish. Following on from a Hayek Memorial lecture given in 1993 under its auspices by the prominent American Catholic theorist of market morality, Michael Novak, the Institute began in 2000 a series of annual lectures, the Templeton Forum on Markets and Morality. Brian Griffiths gave the first lecture of the series, reiterating his long-standing critique of Hayek's understanding of ethics as simply part of cultural evolution, and at the same time calling for the exercise of specifically Judaeo-Christian *judgement* to shape economic values.[17] While the exclusivism of his Christian position and his stress on evangelism to support it characterises a particular evangelical position, his critique of both capitalism and socialism as rooted in false Enlightenment values finds wider affinities. Geoff Mulgan, the founder of Demos, wrote in 1998 of communism and liberal capitalism both having promised the good life through deception. He too argued for the need to leave behind a terror of making judgements. Pointing to the common features of a good life across time and place (in which he included a spiritual understanding of transcendence and connectedness) he made a strong claim for human capacity to make judgements about the goodness of a life.[18]

Other Christian voices, speaking both within the institutional churches and outside them, have developed increasingly close engagements with economic theory, in order to build in appropriate quality of life goals at the most fundamental level, not just leaving them to a residual welfare choice.[19] The revival of many questions of the interrelationship between religious values and economic norms has begun to be expressed also in an interfaith and global context. The recent publication of a dialogue between Marcus Braybrooke, an Anglican theologian, and Kamran Mofid, an Iranian economist, with a preface by Richard Harries, the Bishop of Oxford, and an epilogue by Bhai Sahib Mohinder Singh, the Chairman of GNNSJ, a leading Sikh religious, cultural and civic centre in Birmingham, builds on Mofid's establishment in 2002 of an annual international conference, 'An Inter-faith Perspective on Globalisation for the Common Good'.[20] Rufus Black, the author of the second essay in this section, has suggested the application of John Finnis's practical reasoning approach to the identification of core criteria of human flourishing to complement and refine Amartya Sen's and Martha Nussbaum's development ethics project.

In his essay in this book, Black covers a broader canvas in reflecting on the role of Christian values in economic debate since 1945. A moral theologian who is also a minister in the Uniting Church in Australia, his own career is a striking example of Christian conversation about the good life in the heart of a secular organization. Since 2000 he has worked as a partner for the international management consultancy firm McKinsey. When he was hired, there was a growing recognition at McKinsey that the solutions to a whole range of challenges facing its clients involved understanding people's mindsets – their interpretations of their environment, the needs they wanted to fulfil through work, their sense of identity. There was a realization of the centrality of stories and rituals in shaping the way in which organizations function. A moral theologian has found a fruitful and creative role in helping people to understand, work with and transform their mental maps. As an adviser to CEOs and senior executive teams of large companies and multinationals, he has found that he spends a large part of his time in exploring questions of meaning and value beyond the economic. A significant and expanding group of colleagues regard tackling these questions as central to the work of the organization.

The recognition that the ethos of a business or corporation – its capacity to inspire commitment and a sense of common purpose – is a fundamental factor in its success immediately confronts the distinction between intrinsic and instrumental goods. It is based on the premise that neither employees nor employers are driven by narrowly functional economic motives, and that values of trust, integrity and consistency of behaviour play a key role in making working relationships flourish precisely *because* they are seen to represent intrinsic value, not just the treating of persons as parts of a machine. Neither a liberal economy nor a liberal society is morally neutral. But where are the values that underpin them cultivated, and on what criteria? This very old question has taken on new forms in the last 60 years, as on the one hand thinking about the working of the economy has developed, and on the other British society has become more culturally pluralistic. Debates about school education have focused questions of value particularly sharply. As enterprise and entrepreneurialism became increasingly promoted as social and economic virtues in the late 1970s and 1980s, the same conceptual framework began to be transferred to education. The language of measurable targets, of teachers as delivering a product, and pupils as clients or consumers, began insidiously to challenge fundamental conceptions of what education was about. The long-established premise of a liberal education – that education was a process within which people learned to assess and evaluate the goals themselves, and not just the means of achieving the goals – seemed to be in question. The educational theorist Richard Pring used the metaphor of the habit of critical conversation – a process without a clear or easily measurable outcome – to characterize true education; an education of the sort which would produce creativity and integrity in business as much as in the practice of citizenship.[21] Such a notion has been in continual tension with more functional and vocational emphases.

At the same time, governments and educationalists have reflected on the specific role of religious education in schools in the development of ideas of value. Compulsory RE (a legal requirement from 1944) has retained its place in the curriculum over this period, while there has been a great variety of conceptions of what it should involve and of whether/how it should be defended. Ashley Rogers Berner argues in her essay that the embedding of child-centred educational psychology already in the interwar period, linked to a more general loss of confidence in the metaphysical ambitions of education, helped to contribute to an internal secularization of post-war religious education. However, her case study draws attention to an important recurring theme in this book – that of shifting generations and their roles in the transmission of values and ideas. In the field of education this is obviously especially pertinent: those who were teaching in the post-war decades had been trained in the 1920s and 1930s. She concludes by pointing to some current signs of reaction away from the predominant trend which she had identified for the earlier post-war period, analogous to those which we have noted in other contexts. The attempt at moral and religious neutrality in RE in schools in the 1970s gave way to the attempt of the 1988 Education Reform Act to reinforce the religious education and worship provisions of the 1944 Education Act.[22] Although this section of the 1988 Act was controversially pushed in a more explicitly Christian direction than had originally been intended, it dovetailed with the overall Thatcherite project to reinforce Christian values at the level of personal morality. As Terence Copley has argued, the injunction to the re-articulation of a broadly Christian value system, and even broadly Christian worship in schools, while confused and difficult to implement with any integrity in a multi-faith and multi-cultural context, did refocus critical attention on the role of education in the cultivation of spirituality and moral values. But, in analysing (and contributing to) the debates as they have developed since, he has pointed to the problems involved in aiming at a lowest-common-denominator consensus – an abstracted and vague concept of spirituality which has no demonstrable roots in particular (diverse) traditions – either religious or non-religious.[23] This issue looks set to become more sharply focused in the context of growing controversy about faith schools, and whether they contribute to a society of plural monoculturalism rather than a fully integrated multicultural society.[24] As Copley and others have argued, a much more sophisticated understanding of the significance of religious belief in contemporary society needs to underpin what has been termed 'positive pluralism', as opposed to negative pluralism which either leaves religion out of education or confines religious teaching to separate faith groups.[25] At the time of writing, this issue has become unhelpfully polarized as a result of a widespread paranoia about the perils of religious indoctrination. It is not going to be seen clearly through such a reductive and simplifying lens. At the same time, rising numbers of secondary school pupils are opting to take RE courses at GCSE and A-Level, a marked shift from the situation 20 or 30 years ago.[26] This could have real implications at least for the religious literacy of the next generation.

The Parekh Report on *The Future of Multi-Ethnic Britain* (2000) outlined two sets of values that all people in Britain could be expected to hold – procedural values which 'maintain the basic preconditions for democratic dialogue', and substantive values underpinning 'any defensible conception of the good life'. Substantive values were held to include the equal moral worth of all, and the freedom of all to plan their own lives and lead fulfilling lives (within a framework of international human rights). Procedural values included 'people's willingness to give reasons for their views, readiness to be influenced by better arguments than their own, tolerance, mutual respect, aspiration to peaceful resolution of differences, and willingness to abide by collectively binding decisions that have been reached by the agreed procedures'.[27] This latter definition has clear affinities with a Habermasian idea of consensus rooted in rule-based dialogue, relying on the mutual recognition of the plausibility of different truth claims, and begs the same questions that Habermas begs about the basis of motivation, and about how to deal with narratives that are not in harmony with each other. Procedural approaches can avoid confronting those definitions of the content and destination of the good life that actually inspire people. In an Aristotelian idiom, Mark Young has recently observed that in ordinary life nobody works from an impartial view, and that it is not so much overlapping consensus which serves as a surrogate for Truth, as the notion of an 'enlarged self' – a 'deliberating being enriched by conversation and conflicts'.[28] The Christian theologian Nicholas Adams has developed an analogous critique of Habermas's combination, on the one hand, of respect for traditions for their ability to reinforce identities, and on the other of the reserving of rational authority and real agreement to a procedural ethics stripped of all particular notions of the good. He points out that no Christian or committed believer in any other religious tradition could subscribe to this. He puts forward the specific practice of scriptural reasoning – the mutual discussion between members of different faiths of key texts in each religious tradition – as a model for a practice of deep reasoning which can conduce to friendship and mutual understanding. 'Scriptural reasoning models the discovery that making deep reasoning public is not only risky – because one makes oneself vulnerable when revealing what one loves – but time-consuming. It is a non-hasty practice, and is thus a kind of beacon in our "time-poor" world.'[29]

To generalize from this discussion, a context is required within which the virtue of tolerance itself is carefully defined. Tolerance must mean a quality both positive and engaged – rather than a live-and-let-live indifference. As Nigel Biggar has emphasized, a tolerance which is engaged and cares will take the trouble to investigate differences, while also caring for truth.[30] Where in the past tolerance was opposed as a positive liberal value to dogmatism or normative authoritarianism, which frequently took a religious form, the positive role of religious belief in modern liberal British society now demands to be taken seriously. The educational sphere is one important context in which this is beginning to happen, but there needs to be much clearer-headed thinking in public debate about it. It has been pointed out that if productive dialogue is to develop, it requires the reaffirmation of a set of complementary virtues: humility (both personal and epistemological), vulnerability, honesty, trust and generosity.[31] These virtues underpin mutuality and friendship, while they are also sensitive to what has been termed the 'hermeneutics of the strange' – the recognition of difference as well as closeness, of what can and must, and what cannot and need not be shared.[32] Again, these virtues are not necessarily religious in their foundation; religious believers have no monopoly of value. But Christians, along with other religious groups, have a long tradition of thinking about values, and the fact that many values are shared across traditions, both faith and non-faith, perhaps paradoxically enhances the perceived public relevance of religious contributions to moral debate. Christian identity, like that of other religious and cultural traditions, has always developed in a dialectical process of change and preservation through interaction with other traditions, religious and secular.

Notes

1 *The Good Life*, 1998, London: Demos Collection issue 14, p. 4.

2 *The Good Life*, pp. 3 and 8.

3 In 1997, Channel 4 showed a 6–part series called *The Feel Good Factor*, published as *A Citizens' Handbook for Improving your Quality of Life*, London: Channel 4 and focusing on crime, education, the environment, health, leisure and transport. See also Avner Offer, 1996, *In Pursuit of the Quality of Life*, Oxford: Oxford University Press.

4 *Citizens' Handbook*, p. 30.

5 Robert Lane, 1996, 'Quality of Life and Quality of Persons: A New Rule for Government?', in Offer (ed.), *Quality of Life*, pp. 256–93.

6 Martha Nussbaum and Amartya Sen, (eds), 1993, *Quality of Life*, Oxford: Clarendon Press.

7 Amartya Sen, 1990, 'Development as Capability Expansion', in Keith Griffin and John Knight (eds), *Human Development and the International Development Strategy for the 1990s*, London: Macmillan, cited in S. Alkire and R. Black, 'A Practical Reasoning Theory of Development Ethics: Furthering the Capabilities Approach, *Journal of International Development*, Vol. 9(2) (1997), p. 263.

8 World Bank, 1996, *Ethics and Spiritual Values: Promoting Environmentally Sustainable Development*, p. 1, cited in Alkire and Black, 'Practical Reasoning', p. 263.

9 See, for example, Roger Crisp (ed), 1996, *How Should One Live? Essays on the Virtues*, Oxford: Clarendon Press; Roger Crisp and Michael Slote (eds), 1997, *Virtue Ethics*, Oxford: Clarendon Press; Christopher Cowton and Roger Crisp (eds), *Business Ethics: Perspectives on the Practice of Theory*, Oxford: Clarendon Press; Nigel Biggar, 1997, *Good Life: Reflections on What We Value Today*, London: SPCK; Robert Gascoigne, 2001, *The Public Forum and Christian Ethics*, Cambridge; Cambridge University Press; David Fergusson, 1998, *Community*; David Fergusson, 2004, *Church, State and Civil Society*, Cambridge: Cambridge University Press; Rebecca Todd Peters, 2004, *In Search of the Good Life: The Ethics of Globalization*, New York and London: Continuum; Herbert McCabe, 2005, *The Good Life: Ethics and the Pursuit of Happiness*, London: Continuum.

10 L. S. Cahill, 2000, 'Grisez on Sex and Gender: A Feminist Theological Perspective', in Nigel Biggar and Rufus Black (eds), *The Revival of Natural Law: Philosophical, Theological and Ethical Responses to the Finnis-Grisez School*, Aldershot: Ashgate, pp. 242–61, at p. 243.

11 Gascoigne, *Public Forum*, pp. 153–5, citing *inter alia* Andrew Shanks, 1995, *Civil Society, Civil Religion*, Oxford: Blackwell, as part of a critique of John Milbank.

12 Gascoigne, *Public Forum*, p. 167.

13 *Sunday Times*, 7 May 1988, cited in Paul Heelas and Paul Morris (eds), 1992, *The*

Values of the Enterprise Culture: The Moral Debate, London and New York: Routledge, p. 7.

14 David Nicholls, 1992, 'The Invisible Hand. Providence and the Market', in Heelas and Morris, *Enterprise Culture*, p. 232.

15 *Daily Telegraph*, 25 May 1988 and Radio 4, quoted in *Daily Telegraph*, 4 April 1988, cited in Heelas and Morris, *Enterprise Culture*, pp. 11–12.

16 See, e.g., Brian Griffiths, 1982, *Morality and the Market Place: Christian Alternatives to Capitalism and Socialism; London Lectures in Contemporary Christianity*, London: Hodder & Stoughton.

17 Brian Griffiths, 2001, 'The Business Corporation as a Moral Community', in R. A. Sirico, N. Barry, F. Field, *Capitalism, Morality and Markets*, London: Institute of Economic Affairs, pp. 17–40.

18 G. Mulgan, 1998, 'Timeless Values', *Good Life*, pp. 99–104.

19 See, e.g., Donald Hay and Alan Kreider (eds), 2001, *Christianity and the Culture of Economics*, Cardiff: University of Wales Press; Donald Hay, 1989, *Economics Today: A Christian Critique*, Leicester: Apollos; M. Hirschfeld, 'Standard of Living and Economic Virtue: Forging a Link between St Thomas Aquinas and the Twenty-First Century', *Journal of the Society of Christian Ethics*, Vol. 26(1) (2006), 61–77.

20 Marcus Braybrooke and Kamran Mofid, 2005, *Promoting the Common Good: Bringing Economics and Theology Together Again*, London: Shepheard-Walwyn.

21 R. Pring, 1998, 'Education and Business', in Cowton and Crisp, *Business Ethics*, p. 172.

22 Edwin Cox and Josephine M. Cairns, 1989, *Reforming Religious Education: The Religious Clauses of the 1988 Education Reform Act*, London: Kogan Page.

23 Terence Copley, 2000, *Spiritual Development in the State School*, Exeter: University of Exeter Press, pp. 88–107.

24 See Amartya K. Sen, 2006, *Identity and Violence. The Illusion of Destiny*, London: Allen Lane, for this argument.

25 Copley, *Spiritual Development*; Terence Copley, 2005, *Indoctrination, Education and God: The Struggle for the Mind*, London: SPCK; R. Jackson, 2004, *Rethinking Religious Education and Plurality: Issues in Diversity and Pedagogy*, Abingdon: RoutledgeFalmer, p. 166, citing D. Cush, 1999, 'Models of Religious Education in a Plural Society: Looking to the Future', in I. Borowik (ed), *Church-State Relations in Central and Eastern Europe*, Krakow: Nomos, p. 384.

26 http://www.cofe.anglican_org/news/pr8706.html – accessed 24.08.06, on the 7.5% rise in the number of students taking GCSE in RE in the summer of 2006, which was being used by the Church of England to press for the inclusion of RE in the Government's proposed 14–19 framework.

27 Runnymede Trust, 2000, *The Future of Multi-Ethnic Britain: The Parekh Report*, London: Profile Books, par. 4.30:53, p. 54.

28 Mark A. Young, 2005, *Negotiating the Good Life: Aristotle and Civil Society*, Aldershot: Ashgate, pp. 178–81.

29 Nicholas Adams, 2006, *Habermas and Theology*, Cambridge: Cambridge University Press, pp. 225–26, 242

30 Biggar, *Good Life*, pp. 84–92.

31 Biggar, *Good Life*, p. 100; cf. David Hollenbach, SJ (2003), *The Global Face of Public Faith: Politics, Human Rights, and Christian Ethics*, Washington DC: Georgetown University Press, pp. 43–9.

32 S. Bergmann, 'Transculturality and Tradition – Renewing the Continuous in Late Modernity', *Studia Theologica* 58 (2004), p. 144.

Case Studies

Ambivalence over Virtue
  Harriet Harris

Is English Education Secular?
  Ashley Rogers Berner

Christianity and Economics: The Conversation in Zacchaeus'
House
  Rufus Black

CASE STUDY

Ambivalence over Virtue

HARRIET HARRIS

The promotion and demotion of virtue

Despite the renaissance in virtue ethics among moral philosophers since the late 1950s, and a burgeoning interest in virtue epistemology,[1] 'virtue' remains an old-fashioned, barely-used concept in public discourse, and a surprisingly under-represented concept in twentieth- and twenty-first-century theology. Christian theologians appear ambivalent about virtue. This may seem odd, given the potential of Christianity to foster virtue, and the efforts of some current theologians to do just that. After all, if being trained in virtue is like learning the skills for practising a craft, or for making and appreciating good music or art, or becoming aware of how to eat health-ily, then Christianity can provide teaching, practices and disciplines, mentors and communities in which to be so trained.

Virtuous living is learned by being practised. It is nurtured, or fails to be nurtured, in the communities and institutions that shape our lives, especially families, schools, churches and other religious institutions, colleges, places of work, community groups, and political and charitable organizations. To enhance the potential of institutions to form people in accordance with virtue, Christian educationalists draw on the classical understanding of *paideia* (education).[2] *Paideia* for Plato and Aristotle meant being educated to be good at being human; in other words, being educated to acquire the virtues. For virtue to be fostered, this concept of education must not be totally eclipsed by *Wissenschaft*, critical enquiry, which tests claims to authority and truth by means of reason and empirical experimentation. Critical enquiry is often treated as an end in itself so that it is hard to see how it serves a richer process. The concept of *paideia*, which is a matter of con-sciously attempting to develop people's character, only occasionally overlaps with public educational aims,[3] such as the training in citizenship, or in the management of one's finances, that schools are called on to provide, or when schools are encouraged to work alongside family nurturing programmes to promote healthy personal and interpersonal development. We expect schools and families to try to shape people for the good, but this expectation sits within a 'predominant ideology . . . that it is no business of society to try to interfere with or influence anybody's morals', because morality is a matter of individual conscience.[4] We live with societal anxiety about public prescriptiveness.

Christian moral theologians and philosophers, notably Stanley Hauerwas, Alasdair MacIntyre and Herbert McCabe, have promoted virtue morality as the way to address what MacIntyre diagnoses as a confusion of moral language and a lack of a coherent moral community in Anglo-American society.[5] Given such concerted efforts by certain Christian thinkers to shape public morality in accordance with virtue, it may indeed appear strange to posit theological ambivalence over virtue.

Yet, although virtue has been discussed, it has not been interrogated. Even the seven virtues of medieval Christian tradition, which emerged from Aquinas's attempt to integrate the natural virtues of antiquity – wisdom, fortitude, temperance and justice – with the 'theological' virtues of faith, hope and love, receive almost no discussion in present-day theological works. Nor do the accompanying vices, the seven deadly sins, despite their becoming a focus of popular interest.[6] A number of theological interests consonant with virtue morality have developed in recent decades, including explorations of narrative in relation to personal and communal development, and emphases upon community, theology in practice, and worship as shaping our moral selves. There is also lively theological consideration of wisdom, in conjunction with the exploration of the Wisdom tradition in Scripture, and of associations of Wisdom with the Second or Third Person of the Trinity. But, interest in wisdom aside, mention of particular virtues and exploration of their qualities are wanting even in the work of most Christian virtue theorists, who concentrate precisely on theory (metaethics and methodology) or, ironically, organize their discussions around moral issues rather than around moral character.

MacIntyre and McCabe extol the benefits of virtue theory. Hauerwas has devoted much attention to promoting pacifism, and therefore to the quality of Christian life that lends itself to non-violence. His work is intimately bound up with consideration of character. Nonetheless, he presents his work around issues, including the preoccupations of sexual ethics – abortion and homosexuality – that dominate politicized moral debate in the US. There is a corresponding lack of effort to trace the nurture, characteristics and fruit of such virtues as fortitude or hope in people's lives, and their impact within communities. This is significant, because the exploration of particular virtues is the essence and substance of virtue morality. Moreover, the moral philosopher Elizabeth Anscombe promoted virtue theory partly because she judged concepts such as just, courageous or truthful to be conceptually rich,[7] or 'thick' as Bernard Williams later put it, in comparison to the 'thin' primary notions of modern moral discourse: right, wrong, duty and obligation. If an advantage of virtue theory is that it gives us richer moral concepts, we would expect virtue theorists to explore those concepts by means of exploring the virtues.

This situation in theological discussion, where virtue theory may feature quite highly, but not the unpacking of particular virtues, is the reverse of the situation in public discourse. There is public interest in some particular virtues, even though the language of virtue is not back in fashion.[8] The virtue of integrity greatly exercises people today – perhaps because an interest in integrity is related to quests for authenticity and holism. Integrity involves being true to all aspects of oneself, including one's moral values and evaluations. It is intimately related to virtue, because it concerns achieving whole moral personhood. Integrity has received much attention from philosophers since the 1950s, because of a concern that modern moral theories that urge us to act either according to duty or for the optimum outcome, lead us to sacrifice our deeply held commitments and values.[9] But despite philosophical and popular interest in this virtue, it is not much discussed by theologians, with the exception of Ramsey.[10]

Some of the traditional virtues are also of public concern. Justice remains a priority for our culture. It is a major focus of liberation theologians, in addressing systemic social injustice, but gaps have yet to be bridged with virtue theorists in investigating the nature of just character. Prudence is back on the socio-political agenda, due to concerns over spiralling debt amongst the under-35s in Britain. Schools are encouraged to teach 'personal finance' in a sufficiently practical and sustained way as to inform people's behaviour, and not just their mathematical understanding. Love is continually extolled in secular and Christian discourse, though in ways that lack content, rather along the lines of the Beatles song 'All you need is love'. Without theological exploration of the shape of love in Christian discipleship, in terms of the costliness of the cross, theologians are not helping to address the vagueness of our concept of love, which has 'lost its power of discrimination' so that we can convince ourselves that it is loving even to tolerate violence.[11]

Christianity as detrimental to virtue?

Elizabeth Anscombe, who has been integral to the twentieth-century renaissance of virtue ethics, regards the Christian emphasis on duty and law as critical in undermining virtue. According to Anscombe's analysis, virtue theory acquired a legalistic bent through the influence of Christianity, which eventually undercut it. Both Anscombe's analysis and that of Hauerwas[12] and MacIntyre,[13] rest on an Aristotelian, teleological account of virtue.[14] According to this account, all things have a *telos*, an end, purpose or goal. Identifying the *telos* of something enables us to understand what makes that thing good. The *telos* of an eye is to enable a creature to see. An eye that enables its creature to see well is a 'good eye', a concept which, in this case, we can understand both biologically and aesthetically. Moreover, that which contributes to the eye performing its function well, such as good diet, sufficient rest, and training in what to look for, is good for the eye.

Anscombe points out that notions at the heart of an Aristotelian teleology, concerning what 'should' or 'ought' to be done, can be held in ways that do not imply obligation in law. For example, an engine ought to be oiled because then it can function well; it is bad for an engine to run without oil. But Christianity, bringing with it a law conception of ethics from the Torah, instilled in us notions of guilt and unlawfulness, with the implication that conformity to the virtues is required by divine law.[15] It is rather like the difference between regarding cream cakes as bad for you insofar as they may clog up your arteries, and regarding them as 'naughty', in the sense that you would be guilty if you ate them. Failure to conform to the virtues came to be seen as a matter of being 'bad' – not in the sense of doing something bad for you, in that you impede your well-being and do not function according to your purpose – but in the sense that you are contravening divine law and are therefore guilty. This changed the profile of virtue ethics, and sowed seeds that would undermine it.

An account of the development of Christian moral traditions is missing from Anscombe's thesis. She makes no mention of patristic, medieval or Roman Catholic developments, although many scholars writing in these areas would agree with her that in the development of Christian moral thinking, law has compromised virtue.[16] Hers is more of a linguistic analysis. She focuses on the shift in language: from Aristotle, 'who has terms like "disgraceful", "impious" . . . [and] "unjust"; but no term corresponding to "illicit"; to Christian preoccupation with "sin", "guilt" and what is "illicit" or "unlawful"'.[17] She mentions briefly the Protestant Reformers, who re-interpreted the existence of divine law, seeing it not as something to be obeyed, but as something given to humanity to reveal our inability to obey it. This underlay the Protestant emphasis on our need for Christ's atoning work. At the same time, the Protestant impulse was to place greater emphasis on duty. Within this context, the quest for 'happiness', or beatitude, which characterized Thomist moral theology, could be made to seem inappropriate and unworthy.[18] Luther saw in both Aristotle and Aquinas a tendency towards narcissism, insofar as the intentionality of subjects is directed towards their own self-realisation.[19] Kant held that what he derisorily called 'happiness theory' (*Glückseligkeitslehre*) leads to egoism as it places the determining principle of action in the individual's desire. He sought to counter this danger by developing a duty-based ethic, according to which the agent chooses maxims that conform to universal moral law, and is thereby able to disregard inclinations or thought of personal happiness.

Virtue in coherence with law

Trends that favour emphases on law and duty have been detrimental to virtue morality, and always carry the potential to undermine it, but the matter is more complex than Anscombe's analysis might lead us to believe. It is not the case that Kant strongly opposed duty to virtue, nor, as MacIntyre implies, that Kantian ethics disregard virtue.[20] Out of concern not to undermine true virtue, Kant ceased linking the practice of virtue to a rewarding happiness. Moreover, major strands of Christian tradition that promote virtue do not envision something more legalistic than Anscombe's own ideal. For example, the *Catechism of the Catholic Church* quotes Gregory of Nyssa in its teaching on virtue: 'The goal of a virtuous life is to become like God.'[21] Significantly, Gregory did not say that the goal is to please God by obeying God's will.

Consideration of the ways in which Augustine and Aquinas drew upon and modified Greek conceptions of virtue is significant. For example, Augustine proposed that the four-fold division of the virtues posited by the Greeks could rightly be understood only as forms of love whose object is God.[22] For Augustine and Christian virtue traditions, acting out of a sense of lawfulness or duty is second-best. If a person does what is virtuous out of a sense of duty, rather than for the sake of loving the good itself, which is ultimately a matter of loving God, he or she has not been educated adequately in virtue.[23] The cardinal virtues can be understood in this light:

> Temperance is love keeping itself entire and incorrupt for God; fortitude is love bearing everything readily for the sake of God; justice is love serving God only, and therefore ruling well all else, as subject to man; prudence is love making a right distinction between what helps it towards God and what might hinder it.[24]

It may seem to support Anscombe's analysis that, since she wrote her essay, there has been a revival of interest in Aquinas's ethics in which scholars have tended to formulate his ethics as either a theory of virtue or a theory of natural law. They debate whether Aquinas emphasized action in accordance with the intellectual virtue of *prudentia* and with moral virtues, or action in accordance with right principles.[25] But this debate polarizes matters unnecessarily. Even to the extent that Aquinas promotes a natural law tradition, he does not model the moral life primarily on an analogy with law, but on a life sustained by fidelity and grace. It is instructive to see how he draws on Augustine to make this point:

> There is a twofold element in the Law of the Gospel. There is the chief element, namely, the grace of the Holy Ghost bestowed inwardly. And as to this, the New Law justifies. Hence Augustine says: 'There (that is, in the

Old Testament) the Law was set forth in an outward fashion, that the ungodly might be afraid; here (that is, in the New Testament) it is given in an inward manner, that they might be justified.' The other element of the Evangelical Law is secondary; namely, the teachings of faith, and those commandments which direct human affections and human actions. And as to this, the New Law does not justify. Hence the Apostle says: 'The letter killeth, but the spirit quickeneth' (2 Cor. 3.6), and Augustine explains this by saying that the letter denotes any writing that is external to man, even that of the moral precepts such as are contained in the Gospel. Therefore the letter, even of the Gospel, would kill, unless there were the inward presence of the healing grace of faith.[26]

The necessity of grace

Aquinas is here discussing Law not in relation to virtue, but in relation to grace. Grace is the divine, enabling, transforming presence that can shape us in conformity to God's will. All Christian theology must make room for grace, and understand both law and virtue in relation to it.[27] As Anscombe identified, an emphasis on grace can cause virtue to fall from favour. The concept of virtues as 'acquired by human effort', implicit within parts of the *Catechism of the Catholic Church*,[28] runs counter to the Reformed emphasis on our fallen condition and need for special grace, and one might expect a discussion of virtue to polarize Reformed and Catholic positions. However, the necessity of grace concerns our need for transformation, and our transformation is the subject of virtue morality. Therefore, when law is understood in relation to grace, the way is opened rather than closed for the development of virtue morality. This can be illustrated from within the Reformed tradition.

The Reformed theologian Serene Jones does not explicitly write about virtue, but her theology of excellence and freedom, understood in terms of performing and being performed by grace, contains the same essential insights as virtue traditions, regarding the ways that we embody practices and are shaped by them. Jones shares with virtue theorists the essential concern with how selves are formed. She follows J. L. Austin and Judith Butler in theorizing how human beings become 'certain types of persons by learning to perform the often unconscious but socially constructed scripts of personhood embedded in the language and cultures in which they live'.[29] *Paideia* takes place through performance. She uses the image of sanctification to explore the shape this can take in a Christian context: 'practices are the things that Christians do as their lives are conformed to the patterns of living that embody God's will, patterns embedded in the Law and manifest in the life of Christ, patterns of holiness – *sanctus*'.[30] Following the law becomes a matter of joy and freedom, rather than an expression of a duty not to fall into sin. In this respect, her Calvinist theology is not far removed from the Catholic *Catechism*'s position that the 'virtuous man is he who freely practises the good'.[31] Her work suggests a compatibility of virtue morality with both grace and an understanding of law as that which is freely and joyfully lived out by those who are transformed by grace.

Colin Gunton, also from the Reformed tradition, shares Jones's emphasis on grace, yet is heavily suspicious of 'historically and morally implausible claims that the Church is a community of character and focus for training in virtue'.[32] He is wary of virtue morality in its potential to be inward looking and self-regarding; the worry that leads theologians to remind us of our duty to love God and neighbour. Gunton emphasizes that God alone can turn our focus outwards, away from self-preoccupation, to being conformed to the image of God in Christ – from whence love of neighbour flows. He stresses that moral goodness comes as a gift, and is not something we attain by ourselves. But within this framework, he understands worship, which is also a gift from God, as the primary, communal act of the Church, which serves the cause of virtue by morally shaping the community.[33] This economy resides in the gift of the freedom Christ has won for us.

Gunton's position is evidence that even where Reformed theologians manifest the concerns about virtue that Anscombe expects, the potential of law and duty to undermine virtue ethics is removed once law is understood as that which, by the transforming power of grace, we are free to enjoy. As Augustine put it: to live virtuously is to have become free to 'love and do as you will' (*In Epist. Joann Tractatus*, vii, 8). Moreover, Gunton has been persuaded by Hauerwas to reflect upon the processes of our moral formation. As a Reformed theologian, he focuses on the Word and sacraments as the two constitutive features of the Church's worship, and therefore its mode of shaping its people.[34] Theologians of other traditions write about the transforming power of disciplined prayer,[35] or ritual,[36] or liturgy and the Eucharist,[37] or the richness of our daily communal living.[38] Some, notably Hauerwas and Colwell, have become more worship- and specifically Eucharist-focused as their awareness of the forming power of practices has grown.

Theological reticence and public discourse

The work of these diverse theologians show that developments consonant with virtue morality are currently gaining interest in various theological quarters. Yet, it remains the case that exploration of particular virtues is still almost entirely absent from theological reflection. By contrast, virtue epistemologists, such as Linda Zagzebski, make exploration of the quality of intellectual and other virtues central to their task. Just as virtue ethicists reject act-based moral theories, which assess the rightness or wrongness of particular acts, virtue epistemologists reject belief-based epistemological theories, which evaluate the justified or unjustified nature of beliefs. Belief-based theories make epistemic duty – such as one's duty to know the grounds of justification for one's beliefs – the primary normative concept, just as act-based moral theories make doing right or wrong the primary normative concept. Zagzebski broadens the notion of epistemic impropriety to include being narrow-minded, careless, intellectually cowardly or prejudiced.[39] Zagzebski's consideration of wisdom, open-mindedness, faith, hope, humility, justice, trustworthiness, carefulness and benevolence, forms much of the substance of her rich inquiry into the foundations of knowledge. The Aquinas scholar and moral theologian Jean Porter is similarly refreshing for her study of gentleness in *The Recovery of Virtue*, and thereby for moving Christian moral thinking away from a focus on methodology, meta-ethics or particular social issues, and towards a substantive study of character.

Fuller theological exploration of virtue now seems timely, especially given the level of popular interest in the matters to which virtue pertains: happiness, well-being and the good life.[40] The question of how we should live in order to be happy is a live one, spawning a new science of happiness, practised not only by psychologists,[41] but by economists, social policy makers,[42] and self-help gurus.[43] There seems to be general agreement that riches and the ability to consume do not make us happy, despite our vulnerability to the marketing of moneyed and consumerist lifestyles. Happiness studies also agree that helping others, feeling part of something larger than oneself and belonging within a community, including a religious belief system, are conducive to happiness. So concern for one's own happiness or well-being is situated in the context of concern for the happiness of others, which has at least the potential to connect with theological anxieties about the extent to which motivation within virtue morality is towards self-realization. Current interest in theories of happiness should be an encouragement to virtue theologians to flesh out their thinking with substantive examples of character formation. Since virtue morality is concerned with personal development and personal freedom, and promotes integrity insofar as it pertains to all aspects of a person's life, it speaks to precisely those areas of concern that are the focus of happiness studies.

Moreover, virtue morality expresses ways in which we can care for ourselves by caring for others, or vice versa, and being able to hold these two together could aid us in our social awkwardness about public morality. We worry, in our society, about the extent to which morality has become a matter of individual conscience, with journalists and commentators articulating anxiety about the decline of duty and the increased selfishness of society.[44] For example, it is pointed out in numerous media and philosophical debates over human rights, that we are too quick to claim our rights and too slow to recognize our duties and responsibilities.[45] Moreover, we are grateful to have people towards whom we have duties: dependents, if we have them, others within institutions, if we are plugged into institutions. People are cast adrift when they have no such relational ties, and this is a concern relating to social patterns and policies that effect or increase the isolation of individuals. However, we flinch whenever a duty is implied, such as when the Bishop of London proposed in 2006 that it is a sin to fly around the world as a luxury when this is detrimental to the earth's ability to sustain itself. We flinch even when a duty is not necessarily implied but we suspect that it might have been, such as in the sensitive debate over whether women who are classified as obese should receive NHS-funded fertility treatment. This is primarily a debate about economic resources and the giving of treatment to people in whom there is a higher risk of the treatment failing, but there is social anxiety about an implied duty to lose weight.

These mixed feelings regarding duty suggest that as a society we are looking for a stronger sense of common morality, but do not warm to legalistic or prohibitive approaches. Evidently we do warm to the plethora of parenting programmes, such as those developed by Family Nurturing Network and Family Links, as well as the hugely popular television broadcasts, *Supernanny*, *Little Angels*, *Teen Tamer*, and others, which give guidance over how to promote healthy relationships at home and beyond. They are explicitly concerned with the nurture and transmission of certain types of behaviour, and are unashamedly prescriptive, but they do not use the language of duty. They are not morally uncontested,[46] but in a society wary of public prescriptiveness, they have a remarkably high consumer rate. Their message is that by constancy in implementing clear responses to good or bad behaviour, the contemporary modulations of *paideia*, parents can gain greater control and thereby greater freedom for themselves and their family to enjoy life. Their popularity may stem from our tendency, like the Victorians, to prize the family as a haven in a heartless world.[47] But these programmes reveal all that is dysfunctional in family life, in order to try to make it more functional. Their approach is not theological, or even teleological, but they successfully engage the population in the quest for how to live.

Their popularity may suggest that placing prescriptions into an account of human well-being, as virtue morality does, alleviates some of the anxiety about public morality. If so, this should be an encouragement to Christian theologians further to develop the virtue tradition for our times. In responding to Anscombe's challenge to Christianity, we can see how even law and duty can cohere with virtue in an economy of grace. In Christian theology at present, there is a significant renaissance in virtue theory and a growing interest in the transforming power of practices. Still, there is a dearth of attention to any virtues themselves, which leaves a gap, ready to be creatively filled, in contemporary Christian efforts to foster virtue.

Notes

1 Virtue epistemology explores how the development of intellectual and moral virtues bears on the development of understanding. See Abrol Fairweather and Linda Zagzebski (eds), 2001, *Virtue Epistemology: Essays on Epistemic Virtue and Responsibility*, Oxford: Oxford University Press.

2 Peter C. Hodgson, 1999, *God's Wisdom: Toward a Theology of Education*, Louisville, KY: Westminster John Knox; McCabe, *Good Life*.

3 McCabe, *Good Life*, p. 9.

4 McCabe, *Good Life*, pp. 9–10.

5 Alasdair MacIntyre, 1981, *After Virtue: A Study in Moral Theory*, London: Duckworth.

6 The ESRC used the seven deadly sins 'as a way of looking at some pressing issues of modern life: religious conflict, rage in kids and adults, sexual behaviour, corporate greed, binge drinking, rising personal debt and political apathy', www.esrcsocietytoday.ac.uk/ ESRCInfoCentre/PO/releases/2005/June – accessed 31.08.06. Oxford University Press has published a series of short books by well-known philosophers on the seven deadly sins. See Simon Blackburn, 2004, *Lust: The Seven Deadly Sins*, Oxford: Oxford University Press.

7 G. E. M. Anscombe, [1958] 1997, 'Modern Moral Philosophy', reprinted in Crisp and Slote, *Virtue Ethics*, pp. 26–44.

8 For a reactionary assessment of the relativizing effects of the language of 'values' replacing the term 'virtue' in our moral discourse, see Gertrude Himmelfarb, 1995, *The De-Moralizing of Society: From Victorian Virtues to Modern Values*, London: IEA Health and Welfare Unit.

9 Gabriele Taylor, 1985, *Pride, Guilt and Shame: Emotions for Self-Assessment*, Oxford: Clarendon Press; Bernard Williams, 1973, *Utilitarianism: For and Against*, New York: Cambridge University Press and *Problems of the Self*, New York: Cambridge University Press; Bernard Williams, 1981, *Moral Luck*, New York: Cambridge University Press; Michael Stocker, 'The Schizophrenia of Modern Ethical Theories', *Journal of Philosophy*, 73 (1976), 453–66.

10 Hayden Ramsey, 1997, *Beyond Virtue: Integrity and Morality*, Basingstoke: Macmillan.

11 Richard B. Hays, 1996, *The Moral Vision of the New Testament: Community, Cross, New Creation: A Contemporary Introduction to New Testament Ethics*, Edinburgh: T&T Clark, p. 202; cf. Stanley Hauerwas, 1981, *Vision and Virtue: Essays in Christian Ethical Reflection*, Notre Dame: University of Notre Dame Press, p. 124.

12 Stanley Hauerwas, 1985, *Character and the Christian Life: A Study in Theological Ethics*, 2nd edn, San Antonio: Trinity University Press.

13 Alasdair MacIntyre, 1988, *Whose Justice? Which Rationality?* London: Duckworth; 1990, *Three Rival Versions of Moral Enquiry*, London: Duckworth.

14 Edmund Pincoffs, 1986, *Quandaries and Virtues*, Lawrence: University of Kansas Press. For examples of non-teleological accounts of virtues and human goods, see Martha C. Nussbaum, 2000, *Women and Human Development: The Capabilities Approach*, Cambridge: Cambridge University Press.

15 Anscombe, 'Modern Moral Philosophy', pp. 31–2.

16 Jerome B. Schneewind, 1997, 'The Misfortunes of Virtue', in Crisp and Slote, *Virtue Ethics*, pp. 180–2; Fergus Kerr, 2002, *After Aquinas: Versions of Thomism*, Oxford: Blackwell, pp. 130–1; Romanus Cessario OP, 1991, *The Moral Virtues and Theological Ethics*, Notre Dame: University of Notre Dame Press, p. 3; Charles C. Curran, 2002, *Catholic Social Teaching 1891 – Present: A Historical, Theological and Ethical Analysis*, Washington DC: Georgetown University Press, p. 3; John Berkman and Michael

Cartwright (eds), *The Hauerwas Reader*, Durham and London: Duke University Press, pp. 39–40.

17 Anscombe, 'Modern Moral Philosophy', pp. 30–1.

18 Roger Guidon, 1956, *Béatitude et théologie morale chez saint Thomas d'Aquin: origines – interpretation*, Ottawa: Editions de l'Univeristé d'Ottawa; Kerr, *After Aquinas*, pp. 130–1.

19 Colin Gunton, 2000, 'The Church as a School of Virtue: Human Formation in a Trinitarian Framework', in Mark Theissen Nation and Samuel Wells (eds), *Faithfulness and Fortitude: In Conversation with the Theological Ethics of Stanley Hauerwas*, Edinburgh: T&T Clark, pp. 211–31.

20 MacIntyre, *After Virtue*, pp. 43–7. Contra MacIntyre, see Onora O'Neill, 1989, *Constructions of Reason: Exploring Kant's Practical Philosophy*, Cambridge: Cambridge University Press and 1996, 'Kant's Virtues', in Roger Crisp, 1996, *How Should One Live? Essays on the Virtues*, Oxford: Clarendon Press; John D. O'Connor OP, 'Are Virtue Ethics and Kantian Ethics Really so Very Different?', *New Blackfriars*, 87(2006), 238–52 and Robert B. Louden, 1997, 'Kant's Virtue ethics', in Daniel Statman (ed.), *Virtue Ethics: A Critical Reader*, Edinburgh: Edinburgh University Press.

21 *De beatitudinibus* I: Migne, *Patrologia Graeca*, 44, 1200D, *Catechism of the Catholic Church*, 1999, revised edn, London: Geoffrey Chapman, para. 1803.

22 Augustine, 1955, 'On the Morals of the Catholic Church', in Waldo Beach and H. Richard Niebuhr (eds), *Christian Ethics: Sources of the Living Tradition*, New York: Ronald Press, pp. 110–18.

23 Cf. McCabe, *The Good Life*, pp. 44–51.

24 Augustine, 'On the Morals', p. 115.

25 John Casey, 1990, *Pagan Virtue*, Oxford: Oxford University Press; John Finnis, 1991, *Moral Absolutes: Tradition, Revision and Truth*, Washington, DC: Georgetown University Press; MacIntyre, *After Virtue: Three Rival Versions*; Jean Porter, 1990, *The Recovery of Virtue*, London: SPCK.

26 Thomas Aquinas, 1946, *Summa Theologica*, trans. Fathers of the English Dominican Province, New York: Benzinger Brothers, I-II.106.2

27 Gunton, 'The Church as a School of Virtue', pp. 223–4, 227.

28 *Catechism of the Catholic Church*, para. 1804.

29 Serene Jones, 2002, 'Graced Practices: Excellence and Freedom in the Christian Life', in Miroslav Volf and Dorothy C. Bass (eds), *Practicing Theology: Beliefs and Practices in Christian Life*, Grand Rapids, MI; Cambridge, UK: Eerdmans, p. 60.

30 Jones, 'Graced Practices', p. 60.

31 *Catechism of the Catholic Church*, para. 2500.

32 Gunton, 'Church', p. 230.

33 Gunton, 'Church', pp. 228–9.

34 Gunton, 'Church', pp. 211, 230. See also Jones, 'Graced Practices', p. 56.

35 Sarah Coakley, (2002), *Powers and Submissions: Spirituality, Philosophy and Gender*, Oxford: Blackwell.

36 Amy Hollywood, 'Practice, belief and feminist philosophy of religion', in Pamela Sue Anderson and Beverley Clack (eds), *Feminist Philosophy of Religion: Critical Readings*, London and New York: Routledge, pp. 225–40.

37 Stanley Hauerwas and Samuel Wells (eds), 2006, *The Blackwell Companion to Christian Ethics*, Oxford: Blackwell; John E. Colwell, 2001, *Living the Christian Story: The Distinctiveness of Christian Ethics*, Edinburgh and New York: T&T Clark; John E. Colwell, 2005, *Promise and Presence: An Exploration of Sacramental Theology*, Milton Keynes: Paternoster.

38 Gilbert Bond, 2002, 'Liturgy, Ministry and the Stranger: The Practice of Encountering the Other in Two Christian Communities', in Miroslav Volf and Dorothy

Bass (eds), *Practicing Theology: Beliefs and Practices in Christian Life*, Cambridge, UK: Eerdmans, pp. 137–56.

39 Linda Zagzebski, 1996, *Virtues of the Mind: An Inquiry into the Nature of Virtue and the Ethical Foundations of Knowledge*, Cambridge: Cambridge University Press, p. 20.

40 Alain De Botton, 2000, *The Consolations of Philosophy*, London: Penguin and 2004, *Status Anxiety*, London: Hamish Hamilton; Darrin McMahon, 2006, *The Pursuit of Happiness: A History from the Greeks to the Present*, Allen Lane; Brian Mountford, 2006, *Happiness in Ten Minutes*, Winchester; New York: O Books; Richard Schoch, 2006, *The Secrets of Happiness: Three Thousand Years of Searching for the Good Life*, Profile; Alison Webster, 2002, *Wellbeing*, London: SCM Press; Nicholas White, 2006, *A Brief History of Happiness*, Oxford: Blackwell.

41 Michael Argyle, 2001, *The Psychology of Happiness*, 2nd edn, Hove: Routledge; Daniel Gilbert, 2006, *Stumbling on Happiness: Why the Future Won't Feel the Way You Think it Will*, San Francisco: Harper.

42 R. Layard, 2005, *Happiness: Lessons from a New Science*, Allen Lane.

43 David Niven, 2000, The *100 Simple Secrets of Happy People: What Scientists Have Learned and How You Can Use It*, San Francisco: Harper.

44 In July 2006, the Henley Centre published the results to the question it has been asking for 20 years: 'Do you think the quality of life in Britain is best improved by a) looking after the community's interests instead of your own; or b) looking after ourselves, which ultimately raises standards for all?' From 1994 to 2000 a) received a clear majority vote. Since 2000 the gap has been closing, and in 2006 a majority (53%) chose b). For media comment, see Decca Aitkenhead, 2006, 'It's all about me', *Guardian*, Saturday July 8, 2006.

45 Jonathan Dancy, 1993, 'An Ethic of *Prima Face* Duties', in Peter Singer (ed.), *A Companion to Ethics*, Oxford: Blackwell.

46 Stephen Law, 2006, *The War for Children's Minds*, Abingdon; New York: Routledge.

47 Christopher Lasch, 1977, *Haven in a Heartless World: The Family Besieged*, New York: Basic.

CASE STUDY

Is English Education Secular?

ASHLEY ROGERS BERNER

Is English education secular? The answer is not straightforward. On the one hand, academic educational philosophy has been bereft of a religious framework since before World War Two. On the other hand, English educational practice mandates religious education in state schools, and the national government supports all manner of confessional schools.[1] This practice is entrenched in legislation, if not universally approved.[2] How do we make sense of this juxtaposition? Clearly, any response must be highly nuanced. It must recognize the gap in any educational system between theory and practice, legislation and reality. It must also be chronologically wide-ranging. The forces that shaped post-war education were not created in 1944 with Butler's Education Act and its commitment to religious education, church schools, and a daily act of worship. Rather, by exploring how academic educational philosophy evolved from the early years of the twentieth century onwards, we can explore the tensions at the heart of the English education system and relate current practice to the evolution of theory.

Educational Philosophy

The metaphysics of educational philosophy engage with such questions as, what is the purpose of the classroom? What role should the teacher play? What about the nature of the child? Most importantly, and this is really the thrust of this case study, how should teachers answer these questions? How should teachers frame their life's work? I focus on academic educational philosophy not because extra-mural theories of education did not exist (they did), nor because academic philosophy guided legislative policy single-handedly (it did not), but rather because in academic philosophy we are given a window into how teachers are taught to understand their work. I want to argue that it is *here*, in the ways in which the academic establishment thinks about the meaning and purpose of education, that we find what amounts to secularism.

A psychological, as opposed to theological, orientation was in place well before World War Two. Academic educational philosophy changed profoundly between 1880 and 1920, from a discourse guided by theology and metaphysics to one that relied upon naturalistic psychology. There are many ways to demonstrate this point. For illustrative purposes, I will focus on the foremost teacher-training textbooks, one from the Victorian and one from the inter-war period. The first is John Gill's *Introductory Text Book to School Education, Method, and School Management*. This training book for teachers ran through 50,000 copies between 1857 and 1882 and remained influential throughout that time period.[3] It was the standard manual of educational ideas and practice throughout the Empire.[4] Gill taught intending teachers at Cheltenham Training College, which was evangelical, Anglican, and funded by the State. My second example, Percy Nunn's *Education: Its Data and First Principles* (1920), enjoyed a similar influence in a later age. Between 1920 and 1945 the book was printed some twenty times and 'was designed for teachers and students in training'.[5] It was, wrote historian R. J. W. Selleck, 'certainly the book teachers were most likely to have read'.[6] And, of course, it was the book that the generation of teachers working after 1944, and implementing the 1944 Act, would have been taught from themselves. Nunn and his colleagues John Adams and Cyril Burt were the leading theorists at the London Day Training College, which was an appendage of the University of London and the most influential teacher training college in the country, possibly throughout the Empire.[7] Together they championed the shift from a theological or metaphysical to a psychological ('scientific') approach to education.[8] They supervised PhDs, examined teachers in training all over the country, and guided government policy for the Department of Education. These two works – Gill's *Textbook* and Nunn's *Education* – present entirely different views of human nature, destiny and purpose, and therefore of education.

Gill's theory of education emanated from a Biblical ontology. 'In the child's mind,' he wrote, 'there is the image of Deity defaced . . . and education . . . is to be employed to restore it. Hence [education] embraces both time and eternity.'[9] The child's body, mind, and will are inextricably related, and 'there must be no vain attempt to separate them. As a matter of fact it cannot be done'.[10] Education must nurture the *whole* child. Second, Gill's theory assumed a universally applicable vision of 'the good life'. The point of education for Gill was to impart *both* knowledge and moral training. His notions of the true, beautiful, and good, came from the Bible, 'a book', he wrote, 'whose aim is to bring man back to God; it exhibits a plan whereby he might be saved; it points him to a Saviour'.[11] Third, the teacher's job was to *lead* the child into these rightly ordered pleasures and socially negotiated duties. Gill had all kinds of instructions for the teacher, but the final goal of pedagogy was to direct the child into the *right kind of life*.

Percy Nunn's textbook is completely different. First, Nunn permitted a *teleological* free-for-all. 'There can be no universal aim of education if that aim is to include the assertion of any particular ideal of life . . . Educational efforts must . . . be limited to securing for everyone the conditions under which Individuality is most completely developed.'[12] That is, the classroom must not aim at something universal, such as Ethics or Character or Learning or Citizenship or Godliness. It must only permit each individual the maximum opportunity to develop as he or she chooses. Second, Nunn encouraged a *moral* free-for-all between competing claims about the good life. While he wanted education to urge the individual towards 'loves', he was unwilling to state *which* loves ought to be encouraged. Rather, human morality might only be judged by the degree to which it welcomed individual 'expressiveness'.[13] Third, Nunn championed a *pedagogical* free-for-all in the classroom. A teacher must not claim to be wiser than her pupils but must, rather, foster a 'community of feeling' between herself and them. Rather than guiding pupils towards a normative end, a teacher must seek to 'put his own experiences into the common stock'.[14] The arresting aspect of Percy Nunn's psychological approach is that, beginning in the 1920s, it dominated the landscape of teacher training programmes – even those with religious foundations. His books, along with those of his friends and companions (J. S. Ross, John Adams and Susan Isaacs, all associated with the University of London), formed the core curriculum of teacher training between the wars. How did this happen?

The landscape of educational theory was vast and complex in the last half of the nineteenth and first half of the twentieth century. There were traditional voices (David Stow and John Gill), utilitarian spokesmen (Herbert Spencer) and idealists and romantics (Pestalozzi and Froebel), with disparate views of human nature and educational philosophy. Not all were theological, by any means, but most carried overt notions of normative educational ends. All were overtaken by another voice which declared that there *were* no educational ends apart from self-expression and self-discovery. This voice was explicitly anti-metaphysical, which in this context means that it rejected the notion, shared equally by those with a theological and a utilitarian bias, that there was an end or purpose to human life and community which could be identified and nurtured by education.

Several factors enabled naturalistic psychologists to disseminate their views. First of all, the leading proponents operated within the universities, not the training colleges, particularly the University of London, which carried far greater prestige than the religious training colleges. University-based training colleges, funded by the government from 1890, had been acknowledged to be non-religious from the very beginning.[15] Second, they wrote within the newly segregated discipline of psychology, which had by then rejected its roots in theology and philosophy and sought recognition as a discourse of science.[16] Therefore, it claimed neutrality. Third, they operated within close-knit intellectual and professional circles, organizations, and institutions which were mutually reinforcing and contributed to the type of 'school of thought' which Randall Collins analyses in *The Sociology of Philosophies* (1998).[17] Fourth and finally, these men and women benefited from decades of hammering of intellectual work their predecessors had done to remove metaphysics from the faculties of education and psychology.

An early example of this intellectual project is Alexander Bain (1818–1903), an openly agnostic professor of logic at Aberdeen who insisted that both psychology and education be severed from metaphysics. In *Education as a Science* (1879), Bain argued that educators must refuse to answer questions of meaning, insisting that an honest and thoroughgoing pedagogy must be grounded in physiology (how does the brain work?) and to the proper subject matter (which information do we wish to impart to the brain?) 'Science', not metaphysics, must guide the classroom.[18] His preference for a supposedly neutral, 'scientific' approach was swiftly adopted by the newly created departments of education and psychology and simultaneously around the world.[19] This strand of thinking met Sigmund Freud, so that by the 1920s one of the burning educational questions was whether or not teachers should psychoanalyse their students.[20]

A second example is William McDougall (1871–1938). McDougall was a founder of the British Psychological Society (1901) and held the Wilde Professor of Mental Philosophy at Oxford (1904) and the William James Chair of Psychology at Harvard (1920), writing a book on social psychology which went through 23 editions between 1908 and 1936. McDougall's work focused on instinct, on what he called '*horme*' or will, on suggestion, and on moral development, which he pictured as a naturalistic expansion of the human ego, culminating in a final stage of pure 'self-regard'. His anthropology presented a 'self' which was mellifluous, mysterious, and above all, self-created.

This sort of naturalistic psychology found its way into the most prestigious teacher-training institutions. It dominated the work of the London Day Training College, which in turn dominated the entire educational landscape.[21] In John Gill's former lecture rooms at (evangelical) Cheltenham, for instance, students dutifully reiterated McDougall's stance, at times verbatim, in the 1930s and 40s.[22] The notable exceptions to this trend were the Roman Catholic training colleges in which, before 1939, McDougall's stance was framed by reference to papal writings on education and seasoned with talk of 'the soul' and the spiritual mandate of the teacher.[23] After the war, however, Roman Catholic training similarly shifted in emphasis, while the other denominations secularized significantly. Even a cursory review of the syllabuses of training college classes on education after 1945 reveals the absence of a metaphysical, not to mention theological, framework. For instance, Westminster Training College, a Wesleyan institution, presented the discipline of education as, essentially, a psychological enterprise throughout the 1940s and 1950s.[24] The same was true of the (Anglican)

Culham College, whose internal syllabus of 1953 raises such questions as intelligence tests, child study, and personality, but neither *telos* nor transcendence.[25] In 1950, the University of Bristol's Institute of Education included the education syllabuses of nine constituent colleges, four of which had religious foundations: none of them mentioned theology as a resource for educational study.[26] In the 1960s and 1980s, the Roman Catholic St Mary's College required a divinity course for its students, but the education syllabuses derived their narratives from sociology and psychology and made no reference to a religious sanction for education.[27]

Teacher-training programmes, shaped by the inheritance of generations of educational philosophy, have since World War Two thus emphasized psychological development but not spiritual ontology. They have looked to sociology, psychology, and history as the intellectual resources of educational studies, but not to philosophy and certainly not to theology. Religious education, still a fertile area of study, is seen as a separate entity and not the thing itself. Its segregation from the discipline of education, broadly construed, is indicative of the latter's secularity.

Statutory Mandate for Religious Instruction

Despite the loss of emphasis on a religious sanction for education as a whole within the academy, religious education in England persists to this day. Indeed, English education reflected a religious orientation from the beginning. When Parliament passed its first grant for elementary education in 1834, it channelled the money through religious societies which Anglicans and Nonconformists had established for the purpose of creating schools (the National Society and the British Foreign School Society, respectively). In 1847 this was extended to Roman Catholics, and in 1853 the first Jewish school received a grant.[28] The formal training of teachers, initially, took place in the context of close-knit, residential religious communities.

In 1944 Parliament forged the first statutory obligation of every state-aided school in England and Wales to provide religious instruction, by which was meant both cognitive information about religion and a daily act of worship. Subsequent legislation (the Education Acts of 1988 and 1996) explicitly privileged *Christianity* within religious education. While the mandate for RE is national, the formulation of syllabuses is local and therefore, potentially, recognizes local religious variations. It is worth asking how this works in practice. For even if the legislation compels one thing, this may be undercut by the personal preference of the teacher, by the policy of the school, by the training the teacher has received, or even – more insidiously – by the curriculum itself. Indeed, it is worth asking whether the Agreed Syllabuses sponsor an appreciation of religious life, or in fact diminish it.

Terence Copley, Professor of Religious Education at the University of

Oxford, suggests in his recent book *Indoctrination, Education, and God* (2005), that religious education, badly done, *promotes* the secularization of the mind. After eight years of analysis, Copley concluded that many syllabuses inadvertently teach children to trivialize religious differences, to secularize the subject material, and to reduce stories about God to banal moralizing. For instance, when English children are asked if they 'believe' in God, he writes,

> The question is loaded against God and religion for various reasons. One is that whoever or whatever God may be, God is not an object like a distant planet or a UFO or an alleged Queen Anne chair, that one 'believes in' or not according to evidence and the exercise of a personal choice . . .[29]

More than this, in the classroom, the divine itself is often excised from the heart of religious narrative, an omission which, Copley writes, cannot be done without removing all religious meaning. 'David and Goliath' becomes a morality tale about bullying, not about God's presence in Israel, which was, after all, the real point of the Jewish story.[30] The effect of this model of teaching religions, Copley argues, results in a secularization of the mind. It does not result in religious understanding.

Marius Felderhof of the University of Birmingham Department of Theology and Religion argues that the National Framework for RE carries the same potential to secularize that which it putatively honours. First, the Framework urges an unrealistic breadth of religious knowledge within a short space of time, which results in a superficial overview of religions which may already be outside the pupils' cultural experience.[31] Second, the concept of a National Framework flies in the face of the mandates themselves, which call for local attention to *local* diversity and, therefore, to the diverse religions as practised by the parents. Third, the theory behind these practices implies that religions are 'discrete, reified entities that must be treated "fairly" by some egalitarian model', which amounts to a misunderstanding of religious life itself. Religious life focuses on God and on worship, not upon 'religion' rationally construed:

> The [believers'] prime object is neither skills nor concepts nor understanding, except as a means to faith. If faith is described as a trust and loyalty, it is certainly not a trust and loyalty to a religious tradition, or to a religious institution *per se* . . . In Christian terms the trust is in, and the loyalty is to, God. In Platonic terms it is in and to Truth, the Good, and Beauty to the One. Each tradition may express it differently and mean something different by it, but I dare say none of the adherents would make their 'religion' an end in itself.[32]

Insofar as RE rests upon a 'religious studies' model, paying equal attention to religious traditions which themselves appear as abstract and separated from community life, it is biased towards a secular understanding of religious life.

What is one to make of this? On the one hand, a national mandate for RE in maintained schools suggests that English education, at least theoretically, makes space for the sacred. That RE 'on the ground' may do just the opposite (even if unintentionally) suggests that the whole project could be in danger of undoing what it was intended to accomplish.[33] This is not to suggest that the mandate itself is unworkable or inevitably self-defeating. People like Copley have been able, under its terms, to present more vital models of teaching RE.[34] Penny Thompson recently argued that since *all* learning takes place 'within traditions which are circumscribed by their own particular boundaries and undergirded by particular assumptions', it is fully appropriate for RE to be explicitly confessional, not 'neutral'.[35] I suggest merely that some RE practices may unwittingly sponsor secularity. Thus, while the national mandate may be marshalled as evidence of an ongoing State commitment to religious values, its *practice* supports this claim on shakier ground.

Confessional Schools

What about confessional schools? Here we find the strongest argument that English education is *not* secular. The Government has widened its support for confessional schools of all types. There are eight Muslim schools following the first distribution of grants in 1998, with a further 120 seeking state support. Sikhs and Seventh-Day Adventists have their own schools with state funding. The number of students in full-time Jewish education has increased from 11,000 in 1975 to 22,800 in 2001 – a figure which represents over half of the Jewish children in the country.[36] Significantly, while parents cite academic achievement as *one* reason to support Jewish education, they insist that fostering religious identity is far and above the *primary* cause of such support.[37] Catholic education was defended in Parliament as recently as autumn 2006, when an attempt to prescribe a percentage of non-members of faith communities to be admitted to faith schools was rejected after a particularly forceful campaign from the Roman Catholic Church.[38] Government grants to the capital costs of Catholic schools now stand at 85%.[39] Faith-based schools continue to be accused of fostering division, but they persist.[40] None of this suggests a contraction in religious commitment on the part of the state, but rather the opposite.

Conclusions and Further Questions

The Catholic Church's successful defence of confessional schools in and of itself demonstrates that English education cannot be said to be secular *in toto*. While academic educational philosophy no longer refers to transcendence (at least for now), England's commitment to the existence of confessional schools, and to the prevention of a purely materialist vision of education, remains. Secularism does occur but not inevitably and not evenly. In his recent book *The Secular Revolution* (2003), Christian Smith emphasizes the role of human agency in the secularization process. Smith compares Western secularization to *political revolutions*. He argues, quite convincingly, that human agency (through tightly-knit interest groups which present a coherent agenda, possess substantial monetary capital and have access to political power) plays much more of a role in secularization than do impersonal social forces.[41] This model offers a reasonable way of understanding the partial secularization of English education: academic psychologists were able to secularize the discipline of education, but at the same time the broader community's support for religious schools persists, and is, in some quarters, increasing.

Does it matter that educational practice is open to religious thought but educational philosophy is not? The Religious Education Council believes that it does matter. More students now opt for external examinations in religious studies than in history, geography, or French, but there are not enough teachers prepared to instruct them.[42] The Religious Education Council proposed on 30 September 2005 a national strategy for religious education which calls for extensive government resources to train more teachers, and to train them better. In this it has the support of over fifty religious groups, including the Association of Jewish Teachers, the Buddhist Society, the Catholic Education Service, the Institute of Jainology, the Muslim Council of Britain.[43]

Inevitably, the *model* of understanding religious life into which the teachers are trained becomes profoundly important here. As Felderhof noted recently, any attempt on the part of RE professionals to see themselves as 'neutrals', standing outside of, and explaining, 'competing loves', needs to be seen as epistemologically untenable,[44] postmodern philosophy having closed the door to the modernist faith in a neutral pedagogy. The challenge that religious educators in non-sectarian schools face is that of helping children glimpse the *possibility* of divine existence without promoting *any one* particular religious life stance. Confessional schools have an easier time of it here, for theoretically they may hire teachers who view *all* of education, not just religious education, from within a particularist framework.

The broader question, of course, is that of sanction. On what basis, and to what end, does a modern, Western, pluralist, society educate its children? Is a theological renovation of educational philosophy in the Academy possible or desirable? How should the Government honour the persistent and varying religious commitments of its citizens: by bringing more resources to bear in the training for religious educators, or by enabling more confessional schools to flourish? Or both? However one answers these questions, the fact that we are still, at the beginning of the twenty-first century, engaging them, indicates the complex and unpredictable nature of religious belief, the inadequacy of the secularization thesis to explain it, and the necessity of considering how *both* educational philosophy *and* educational practice may best honour and reflect these complexities.

Notes

1 Throughout this case study, the focus will be on education in England and Wales. Legislation and tradition have produced importantly different systems in Scotland and Northern Ireland.

2 See C. Cannon, 'The Influence of Religion on Educational Policy, 1902–1944', *British Journal of Educational Studies* 12(2) (1964), 143–60 and Terence Copley, 2000, *Spiritual Development in the State School*, Exeter: University of Exeter Press, pp. 57–82.

3 Charles More, 1992, *The Training of Teachers, 1847–1949: A History of the Church Colleges at Cheltenham*, London: Hambledon Press, p. 71.

4 John William Adamson, 1930, *English Education 1789–1902*, Cambridge: Cambridge University Press, p. 136.

5 G. Z. F. Bereday and J. A. Lauwerys, 1963, *The Education and Training of Teachers*, New York: Evans Brothers, p. 91.

6 Richard Joseph Wheeler Selleck, 1972, *English Primary Education and the Progressives, 1914–1939*, London: Routledge and Kegan Paul, p. 121.

7 From 1926 the LDTC ran a colonial programme which became influential across the Empire. See R. Aldrich, 2002, *The Institute of Education: 1902–2002*, London: University of London Institute of Education.

8 A. Wooldridge, 1985, 'Child Study and Educational Psychology in England, 1880–1950', *Modern History*, Oxford, Oxford University, pp. 84–5.

9 John Gill, 1882, *Introductory Text Book to School Education, Method, and School Management: A Treatise on the Principles, Aims, and Instructions of Primary Education*, London: Longmans, Green and Co., p. 1.

10 Gill, *Introductory Text Book*, p. 8.

11 Gill, *Introductory Text Book*, p. 290.

12 Percy Nunn, 1920, *Education: Its Data and First Principles*, London: Edward Arnold, p. 5.

13 Nunn, *Education*, p. 197.

14 Nunn, *Education*, p. 128.

15 See the comments of Chief Inspector of Training Colleges, Sir William Scott-Coward, in his General Report to the King on elementary schools and training colleges in 1901, D/1/c/1 (1901) Board of Education Report on Elementary Schools and Training Colleges, p. 181. For further evidence, consult the reports of the Moral Instruction League's international inquiry on moral education: Michael Sadler (ed.), 1908, *Moral Instruction and Training in Schools: Report of an International Inquiry, Volume 1*, London: Longmans, Green and Co., p. xlix.

16 For a robust discussion of the role of psychology in Victorian intellectual life, see Rick Rylance, 2000, *Victorian Psychology and British Culture 1850–1880*, Oxford: Oxford University Press.

17 For details of their social networks, see in particular Adrian Wooldridge, 1994, *Measuring the Mind: Education and Psychology in England, c.1860–c.1990*, Cambridge: Cambridge University Press.

18 Alexander Bain, 1879, *Education as a science*, London: Kegan Paul, p. 161.

19 T. A. Ribot, 1873, *Modern English Psychology*, London: Henry S. King and Co., pp. 23–4.

20 John Adams, 1922, *Modern Developments in Educational Practice*, London: University of London Press, Ch. 11 ('Psycho-Analysis in Education') for a discussion of this question.

21 See Wooldridge, 'Child Study', for a good account of the influence of the University of London.

22 See the lecture notes found at Cheltenham Training College, in particular: UAD402 (1938–40) Student notebooks G. C. Reeves; UAD408 (1946–8) Student notebook J. Bainton; UAD394 (1947–49) Student notebooks P. J. Howell; UAD375 (1949–51) Student notebooks T. Mayhew. These lecture notes are from the archives of the Cheltenham Colleges.

23 See the lecture notes found at St. Mary's College, Twickenham, in particular: DDP/7/1 (1938–9) Lecture notes of D. P. McPherson; DDP/9/1 (1938–40) Lecture notes of William McGregor.

24 G/1/a/1 (1937–59). Westminster College and London University Syllabuses.

25 CU4132 (1953). Culham College syllabus for Education.

26 UA20/11/2 (1950). University of Bristol Institute of Education, HANDBOOK.

27 PUB2/3 (1960–61) St Mary's Prospectus, PUB2/11 (1981–2) St Mary's Prospectus.

28 H. Miller, 2001, 'Meeting the Challenge: The Jewish Schooling Phenomenon in the UK', *Oxford Review of Education*, 27(4) (2001), 501–513, p. 502.

29 Terence Copley, 2005, *Indoctrination, Education and God: the Struggle for the Mind*, London: SPCK, p. 19.

30 Copley, *Indoctrination*, p. 125.

31 Marius Felderhof, 'RE: Religions, Equality and Curriculum Time', *Journal of Beliefs and Values*, 26(2) (2005), p. 204.

32 Felderhof, 'RE: Religions, Equality and Curriculum Time', p. 211.

33 For a rich discussion of the nuances which inhere in the statutory mandate that local authorities foster children's spiritual side, see Copley, *Spiritual Development*.

34 For Copley's concrete proposals, see Copley, *Indoctrination*, ch. 6. For other resources, see also the material, videos and training presented by the Culham Institute at www.culham.ac.uk – accessed 31.08.06.

35 Penny Thompson, 2004, *Whatever Happened to Religious Education?*, Cambridge: Lutterworth Press, p. 150.

36 Miller, 'Meeting the Challenge', p. 501. The numbers are 11,000 and 22,620 respectively.

37 Miller, 'Meeting the Challenge', p. 506.

38 'Johnson backtracks in row over faith schools', *Guardian*, 27 October 2006. For an exploration of these issues, see Jeremy Hurst, 'Religious Requirement: The Case for Roman Catholic Schools in the 1940 and Muslim Schools in the 1990s', *Journal of Beliefs and Values*, 21(1) (2000), 87–97.

39 Hurst, 'Religious Requirement', p. 91.

40 H. Judge, 'Faith-Based Schools and State Funding: A Partial Argument', *Oxford Review of Education*, 27(4) (2001), 463–74.

41 Christian Smith, 2003, *The Secular Revolution: Power, Interests and Conflict in the*

Secularization of American Public Life, Berkeley: University of California Press, introduction.

42 Copley, *Indoctrination*, p. 8 – Religious studies (350,000), history (218,565), geography (232, 830), French (331,089).

43 The Religious Education Council of England and Wales, 'Towards a National Strategy for Religious Education' – author's copy (from Dr John Gay, the Church of England's official spokesman on education).

44 Marius C. Felderhof, 'Professionalizing (Religious) Education', *Journal of Beliefs & Values*, 26(2) (2005), 119–122.

Christianity and Economics:
The Conversation in Zacchaeus' House

RUFUS BLACK

Tectonic shifts in economic thought and their effects on public policy have played a defining role in the ordering of the world for the past half-century. Since the end of World War Two, the middle ground of Christian thought and its public expression in Britain has moved from practical collusion, through division and protest, to a cause-based critique searching for a more systemic response. Today the 'continental plate' of economic thought is on the move again. If the authors of moderate Christian thought are to learn from the history of the engagement between Christianity and economics, they could be positioned to shape this shift because of the reconvergence of economic and theological thought in interesting new territory. Shaping this shift will require theologians to risk associating with people often seen by the church as the tax-collectors of our time – they will need to risk the opprobrium of a conversation in Zacchaeus' house.

If theologians and economists do not connect in creative conversation, the opportunity will be lost to furnish the fashioners of the commercial world with fresh frameworks and theories, to shape a more humane and environmentally sensitive world. Some may be surprised or cynical that such a refashioning is possible, but a reservoir of desire for a different agenda is building as Generations X and Y flow into the global workforce.[1]

Stepping back, the engagement of Christian theology and economics that has brought us to this period, so pregnant with possibility, can be understood as the interplay of the 'two kingdoms' tension of Christian political thought and the two architectonic questions for economic thought.

The 'two kingdoms' tension of Christian political thought emerges from its need not only to speak about the governance of the world now – the created world whose inherent value it is theologically committed to affirm – but also to witness in the present the radically transformed future world of the Kingdom of God. This inherent tension is why Oliver O'Donovan observes that Christian political thought always needs a 'doctrine of the two'[2] to accommodate the fact that people live in relation to two realities, whether they are characterized as 'two realms', 'two forms of rule' or 'two kingdoms'. A well constructed 'doctrine of the two' creates three coherent sites in which the theological and secular worlds can converse. We will see that each has been a locus for engagement between Christianity and economics.

The first site of engagement is *the public square*. Here, Christians dress in their everyday work clothes, and use categories and language grounded in a distinctive Christian epistemology which requires no translation for a secular audience and does not demand belief in Christian reality to be plausible. For example, a translator was not required to explain the Christian critique of economic development, and its focus on Gross Domestic Product rather than on a broader conception of the human good.

The second site is *the cathedral*, a site of twentieth-century socio-economic engagement whose contemporary significance was marked by the martyrdom of Oscar Romero. Here, Christians identifiably gather in the discourse of a distinctive Christian epistemology and its categories. They gather in reminder that public square life participates in a wider sacred realm and that the priorities of political posturing may need radical re-ordering, when viewed from this vantage point. From this look-out on life, for example, the planet's natural abundance belongs to the category of 'gift', which should be approached according to the principle of 'stewardship' rather than the economic category of 'resource', which is approached with a principle of 'efficient exploitation'.

Finally, there are *sites of radical witness*. This is anywhere Christians gather as Christians to call for or engage in radical acts of witness to the Kingdom of God – acts that do not aim to replace the secular world's logic, but rather to demonstrate that it is provisional and does not provide the basis for the ultimate ordering of relationships. The Jubilee 2000 Campaign's call for the forgiveness of third-world debt is a good illustration of this sort of witness. The economic system could not be premised on the regular forgiveness of debt, as it would create myriad problems of moral hazard; but it could contemplate a one-off act. Importantly, for all the good created by taking debt out of the saddle bags of third world economies, from a Christian perspective, it is the act of forgiveness that really matters. This act witnesses the fact that ultimately, economics do not order human relationships. This animating idea of radical witness has also given rise to serious confusion. It is easy to slide from a theology of witnessing to a vision of a Kingdom that lies on the other side of the *eschaton*, to a theology in which that vision becomes a social and economic programme for today.

If the question of 'two kingdoms' has shaped the Christian side of the engagement for economics, two architectonic questions for economic thought have formed the other side of the conversation. First, what is the central concern of economics? And, second, what role does government have? We will see in the post-war history below that as economics' answers to these questions have moved further away from a Christian perspective, so has Christian engagement moved further towards the site of radical witness.[3]

Keynesian consensus in the Public Square (1945–68)

The interplay of economics and Christianity began harmoniously enough. In post-war Britain, the dominant role given to the state by the Labour Party was with respectability baptized by the economic thought of John Maynard Keynes. Keynesian economics went on to provide a rationale for a mixed economy to which both sides of politics could assent.

Keynesian thought framed the central problem of economics – to achieve full employment, and its proposed solution – government intervention to solve the problems to which free markets give rise when individuals simply pursue self-interests. This created an architecture of ideas whose themes resonated with Christian thinkers. Christian ears, attuned to such memorable scriptural sayings as the reminder that Jesus' mission is 'to bring good news to the poor' (Luke 4.18), could interpret Keynesian ideas as placing the problem of the poor at the centre of economic policy, and making collective action to address it, a clear responsibility. While there were important Roman Catholic thinkers who resisted what they saw as the overreaching of the welfare state,[4] collaboration with a cosy Keynesian consensus was the state of mind for most Christians.

New paradigms from the Cathedral and the Academy (1968–79)

It was in the developing world where material progress was not being made that a radical change occurred in the field of engagement. Amid poverty, injustice and repression, a theological critique of the economic order exploded, setting off reverberations that would eventually make a concern about the justice of the global economic order a placard around which Christian thought in the developed world could rally. That first eruption, which occurred in Latin America at the 1968 Catholic Bishops conference in Medellin, launched the agenda of liberation theology.

Critically, this agenda reoriented the whole theological engagement with economics by demanding that reflection begin with the experience of people suffering under economic systems. Unlike the previous practice of taking a few promising categories like 'the Kingdom of God' and fashioning them to contribute to public debate, this new approach reinterpreted all theological categories, and indeed the entire theological system in response to that experience. The category which remained unchanged was 'the poor': they were unambiguously the central economic issue and government's role was to be more active than ever.

During this period, however, long dismissed rumblings deep in the heart of economics also started to be taken seriously. Friedman and his colleagues at the Chicago school argued that it was the growth of wealth, not the poor, that was the issue, and free markets were the way through. This thinking, in part because of the failure of Keynesian policy prescriptions to meet the economic problems of the 1970s, would unleash forces that set economic and Christian thought on a direct collision course.

Free-market economics and a Cathedral divided (1979–88)

Britain in 1979 saw the Thatcher government elected, free-market economics take a grip of public policy, and the state start to retreat. Battle-lines were drawn and a deep rift in Christian thought hidden in the post-war shadows was suddenly thrown into relief by the political glare. Rallying to the free-market banner of individualism came evangelical voices with a theology strongly themed around individual accountability and destiny.

This sudden rallying on the right was a move for which liberal Christian thought was ill-prepared. There was no liberation theology for the developed world. Their responses were reduced either to engaging the secular world with socialist hand-me-downs or calling upon a handful of Christian categories. In public policy confrontation, their categories were crushed under the wheels of an entire and renewed system of thought. A symbol of their impotency is that the protesting hero whom Britain would honour from this period with a statue on the façade of Westminster Abbey was not a local challenger to the socio-economic order, but Oscar Romero.

Globalization and sites of radical witness (1988–today)

Free-market economics soon had a momentum of its own and when the dyke of the Berlin Wall broke, it flooded east. Not only did it wash away the political edifices of communism but also its intellectual foundations – the very same foundations upon which liberation theology had been built. As a result, Christianity's greatest challenge to economics was largely swept away.

Many Christians now faced a world shaped by an economic ideology whose central concerns did not sit well with them, but who lacked the theological resources to offer comprehensive critique. Only adding to the disquiet were fundamentalist Christians in Cadillacs, baptizing free-market economics on television. Their response was to move more clearly to radical witness. The cause was debt forgiveness, and the language of 'Jubilee' signalled the introduction of a radical theological category into public policy debate. In Britain, this move enabled Christianity to shape the global economic agenda, even if little continues to be said about the domestic agenda.

Christianity's role in transforming economics

From the chapters of its conversation with economics a lesson for Christianity emerges: if it is to play a shaping role it needs a substantial, systematic, moral theology whose agenda emerges from a distinctively theological account of reality. Otherwise, it risks either being lulled into sleepy collusion with ideologies that appear to share its agenda or simply overwhelmed by a more comprehensive construct of reality. Integral to that theology needs to be both a conceptual power to contend with economics in the public square and poetic power in its cathedral catechism to unsettle economics' self-confident categories.

The time for fashioning such a theology is at hand because for some time now the signs of a tectonic shift in economics have been registering on the seismographs of intellectual change. The clearest register of these rumblings has been the awarding of Nobel prizes in economics to the welfare and development economist Amartya Sen (1998) and the behavioural economists Daniel Kahnemann and Vernon Smith (2002). The movement signalled by those awards is from the traditional economics of 101 courses and textbooks, to what former Stanford and Sante Fe Institute economist Brian Arthur calls 'complexity economics',[5] a title that seeks to capture what is common in the agendas in contemporary movements in economics that challenge the discipline's traditional assumptions including: evolutionary economics,[6] interactions economics and behavioural game theory.[7] This shift has recently been brilliantly synthesised by Eric Beinhocker in *The Origin of Wealth*.[8] Two pivotal elements from his account can be usefully highlighted to discuss the engagement with Christianity.

First, there is a shift from the laws of Newtonian physics inspiring economic analysis, to the claim that economic systems are governed by the same evolutionary laws as natural, biological systems. Practically, this means there is a shift from viewing economic systems from a paradigm in which they are characterized as '[c]losed, static, linear systems in equilibrium' to one in which they are understood as '[o]pen, dynamic, nonlinear systems, far from equilibrium'.[9] This shift also locates economic thought in a broader atheistic description of reality by arch-secularists like the evolutionary biologist Richard Dawkins.

Second, there is a move from the startlingly unrealistic assumptions of *Homo economicus* which sees everyone 'use complex deductive calculations to make decisions; have complete information; make no errors and have no biases; have no need for learning or adaptation (because they are already perfect)'[10] to a humanly realistic one informed by anthropological and psychological knowledge in which most people's decisions are shaped by rules of thumb, very limited information, and their rich and complex emotional lives.

Complexity economics is still wet clay on the intellectual potter's wheel and there is time for the hand of the theologian to shape it. Where that hand can be best applied is in enhancing critiques of traditional economics, providing more sophisticated building materials for the complexity economics project, like a better non-utilitarian decision-making theory, and offering a theological account of reality to cradle it. Such an account would increase the plausibility of complexity economics itself by providing an even more consistent background account of reality. The account would also enable complexity economics to have a legitimate place for the commercial world's spiritual questions and open it to theological critique. Applying its hand in this way will challenge theology itself because the resources required need to be drawn from fields currently balkanized behind several of its ideological battle lines. Therefore, the possibility also exists that Christianity's renewal of economics could renew theology. From here we will briefly map a possible agenda for a renewed and reconverging conversation across Christianity's three sites of engagement with economics.

The Public Square

In the public square, Christian thought can play a vital role both in hastening the demise of traditional economics and in providing a philosophically robust and anthropologically sound foundation for a decision-making theory of complexity economics. Traditional economics is dependent on utilitarianism to provide the philosophical basis for how people make decisions. Contemporary natural law theorists have mounted a powerful and sustained critique of utilitarianism that extends the complexity economists' critique by demonstrating that not only is it practically impossible for people to make the calculations required but also that it is logically impossible.[11] In its place they have developed a very substantial theory of the human good – of what it is that leads to a fulfilled life – and a theory of how people decide which goods to pursue that which allows for their emotional life.[12] Already, this account is coming into dialogue with development economists like Amartya Sen.[13]

The further development of a non-utilitarian theory of the good offers the prospect of bringing human welfare rather than wealth back to the centre of economics. The promise of reconverging theological and economic agendas is already present in the contribution Sen and his thought have made to the creation of the United Nations Human Development Index, which seeks to measure development in terms of advancement of human welfare rather than the advancement of wealth, as measured by Gross Domestic Product.

Where the convergence of theological and economic agendas will need tough dialogue is on the question of the role of government. The new natural law theorists Finnis, Grisez and George, do provide a powerful restatement of the expansive role of government in the creation of the common good – albeit one that is often hard to see through the incendiary consequences of their application of it to bodily matters like homosexuality and abortion.[14]

The Cathedral

As we move from the public square to the cathedral, those gathered there first need to find a resonant language to express that the cathedral is not a museum of antique attitudes but a living symbol of the reaches of reality that go beyond the material. They need to provide a theological account of reality that extends and enriches the secular, scientific account that complexity economics relies upon, so that those who reach the edge of that secular account are not forced, by the lack of any viable alternative perspective, to believe that they stand on the edge of a void.

There are theologians like Keith Ward who have taken very seriously the task of reconfiguring theology by engaging with the very same scientific account of reality that has guided and inspired complexity economics.[15] Their theology speaks in the same categories of complexity economics about the nature of reality as emergent, dynamic and multiform. What we are seeing here is an exciting epistemological convergence as two separated continents of thought realign to restore a long-lost unity between their fields – a kind of reforming of the Gondwanaland of Western thought.

A reason for highlighting the theology of Keith Ward in particular is that he has a gift for communicating a Christian account of the spiritual realm in a language sympathetic to secular inquirers who do not want to be entrapped in 'organized religion'.[16] There is plenty of such inquiry in the commercial world, especially with the arrival of Generations X and Y into Western workforces with their desire for a life of broader experience and meaning than that of their materialist parents. Equally, there is a New Age industry already starting to meet this need with early signs of management thought seriously questioning the place of spirituality and meaning in the modern corporation.[17] The Zacchaeuses of our time are already climbing trees to seek a glimpse of the numinous.

Christians in the cathedral need to go beyond a conversation at the converging rim of the two great continents of thought, to create a systematic, moral theology with categories and questions that can reach deep into the economics heartland. The integrity of distinctive Christian epistemology requires what Oliver O'Donovan has called a liberation theology of the North.[18] An analogue for this type of critique already exists in the thought of

sociologists like Zygmunt Bauman who have fashioned theologically resonant[19] categories of critique – perhaps because they are ultimately grounded
in a substantive anthropology that is attuned to the same abstract categories
of time, space and history as theology. Drawing on this analogue one can
speculate that the agenda for this theology might be the liberation of people
and the planet from a narcissistic culture of consumerist individualism by
re-embodying them in neighbourly communities and reconnecting them to
the planet's dynamic web of life. Such a theology is likely to challenge the
instrumentalizing category of resources, human and material, with notions
of gift and stewardship; emphasize the physicality of neighbourliness against
the virtual world; challenge the reduction of human interaction to the economic constructs of transaction; take on the technocratic concealment and
denial of human limits and its culture of bodily perfection with a celebration
of the haptic nature of human life; and respond to the restless anxiety of
consumerism with the stillness of prayer.[20]

Sites of radical witness

The greatest challenge for a liberation theology of the North will be for it to
find a voice. The clue suggested by the Jubilee 2000 Campaign is that this
voice is likely to come from grass-roots political movements inspired by a
galvanizing idea for liberation. The challenge for the Christian religious
imagination is what would be the acts of radically peaceful witness that set
the world on a path to liberate people and the planet, or at the very least, to
provide a hint of an alternative route to the path on which we currently
travel. Perhaps, that act of witness will be to dare an invitation inside the
glass towers of global capitalism and to risk a conversation with those
Zacchaeuses who are already straining in the crowd to glimpse a larger
whole.

Notes

1 For an excellent account, see Hugh Mackay, 1997, *Generations*, Sydney:
Macmillan.

2 Oliver O'Donovan, 1996, *Desire of the Nations*, Cambridge: Cambridge University
Press, pp. 193–242.

3 See Daniel Yergian and Joseph Stanislaw, 2002, *The Commanding Heights*, New
York: Touchstone, which explores this period of economics and its impact on public
policy.

4 Joan Keating, 'Faith and Community threatened? Roman Catholic Responses to the
Welfare State, Materialism and Social Mobility, 1945–62', *Twentieth Century Social
History*, 9(1) (1998), 86–108.

5 Brian Arthur, 'Complexity and the Economy', *Science* 284 (1999), 107–9. See also

P. W. Anderson, K. J. Arrow, and D. Pines (eds), 1988, *The Economy as an Evolving Complex System*, Redwood City, CA: Addison-Wesley.

6 J. Lesource and A. Orlean, 1998, *Advances in Self-Organisation and Evolutionary Economics*, London: Economica.

7 C. F. Camerer, 2003, *Behavioural Game Theory: Experiments in Strategic Interaction*, Princeton, NJ: Princeton University Press.

8 Eric D. Beinhocker, 2006, *The Origin of Wealth*, Boston: Harvard Business School Press.

9 Beinhocker, *Origin*, p. 97.

10 Beinhocker, *Origin*, p. 97.

11 John Finnis, 1983, *Fundamentals of Ethics*, Washington: Georgetown University Press, pp. 87–105.

12 Germain Grisez, Joseph Boyle, and John Finnis, 'Practical Principles, Moral Truth, and Ultimate Ends', *American Journal of Jurisprudence* 32 (1987), 99–151.

13 Amartya Sen, 1999, *Development as Freedom*, New York: Random House Press, pp. 75, 310.

14 John Finnis, 1980, *Natural Law and Natural Right*, Oxford: Clarendon Press; Germain Grisez, 1997, *The Way of the Lord Jesus: Vol 3: Difficult Moral Questions*, Illinois: Franciscan Press; Robert George, 1993, *Making Men Moral*, Oxford: Oxford University Press.

15 Keith Ward, 1996, *Religion and Creation*, Oxford: Oxford University Press.

16 Keith Ward, 2002, *God: A Guide for the Perplexed*, Oxford: Oneworld Publications.

17 E.g. Danah Zohar, 2000, *SQ: Spiritual Intelligence: the Ultimate Intelligence*, London: Bloomsbury Press. Zohar has used this best-seller to consult to a range of large multinational companies.

18 O'Donovan, *Desire of the Nations*, pp. 12–19.

19 Zygmunt Bauman, 1998, *Globalization: The Human Consequences*, Polity Press: Cambridge.

20 Others besides Bauman who are important in setting this agenda include Robert Putnam, 2000, *Bowling Alone: The Collapse and Revival of American Community*, New York: Simon and Schuster; Richard Sennett, 1998, *The Corrosion of Character: The Personal Consequences of Work in the New Capitalism*, New York: W.W. Norton & Company; and Theodore Zeldin, 1998, *An Intimate History of Humanity*, London: Vintage. I start to explore this agenda in my essay, Rufus Black, 'Community in an Electronic Age', *Eureka Street*, 14/1 (2004), 30–32.

6

The Common Good

In March 2001 the *Guardian* newspaper ran a series of articles entitled 'The Common Good', about the public services in Britain. Under the provocative headline, 'Once they wanted to help others. Now they want to be Britney Spears,' the columnist Madeleine Bunting opined that 'public service is a concept which means little to anyone under 20'. What had destroyed public service, she argued, was the demise of three factors which had sustained it throughout much of the twentieth century – patriotism, socialism and Christianity. 'Questioned, scrutinised, debunked; these big three can no longer rally a new generation to devote their lives to the common good,' she said. 'The decline of collective identities – of nation, faith and ideology – has left a vacuum which has been taken over and exploited by consumer culture.'[1]

Was it true, as Bunting claimed, that young people no longer had any sense of the common good? The series of interviews with public servants, many of them not much older than 20, which accompanied her article, suggested not. Although many of the public servants complained at the conditions in which they worked, most were adamant that they were motivated not by material reward, but by a sense of vocation. The survey provided ample evidence of the existence of a sense of the common good, even if it was not always expressed in exactly those terms. Moreover, by restricting itself to the public sector, it did not include the large number of members of the 'Y Generation' (referred to in our Chapter on Generation), who are involved in the voluntary sector and pressure groups. This chapter will argue that the concept of the common good retained its salience in the second half of the twentieth century, in spite of onslaughts from expressive individualism and consumerism, but that it has mutated. Having been primarily conceived in terms of the nation or state in the 1940s and 1950s, it increasingly came to be seen in global or very local terms, and in opposition to the sectional interests of the state.

In spite of its faults, Bunting's article did raise the interesting, and neglected, question of how the decline of religious observance was connected with the declines of other forms of collective identity. Historians of British religion have been slow to consider how changing conceptions of the public – whether of state, nation, community, empire or law – have affected religious commitment.[2] This is in stark contrast to the history of religion in France, which as Thomas Kselman has recently pointed out is still largely written in terms of church-state relations.[3] There are a number of reasons for this neglect. One reason is the influence on sociologists and social historians in the 1960s and 1970s of Marxism, which assumed that the fundamental structural processes in religious change were economic, and which dismissed state and nation as superstructural. Another reason is the concentration of historians of religion (whether secularization theorists or revisionists) on urban working-class communities, which has led to an over-emphasis on local identities at the expense of national, international, or imperial ones.[4] A third reason is the pervasiveness in recent accounts of the theory of privatization, which asserts that religion migrated from the public to the private sphere, without considering in any detail the process whereby this happened.[5] The idea of privatization has been challenged by José Casanova and Grace Davie, who have argued in a global context that religion has retained, and even increased, its public role in recent years.[6] The public role of Christianity in Britain, however, remains an under-explored topic.[7] The case studies in this section of the book seek to remedy this neglect, and to offer some pointers as to how changing conceptions of state, society and citizenship have altered Christianity's public role.

The common good as it was conceived in 1945 was strongly tied up with the nation state. This was partly a result of the artificial elision of state, nation and common good during wartime. Unity against a common enemy, and the language of equality of sacrifice, had meant that the rhetoric of common good was almost universal; even the party that broke the wartime political truce was called the Common Wealth Party. But ideas of national community had also been central to the appeal of all three main parties before World War Two. Idealist conceptions of community and the common good had proved remarkably resilient in political rhetoric and social policy in the 1930s, in spite of attacks on their philosophical basis from positivist philosophers who argued that it was impossible to talk meaningfully of the common good. At the end of World War Two, the idea of the common good found new expression in the welfare state, with its emphasis on universal provision and 'fair shares for all', while the emphasis on spiritual values in the 1944 *Education Act* recalled the idealists' insistence that the common good was spiritual rather than material. The common good also had analogues in the idea of a common culture, as expressed in the BBC, and in J. M. Keynes's creation of the Arts Council.[8] Labour's appeals to the common good actually intensified during its years in power after the war, and its 1950 manifesto stressed the duty of the individual to 'contribute to the good of the community according to their abilities'.[9]

The language of the common good was shared by Christians and non-Christians alike, and represented a common frame of reference for those from different intellectual traditions. It had pagan as well as Christian antecedence.

But its currency was of inestimable benefit to the Christian churches, because it provided a framework in which Christian morality was both comprehensible and largely uncontested. Whether or not they were themselves Christian, the proponents of a moralized citizenship required a consensus in favour of Christian morality, and needed the churches as teachers of that morality. What is striking in some writing on this subject from the 1950s is its certainty that a Christian moral consensus existed. In their article on 'The Meaning of the Coronation' in 1953, Edward Shils and Michael Young described the coronation ceremony as evidence of Britain's shared conception of virtue, 'a degree of moral consensus such as few large societies have ever manifested'. For Shils and Young, it was natural that this moral consensus had been expressed in Christian ritual, because 'Britain is still generally a Christian country'.[10] A similar belief in the necessity and reality of moral consensus was expressed by the Catholic judge, Lord Devlin, in his lecture 'Morals and the Criminal Law' in 1959. Devlin argued that no society could exist 'without shared ideas on politics, morals and ethics', and that Christianity should provide these moral ideas, because 'morals and religion are inextricably joined', and the majority of the country was Christian. Devlin assumed that on most issues there was 'no practical difference' between Christian morals and 'those which every right-minded member of society is expected to believe'.[11]

However, during the 1950s several aspects of the common good began to be questioned. The common good had often been tied up with exhortations to sacrifice, but these were increasingly resented by an affluent populace exasperated at the peacetime continuance of wartime austerity and regulation. The Conservatives successfully capitalized on this feeling in the late 1940s and 1950s, offering deregulation and personal betterment. Appeals to the common good were replaced by the promise of consumer goods. Harold Macmillan's famous speech at Bedford football ground in 1957, in which he stated that 'the British people have never had it so good', appeared to identify 'good' with private affluence, though in private Macmillan harboured his own doubts about the absence of a moral basis to consumer society.[12] In a memorandum to Macmillan in 1961, the Christian cabinet minister Sir David Eccles questioned what sort of good was being pursued. 'They have never had it so good, but what is good? Does it include happiness and a conviction that life has a purpose? If so, there is much that is wanting before we can be satisfied.'[13] But Conservative victories in successive elections by and large quieted these doubts.

A similar reconsideration of the meaning of 'good' was occurring among revisionists in the Labour Party. During and after World War Two, some on the left came to believe that the common good was material rather than spiritual, and that it did not require a shared conception of the good, merely shared economic goods. State planning and expertise would obviate the need for the sort of participatory citizenship envisaged by the Idealists.[14] The defeats of the 1950s prompted Tony Crosland to attack the drabness and joylessness of Labour's communitarianism. In *The Future of Socialism* (1956), he criticized the 'public virtues' of socialist moralists like Beatrice and Sidney Webb, arguing that these needed to be replaced by 'a greater emphasis on private life, on freedom and dissent, on culture, beauty, leisure and even frivolity'.[15]

Another reason why the old version of the common good came under threat in the later 1950s was a new uncertainty about the nation with which that common good had been identified. From the 1920s to the early 1950s, an idea of national community had been underpinned by a discourse of shared national character, as well as by a sort of low-key providentialism which saw British victory in the two world wars as evidence of divine favour.[16] But as Chris Waters has shown, the belief in a common national character went out of fashion in the 1950s, as New Commonwealth immigration posed a challenge to some of its glibber generalizations.[17] One of these generalizations was that England was a Protestant (or even a Christian) country; always questionable, it became unacceptable after the incorporation through immigration of a substantial non-Christian religious population. At the same time, the rapid decline of the British Empire punctured popular providentialism. Progressive imperialism, with its rhetoric of trusteeship, had drawn heavily on the idea of the common good, as the gradual renaming of the Empire as the Commonwealth implied, but this no longer looked sustainable after the Suez crisis.[18] The consolidation of rival power blocs, and the threat of nuclear war, meant that a common good vested in a single nation seemed too limited; for many intellectuals, a more attractive common good seemed now to lie in new internationalist movements such as the United Nations and the European Common Market.

All these critiques had to some extent continued to approve the existence of a common good, differing only about what it was. But from the early 1960s there was a new argument that the common good might be a bad thing, because it was potentially repressive to minorities. This was not, of course, actually a new argument at all; H. L. A. Hart's debate with Lord Devlin on this subject was essentially a reprise of J. S. Mill's argument with James Fitzjames Stephen a century before.[19] As Raymond Plant's case study shows, the fear that the common good could be repressive led some liberal theorists to espouse a rather thin, procedural version of it which simply enabled people to pursue their own goods.[20] But the renewed emphasis on the sinister aspects of the common good was damaging to the language of sacrifice and citizenship which had accompanied it. As Raphael Samuel later put it, .

> collectivity, instead of being the means of realising the common good – as, say, in notions of solidarity or service, fair shares or equality – is seen rather as an instrument of coercion, producing uniformity rather than

diversity, intimidating the individual, and subordinating the minority to the unthinking mass. All unifying institutions and totalising concepts are subject to this attack.[21]

This attack continued between the 1960s and the 1980s, eroding the language of citizenship. The barrage came on different fronts. Social problems like juvenile delinquency were no longer treated as the estrangement of the citizen from the national community, but instead came to be seen in terms of healing the individual.[22] The radical left's new espousal of the recognition of minorities led it to celebrate difference rather than sameness, leaving little room for the language of the common good.[23] Disenchantment with the welfare state led critics on both the left and the right to repudiate the communitarian language in which it had been framed. Thatcherism eventually drew on this disenchantment. Although, as our chapter on the Good Life points out, Thatcherism set out to remoralize society, it lacked what Eugenia Low has described as 'a conception of a unified moral framework within which both state and citizen found their being' – in other words, a sense of the common good.[24] Instead, Thatcherites sought to replace the language of the common good with that of customer service.[25]

This decline of civic discourse was noted by academics. Richard Sennett's *The Fall of Public Man* (1977) was the first of a number of titles bewailing the decline of civic engagement, of which the most recent is David Marquand's *Decline of the Public* (2004).[26] Significantly, the introduction to Sennett's book was written by the secularization theorist, Harvey Cox, and the declinist narratives of civic disengagement and secularization have to an extent fed off one another.

But as with the secularization thesis, it is possible to question how far the civic disengagement thesis overstated the decline of the common good. Much of the counter-culture of the 1960s onwards was in fact communitarian rather than individualist in aspiration. The impulse to form the perfect community was still present in many distinctive aspects of radical culture – whether the hippy commune, the tenants' association, or the comprehensive school. What was new was that the community was no longer identified with the power structures of the nation or the state, and was now variously conceived as local, international, or embodying an identifiable minority. The lyrics of John Lennon's song 'Imagine' (1971) were a rather banal example of this new communitarianism, envisaging a utopian global community without countries or religions. The critique was not so much of the common good itself, but of institutional bearers of the common good such as churches and nations. Political participation and the voluntary impulse did not suddenly give way to rampant individualism or consumerism; they survived, but they sloughed off what they saw as the repressive connotations of citizenship.

This left the way open for churches to attempt to portray themselves as part of the counter-culture, and to identify themselves with more unofficial expressions of the common good. Here the amphibiousness of Christianity – its capacity to be either establishment or counter-culture – came in useful. All the main denominations, including Catholics, had been at pains to identify themselves with the nation in the mid-twentieth century, but now they increasingly sought to distance themselves from it. Many clergy, especially in the established church, felt that they no longer wanted to perform the role of moral conscience of the state – a role which seemed to them to be compromising and *inauthentic*. As Bernice Martin has pointed out, some clergy came 'to resent their role as hapless providers of the rituals which go along with mere citizenship', and attempted to raise the bar of church membership by restricting baptism to regular churchgoers.[27] All the main denominations emphasized their internationalism, and their commitment to international causes like peace and the poor. This did not mean, of course, that the Church of England sought to disavow establishment; as Mark Chapman's case study shows, some Anglicans tried to have it both ways, utilizing their national status while at the same time attempting to be counter-cultural. More recently, there have been nuanced defences of establishment from evangelicals and liberals, which acknowledge the dangers of too close a relationship with power structures, while nevertheless arguing for the importance of a national recognition of Christianity.[28]

In reconceiving the common good to remove the contagion of association with the nation, Christians of all denominations were influenced by developments in Catholic theology.[29] In works like *The Person and the Common Good* (1948), the neo-Thomist Jacques Maritain tried to produce a version of the common good that emphasized individual personality, and these ideas influenced the Second Vatican Council. In his 1963 encyclical *Pacem in Terris*, Pope John XXIII insisted that the common good must safeguard the interests of minorities. He argued that while

> every civil authority must strive to promote the common good in the interests of all, without favouring any individual citizen or group of citizens ... Nevertheless, conditions of justice and equity can at times demand that those in power pay attention to the needs of the weaker members of society, since these are at a disadvantage when it comes to defending their own rights and asserting their legitimate interests.[30]

The implication of this emphasis on the weakest in society was that the common good should involve a bias to the poor, and Vatican II also saw the concept being used to criticize market economics. In *Mater et Magistra* in 1961, John XXIII had argued that the need for all to share in the common good justified employee share ownership and state intervention, including nationalisation.[31] In line with wider developments in Western culture, Vatican II conceived the common good in global, rather than national, terms. *Pacem in Terris* said that nations were 'unequal to the task of promoting the common good of all peoples', and instead called for international authorities to do this job.[32]

As Rufus Black has already shown, a number of theorists (most, but not all, of them Catholics) have developed these ideas on the common good in recent years. Two aspects of the Vatican II idea of the common good – its globalism and its critique of market economics – proved particularly influential. The global idea of the common good found expression in the activities of pressure groups and aid organizations like Oxfam, founded by a group of Oxford Christians in 1942. The rise of the term 'non-governmental organization' to describe charities and international bodies shows how their moral status was invested by their distance from governments. Holger Nehring's essay in this book shows how the idea of a global common good was also pursued in the Campaign for Nuclear Disarmament, and when fear of nuclear war receded somewhat after 1989, it was replaced by alternative fears about global warming, which also lent itself to a global conception of the common good. As Jane Garnett's essay shows, the rise of the internet has recently offered both a technological means towards, and a utopian avatar of, the global common good.

The common good's potency against market capitalism meant that it resurfaced in British political debate in the 1980s and 1990s. It filled a hole in Thatcherite discourse, and highlighted the poverty of that discourse. The Anglican *Faith in the City* report in 1985 followed Catholic thought in asserting that 'the Church has to be ready to challenge any understanding of community . . . which is concerned with individuals' rights and material possessions at the expense of the common good'.[33] The power of this critique impressed those (some of them Christian socialists, including Tony Blair) who sought to reform the Labour Party in the 1990s. For them, the common good was attractive not just because it offered a critique of Thatcherite economics, but because it offered a holistic alternative to the fragmented identity politics which had rendered Labour unelectable.[34] It was also a conveniently vague formulation to mask the fact that the party had dropped its commitment to nationalization; in the 1994 rewritten Labour Party Constitution, the old Clause IV commitment to 'common ownership of the means of production, distribution and exchange' was replaced by a commitment to 'a thriving public sector and high quality services, where those undertakings essential to the common good are either owned by the public or accountable to them'.[35] The re-emergence of the term in domestic politics was underlined by the fact that the Catholic Bishops of England and Wales entitled their letter to voters before the 1997 election *The Common Good*.[36]

The revival of ideas of the common good has been tentative and contested. Liberals remain concerned at the term's normative and coercive potential, and it was recently dropped from the National Curriculum, to the anger of Roman Catholic teachers.[37] Nevertheless, the common good does represent one sort of Christian discourse which is intelligible and largely acceptable to non-Christians. The success of charitable campaigns like Jubilee 2000 shows that it is possible for campaigns rooted in a specifically Christian commitment to attain a salience with a wider public; this is an aspect of Bhikhu Parekh's idea of 'mixed discourse', which is further discussed in Matthew Grimley's case study. The mission statements of aid agencies like Christian Aid, CAFOD and the microcredit agency Opportunity International all affirm that they are Christian in inspiration, but that they do not seek to discriminate between recipients on grounds of religion.[38] Both in the international sphere and in domestic politics, the rhetoric of the common good is a useful umbrella for collaboration between Christian and Muslim bodies because of its closeness to the concept of *maslaha*, or public good, in Islamic law.[39] Significantly, the Muslim Council of Britain has chosen 'The Common Good' as the title of its newsletter, while a Home Office-funded report for the Inter-Faith Network in 2003 was entitled 'Partnership and the Common Good'.[40] In a sense, this is a return to the late nineteenth-century idea of the common good, which Idealists like T. H. Green envisaged as an ideal which could unite Christians and agnostics alike in the pursuit of a common programme of social service.[41]

The common good, then, was not replaced by consumerism – or by the desire to be Britney Spears. Rather, what happened to the common good is an example of David Martin's argument that far from being lost, Christian language has mutated and migrated.[42] The following three case studies explore the mutation of ideas of the common good in, respectively, state, civil society, and nation. Raymond Plant's case study describes in detail the process by which the British state has come to assume a position of neutrality between different conceptions of the good. Drawing on his own experiences of recent debates in the House of Lords, he points out some of the difficulties of this neutrality for church leaders, who have had to frame their contributions to public debate in terms of a Rawlsian overlapping consensus, rather than by appealing to their own traditions. He also reflects on how the 1998 Human Rights Act might complicate the traditional collaboration between the state and religious organizations in welfare and education, by forcing the religious bodies to subscribe to liberal tenets which go against their own doctrines. He does not find the natural law tradition a convincing bridge between Christianity and the emerging modern liberal state.

Plant writes as a political theorist who is a defender of Rawls' vision of a neutral public sphere. His argument that church leaders are no longer able to make public utterances based on their own doctrines is challenged by Matthew Grimley in his case study 'Public Intellectuals and the Media'. Grimley suggests that the public have in fact been willing to listen to, and take moral guidance from, religious leaders, even when they do not espouse their belief systems. This is an example of how the public sphere has not, in fact, become secular in a pluralistic society, but has instead accommodated a diversity of religious voices. Multiculturalism has involved the extension, rather than the diminution, of state support for religion. This process has in general been beneficial to Christianity because it has increased the visibility and recognition of religion in general, though it also carries some pitfalls. Grimley argues that the relationship of public intellectuals and the media with Christianity has not been as oppositional as the rhetoric of both sides has sometimes seemed to suggest, and that secularism has in fact generally been weak among the intelligentsia.

Robert Tobin's essay explores how the old elision of national religion and national identity has given way to a more pluralistic and negotiable sort of identity – but in the different context of Britain's neighbour, the Republic of Ireland. Many of the same social changes have affected the two countries in recent years, in particular the impact of mass immigration, though Tobin shows that the Irish have more readily embraced the European Union as an international model of the common good, not least because it offers an attractive alternative to old sectarian labels. While this introduction has argued that Catholic versions of the common good have provided an alternative to the old elision of Protestantism and nation in Britain, Tobin demonstrates a fascinating reverse process taking place in Ireland, where the pluralistic model of community espoused by the Church of Ireland has seemed to many outsiders to offer an attractive alternative to Catholic monoculturalism.

Notes

1 The Common Good supplement, *Guardian*, 22 March 2001, p. 1.

2 A point made recently by Jeffrey Cox, 2003, 'Master Narratives of Long-Term Religious Change', in Hugh McLeod and Werner Ustorf (eds), *The Decline of Christendom in Western Europe, 1750–2000*, Cambridge: Cambridge University Press, pp. 201–17; and Jeremy Morris, 'The Strange Death of Christian Britain; another look at the secularisation debate', *Historical Journal* (2003), 968.

3 Thomas Kselman, 'Challenging Dechristianization: The Historiography of Religion in Modern France', *Church History* 75 (2001), 130–9.

4 See Susan Thorne, 1999, *Congregational Missions and the Making of an Imperial Culture in Nineteenth-Century England*, Stanford: Stanford University Press, p. 3.

5 For early formations of this theory, see Berger, *Social Reality of Religion* and Thomas Luckmann, *The Invisible Religion: The Problem of Religion in Modern Society*, New York: Macmillan, 1963.

6 Casanova, *Public Religions*; Davie, *Memory Mutates*.

7 For attempts at remedying this deficiency, see Grimley, *Citizenship*; S. J. D. Green, 'Survival and Autonomy: On the strange fortunes and peculiar legacy of ecclesiastical establishment in the modern British state, c. 1920 to the present day', in S. J. D. Green and R. C. Whiting (eds), 1996, *The Boundaries of the State in Modern Britain*, Cambridge: Cambridge University Press, pp. 299–324.

8 D. L. LeMahieu, 1988, *A Culture for Democracy: Mass Education and the Cultivated Mind between the Wars*, Oxford: Oxford University Press, esp. pp. 227–36; S. Fielding, P. Thompson and N. Tiratsoo, 1995, *England Arise! The Labour Party and*

Popular Politics in 1940s Britain, Manchester: Manchester University Press, Ch. 6; see also Lawrence Black, 2003, *The Political Culture of the Left in Affluent Britain, 1951–64*, Basingstoke: Palgrave, pp. 85–6.

9 *Labour and the New Society* (1950), p. 16, quoted in Lawrence Black and Hugh Pemberton, 2004, *An Affluent Society? Britain's Postwar Golden Age Revisited*, Aldershot: Ashgate, p. 72.

10 Edward Shils and Michael Young, 'The Meaning of the Coronation', *Sociological Review*, new series, I (1953), 64–5, 69, 77.

11 Devlin, 'Morals and the Criminal Law' (1959) in Patrick Devlin, 1965, *The Enforcement of Morals*, Oxford: Oxford University Press, pp. 4, 23.

12 Mark Jarvis, 2005, *Conservative Governments: Morality and Social Change in Affluent Britain, 1957–1964*, Manchester: Manchester University Press, pp. 13, 163.

13 TNA:PRO;PREM 11/3264, Eccles to Macmillan, 3 July 1961.

14 Eugenia Low, 2000, 'The Concept of Citizenship in Twentieth Century Britain: Analysing Contexts of Development', in P. Catterall, W. Kaiser and U. Walton Jordan (eds), *Reforming the Constitution: Debates in Twentieth Century Britain*, London: Frank Cass, p. 196; Jose Harris, 'Political Thought and the State', in Green and Whiting, *Boundaries of the State*, pp. 15–28, at p. 27; Andrew Vincent and Raymond Plant, 1984, *Philosophy, Politics and Citizenship: The Life and Thought of the British Idealists*, Oxford: Blackwell, pp. 180–1.

15 Tony Crosland, 1956, *The Future of Socialism*, London: Jonathan Cape, p. 524. But Crosland was not consistent in this repudiation of public virtue; in wartime Italy, he had decried the fact that the Italians 'lack a social conscience; the common good takes precedence over the individual good'. He continued to use a heavily moralized political rhetoric after publishing *The Future of Socialism*. See Jeremy Nuttall, 'Labour and the Improvement of Minds', *Historical Journal* (2003), 133–53.

16 Matthew Grimley, 'The Religion of Englishness: Puritanism, Providence and National Character, c 1918–1945', *Journal of British Studies*, forthcoming, 2007.

17 Chris Waters, '"Dark Strangers" in our Midst: Discourses of Race and Nation in Britain, 1947–1963', *Journal of British Studies*, 36 (1997), 207–38.

18 For the ideology of the Commonwealth, see John W. Cell, 'Colonial Rule', in Judith M. Brown and Wm Roger Louis (eds), 1999, *The Oxford History of the British Empire IV: The Twentieth Century*, Oxford: Oxford University Press, pp. 251–3.

19 H. L. A. Hart, 1963, *Law, Liberty and Morality*, London: Oxford University Press.

20 For two introductions to these debates, see Alasdair MacIntyre, 'The Privatisation of the Good: An Inaugural Lecture', *The Review of Politics*, 52 (Summer, 1990), 344–77; Raymond Plant, 2001, *Politics, Theology and History*, Cambridge: Cambridge University Press, Ch. 8.

21 Raphael Samuel, 'The Lost World of British Communism', *New Left Review*, I/154, November–December 1985, p. 8.

22 Abigail Wills, 'Masculinity and Citizenship in England 1950–1970', *Past and Present* (May 2005), 159–85.

23 Julia Stapleton, 'Citizenship versus Patriotism in Twentieth Century England', *Historical Journal* 48 (2005), 174–5.

24 Low, 'The Concept of Citizenship', p. 197.

25 On linguistic shifts, see John Sutherland, 'How the Potent Language of Civic Life was Undermined', *Guardian*, 21 March 2001, Common Good supplement, p. 10.

26 Sennett, *Fall of Public Man*; David Marquand, 2004, *The Decline of the Public: The Hollowing Out of Citizenship*, Cambridge: Polity.

27 Martin, *Sociology*, p. 194; Bernice Martin, 2003, 'The Non-Quantifiable Religious Dimensions in Social Life', in Avis (ed.), *Public Faith?*, pp. 1–18, at p. 4.

28 See John Habgood (ed.), 1983, *Church and Nation in a Secular Age*, London:

Darton, Longman & Todd, Ch. 6; *Faith and Nation: A Report of a Commission of Inquiry to the UK Evangelical Alliance (2006)*, available at http://www.eauk.org/faithandnation – accessed 03.11.06.

29 Charles E. Curran, 2002, *Catholic Social Teaching 1891–Present: A Historical, Theological and Ethical Analysis*, Washington, DC: Georgetown University Press; Paul Vallely (ed.), 1998, *The New Politics: Catholic Social Teaching for the Twenty-First Century*, London: SCM Press.

30 *Pacem in Terris* (1963), paragraph 56, reprinted in Michael Walsh and Brian Davies (eds.), 1984, *Proclaiming Justice and Peace: Documents from John XXIII to John Paul II*, London: Collins, p. 56.

31 *Mater et Magistra* (1961), in Walsh and Davies, *Proclaiming Justice and Peace*, pp. 1–44.

32 *Pacem in Terris*, paragraph 131, in Walsh and Davies, *Proclaiming Justice and Peace*, p. 69.

33 *Faith in the City*, p. 59.

34 Mark D. Chapman, 2005, *Blair's Britain: A Christian Critique*, London: Darton, Longman & Todd, pp. 62–4.

35 For a comparison of the two texts, see thecitizen.org.uk/views/clause4.htm – accessed 28.10.06.

36 www.catholicchurch.org.uk/sources/cg/index.htm – accessed 27.10.06.

37 *The Tablet*, 5 August 2006, p. 44.

38 See www.christian-aid.org.uk/aboutca/index.htm;www.cafod.org.uk/about_cafod/vision/vision_mission_and_values;www.opportunity.org.uk/about-us.htm – accessed 03.11.06.

39 We are grateful to Professor Francis Robinson for his advice on this point.

40 http://www.mcb.org.uk/media/newsletters.php – accessed 29.10.06; Partnership and the Common Good: Inter-faith Structures and Local Government' (2003), www.interfaith.org.uk/publications/goodpracticeguidelines.pdf – accessed 27.10.06.

41 For the Idealist version of the common good, see his 'Green and the Common Good', in Peter Nicholson, 1990, *The Political Philosophy of the British Idealists*, Cambridge: Cambridge University Press, pp. 54–82; Sandra Den Otter, 1996, *British Idealism and Social Explanation: A Late Study in Late Victorian Thought*, Oxford: Oxford University Press; Vincent and Plant, *Philosophy, Politics and Citizenship*.

42 David Martin, 1997, *Does Christianity Cause War?*, Oxford: Clarendon Press; and Martin, *Christian Language*.

Case Studies

Liberalism, Religion and the Public Sphere
  Raymond Plant

Public Intellectuals and the Media
  Matthew Grimley

The Evolution of National and Religious Identity in
Contemporary Ireland
  Robert Tobin

CASE STUDY

Liberalism, Religion and the Public Sphere

RAYMOND PLANT

The cardinal fact which faces us today is the religious heterogeneity of the modern State. Toleration has not yet produced all its fruits; perhaps it is nowhere quite complete. Still it is clear that a uniform State religion has departed.

J. N. Figgis, *Churches in the Modern State* (1913)

The establishment of the Church of England has, from its inception, posed central questions about the relationship between church, nation, politics and society. These questions have engaged divines as diverse as Hooker, Pusey, Coleridge, Creighton, Keble, Temple, Gore, Figgis, and Scott-Holland. Some of these thinkers have adopted a 'Christian Nation' approach, which embodies a high doctrine of the place and vocation of the church in society, claiming that the church has the task and the duty to define and articulate the fundamental ethical principles that should govern both private and public morality. Protagonists of the Christian nation approach to the relationship between church and state differ in the intensity with which they organize their case, but their message is essentially the same. In *The Idea of a Christian Society*, T. S. Eliot argued in favour of the idea of a natural order which the church could articulate, and which even non-Christians could accept, just because it would be an appeal to a *natural* order and that this would be the basis of what he called a 'Christian organisation of society'.[1] Such a view requires considerable theological justification. There has to be a basis to the claim that the church has a morally privileged position in society, such that it can claim some moral authority not just over its own members, but in the nation as a whole. This cannot just be understood as being the result of historical contingency. Rather it also has to rest on some theological claims about the nature of the church and of the society and state to which it ministers and witnesses. A church aspiring to speak for the nation and having a privileged position in the state needs to have a social and political theology: a theological understanding of the nature of the society and the state within which it operates. Any such social and political theology now will have to take full account of the degree of ethnic, religious and cultural pluralism in modern society. Unless the church has a clear grasp of the political impact of this pluralism it is not likely to be able to relate to it and its consequences in a constructive and realistic manner. One central element of a concern with the growing pluralism of modern society is with what could be the basis of social unity in a society marked by this diversity. A national church ought to have this question high on its agenda, because it is not at all clear how social unity in a pluralistic society relates to specifically religious understandings of the unity of society.

One very plausible answer to the question about social unity is given by modern liberalism: that the unity of modern society is not to be found in shared substantive ideas about what the human good and human flourishing consist in, but rather in the framework within which individuals pursue their diverse goods. This framework will concern the basic rights that people should have, the equal concern and respect with which they should be treated, the claim that the state should be as neutral as possible between different and divergent conceptions of the good, and with protecting human choice and autonomy. In this sense the focus of social unity has moved from the *good* to *procedure*, or *rules*: from a sense of a common good to shared procedures facilitating the pursuit of individual goods. The common good is this framework, rather than shared substantive goals. From the perspective of political liberalism this is what we share in common, not a substantive idea of the good and human flourishing and human virtue. If this is becoming an important conception of what it is that gives unity to society, then a national church has to learn how to address this issue if it is to speak about what we do and do not have in common as citizens. On this view of political liberalism, it is important to distinguish between what we have in common as citizens – the framework of laws and rights protecting freedom – and what we might or might not have in common as private adherents of particular faiths. Citizenship and the religious life are not co-extensive and the virtues relative to each are not at all the same.

A new form of public philosophy is becoming increasingly prominent in British society, which is dominated by modern liberal principles, particularly relating to human rights, the relative moral neutrality of the state and the centrality of the idea of individual autonomy. Earlier forms of liberalism had not detached liberal principles so much from substantive moral values; they were highly moralized and often indebted to natural law and ideas about the natural goods of human life. Modern liberalism contains far less of this, and, from the point of view of modern liberal thinkers, for very good reasons. The closer liberal principles are allied to conceptions of the good, the less likely will it be that liberalism can act as the basis of social unity in a society which is marked by a high degree of dissensus over substantive moral views. The liberalism with which I am concerned in this case study is primarily a response to pluralism and not a developed and rich moral doctrine on its own, which might well preclude it from dealing with the problems of pluralism.

It can be argued that such liberalism as is developing in the UK responds to a situation in which traditional values and institutions, including those involving religion, are either changing or eroding at least so far as the public world is concerned. Since the Reformation, the Church of England has been inextricably linked with a political and social settlement which has over the centuries received a substantial degree of historical and traditional legitimacy. It is represented in Parliament; the monarch is its Supreme Governor, its rites are used in state occasions. There are also many studies, such as Peter Laslett's *The World We Have Lost*,[2] and Gordon Schochet's *Patriarchalism in Political Thought*,[3] which demonstrate the close relationship of the Church of England to social organization and how over a very long period its catechism played a significant role in the shaping of social and political attitudes. The church was also, and still is, heavily involved in education, and for a very long time the role of the parson was central in organizing simple types of schooling in his parish. Thus the church has been part of a traditional and habitual way of life. It was part of what Hegel called *Sittlichkeit* – the ethical life of the community. Of course, tradition is not just some kind of homogenous given. Traditions can be interpreted in more than one way. There has, however, been an appeal to tradition by both church and state as a basis for legitimacy. Pluralism makes such appeals much more problematic in the modern world. Why is this so?

We can no longer appeal to tradition as the sole or primary basis of a public philosophy. The authority of tradition has become highly problematic. Once you can ask the question 'What authority does tradition have?' then tradition has lost its authority, because if we answer the question by invoking reasons why we should carry on in the traditional manner, then the authority of the tradition has actually transferred itself to *those* reasons, and will depend on the plausibility of those reasons. I am not decrying the power of the evocation of a tradition. Indeed evocations of tradition can be very moving – but only because they make explicit what is still present in a habitual way of life to which people are attached or are laments for a lost way of life. Nonetheless, once an understanding of a tradition has become contested and subject to widely different interpretations, as happens in a pluralistic society embodying a wide range of standpoints, then it cannot be appealed to in a straightforward way as the basis of legitimacy. Thus, the argument for a purely traditional approach to the legitimacy of institutions and as a basis for social unity is now deeply problematic. Second, to be a basis for public life and its unity, tradition has to embrace the whole of the community, but in modern Britain there are now many religious, ethnic and cultural communities which either do not share, or have not shared, in a traditional understanding of the public life of Britain. Such pluralism makes it very difficult to appeal directly to an established tradition.

We still need some basis for social unity in a diverse society, and tradition can no longer fulfil that role. One possibility that is emerging and developing in Britain is the liberal approach. The liberal position as a basis for social unity means essentially that the basic institutions and policies of the state find their legitimacy not in habit, tradition, or a uniquely religious justification, but in terms of protecting equal rights. These rights are in turn justified in the protection that they afford to significant human choices and human interests which serve the goal of human autonomy. In addition, the state should be as neutral as possible between different and self-chosen conceptions of the good. The only justification for the state intervening to prevent the pursuit of a conception of the good by an individual would be that that conception of the good would, if realized, prevent other people from pursuing their conception of the good. Liberty is to be restricted only for the sake of liberty. Institutions and policies are not to be justified in terms of some dominant conception of the good or some specific conception of human flourishing, as might be found in a Christian perspective. Rather the central thing is autonomy and the set of rules which provide the framework within which autonomous choice can be pursued. To quote John Rawls, a fully articulated liberalism will put the 'right before the good'.[4] It is concerned with the rules or framework for individual autonomy rather than with the goals and purposes of society. These are a matter of individual choice. Hence liberalism in this sense is deontological rather than teleological; nomocratic rather than telocratic.

If this is so, then several things follow. First of all it means that a concern for equal rights and autonomy is the default position of public debate within a liberal society. Thicker and, for example, religiously based ideas about virtue and the good get edged out of social and political debate, whether it is about the age of consent for gays, abortion, assisted suicide or Sunday trading. The question is no longer about the rightness or wrongness of gay sex so much as the issue of equal rights: why should the age of consent for gay sex be different from that of heterosexuals? We are no longer talking about virtue, but rather about equal rights which, it might be claimed, are the dominant 'virtue' of liberalism.

The only justification for resisting equal rights from the point of view of political liberalism is to be found in making a case that lowering the age of consent will produce some kinds of objective harms to other people – harms which can be acknowledged by all independently of any system of belief. For example, some religious critics of the liberalization of the age of consent for gay sex have joined forces with secular critics by arguing that the rate of sexually transmitted infection will increase. The argument based upon a specifically religious conception of the good has been displaced by arguments about objective harm which do not depend particularly on religious belief. Religious critics of assisted suicide have also used secular arguments against it, rather than thicker religious arguments based upon a conception of the good. These include arguments about the coarsening of the doctor–patient relationship, or the fear that people in this position might be pressurized by avaricious relatives into seeking to terminate their lives. Common cause is made with secular views to produce a kind of universal or common set of reasons, rather than invoking reasons of a specifically religious character. There are many other public policy issues where this logic also applies.

We can see, then, some reticence within the British churches about using specifically religious arguments in pursuit of policy objectives. At the same time, this has been set in a theoretical context by a number of liberal thinkers, particularly John Rawls, who focuses on the fact of pluralism in modern societies.[5] By this he means that people in modern societies differ in their conceptions of the good, and therefore social unity and the legitimacy of social and political institutions cannot be founded on just one conception of the good. Rawls calls religious and metaphysical beliefs in which ideas of the good are embedded 'comprehensive doctrines', and in our society no comprehensive doctrine can be taken as the sole source of legitimacy.

In this situation, the best that we can look for is an 'overlapping consensus' in which institutions and public policy are justified in terms of conceptions which can (not necessarily will) be affirmed by individuals and groups from the point of view of the comprehensive doctrines which they affirm. So, for example, there might well be an overlapping consensus about basic rights in the modern world, including the right to life and religious freedom. There will not be one unique justifying conception of the good underlying such a rights-based doctrine, rather it may be affirmed from people each within their own comprehensive doctrine. Allied to this is the idea of public reason: namely, a set of reasons that will be taken to count in public debate irrespective of which comprehensive doctrine an individual accepts, if any. In a sense this gives the philosophical reason why religious people in public forums like the House of Lords have founded their arguments in relation to contentious issues of public policy on arguments which one does not to have to be religious to accept. Discussions about the relationship between gay sex and public health, or the effect of assisted suicide on the doctor–patient relationship, might be seen as part of public reason in that they can be debated and tested by empirical evidence, a process which is independent of one's world-view or comprehensive doctrine. Nevertheless, they are reasons that can be accepted within different and incommensurable comprehensive doctrines. In a society marked by a high degree of pluralism, it is necessary to develop a conception of public reason which will transcend the reasons embedded in first-order comprehensive doctrines over which, given the fact of pluralism, we cannot expect agreement.

Adherents of comprehensive doctrines may, in their own communities of belief based upon those doctrines, still deploy the reasons which are specific to those doctrines, for example disciplining members whose actions may have flouted those doctrines. Such disciplining might, for example, mean exclusion, excommunication, or the denial of access to religious rites, and these sanctions will be justified by reasons and conceptions of virtuous conduct internal to these communities. The matter is, however, quite different in the public sphere. While a church might want, for example, to discipline a member on the grounds of homosexuality because such activity contravenes the conception of sexuality endorsed within that religious group, nevertheless, in the public sphere deliberation about public policy in relation to gays has to be based upon public reason and not on conceptions of virtue and vice drawn from comprehensive doctrines.

What follows is that religious beliefs have to be seen essentially as a *private* matter, since conceptions of virtue and human flourishing central to those religious beliefs have to be understood as internal and to have no direct purchase on the public realm. This is the case even when adherents of a religion interpret it to make intrinsic demands about the organization of the social and political order. These demands might be as general as a concern with basic forms of political organization or with what types of conduct might be permitted in society: for example abortion, gay sexuality, and assisted suicide. In so far as the arguments deployed in favour of these positions are drawn from comprehensive doctrines, they can have no purchase in the pluralistic public realm. In this sense the liberal position might be thought to endorse the privatization of religion.

It could be argued that the passing of the 1998 Human Rights Act (HRA), which came into force in 2000, is (along with related legislation like the 2004 Civil Partnerships Act) the clearest endorsement of the development of a liberal polity in Britain. Many of the issues that have historically been linked to particular accounts of the virtues and human flourishing within comprehensive doctrines are now to be seen as matters of basic and equal rights. The HRA provides an institutional basis for the idea of public reason, in that many social and political issues now have to be debated in the terms set out in the Act, rather than in terms of reasons embodied in disputed comprehensive doctrines. In so far as religious people do not engage with the reasons underlying the Act, and made explicit in the European Convention on Human Rights (ECHR), their views will, in effect, be ignored in the public realm. While the churches gained some exemptions from the HRA in relation, for example, to church schools where it would be possible to deny appointments on religious grounds without being regarded as being discriminatory, this does not breach the public–private divide which a liberal polity sets up because the school might be seen as not being a public authority in the full sense to which the Act applies. It is likely that such exemptions will not survive for long. At the time of writing, the government has proposed new Sexual Orientation Regulations which forbid any religious group offering services from discriminating against customers on the grounds of their sexual orientation.[6] In due course, government may also seek to force religious groups which are in receipt of state funding for welfare activities to follow the terms of the HRA concerning non-discrimination in employment. In this sense the public sphere may come to shape the private sphere, but *not* the other way round.

It might be thought that some of these difficulties for religious belief in a liberal society are overdone, because there is in fact a bridge between public and private reason available through natural law. The natural law is accessible for those who believe through faith and revelation, but it is available also to the secular intelligence through deliberation. Aquinas argued in *Summa Contra Gentiles*[7] that in using his intellect, he was deploying a universal faculty shared with pagans, and therefore he could share a perspective with them. This approach might lead us to recognize that in a pluralistic society there is a need for public reason as the basis of social unity but that, properly understood, the demands of public reason will cohere with religious conceptions through the idea of natural law and indeed natural rights. There is a bedrock of values lying either *behind* different pluralistic moralities or *implicit* within them, and from these deep shared 'natural' conceptions we could distil a sense of public reason which would not divide the public and the private. The churches could articulate this natural law-based public reason and still witness to social union from a specifically religious standpoint. This is very much a modern form of the conception lying behind the views of T. S. Eliot and others.[8]

Critics of this approach will, however, argue that while it might very well be possible to agree on a very basic set of natural values, these will be very far from constituting a workable idea of public reason in a pluralistic society. There are two reasons for this. Agreement on 'natural' principles might only be possible in virtue of their almost total vacuity. We might well all accept that murder is wrong and agree that this is not disputed whatever the degree of pluralistic disagreement. However, as it stands, this principle helps us very little because the dispute between pluralistic positions is about what actually counts as murder. Is abortion murder? Is assisted suicide murder? Capital punishment? Different pluralistic moralities will find different answers to these questions from within their own comprehensive doctrines, and agreement on the thin 'natural' principle will not survive attempts to 'thicken' up that principle into a set of values to underpin public policy.

The second reason is that such natural principles and values do not cover the whole field of pluralistic contention in modern societies. First of all, in respect of sexuality, some comprehensive doctrines will regard gay sexual relations as unnatural and to be condemned on that basis, while others in society will not see the issue in that way at all, and will in any case want to question the whole assumption that what is natural is good and what is unnatural is wrong. There are many natural things in this world which we can hardly regard as good – death being one example. Second, we may just have a straight dispute between a claim that one protagonist regards as natural, which is rejected by the opposing side. There is nowhere else to go in terms of a moral resolution of the problem. One person may regard a woman's right to control her own fertility and to choose whether or not to carry a foetus to term as a natural right; others will dispute the moral basis of this position. So it would be very difficult to justify the claim that there is a bridge available between public reason and private comprehensive doctrines via the notion of a natural set of goods and rights. It seems that even if such goods and rights are recognized in a 'thin' sort of way, issues of dispute and incommensurability will return once the attempt is made to make such principles more substantial.

A number of problems about the liberal polity which I have described remain for its protagonists to address. One problem for liberals is how adherents of comprehensive doctrines can come to feel a sense of loyalty to, and the legitimacy of, a liberal polity whose public sphere is marked by public reason, the central elements of which are not the reasons with which adherents to comprehensive doctrines feel the greatest sense of identity. To put the matter bluntly: why should an adherent of a comprehensive doctrine which embodies the belief, say, that gay sex is wrong, unnatural or perverted be prepared to subordinate this judgment to the demands of public reason? It is the comprehensive doctrine, after all, to which the adherent has the greatest sense of loyalty.

It might be argued that we have to distinguish here between two different points, the first being the justification of the basic constitutional structure of a liberal polity, the second being the justification of particular policies produced after deliberation within the institutions of that constitutional structure. Given the salience of this distinction, it could then be argued that there might be questions about loyalty at the constitutional level which are not the same as loyalty at the level of accepting policy outcomes from within that constitutional settlement. I may accept for good reasons a liberal constitutional structure and yet from within my comprehensive doctrine object very strongly to a particular policy outcome of the political process – for example the liberalization of the law governing the age of consent. However, this will not really do. Both of these levels engage the same issues that I have been discussing because there is not a clear distinction between policy and constitution in the areas on which I have focused. We might take the policy issues that I have raised, such as homosexual rights, as examples of particular policies, but they are likely to be resolved in terms of conceptions drawn from the HRA and ECHR, which are constitutional documents. There is no sharp demarcation between policy and constitutional structures and procedures in such cases. Both will engage public reason and neither can be regarded as being legitimated by just one comprehensive doctrine – although the Rawlsian hope as outlined is that they will be endorsed by comprehensive doctrines in their own ways and from perspectives arrived at through an overlapping consensus. So we cannot respond to the question about legitimacy and loyalty by saying that basic adherence is to constitutional structures rather than to particular policy outcomes developed within that constitutional structure because both engage public reason (despite Rawls' hesitation about constitutional principles in this regard). In so far as they still lead to the privatization of comprehensive doctrines and beliefs, the question of loyalty and legitimacy remains.

It seems that the liberal has two ways of answering this question. The first is easily stated. It is that we have to find a firm basis for social unity in a modern complex and pluralistic society in public reason. We cannot find it in comprehensive doctrines, just because it is precisely the plurality and incommensurability of comprehensive doctrines that gives rise to the problem of social unity in the first place. If this is so, and if the adherent of a comprehensive doctrine is concerned about social unity and solidarity, then so far as public policy is concerned he or she will be prepared to subordinate the demands of his/her comprehensive doctrine to the demands of public reason. So while I may regard abortion as killing or even murder, I will be prepared to entertain this as a private belief and as a citizen subordinate that private belief to the demands of public reason and social unity. A great deal depends on whether or not a concern for social unity plays the central role that the liberal believes that it does in a modern pluralist society and whether this concern is part of what reasonableness means. It is, of course, open to the adherent of a comprehensive doctrine to say that what matters to him or her is to witness in the public realm to the truth of that doctrine irrespective of the effect that this will have on social unity. From this point of view, the place of social unity in the scheme of liberal values raises exactly the same questions as public reason: what is the basis for subordinating private belief to public reason and its demands? The same is true of social unity.

The second point is, as we have seen, to appeal to the idea of reasonable comprehensive doctrines. However, in this context the issue is rather different. An adherent to a comprehensive doctrine may take broadly one of two attitudes to his/her belief in that doctrine. The first is when the belief is a fundamentalist one. This stance entails first, that I know (from my own point of view) that my doctrine is true, and second, that I do not recognize that it is reasonable for others to disagree with it. There are, in my view, no good grounds for that disagreement. The second attitude of belief is that, while I believe my comprehensive doctrine to be true, I can recognize that it is reasonable for others to disagree with it: it may after all be based on more than empirical evidence, on faith, on revelation, etc. These are not problematic for *my* belief but I can recognize that they are for *others*. Belief in this second sense is 'reasonable' (to use Rawls' terminology) in contrast to a fundamentalist approach to belief which cannot accept that it is reasonable for others to disagree with it. If we adopt the reasonable approach to belief then we may also adopt what Nagel calls epistemological restraint.[9] That is to say that, while from my own point of view I may live my life according to my basic beliefs, nevertheless I recognize that it is not reasonable for me to demand the same of others in society who reasonably disagree with my belief system. Hence, so far as public deliberation is concerned, we have to shift from private comprehensive beliefs to concepts and evidence which have a degree of inter-subjective endorsement, or public reason. Public reason as a basis for social unity follows from the idea of holding beliefs in a reasonable manner.

This means that the ideal of public reason will appeal to, and provide, a basis for the legitimacy of, and loyalty to, both constitutional principles and policies on the part of those who hold to their comprehensive doctrines in a reasonable way. Another way of making the point is that the ideal of public reason will appeal to those who hold their comprehensive beliefs in a *liberal* way – that is recognizing the reasonableness of disagreement. If this is so then there are two problems for the liberal here. The first is that this seems to imply that the argument about public reason is part of a *circle* of justification rather than being in any sense *foundational*. Liberal-minded people will hold their comprehensive doctrines in a liberal-minded way and will endorse public reason as the liberal response to reasonable pluralism. Those who do not hold their beliefs in this way – the unreasonable or fundamentalists – may of course end up being coerced by liberal policies based upon the demands of public reason. Indeed, at the time of writing this is a very live issue in British politics when all sorts of institutions are being urged by the Government to challenge fundamentalist Islamic beliefs. Does the liberal position possess the moral resources to justify this coercion of the unreasonable? The more liberalism is seen as a way of coping with diversity, the thinner its authority might be seen to be, particularly by those who hold comprehensive doctrines in an unreasonable manner; the richer and thicker liberalism is, however, the more it will seem to be one among a range of competing comprehensive doctrines and may be seen as part of the problem of pluralism rather than the solution to it.

The same issue about reasonableness applies also to liberalism in a more positive way. A liberal may well accept that communities of all sorts, among them communities of faith, are a very important setting for human development, including the development of autonomous choice which might be seen as a central value of liberalism.[10] It might be seen as a necessary background for choice in that individuals are not just born, but develop in all kinds of social settings including communities. They derive a sense of identity and worth through this developmental process and the intellectual and moral resources to make choices and to follow a conception of the good. At least they do if the communities in which they develop are of a reasonable sort – that is if they teach the comprehensive doctrines on which they are based in a reasonable, tolerant and open manner. Within a liberal society the value of community as essential to human development may well be recognized but such communities have to be liberalized. There may be a programme for the liberalization of faith groups – for example, requiring that faith schools adhere to the National Curriculum founded on the development of choice, autonomy, tolerance, respect for other faith groups, or in other words 'reasonableness'. But liberal political thought has to have some basis for justifying this liberalization to the adherents of faith groups who might not otherwise communicate their faith to a new generation in a reasonable way.

It would be quite wrong to think that liberalism as a developing public philosophy in the UK is without its problems and that all the problems are on the side of faith groups. In some sense, as I suggested earlier, if we see liberalism as the emerging public philosophy, it is a public philosophy which, whether intentionally or unintentionally, will reshape the nature of private belief too. The difficulty for liberalism is that the richer it becomes as a moral and political belief system, the more like one of the competing comprehensive doctrines it becomes. Yet it is often proposed as a way of dealing with the clash of comprehensive systems. Obviously it cannot do that if it too has become one of the comprehensive doctrines itself.

As we have seen, for the liberal all of this is a consequence both of the fact of pluralism and the decline of a traditional public philosophy which has lost its legitimacy with the demise of the way of life that engendered it. Both of these pose fundamental questions for the Christian churches, and most acutely for the Church of England as the established church in England. It is the embodiment of a comprehensive doctrine and is also at the heart of national institutions in Parliament and in relation to the monarchy. How does it respond to the fact of pluralism and the challenge of a new public philosophy? It somehow has to speak to a pluralistic nation from within a comprehensive doctrine, and in a situation in which public morality and the law have moved decisively away from an understanding of public life and institutions as being founded on a particular comprehensive doctrine.

There are certainly no easy answers to these questions. Appeal to tradition is unlikely to help. Take for example the reform of the House of Lords. If there is a further reform taking the Lords in a more democratic direction, this is going to raise basic questions about the role of the bishops in the Lords in the face of a more, or indeed wholly, democratic House. If the argument is put for religious, but not exclusively Anglican, representation, that is bound to raise the question of what types of religious beliefs should have *ex officio* representation in the legislature and what role the Church of England would then have as the national church if other religions (and not just other Christian denominations) had such a role. It would also mean confronting head-on many of the points made in this case study about whether the adherents of comprehensive doctrines should have a public and political voice as *adherents* of such doctrines as opposed to *citizens* with a commitment to public reason.

It might be argued that Anglicanism has the moral and theological resources to address these problems, because while the Christian Nation approach has, at various times, been important to the church's understanding of its mission as the established church in England, there has nevertheless been an important alternative strand of more pluralistic thinking in the history of the church. The most vigorous defender of a pluralist conception of both the church and politics was the Mirfield monk J. N. Figgis, and it is worth considering what his thought, developed in the early twentieth century, can contribute to the modern debate about the Anglican church, pluralism and the unity of society. There is certainly quite a bit of overlap between his conception of modern society and Rawlsian political liberalism, although their routes to these not dissimilar views are very different. It was central to Figgis' view that the church was no longer coextensive with the nation.[11] He argued that the modern state should provide the framework within which different and competing religious groups and denominations should have the greatest degree of freedom subject to similar freedom for other groups. They should be free and autonomous in their beliefs, liturgies, rituals, and internal order and discipline. It was not for the church to seek laws to impose its own conception of the good or virtue on the nation as a whole. For example, the church could have a very high doctrine of marriage, and could impose draconian sanctions on its own members who divorced, but it was not the function of the church, no longer coterminous with the nation, to impose that 'thick' doctrine on the rest of society. So far this looks quite like Rawlsian public reason and the distinction between the citizen and the adherent to private comprehensive doctrines.

There is however a difference, although Figgis is very inexplicit about the crucial detail of this. Namely where do we draw the line between crime and sin? A sin is defined religiously within the religious group whereas crime has to reflect the values of society as a whole, which almost certainly will not be dominated by religious conceptions. Divorce might be a sin within a comprehensive doctrine but we should not seek to criminalize it; murder is a sin within a comprehensive doctrine but so it is across society. Lying behind Figgis' pluralism is still some idea of a substantive social morality which would transcend group differences, including group differences about morality. As David Nicholls argues in *The Pluralist State*: 'Figgis' theory of a secular state assumes that Christians and non-Christians can agree on a broad political ethic, while disagreeing in their theological or metaphysical pictures of the world.'[12] For Rawls, such a political ethic arises out of public reason and has no metaphysical foundation, although people from different comprehensive doctrines may endorse it each from their own point of view. Figgis, however, has nothing like this to hand. Nicholls argues that he may implicitly be appealing to a natural law/natural order conception supporting his pluralism as the basis of a political ethic and the unity of society, but he certainly does not make this clear. If, however, that is what he has in mind, it would be necessary to tackle some of the deep problems with natural law to which I referred earlier. This does, however, look to be the only coherent approach to a religious view of pluralism if one wants to reject Rawlsian public reason on the theological grounds that it privatizes religion, or more tendentiously turns religion into a hobby. Transforming religion into a hobby, or reinstating it to a proper place within a liberal society, is a problem with which the church will have to grapple and it will not do so by ignoring the deep problems with the standard intellectual resource open to it in this context – namely the natural law and natural order as the basis for political morality and social union, and as the bridge between those of faith and those without.

Notes

1 T. S. Eliot, 1939, *The Idea of a Christian Society*, London: Faber & Faber. See also 'Towards a Christian Britain', *The Listener*, 10 April 1941, pp. 524–5; 1943, 'Christianity and Natural Values', *Christian Newsletter*, 3 September 1943.

2 Peter Laslett, 1965, *The World We Have Lost*, London: Methuen.

3 Gordon Schochet, 1975, *Patriarchalism in Political Thought*, Oxford: Oxford University Press.

4 John Rawls, 1972, *A Theory of Justice*, Oxford: Oxford University Press.

5 John Rawls, 1996, *Political Liberalism*, New York: Columbia University Press.

6 'Emboldened Churches join Forces to Scupper New Law on Gay Rights', *The Times*, 2 December 2006; ' The Government must not buckle over Gay Rights', *Observer*, 3 December 2006.

7 Thomas Aquinas, 1988, *St. Thomas Aquinas on Politics and Ethics*, trans. and ed. Paul E. Sigmund, New York: Norton, pp. 1–13.

8 Eliot, 'Christianity and Natural Virtues'.

9 Thomas Nagel, 'Moral Conflict and Political Legitimacy', *Philosophy and Public Affairs*, 16(3) (1987), 215–240.

10 Will Kymlicka, 1989, *Liberalism, Community and Culture*, Oxford: Oxford University Press.

11 J. N. Figgis, 1913, *Churches in the Modern State*, London: Longmans, Green and Co.

12 David Nicholls, 1975, *The Pluralist State*, London: Macmillan, p. 105.

CASE STUDY

Public Intellectuals and the Media

MATTHEW GRIMLEY

Bel Mooney: Do you think it's true that religion is sneered at among people you would consider your peers?
Melvyn Bragg: I don't think so. I think that people are effectively indifferent to it, mostly.

(BBC Radio 4 interview, *Devout Sceptics* (1995))[1]

In July 2004, *Prospect* magazine produced a list of the top 100 public intellectuals in Britain. It included only two religious leaders, the Archbishop of Canterbury, Rowan Williams, and the Chief Rabbi, Jonathan Sacks, and no other theologian. When the magazine asked its readers to rank the top 100, the runaway winner was the evolutionary biologist and prominent atheist Richard Dawkins.[2] The same magazine's exercise to discover the world's top 100 intellectuals in November 2005 yielded only two Christian theologians, those unlikely bedfellows Pope Benedict XVI and Hans Küng.[3] Both the British and global lists included a large number of avowed atheists or secularists, but few professed Christians. They appeared to bear out the idea that by the start of the twenty-first century, the intelligentsia had become completely secular. But commenting on the original list of British intellectuals, the *Prospect* writer David Herman raised a note of doubt. 'Are we as secular as this list suggests?' he asked. 'Or are religious thinkers failing to reach out beyond their congregations or faiths?'[4] This case study takes up both these questions, and argues that the image of a secular public intelligentsia, and media, has been overdrawn.

The idea of a secular intelligentsia is an attractive one for various different groups, which share an interest in perpetuating it, but little else. It is undoubtedly true that for many secularists, the idea of the intellectual is inexorably bound up with traditions of Enlightenment rationalism and anti-clericalism, and to speak of a 'religious intellectual' is a category mistake. Equally, many Christians have liked to portray themselves in oppositional terms as a remnant buffeted by a rampantly secular national culture. Evangelicals are especially prone to this self-image, but it has plenty of scriptural validation, and is attractive to Christians of all parties; most recently it has been espoused by the Radical Orthodoxy movement. A third group consists of conservative commentators, who have liked to accuse the intelligentsia, including the clergy, of a gigantic *trahison des clercs*, which has led to the abandonment of Christian traditions and the secularization of national life.[5] A fourth group who have colluded in the idea of a secular intelligentsia are historians and sociologists, who have tended to assume that intellectuals were irrelevant to the fortunes of religion (and vice versa) in the twentieth century. In stark contrast to the copious coverage of the relationship between religion and intellectuals in the nineteenth century, almost nothing has been written about this subject. Intellectuals play no role in Callum Brown's thesis about *The Death of Christian Britain*. In Noel Annan's group autobiography of the post-war intelligentsia, *Our Age*, Christianity appears only as a barely residual trace in intellectual life. In his recent *Absent Minds: Intellectuals in Britain*, Stefan Collini finds it hard to mask his distaste at R. G. Collingwood and T. S. Eliot for letting the side down by evincing Christian commitment.[6]

Christian laments about the secularity of the intelligentsia are not new. In 1949, at the start of the period covered in this book, the academic and university administrator Sir Walter Moberly found himself bemoaning the specialization of contemporary intellectuals, and their neutrality on ethical and religious issues, and looking back to a lost era of Victorian moral consensus. 'Whatever the differences on religious and moral issues between Whewell and Mill, Gladstone and Huxley, Newman and Matthew Arnold, they had substantially the same standards of what was good and evil in moral conduct', he said. 'They all believed firmly in a system of objective values . . . But it is the validity of any moral order at all that is in question today.'[7] But Moberly's despair at the moral relativism of the academic world was mirrored by the despair which was expressed for entirely opposite reasons by E. P. Thompson in his essay 'Outside the Whale' in 1960. Thompson's complaint was that, repelled by Stalinism, the post-war intelligentsia had retreated into 'anti-politics', and that for many intellectuals, 'it seemed as though it was within traditional institutions and Christian doctrine that the true values of love and community had been conserved.'[8] The disparity between these views is a reminder that standpoint was all-important; the same intelligentsia which Moberly had attacked as godless was still too God-intoxicated for Thompson's taste.

Nevertheless, if we try to mediate between such polarized views, we can trace the lineaments of some generational changes in intellectuals' attitudes to Christianity in the post-war decades. These different views overlapped in time, so characterizing them by period is an inexact exercise, but we can discern three different attitudes to Christianity, which followed on from, though did not absolutely supersede, one another. During the first period, in the later 1940s and 1950s, there was a vigorous and vociferous Christian presence among the British intelligentsia. The Christian commitment of prominent literary figures, many of them 1930s converts to Anglicanism or

Catholicism, was still conspicuous, taking in Rose Macaulay, Dorothy Sayers, Agatha Christie, Evelyn Waugh, John Betjeman, Graham Greene, John Middleton Murry, and T. S. Eliot. Although some of these individuals were too wayward or spiky to belong to any sort of group, many had found themselves drawn into discussion and collaboration with other Christian writers and academics through wartime projects like the Moot, Sword of the Spirit, and the *Christian News-Letter*. Through these activities, and through their own novels, poems, plays and journalism, they ensured that there was still a public culture of discussion of religious themes in the later 1940s and 1950s.

Although many of these Christian intellectuals felt, like Moberly, that they were becoming marginal in post-war society, they were bolstered by a larger contingent of intellectuals who, whether or not they retained Christian belief, remained well disposed to Christianity out of a sense of convention, a desire to preserve Christian morality, or a feeling that it was part of their national character. Many of them retained a vestigial Christian observance, at least attending religious services when civil (Remembrance Sunday) or educational reasons (school or college chapel) required it. This sort of conventional religion was not restricted to conservative intellectuals. The Labour academic and politician Richard Crossman was once asked by the journalist C. H. Rolph why, as an agnostic, he was prepared to act as godfather to a friend's child, which involved assenting to the Creed. Crossman replied that

> in a Christian country . . . with an established church, the whole of public life, plus a great deal of what should be private life, was prescribed in this type of formula. It was part of the grammar of living . . . You either believed in it, or you paid lip-service to it (as you did at Prayers in the House of Commons or at the funerals of old friends) or you went away and dug a hole for yourself.[9]

Crossman was a good example of how a mid-twentieth century intellectual, having rejected Christianity in his youth, could also remain fascinated and engaged by it, championing the theology of Reinhold Niebuhr, writing a critique of Frank Buchman's Oxford Group in the 1930s, and attending meetings of the St Julian's Group, a short-lived successor to the Moot in the later 1940s. The combination of active Christians and 'fellow travellers' among the intelligentsia helped to maintain the sympathetic intellectual climate towards Christianity which E. P. Thompson lamented in 'Outside the Whale'.

In the later 1950s and early 1960s, as the late-Victorian generation were dying off, a new generation of intellectuals emerged who had no interest in religion, and who assumed its imminent demise. This was not a new phenomenon, but whereas before it had been restricted to self-conscious cadres like the Bloomsbury Group, it was now more pervasive. The biographer of the DNA pioneer Francis Crick has recently described how, in 1960s Cambridge, 'there was a feeling, not of triumphalism, but that religion was in inevitable, though gradual decline'.[10] Such a feeling was not restricted to atheists like Crick (or to Cambridge). It usually manifested itself in a tendency to ignore religion, rather than to criticize it, though some intellectuals affected a skittishness about all forms of religion, particularly Catholicism.[11] Its pervasiveness helps to explain why religion was absent from so much intellectual debate in this period; writing in 1963, the novelist Colin MacInnes remarked on how seldom religion was discussed in serious periodicals such as *Encounter*. 'It is noticeable that the subject is rarely raised', he said. 'It seems to be considered an embarrassment or, at best, an irrelevance.'[12]

This sense of religion as embarrassment or irrelevance suffused many academic disciplines from the later 1950s onwards. This was not just the case in philosophy, where logical positivism had proclaimed the impossibility of any discussion of theological or metaphysical questions.[13] Ashley Rogers Berner has shown how new psychological theories of child development replaced religious world-views in educational theory. Some emerging disciplines in the social sciences in the 1960s and 1970s were also marked by their secular assumptions. In race relations, the assumption that religious identities were transient or epiphenomenal, and that the essential identities were racial, was extremely pervasive. This resulted in the bracketing (and problematizing) of many immigrants under the artificial ethnic category of 'Asian', which many of them (Muslims in particular) found offensive.[14] Historical writing, too, was influenced by positivism. Discussion of religion was virtually omitted from major histories of the twentieth century such as A. J. P. Taylor's *English History, 1914–1945* (1965). In some intellectual histories published in the 1970s, there was a barely suppressed incredulity that their pre-modern subjects could seriously have believed in something as primitive as Christianity, and an indisposition to accept at face value their claims to have been motivated by it.[15] The fact that so many prominent historians ignored or belittled religion set a public tone for the discipline; when the *Times Literary Supplement* gave over three issues to 'New Ways in History' in 1966, none of the contributors (who included E. P. Thompson, Keith Thomas, and Eric Hobsbawm) discussed religious history.[16]

But from the 1960s onwards, there was a reaction against this 'airbrushing out' of religion. As we have seen, much of the new expressive culture rejected the bloodlessness of rationalism and sought to recapture the spiritual or transcendent. This process occurred in the academy as well as within wider popular culture. Anthropologists protested against the Marxist relegation of culture to the sub-structural, and sought to explore the cultural significance of religion.[17] Some theologians and philosophers attempted to reconcile Christianity and Marxism.[18] The new interest in 'history from below,' and a contemporary fascination with mysticism and utopian forms of community, led historians to attempt to recover the mentalities of marginalized religious groups in the past.[19] While much of the revived interest in religion was directed towards the East, this process in turn prompted historians to reconsider Christianity in comparative terms.

This 'return of the sacred' (to quote the title of Daniel Bell's famous 1979 lecture) was a gradual process, and in many disciplines it did not have a great impact until the 1980s or beyond. Events in the 1980s such as the Iranian revolution, the Rushdie Affair, and the fall of the Berlin Wall, forced social scientists to engage (whether critically or sympathetically) with religious commitment and agency. From the early 1980s, a number of historians sought to reinstate religion as a causal factor in events like the English Civil War, and to explain how theology continued to inform 'secular' politics into the modern period.[20] The decline of Marxism as a political system led to a more critical exploration of its intellectual debt (and that of socialism more generally) to Christian eschatology.[21] Some historians found Marxism and other progressive theories wanting in their failure to comprehend belief or identity.[22] Postmodernists and critics of Enlightenment universalism emphasized the foundational importance of Judaeo-Christian narratives in European culture.[23] These diverse threads did not amount to any sort of programme, and certainly not to any revival of Christian belief, but they did betoken a renewed appreciation of Christianity's contribution to culture, and of its seriousness as a subject of academic study.

There were a number of other connections between Christianity and the expressive culture which first emerged in the 1960s. One was the churches' identification with progressive causes. During the 1960s, the support of the Protestant denominations for reform of the law on suicide, divorce, and homosexuality insulated them from criticism. While the Catholic hierarchy lost support among its own university-educated adherents because of its opposition to some aspects of permissive reform, it was able to identify itself with other progressive movements such as international development, campaigns against miscarriages of justice, and the civil rights movement in Northern Ireland. As Holger Nehring's case study shows, a feature of British protest culture was its bringing together of Christians and non-Christians.[24] Despite the decline of political Nonconformity, the language of political dissent remained heavily imbued with Christian symbols and ideals, and (as our introductory chapter on the Common Good shows) was further infused from the 1960s onwards with a reworked Christian communitarianism.

This alliance of secular and Christian progressivism intensified in the 1980s, when clergy and the other expressive professions found themselves standing together in the Thatcherite firing-line. The Anglican *Faith in the City* Report in 1985 was welcomed by many outside the churches because it seemed to offer a critique of Thatcherite economics at a time when the political opposition was notably unable to do so; that it was wrongly denounced as 'Marxist' by a government minister only added to its credibility in *bien-pensant* circles. The Scottish churches played a crucial role in bringing together the political parties in the Scottish Constitutional Convention in 1989 to campaign for Scottish devolution.[25] The alliance between secular and Christian social action has more recently been attacked by secularists who find collaboration with 'faith-based' groups pernicious, but it has been strongly defended on grounds of utility and tradition by atheists like Roy Hattersley and Sir Bernard Crick.[26]

The affinity between Christianity and counter-cultural movements meant that the churches largely escaped unscathed from criticism of the Establishment, even though the term was itself borrowed from an ecclesiastical context.[27] Insofar as the clergy were the butt of satire, it was not for their obscurantism, but for their sometimes hapless attempts to appear 'with it' or 'in touch'. The intellectual contortions of liberal Anglicans were a recurrent target, caricatured in creations like Michael Wharton's Dr Spaceley-Trellis, the 'go-ahead' Bishop of Bevindon, and *Private Eye's* limp liberal cleric Dr J. C. Flannel and the 'Alternative Rocky Horror Service Book'. All these satires were written by church members or sympathetic outsiders, and all were relatively gentle. The same was true of David Lodge's comic novel about 1960s Catholic progressivism *How Far Can You Go?* (1980).[28]

More critical literary treatments of Christianity tended to attack the churches as institutions, rather than individual Christians, or Christianity as a belief system. Bernice Martin has already shown how Philip Pullman's animus in his novels is primarily against institutional religion, rather than the spiritual or numinous *per se*. In Antonia Bird's film *Priest* (1994), about a gay Catholic priest in Liverpool, and David Hare's anatomy of Anglicanism, *Racing Demon* (1990), ecclesiastical hierarchies were presented as sinister and hypocritical, but the heroes of both works were inner-city parish priests whose flaws were presented as evidence of their authenticity. Attacks on institutional churches have also been blunted by the fact that the Church of England has made a rather ineffectual villain of the piece, while Catholicism has more often been portrayed as a minority community rather than a hegemonic power structure. Memoirs of child abuse in Catholic orphanages or schools have been popular among an English middlebrow readership, but have almost all been set in Ireland, not England; two recent autobiographical accounts by English intellectuals of their Catholic upbringings, though not uncritical, are comical rather than recriminatory.[29]

It is also true that many intellectuals' commitment to tolerance has meant that they have eschewed militant attacks on religious belief. While noting that religion was largely ignored by intellectuals, Colin MacInnes also observed 'how rare is any militant expression of anti-religious feeling. Cordial blasphemy there may indeed often be, yet can one imagine anyone getting up anywhere in public, and seriously denouncing the Almighty without violent resentment and indignation?'[30] Since MacInnes wrote these words in 1963, taboos about public expressions of irreligion have significantly weakened, but they have been replaced by new codes of respect for individual authenticity, which preclude attacks on an individual's religious beliefs as they do his or her sexual orientation or ethnicity. The effect is much the same; intellectuals who ride roughshod over religious sensibilities still find themselves upbraided for intolerance or bigotry. The most recent antireligious polemic by Richard Dawkins, *The God Delusion* (2006), has topped the bestseller lists, but it has also been condemned by other nonbelievers, who, while agreeing with much of his critique of religion, have been repelled by its bludgeoning analysis and hectoring tone.[31] A collection of radio interviews with prominent figures in science, politics and the arts, *Devout Sceptics*, reveals the prevalence of a sort of wistful agnosticism, and an aversion to anything smacking of arrogant certainty on either the religious or secular side (though it might be reasonably be objected that a series with that title was more likely to attract agnostics with spiritual leanings than hardline materialists).[32]

Some religious leaders have continued to command a popular following in the post-war period. Here the perception of personal authenticity has played a role. Two of the most effective prelates since 1945, Cardinal Basil Hume and Archbishop Michael Ramsey, were popular with an educated public partly because they were widely perceived as possessing an aura of calm, wisdom, or even sanctity. Through force of personality, and a judicious choice of campaign issues, Hume was able to command a national following greater than any Catholic leader since the Reformation.[33] The popularity of these religious leaders was not restricted to their own followers; their moral and political pronouncements earned respect because they were seen as being rooted in an authentic religious commitment.

Here I would take issue with Raymond Plant when he says that senior clergy have avoided rooting their political pronouncements in any comprehensive doctrine, seeking instead to appeal to a Rawlsian 'overlapping consensus'. In fact, the public seems to have been receptive to appeals made in specifically Christian language on moral and political issues, even when they did not share the theological beliefs in which that language was rooted. It is true that on issues like the recent Assisted Dying Bill, religious leaders have been careful to offer pragmatic arguments against the measure (such as the difficulty of ascertaining whether or not an incapacitated person wants to die) as well as theological ones (the Christian doctrine of the sanctity of life).[34] But the Christian arguments are still voiced. As Bhikhu Parekh points out, this sort of 'mixed discourse' is in fact quite normal, and far less problematic than liberal theorists allow. 'The standard liberal theory finds it difficult to explain how we can communicate across different moral and political languages', he says. 'In fact we manage rather well.'[35] Parekh's idea of 'mixed discourse' explains why the more articulate and incisive Christian leaders have continued to enjoy a national audience beyond their own membership.

A more prosaic (some would even say banal) example of this 'mixed discourse' at work is the continuing popularity of the 'Thought for the Day' slot on Radio 4's *Today* programme. Attempts by BBC executives to axe 'Thought for the Day' have persistently been confounded by audience research which shows that it is more popular than other components of the programme.[36] The most popular presenters are ones in whom the audience discern some sort of authenticity. These need not be Christians; two of them, the Reformed Rabbi, Lionel Blue, and the Sikh journalist Indarjit Singh, represent two of the smaller religions in Britain. The audience does not have to subscribe to the doctrinal tenets of the speaker's religion in order to respond to the message.

The continuing ability of Christian leaders to command a popular audience is an illustration of the broader point that multiculturalism has not led to a secularization of the public sphere. Indeed, in some ways it has actually led to an extension of religion's role, as the state has acceded to Muslim demands for religious schools and (with qualifications) for protection against religious hatred. This has had the incidental effect of placing the privileges of Christian denominations on a firmer footing, because what had seemed rather anomalous privileges (for example, church schools), seem less anomalous when extended to other religious groups. If the proposals of the 2000 Wakeham Committee into House of Lords reform (or some variant on them) are implemented, the representation of religion in the House of Lords will similarly be extended to other religions, rather than ended.[37] Another public body which has continued to offer a protected status to religion while widening it beyond Christianity is the BBC. Here too, despite initial complaints by aggrieved Christians about the inclusion of other religions, it can be argued that the ring-fenced coverage of religion was given a stronger justification by being made in the name of *all* religions rather than just Christianity. The effect of post-1945 immigration has thus not been to create a secular state, but to extend the confessional state so that religion *in general* has been given a protected status.

In recent years, there has been a backlash from some secular-minded intellectuals against this extension of the protection and recognition of religion. Intellectuals who supported multiculturalism when it appeared to be about celebrating ethnic difference have become squeamish about its celebration of religious difference, and there have been a number of liberal critiques of multiculturalism.[38] In the most recent – and elegant – of these, Amartya Sen has warned that what is being created is not multiculturalism at all, but plural monoculturalism, in which communities defined by religious commitment are effectively segregated from one another.[39] For many critics, including Sen, the extension of state-funded religious schooling to include Muslims is an unwelcome development, and this has led them to condemn the whole principle of religious schooling. In recent debates, the discussion of the desirability of faith schools has been extrapolated from the hard case of the

Islamic school, even though there are still only eight of these in the maintained sector, rather than from the 6,850 Christian and Jewish schools. Christians may well reflect ruefully that life was easier in the days when religious schooling was not an issue, because religion in general was a dormant political issue.

The broader problem of some of these critiques for Christians, as for moderate Muslims, is that they tar all religion with the fundamentalist brush. In this analysis, Islamic and American Christian fundamentalism become conflated, and then mapped onto religion as a whole, obscuring traditions of moderation and toleration within the world religions. The crumbling 9/11 Twin Towers are adduced as symbolic evidence for the old argument that religion – *any religion* – causes intolerance and violence. Not all critiques of multiculturalism are this crude, but even as judicious a critic as Amartya Sen assumes an antinomy between faith and reason, criticizing faith schools for giving priority to 'unreasoned faith over reasoning'.[40] Some recent liberal critiques of state concessions to Islam also have the effect of denying the authenticity of religious commitment in general. While the Government's recent attempt to legislate against religious hatred was attacked from a number of standpoints, some of them Christian, some secularists argued that the sensitivities of religious believers should not be protected by law because belief was misguided, a form of false consciousness.[41] Similar arguments were used by defenders of free speech against Muslims who claimed to have been offended by the Danish cartoons of the Prophet; while upholding the artistic authenticity of the cartoonists, they denied the authenticity of the offence caused to believers. Here there has been a failure of empathy from secular towards religious mentalities; as the literary journalist Ian Jack put it during the row over Sikh picketing of the Birmingham Rep: 'the secular world can offer no real analogy for sacredness, nothing to help us understand how the avid religionist feels'.[42] This inability to comprehend religious mindsets has implications for all religions, including Christianity.

We should not overplay the significance of recent challenges to the public role of religion. Some of them are serious attempts to address the problems of segregated communities and alienated Muslim youth, others an affronted *cri de coeur* from secularists who assumed that religion would dwindle inexorably to nothing, and have seen their predictions confounded. But as we have seen, secularism was only one strain, and not the dominant one, in intellectual life after 1945. Indifference and sympathy towards Christianity have been, and remain, more prevalent than opposition. There has been nothing in Britain like the polarization between a religious right and a liberal intelligentsia seen in the 'Culture Wars' of the United States. The complaints of secularists notwithstanding, it seems likely that Christianity, alongside other religions, will continue to contribute to a mixed public discourse, and to enjoy a measure of recognition from the state.

Notes

1 Bel Mooney, 2003, *Devout Sceptics: Conversations on Faith and Doubt*, London: Hodder & Stoughton, p. 42.

2 'Top Intellectuals: The Results', *Prospect*, August 2004, available at www.prospect-magazine.co.uk – accessed 09.11.06.

3 'Top 100 World Public Intellectuals', *Prospect*, October 2005, pp. 24–5

4 David Herman, 'Thinking Big', *Prospect*, July 2004, p. 8.

5 See e.g. Peter Hitchens, 2001, *The Abolition of Britain*, London: Quartet; Theodore Dalrymple, 2005, *Our Culture, What's Left of it*, Chicago: Ivan R. Dee; Roger Scruton, 2006, *England: An Elegy*, London: Continuum.

6 Noel Annan, 1990, *Our Age: The Generation that Made Post-War Britain*, London: Weidenfeld and Nicolson; Stefan Collini, 2006, *Absent Minds: Intellectuals in Britain*, Oxford: Oxford University Press. For a history of intellectuals which does recognize the role of religion in post-war intellectual life, see Julia Stapleton, 2001, *Political Intellectuals and Public Identities since 1850*, Manchester: Manchester University Press.

7 Walter Moberly, 1949, *The Crisis in the University*, London: SCM Press, p. 52.

8 E. P. Thompson, 1960, 'Outside the Whale', in E. P. Thompson *et al.* (eds), *Out of Apathy*, London: Stevens Books, p. 188.

9 C. H. Rolph, 1987, *Further Particulars*, Oxford: Oxford University Press, p. 217.

10 Matt Ridley, 'The Genetic Code Genius who Failed to Kill Faith', *The Spectator*, 30 September 2006, p. 22.

11 See e.g. Hugh Trevor-Roper, 2006, *Letters from Oxford*, ed. Richard Davenport-Hines, London: Weidenfeld and Nicolson.

12 Colin MacInnes, 'A Godless Nation?' *New Society*, 48, 29 August 1963, p. 25.

13 For rejoinders to the positivists, see Antony Flew and Alasdair MacIntyre, 1955, *New Essays in Philosophical Theology*, London: SCM Press; Basil Mitchell (ed.), 1957, *Faith and Logic: Oxford Essays in Philosophical Theology*, London: George Allen and Unwin.

14 Talal Asad, 1993, 'Multiculturalism and British Identity in the Wake of the Rushdie Affair', in *Genealogies of Religion: Discipline and Reasons of Power in Christianity and Islam*, Baltimore and London, p. 255; Tariq Modood, 'Muslims and the Politics of Difference', *Political Quarterly*, 2003, pp. 103–5; Sarfraz Manzoor, 'We've Ditched Race for Religion', *Guardian*, 11 January 2005, p. 22.

15 See e.g. Quentin Skinner, 1978, *The Foundations of Modern Political Thought*, Cambridge: Cambridge University Press; Keith Thomas, 1971, *Religion and the Decline of Magic: Studies in Popular Belief in Sixteenth and Seventeenth Century England*, London: Weidenfeld & Nicolson.

16 *Times Literary Supplement*, 7 April, July 28 and September 8, 1966; see also Lamin Sanneh, 'Religion's Return', *Times Literary Supplement*, 13 October 2006, pp. 13–14.

17 Clifford Geertz, 1966, 'Religion as a Cultural System', in M. Banton (ed.), *Anthropological Approaches to the Study of Religion*, New York: Praeger, pp. 1–46.

18 See Alasdair MacIntyre, 1968, *Marxism and Christianity*, London: Duckworth; Christian Bailey, 'The Quest for a Catholic Marxist Rapprochement in Post-War Britain: the Case of the Slant Group', Oxford University BA thesis, 2001; Peter G. McCaffery, 'Catholic Radicalism and Counter-Radicalism: A Comparative Study of England and the Netherlands', Oxford DPhil thesis, 1979.

19 E. P. Thompson, 1963, *The Making of the English Working Class*, London: Gollancz; E. P. Thompson, 'The Peculiarities of the English' (1965), in 1978, *The Poverty of Theory and Other Essays*, London: Merlin Press, pp. 245–301; Christopher Hill, 1972, *The World Turned Upside Down*, London: Temple Smith. See also Pene Corfield, '"We are all one in the Eyes of the Lord": Christopher Hill and the Historical Meanings of

Radical Religion', *History Workshop Journal* 58 (2004), pp. 110–24.

20 See e.g. John Morrill, 1983, 'The Religious Context of the English Civil War', *Transactions of the Royal Historical Society*, 5th series, 34, pp. 155–78; J. C. D. Clark, 1985, *English Society, 1688–1832*, Cambridge: Cambridge University Press; Boyd Hilton, 1988, *The Age of Atonement: The Influence of Evangelicalism on Social and Political Thought, 1795–1865*, Oxford: Clarendon Press.

21 See e.g. Michael Burleigh, 2005, *Earthly Powers: Religion and Politics in Europe from the Enlightenment to the Great War*, London: HarperCollins, 2005; Gareth Stedman Jones, introduction to Karl Marx, 2002, *The Communist Manifesto*, London: Penguin.

22 Benedict Anderson, 1983, *Imagined Communities: Reflections on the Origin and Spread of Nationalism*, London: Verso, 1983; See also T. J. Clark, 'In a Pomegranate Chandelier', *London Review of Books*, 21 September 2006.

23 See e.g. John Gray, 2003, 'Enlightenment Humanism as a Relic of Christian Monotheism', in *2000 Years and Beyond: Faith, Identity, and the Common Era*, Paul Gifford (ed.) with David Archard, Trevor A. Hart and Nigel Rapport, London: Routledge, pp. 35–50; Slavoj Žižek, 2000, *The Fragile Absolute, Or Why is the Christian Legacy Worth Fighting For?*, London: Verso.

24 David Martin, 1972, 'Great Britain: England', in Hans Mol (ed.), *Western Religion: A Country by Country Sociological Inquiry*, The Hague: Mouton, pp. 229–47, at p. 237.

25 Andrew Marr, 1992, *The Battle for Scotland*, London: Penguin, pp. 32–44.

26 Roy Hattersley, 'Faith does breed charity', *Guardian*, 12 September 2005; Bernard Crick, 'This age of fanaticism is no time for non-believers to make enemies', *Guardian*, 22 October 2005.

27 The churches were omitted from Hugh Thomas's edited symposium on *The Establishment* in 1959, on the grounds that they no longer mattered enough to be included, except under the heading 'Public Schools'. See Hugh Thomas (ed.), 1959, *The Establishment: A Symposium*, London: Anthony Blond, p. 14.

28 David Lodge, 1980, *How Far Can You Go?*, London: Secker and Warburg.

29 Terry Eagleton, 2001, *The Gatekeeper: A Memoir*, London: Granta; John Cornwell, 2006, *Seminary Boy*, London: Fourth Estate.

30 MacInnes, 'A Godless Nation?' p. 25.

31 Andrew Brown, 'Dawkins the Dogmatist', *Prospect*, October 2006, pp. 69–70; Kenan Malik, *Daily Telegraph*, 30 September 2006; Terry Eagleton, 'Lunging, Flailing, Mispunching', *London Review of Books*. 19 October 2006, pp. 32–4.

32 Mooney, *Devout Sceptics*.

33 Anthony Howard, 2005, *Basil Hume: The Monk Cardinal*, London: Headline.

34 See e.g. House of Lords speech by Rowan Williams, 12 May 2006, reprinted at www.archbishopofcanterbury.org – accessed 10.11.06.

35 Bhikhu Parekh, 2006, 'European Liberalism and the "Muslim Question"', in Tariq Modood, Anna Triandafyllidou and Richard Zapata-Barrero (eds), *Multiculturalism, Muslims and Citizenship: A European Approach*, London: Routledge, pp. 189–90.

36 Tim Luckhurst, 2001, *This is Today: A Biography of the Today Programme*, London: Aurum, p. 117; Mark Lawson, 'Three Minutes of Jesus,' *Independent*, magazine section, 22 December 1990, pp. 38–9.

37 *A House for the Future: Royal Commission on the Reform of the House of Lords*, CM4534 (2000), Ch. 15.

38 See e.g. Brian Barry, 2001, *Culture and Equality: An Egalitarian Critique of Multiculturalism*, Cambridge: Polity.

39 Sen, *Identity and Violence*, pp. 156–60.

40 Sen, *Identity and Violence*, p. 160.

41 Polly Toynbee, 'My Right to Offend a Fool', *Guardian*, 10 June 2005, p. 27.

42 Ian Jack, 'Beyond Belief', *Guardian*, Review section, 1 January 2005, p. 7.

CASE STUDY

The Evolution of National and Religious Identity in Contemporary Ireland*

ROBERT TOBIN

On 12 July 1998, the Tour de France came to Ireland. The first stage of the competition was held in and around Dublin, where thousands of spectators lined the streets to catch a glimpse of the cyclists as they raced towards the finish in Phoenix Park. The city had not seen such a major public event since the visit of Pope John Paul II in the autumn of 1979. Yet in the intervening two decades, the Republic of Ireland was transformed, and the nature of this transformation may be glimpsed in the contrast between these two events and their symbolic significance. The Republic that greeted the Pontiff with such adulation in 1979 remained, at least on the surface, the pious, impoverished and long-suffering country it had always been, afflicted by high unemployment and haunted by the apparently intractable sectarian conflict north of the border. By 1998, however, there was a tangible sense that Ireland was now on the cutting edge of the new Europe: energetic, prosperous, increasingly tolerant, and thanks to the recent Good Friday Agreement, actively promoting a framework for lasting peace in Ulster. Metaphorically speaking, then, life in the Republic had gone from standing under leaden skies during an open-air papal Mass to cheering colourful athletes speeding through the sunny streets of Dublin.

Of course, such a contrast of moments serves to highlight the profound shift that has taken place in Irish society, but it does little to illuminate the underlying realities of the moments themselves or the complex and sometimes contradictory forces that have led the country from one point to the other. To begin with, many of the social, political and economic trends associated with the renaissance of the 1990s were already under way by 1979. By the same token, many of the traditional identity-markers of Irishness presumed to have disappeared during the past decade have retained a salience for some people right up to the present day.[1] However tempting it might be to conclude, therefore, that the Republic's experience represents a straightforward case of secularization – a wholesale exchange of agrarian Catholic nationalism for high-tech European cosmopolitanism – life on the

278

ground is not in fact so simple.[2] It would be far more accurate to recognize that while the Catholic nationalist monoculture defining Ireland during most of the twentieth century has eroded dramatically in recent years, neither religion nor nationality has perforce ceased to matter. Rather, an unprecedented material prosperity, in conjunction with the diminishment of the Catholic Church's moral authority and the state's embrace of European integration, have awakened in the Irish a new sense of possibility and of choice.[3] No longer constrained by the former orthodoxies, the country is asserting itself and its values in ways unthinkable a generation ago.[4] To be 'secular' in this context may or may not mean ceasing to be religious, but it does mean recognizing the legitimacy of being something other than Catholic in the old, highly prescribed way. Likewise, to be 'European' may or may not mean repudiating nationalist commitments, but it does mean recognizing the viability of being Irish without constant recourse to anti-Englishness. The speed with which Ireland has undergone this process of social liberalization has indeed been dizzying, and clearly there are those who have been disorientated and estranged by it.[5] But for a far greater number, especially among the young, the essence of being Irish increasingly lies in the very capacity to assimilate and abide in the multiple and overlapping identities of late modernity.[6] As uncertain as this condition must surely be for them as individuals, never have the Irish as a people displayed more confidence in the promise and variety of their own becoming.

The roots of this transformation may be traced back nearly half a century. In 1958–9, two major changes took place that would have far-reaching effects upon Irish society in the years to come. The first was the election of Pope John XXIII in October 1958, which heralded a programme of reforms in the Catholic Church under the auspices of the Second Vatican Council. The impact of these reforms upon a body as profoundly conservative as the Irish Catholic Church remains difficult to overstate.[7] The second major development was the replacement of Eamon de Valera by Seán Lemass as *Taoiseach* [Prime Minister] in June 1959. Lemass's leadership was to become the catalyst for a whole series of initiatives to bolster the Irish economy and rejuvenate national life.[8] Both as economic and foreign policy, the decision to abandon its defensive posture towards Britain and embrace regional free trade led to steady export-driven growth for Ireland throughout the 1960s, culminating in its admission to the EEC in 1973.[9] Meanwhile, a variety of social changes were taking place in the Republic, not least an ongoing process of urbanization.[10] A native television service was introduced in 1961 and increasingly served as a forum for national debate and international awareness, while the much-hated literary censorship was effectively dismantled in 1967.[11] Later the same decade the contraceptive pill became available, heralding the advent of the sexual revolution and the gathering force of feminist concerns. Correspondingly, the open conflict between Irish liberals and conservatives over the 1968 papal encyclical *Humanae Vitae* revealed fissures within a Catholic population previously assumed to be unified on such matters.[12] And the explosion of sectarian violence in Northern Ireland in 1969 in turn provoked a revaluation of church–state relations in the Republic, prompting the successful 1972 referendum to remove the clause from the Irish Constitution according a 'special position' to the Catholic Church.[13]

While all these novelties anticipated the still more fundamental changes yet to come, much about the Ireland of the 1970s and 80s remained familiar. Despite economic modernization, high unemployment continued to afflict the populace, as did high rates of immigration. And notwithstanding the increased co-operation between the two countries, the Troubles in Ulster continued to highlight for many Irish people their ancient and visceral quarrel with Protestant Britain. Moreover, when the Pope visited the island in 1979, more than 90% of Catholics still claimed to attend Mass at least once a week.[14] At the same time, though, the fault-line within the Republic on social matters grew wider, as evidenced by the controversial abortion referendum of 1983. Though anti-abortion advocates ultimately prevailed in the debate, the campaign leading up to the vote demonstrated the growing assertiveness of liberal values and, in particular, of Irish feminism.[15] The unexpected election of Labour candidate Mary Robinson to the Presidency in 1990 confirmed this trend, and her tenure soon epitomized the newfound hope and burgeoning prosperity Ireland started to experience at century's end.[16] Robinson's eloquent espousals of Irish self-belief proved a timely counterpoint to the revelations of financial corruption in government and sexual scandal in the Catholic Church that proliferated during the 1990s. She and her successor, Mary McAleese, worked to encourage a civil society less dependent upon the traditional authority of the priests and politicians with whom there was now widespread disillusionment.[17] The abolition in 1993 of the law forbidding homosexual relations between men, along with the legalization of divorce in 1995, both suggested a growing willingness by many Irish people to tolerate, if not necessarily approve, alternative social values.[18] Yet the exceptionally close vote in the divorce referendum along the lines of conservative-rural versus liberal-urban bespoke the larger polarization underway not only in terms of geography, but class and age as well. Due to the longstanding trend of urbanization, in combination with the influx of educated young people no longer forced to emigrate, almost one-third of the population lived in greater Dublin at the dawn of new millennium. And the modern Ireland they were shaping and being shaped by had less and less in common with a more traditional Ireland still operating on the fringes.[19]

Ireland's transformation during the 1990s made it the darling of Europeanization. Though a significant proportion of the Republic's economic growth was in fact due to Anglo-American corporate investment, it nonetheless became popular to attribute such success to the Republic's wholehearted embrace of the European unification project.[20] This view gained added resonance in 1996 when, for the first time, it was announced that the Irish now produced more wealth per capita than did the unity-shy British. Whatever the underlying facts, Ireland now found itself doing better than its more powerful neighbour, and the reason appeared to be Europe. As this perception began to percolate into the popular consciousness, a fundamental shift took place in the national psyche: for the first time, it was not only possible but necessary to conceive of Ireland as something more than simply the antithesis of Britain.[21] Not surprisingly, diehard Irish Catholic nationalists have resisted claims that the ancient quarrel is past, as have those liberal intellectuals for whom post-colonial theoretical categories retain their Manichean allure.[22] It has even been suggested that far from serving as a liberating manoeuvre by which Ireland might overcome the crippling effects of an outdated preoccupation, Europeanization has merely been a way for the country to deny its colonial history and transfer its unresolved inferiority complex to another arena.[23] But such analysis would appear blind to the fact that, whatever abstract feelings of resentment the Irish may retain towards England about the past, in practice they see contemporary Britons as the people most like themselves.[24] Likewise, the state's political embrace of Europe has not proved so much a slavish lurch from one ideological master to another as a self-conscious attempt to complicate Ireland's regional position. Or, as Northern politician John Hume once put it, the shift should be seen not as a betrayal of Irish nationalism but rather an attempt 'to enjoy properly the inchoate European outlook and vision which was lost in our oppressive and obsessive relationship with Britain'.[25] Current *Taoiseach* Bertie Ahern reiterated the point in 2001 when he referred to Ireland's Europeanization as the best means by which to 'develop a new and more balanced relationship with Britain' by contextualizing it among relationships with others.[26]

Yet despite their remarkable success in using European integration as a platform for economic development and as a counterpoint to nationalist orthodoxy, it is unclear what specific cultural meaning Europe now has for the Irish. Of course, in this respect they are hardly unique among the Union's member states. What is noteworthy, however, is the frequency with which certain advocates of integration have invoked a notion of shared European Christian values and traditions as an ideological basis for Irish participation. In practice such arguments have never been as decisive as the promise of increased prosperity for the country, but nonetheless they have retained a consistent if vague appeal.[27] Belief in the possibility of a pan-European cultural identity is predicated upon the conviction that such a unified entity existed in pre-Reformation, pre-national Europe and is now simply waiting to be recovered and restored.[28] Anticipating that this process of recovery was the next step in the Europeanization project, one Irish commentator predicted in 2003 that 'after decades of torpidity, cultural Europe may just be about to experience its big bang'.[29] This expectation has proven premature, and at least so far, Anthony D. Smith's assessment of Europe as 'merely an arena, a field force, for conflicting identities and cultures' remains an accurate assessment of the reality.[30] Even so, Irish voices from across the Republic's political and religious spectrum have expressed a belief that the European Union should develop a coherent moral vision to match its success as a free-trade area.[31] Whether the population at large shares this commitment is another matter. Although the Irish public's attitude toward integration is currently one of the most supportive in the EU, it is not clear that such enthusiasm will be sustained by idealism if and when the economic benefits become less compelling.[32]

A strong counterpoint to European idealism – or indeed idealism of any kind – in the contemporary Republic has been the belated but forceful arrival of mass consumerism. After generations of material want and communal self-denial, Irish people are now assiduously pursuing a culture of material gratification and individual self-indulgence.[33] An unprecedented atmosphere of personal choice now prevails, buoyed by the ready availability of credit and the rapid introduction of progressive social legislation.[34] Yet the single-mindedness with which the Irish have begun to pursue their newfound freedom and affluence has led some to worry that certain good qualities from the old Ireland have been lost in the process. Writing in 2002, the poet Seamus Heaney worried that 'some kind of metaphysic has disappeared from the common life . . . I think we are running on an unconscious that is informed by religious values, but I think my youngsters' youngsters won't have that.'[35] Though a causal relationship between the new prosperity and the decline in religious observance cannot be straightforwardly postulated, it is nonetheless clear that the Catholic Church's loss of public influence both reflects and has contributed to a widespread diminishment in social solidarity. Shamed throughout the 1990s by revelations of sexual misconduct among its clergy, abuse within the welfare institutions of its religious orders, and subsequent attempts by its hierarchy to cover up the evidence, the church has since been decidedly more modest and conciliatory in its public pronouncements.[36] While many Catholic clergy still see the church as having a key role to play in promoting spiritual values in Irish life, there is a growing recognition that the institution must work to meet people where they are. When interviewed recently about his work among young people in Dublin, for example, the Revd Brendan McManus acknowledged that 'we're trying to bring the message in a different way, through music, through creative, dynamic liturgy, and through participation', adding: 'Many people realize that there is a void there, even with all the affluence and the consumer culture.'[37]

Part of the challenge the Catholic Church now faces, though, is that increasingly people in the Republic do not regard religious observance as intrinsic to their Irish identity but as just another 'lifestyle choice' that this same consumer culture affords them.[38] Or, as Sheridan Gilley has aptly put it, the Irish middle class 'no longer buys its religion wholesale'.[39] So while it is true that the rate of weekly church attendance among Catholics in Ireland remains among the highest in Europe – only in Malta and Poland do people attend Mass more regularly – such a statistic needs to be read contextually.[40] Recalling that 90% of Irish Catholics attended Mass regularly in the 1980s, it is striking that in a 2003 survey, only 44% claimed to do the same, while the figure for young people in Dublin was down to 30%.[41] On the other hand, there is also a case to be made for not relying upon regular Mass attendance as the only criterion for assessing spiritual conviction. Irish Catholics increasingly evince a willingness to differentiate between Christianity's 'core teachings' and the church's teachings about sex and authority, such that belief and practice are no longer correlative.[42] And nowhere is this growing confidence in their own judgement on matters of faith and morals more plainly demonstrated than in the virtual extinction of sacramental confession, once a staple of Irish Catholic practice.[43] Indeed, there is a sense that, save among the ageing rural population, Irish people are now going out of their way to assert their freedom from, if not total indifference to, their religious inheritance. This was particularly evident in their response to the death of John Paul II in April 2005. In marked contrast to the rapturous and universal welcome the Pontiff received when he visited Ireland in 1979, media coverage of his passing was studiously dispassionate.[44] And while 10,000 attended a vigil at the Marian shrine of Knock in rural Co. Mayo on the day of the funeral, life in Dublin was notable for its ordinariness.[45] Perhaps most telling of all was the uncertainty in the Government as to whether it should proclaim an official day of mourning. That the perennially popular Bertie Ahern initially assumed such observance was unnecessary and, when challenged about this, conceded only that it should be optional, demonstrates just how far Irish Catholic piety has moved from public norm to personal choice.[46]

The mixed response by Irish Catholics to the election of Joseph Ratzinger as John Paul's successor was similarly noteworthy, but it was the well-publicized critique of the new Pope by Protestant layman David Norris that bespoke another key shift in Irish social discourse.[47] Since the early 1970s, the Protestant minority in the Republic has gained steadily in collective confidence, having been largely silent during the 50 years following Irish Independence in 1922.[48] Those few Protestants who during this earlier period dared to speak out against the pervasive Catholic nationalist orthodoxy encountered a level of obloquy now difficult to credit.[49] Especially during the last decade, though, Protestant church leaders, intellectuals and politicians have become increasingly vocal in their opinions about the moral and social condition of the country.[50] Far from provoking the sort of Catholic reaction his remarks would have elicited a generation ago, David Norris' attack on Benedict XVI appears to have been accepted as simply another opinion among many about the prospects of the new pontificate. In this respect, the loosening grip of Catholic nationalism upon Irish sensibilities has obviously benefited the Protestant minority. The Church of Ireland's comparatively progressive social teachings have also given it an institutional credibility among younger Catholics that they are rarely prepared to extend to the church of their birth. Yet at the same time, this unprecedented level of acceptance into the mainstream of Irish society is forcing Southern Protestants to revaluate their communal identity as something other than simple resistance to monolithic Catholicism.[51] Writing in the *Irish Times* in August 2005, for example, Michael Webb upbraided his co-religionist Robin Bury for claiming that the Republic remained a 'cold place' for Protestants: 'Any Irish woman or man, Protestant or not, who is prepared to contribute will find modern Ireland a warm place', he insisted. Rather than rake over the past, Webb added, Protestants should instead lead the way in witnessing to just how 'cold' Ireland can often be for the impoverished, the uninsured, and the recently arrived.[52]

The fate of the many immigrants now coming to Ireland is not only a social justice issue for the Church of Ireland but also an increasingly important factor in its own development. For the first time in over a century, Church of Ireland membership in the South is growing, and this is due mainly to the influx of Anglican immigrants from African and Asian countries. And while this resurgence in numbers comes as a boon to a church whose continued viability in the Republic has often been the subject of grave concern, it brings with it the challenge of how to accommodate an unprecedented level of cultural heterogeneity within the community. Acknowledging as much in 2003, the Protestant Archbishop of Dublin, John Neill, called on Irish Anglicans 'to do more to welcome their co-religionists from overseas'.[53] Both Neill and his Roman Catholic counterpart, Archbishop Diarmuid Martin, have affirmed their churches' commitment to the rights of immigrants, encouraging the Government to adopt an 'open, transparent, modern and enlightened national migration policy' and, more specifically, to regularize immigrants' legal status after five years.[54] The importance of immigrants not just to the future of the Church of Ireland but to the future of religion in Ireland generally cannot be underestimated. The most recent Irish census revealed that between 1991 and 2002, the number of people claiming Catholicism rose, even though the number of Irish-born Catholics fell by 15,000 and the Church's membership dropped from 91.6% of the overall population to 88.4%.[55] The three main Protestant churches also saw notable increases, but these were slight compared with the massive jump in the number of Orthodox Christians, who went from 400 in 1991 to 10,400 in 2002, an increase of 2,815%. Similarly impressive in the category of Christian groups has been the proliferation of smaller, independent 'black majority' churches, estimated by the Irish Council of Churches to possess approximately 10,000 members combined. Just as important, though, is the increase in the Republic of non-Christian communities. During the 1990s, the number of self-identifying Muslims rose from 3,900 to 19,100, a climb of 390%. The number of Buddhists and Hindus also increased significantly, while the decline in the Jewish community halted. Almost all these figures are easily attributable to the tremendous growth in immigration since the early 1990s. Among the native-born Irish themselves, though, the trend has been towards non-affiliation: almost 139,000 people now identify themselves as having no religion, making them the second largest block of the population after Roman Catholics.[56]

Is it enough, then, merely to conclude that the native-born Irish are becoming godless consumers, while immigrants are keeping religion alive in a nation whose founders never even imagined their presence? This, like any straightforward explanation, obviously cannot do justice to the complex society Ireland has become. It is true that life in the Republic is now more secular and cosmopolitan than it was 20 years ago, but such changes have been embraced by most Irish people more at the level of practicality than of principle. Manifestly, they have not replaced their old idealism with a new one. If Diarmaid Ferriter was right when recently he characterized the Irish as 'a fat, drunken, indebted people who are also obsessed with healthcare', it may be that such material excess is serving as a necessary corrective to past excesses of other kinds.[57] Church and state are realigning themselves as public actors, and the challenges of a pluralistic future are beginning to replace those of the sectarian past.[58] Or, as Ian d'Alton has succinctly put it, cultural debate and social policy in Ireland are more likely in the coming years to revolve around 'the place of Poles rather than Protestants'.[59] In this sense, the human presence of European integration will remain long after the economic advantages of the EU cease to galvanize Irish enthusiasm for it. Likewise, religion as a daily presence in Irish life will continue to assert itself, even as traditional Catholicism gradually takes its place as but one personal option among many. The negotiation of religious and national identities will thus remain factors with which the new Irish will have to contend, even if the terms under which they do so will have altered beyond all recognition. And their capacity to greet such change pragmatically is now key to who, and what, they understand themselves as people to have become.

Notes

* My thanks go to Roy Foster, Ian d'Alton, Philip Howell, Susan Hood, Alana Harris and William Whyte for their helpful comments and suggestions during the preparation of this article.

1 Tom Garvin, 2001, *Redefining Southern Nationalism: An Academic Perspective*, Dublin: Institute for British-Irish Studies, University College Dublin, p. 8; Andrew M. Greeley, 2003, *Religion in Europe at the End of the Second Millennium: A Sociological Profile*, New Brunswick, NJ: Transaction, pp. 185–6.

2 Michael P. Hornsby-Smith, 1992, 'Social and Religious Transformation in Ireland:

A Case of Secularisation?', in J. H. Goldthorpe and C. T. Whelan (eds), *The Development of Industrial Society in Ireland*, Oxford: Oxford University Press, pp. 267, 285–7.

3 Niamh Hardiman and Christopher Whelan, 1998, 'Changing Values', in Raymond Crotty and David E. Schmitt (eds), *Ireland and the Politics of Change*, London: Longman, pp. 84–5; Mary Kenny, 2000, *Goodbye to Catholic Ireland*, rev. edn, Dublin: New Island, p. 284.

4 Marguerite Corish, 1996, 'Aspects of the Secularisation of Irish Society 1958–1996', in Eoin G. Cassidy (ed.), *Faith and Culture in the Irish Context*, Dublin: Veritas, pp. 140–1.

5 Tom Garvin, 1998, 'Patriots and republicans: an Irish evolution', in Crotty and Schmitt, *Ireland and the Politics of Change*, pp. 144–55, at p. 154.

6 Carmen Kuhling and Kieran Keohane, 2002, 'Celebrity Case Studies in the Localisation of the Global', in Mary P. Corcoran and Michel Peillon (eds), *Ireland Unbound: A Turn of the Century Chronicle*, Dublin: Institute of Public Administration, pp. 103–18, at p. 104.

7 Dermot Keogh, 1994, *Twentieth-Century Ireland: Nation and State*, Dublin: Gill & Macmillan, pp. 261–3; J. J. Lee, 1989, *Ireland 1912–1985: Politics and Society*, Cambridge: Cambridge University Press, p. 655.

8 John Horgan, 1997, *Seán Lemass: The Enigmatic Patriot*, Dublin: Gill & Macmillan, pp. 348–57.

9 Ben Tonra, 2001, *The Europeanisation of National Foreign Policy: Dutch, Danish and Irish Foreign Policy in the European Union*, Aldershot, Hampshire: Ashgate, pp. 107–8, 117.

10 Corish, 'Aspects of the Secularisation', p. 144.

11 Michael Adams, 1968, *Censorship: The Irish Experience*, Dublin: Sceptre, pp. 120–8, 199.

12 Kenny, *Goodbye*, pp. 216–22, 237.

13 J. H. Whyte, 1980, *Church and State in Modern Ireland, 1923–1979*, 2nd edn, Dublin: Gill & Macmillan, p. 389.

14 Sheridan Gilley, 2003, 'Catholicism in Ireland', in McLeod and Ustorf, *Decline of Christendom*, p. 99.

15 See Tom Hesketh, 1990, *The Second Partitioning of Ireland?: The Abortion Referendum of 1983*, Dun Laoghaire, Co. Dublin: Brandsma.

16 Michel Peillon, 2000, 'Carnival Ireland', in Eamonn Slater and Michel Peillon (eds), *Memories of the Present: A Sociological Chronicle of Ireland, 1997–1998*, Dublin: Institute of Public Administration, p. 140.

17 Terence Brown, 2004, *Ireland: A Social and Cultural History, 1922–2002*, rev. edn, London: Harper Perennial, pp. 380–1.

18 Kenny, *Goodbye*, pp. 292–4; *Irish Times* 24 June 2005.

19 Hardiman and Whelan, 'Changing Values', pp. 70–5.

20 David McWilliams, 2005, *The Pope's Children: Ireland's New Elite*, Dublin: Gill & Macmillan, p. 92

21 Fintan O'Toole, 1997, *The Ex-Isle of Erin: Images of a Global Ireland*, Dublin: New Island, pp. 12–13, 18–21.

22 For a summation and critique of this position, see Stephen Howe, 2000, *Ireland and Empire: Colonial Legacies in Irish History and Culture*, Oxford: Oxford University Press, p. 122; and Liam Kennedy, 1996, *Colonialism, Religion and Nationalism in Ireland*, Belfast: Institute of Irish Studies, p. 219.

23 Brian Fallon, 1998, *An Age of Innocence: Irish Culture 1930–1960*, Dublin: Gill & Macmillan, p. 3; Terence McDonough, 2005, 'Introduction', in Terence McDonough (ed.), *Was Ireland a Colony?: Economics, Politics and Culture in Nineteenth-Century Ireland*, Dublin: Irish Academic Press, viii; *Irish Times*, 9 January 2006.

24 *Irish Times*, 23 March 2005.

25 John Hume, 1988, 'Europe of the Regions', in Richard Kearney (ed.), *Across the Frontiers: Ireland in the 1990s*, Dublin: Wolfhound, p. 56.

26 Bertie Ahern, 'Europe: The Irish Viewpoint', speech delivered to 'Wales, Europe and the World' Forum, Newport, 1 Mar. 2001 – see www.taoiseach.gov.ie – accessed 31.05.06.

27 Karin Gilland, 2001, 'Ireland and European Integration', in Kjell Goldmann and Karin Gilland (eds), *Nationality versus Europeanisation: The National View of the Nation in Four EU Countries*, Stockholm: Department of Political Science, Stockholm University, pp. 21–49, at p. 22.

28 Anthony D. Smith, 1995, *Nations and Nationalisms in a Global Era*, Cambridge: Polity, p. 129.

29 *Irish Times*, 29 December 2003.

30 Smith, *Nations and Nationalisms*, p. 131.

31 E.g. Labour politician Justin Keating's article in the *Irish Times* 5 November 2004; Garret Fitzgerald, 1994, 'Ireland, Britain, Europe: Beyond Economic and Political Unity', in James P. Mackey (ed.), *The Cultures of Europe: The Irish Contribution*, Belfast: Institute of Irish Studies, p. 185; Anthony Cronin, 2002, 'Address', in *National Forum on Europe: Report of Proceedings*, n.14, Dublin: Government Stationery Office, p. 64; Kenneth Milne, 2002, 'Church of Ireland submission to the National Forum on Europe', speech delivered at Dublin Castle, 1 February 2002 – www.ireland.anglican.org – accessed 25.05.06; Tony Brown, 2002, *Why Europe?*, Dublin: Institute of European Affairs, p. 28.

32 *Irish Times*, 18 February 2005.

33 Tom Inglis, 2002, 'Pleasure Pursuits', in Corcoran and Peillon, *Ireland Unbound*, p. 35.

34 Corish, 'Aspects of the Secularisation', p. 141; McWilliams, *The Pope's Children*, p. 116.

35 Martin, *On Secularization*, p. 134.

36 Kenny, *Goodbye*, pp. 295–305; Brown, *Ireland*, p. 370.

37 *Boston Globe*, 2 May 2005.

38 Anne Looney, 1996, 'Disappearing Echoes, New Voices and the Sound of Silence', in Seán MacRéamoinn (ed.), *The Church in the New Ireland*, Dublin: Columba Press, pp. 28–9.

39 Sheridan Gilley, 'Catholicism in Ireland', p. 109.

40 *Irish Times*, 24 June 2005.

41 *Irish Times*, 30 September 2003.

42 Greeley, *Religion in Europe*, pp. 156–61; Tom Inglis, 1998, *Moral Monopoly: The Rise and Fall of the Catholic Church in Modern Ireland*, 2nd edn, Dublin: University College Dublin Press, pp. 241–2.

43 Corish, 'Aspects of the Secularisation, p. 164.

44 *Irish Times*, 9 April 2005.

45 *Irish Times*, 4 April 2005.

46 *Irish Times*, 5 April 2005.

47 *Irish Times*, 20 April 2005.

48 Whyte, *Church and State*, p. 385.

49 I have explored this situation in detail in my doctoral thesis, 'The Minority Voice: Hubert Butler, Southern Protestantism and Intellectual Dissent in Ireland, 1930–72', Faculty of Modern History, University of Oxford, 2004.

50 *Church of Ireland Gazette* 11 Dec. 1998; Alan Acheson, 2002, *A History of the Church of Ireland, 1691–2001*, rev. edn, Dublin: Columba Press/APCK, p. 274.

51 John Coakley, 1998, 'Religion, ethnic identity and the Protestant minority in the Republic', in Crotty and Schmitt, *Ireland and the Politics of Change*, pp. 104–5.

52 *Irish Times*, 8 August 2005.
53 *Irish Times*, 20 June 2003.
54 *Irish Times*, 6 January 2003.
55 *Irish Times*, 9 February 2004.
56 *Irish Times*, 10 February 2004, 10 August 2004.
57 *Irish Times*, 17 December 2005.
58 *Irish Times*, 12 October 2004
59 Ian d'Alton, 2004, 'Remembering the future, imagining the past – the journeys of southern Irish protestantism' [revised version of a paper presented to the National Library of Ireland Society, Dublin, 26 Feb. 2004]. Used with permission from the author.

Conclusion

Christian Britain Reconsidered

This book was born out of a shared sense of frustration at conventional analyses of Christianity in modern Britain. Although the vibrancy of current debate is undeniable, what is also clear is that positions have become polarized, as comparatively few starkly delineated accounts, usually of religious decline, are repeatedly rehearsed. What we have sought to do is break out of this debate and reconsider the assumptions on which it is based. Rather than describe the death (or resurrection) of Christian Britain, we have attempted to redefine it, abandoning the existing maps for a more sensitive charting of the contours of modern religion. As a result we have challenged a number of conventional definitions and received opinions, and have raised questions for further development and research, which we highlight in this concluding section. In particular, we have argued that too many recent writers have tended to associate change with crisis and to define Christians only as those people they can count. By contrast, our account of Christianity stresses transmutation and reinvention, and our definition of 'Christian' is both broader and more precise than a simple statistic. The result is a conclusion at variance with much of the mainstream literature. Christian Britain, we have argued, has not died. Rather, it has been transformed. In that sense, our book can be seen as a part of a wider discussion – and, most obviously, as an engagement with Callum Brown's recent work on the same subject.

Like George Dangerfield's 1935 classic *The Strange Death of Liberal England*, Brown's *The Death of Christian Britain* is a history book with a title mimicking a murder story. Any good murder story needs a victim, and a culprit. We have suggested that there are problems with both the victim, Christian Britain, and the culprit, the 1960s 'discourse revolution', in Brown's story. The most obvious problem is that the victim is not actually dead. There is no corpse in the library. Christianity continues to enjoy a numerical base and cultural influence which, though greatly diminished, do not justify the application of the terminal metaphor of death. Brown is careful to qualify his title by pointing out that it is predictive, and insisting that Christian Britain will be dead within the next few decades. But predictive titles have a habit of looking over-blown, and Brown's recalls that of his fellow Scot Tom Nairn, whose *The Break-Up of Britain* was published with great éclat in 1977, but whose predicted break-up has still not happened thirty years later.

What was refreshing about Callum Brown's work was his attempt to move the argument away from mere statistics and the study of the institutional church. He argued that 'what made Britain Christian was the way in which Christianity infused public culture and was adopted by individuals, whether churchgoers or not, in forming their own identities'.[1] Yet, having done so, Brown fell back into the conventional habits of much writing on modern belief. Having sensitively explored the way in which one particular form of discursive Christianity – evangelicalism – evolved and developed, he associated its later transmutation with death rather than change. Having proclaimed that the cultural importance of religion amounted to more than church attendance figures for the period before 1963, he then resorted to the figures to prove decline after 1963, thus ending up extrapolating the cultural decline of religion from its institutional decline.

In this book we have provided countless examples of how Christianity has continued to infuse public culture and to be adopted in identity formation up until the present day. We have demonstrated the continuance of Christian discourses in literature, the arts, and political protest, and their revival in ethics, economics, and political theory. Our findings support the view that the cultural strength of religion must be separated from its institutional strength. Here we follow Daniel Bell's argument that 'secularization is such a muddle, for it mixes two very different kinds of phenomena, the social and the cultural, and two very different processes of change that are not congruent with each other'.[2] We have seen how the cultural influence of religion could continue to be strong, in spite of institutional decline. Christianity was not superseded by other world-views, as figures of speech like the 'death' of Christian Britain, or 'post-Christian Britain', imply.[3] Such a stadial view of any religion is inappropriate; as Bell put it, using a musical analogy: 'Boulez does not replace Bach, or serial music the fugue.'[4]

We have also identified a number of flaws in Brown's depiction of his protagonist and victim, 'Christian Britain'. We feel that 'Christian Britain' is an extremely useful concept, because it calls attention to the degree to which national identity, and public and private morality, have continued to be dominated by Christian assumptions. But we also feel that Brown's version of it is too monolithic, being heavily based on one version of nineteenth-century evangelical piety. It does not allow for sub-cultures within denominations and traditions, such as the new immigrant Christian communities who have established themselves in Britain since World War Two. It does not recognize that the different denominations often behaved in very different ways, as is demonstrated by the radically divergent responses which we have charted to the growth of expressive individualism around the 1960s, or to economic individualism in the 1980s. Moreover, Brown depicts a Christianity which was passive in the face of inexorable cultural change from the 1960s onwards. Our account, by contrast, suggests that it adapted vigorously to the threats it faced. Christianity possessed innate resources and vocabularies for meeting many of them. Perhaps more than any other world religion, it was capable of reshaping itself. It could be variously establishment or counter-cultural, solitary or communal, democratic or hierarchical, sacerdotal or congregational, national or transnational. Although we have been critical of the metaphor of the liquid church, Christianity has always in some ways been a liquid religion, shaping itself to fit the society that contained it. This does not mean that its continuance was (or is) inevitable, but it was better able to respond to changed circumstances than grand narratives of decline have allowed.

This book has demonstrated a number of particular ways in which Christianity adjusted in the decades after World War Two. From the late 1950s, the Protestant churches were in the vanguard of redefining sexual ethics. All the major denominations identified themselves with internationalism, and with the causes of peace and the poor, forging alliances with secular progressives. All of them to some extent reformed their liturgies, drawing on new forms of popular culture. As we have seen, not all of these readjustments were successful. Mark Chapman's case study argues compellingly that South Bank theology was a wrong turning. We have also seen that there was division within the churches about whether changes to music, liturgy and architecture strengthened or weakened them. Nevertheless, the picture we have uncovered is one of innovation and experimentation, not atrophy or paralysis.

Our version of Christian Britain is also more relational than Callum Brown's. Christianity in Britain was affected by global political and social changes – by loss of Empire, by moves towards European unity, and by immigration. All denominations operated in an international, as well as a national, context. The consolidation of power within the Roman Curia, and the growing power of Anglican churches in the developing world, sometimes frustrated the liberalizing instincts of the Anglican and Catholic leaderships in Britain. But there were opportunities here for Christianity as well as threats. Our chapters on Generation, the Good Life, and the Common Good all show how Christianity's traditional universalizing rhetoric could fittingly be harnessed to new global media, and to internationalist causes.

The most significant of these global factors reshaping Christian Britain was Commonwealth immigration. The arrival of significant non-Christian religious populations in Britain ended the old congruence between 'Christianity' and 'religion', and turned Britain into a multi-faith society. This required Christians to consider how exclusive were their claims to truth, and how far they wished to act in partnership with other religions in defence of religion in general. As Raymond Plant's case study shows, it also complicated the relationship of Christianity to the state. There is a great deal for historians to study here, and they might well find it useful to apply to late twentieth-century Britain the insights of historians of nineteenth-century missions, who have shown how the Christian churches in Europe were transformed by the exigencies of operating in a religiously pluralistic context in the colonies.[5] More attention also needs to be paid to the influence of Christian immigrants – not just from the Caribbean, but also from Latin America, South Asia, Africa and, most recently, Eastern Europe – in reshaping British Christianity.

We have also questioned the existence of Brown's culprit, the 1960s 'discourse revolution'. As we have shown in our chapters on Generation, different Christian discourses continued to be widely used throughout and beyond the 1960s, and much of the new culture of expressive individualism and authenticity itself drew on Christian repertoires. We hope that other historians will wish to take this study of popular culture further. In line with other recent historiography, we have stressed that post-war social change occurred incrementally over a long period, and that it cannot be compressed into a single decade – let alone a single year – for the purposes of historical shorthand. But we also feel that further work needs to be done on the role of authority (both civil and ecclesiastical) in promulgating permissive social reforms from the late 1950s onwards.

The Death of Christian Britain was published in 2001, the same year as the 9/11 attacks, and it is worth reflecting on how events since then have changed popular and academic perceptions. Religion has assumed a vastly greater prominence as a subject of public debate. The huge attention paid by the media and politicians to Islam demonstrates that the cultural power of a religion may not be directly correlated to its number of adherents. The phenomenon of the young male fundamentalist has ambivalent implications for the student of contemporary religion. On the one hand, the fundamentalist critique of Western societies is predicated on the belief that they have become secular, and draws heavily on the imagery of the 'secular city' in the Western tradition.[6] On the other hand, fundamentalism also demonstrates the over-simplicity of unilinear theories of secularization, and the possibilities of religious reaction and revival. The profoundly disturbing phenomenon of the young 7/7 suicide bombers has prompted scholars of British Islam to reconsider their own assumptions about the intergenerational transmission of religion.

Public reactions to Islamic fundamentalism have also had ambivalent consequences for Christianity. Religion as a whole has been subject to more strident condemnation, and to the accusation that it is inherently fundamentalist. Secularist attacks on the official recognition of religious difference have led to criticism of faith schools, and a vigorous reaction from the Catholic Church. On the other hand, the desire to define why fundamentalism threatens a British 'way of life' has led some commentators to reflect on how far that way of life is Christian, in origin and in fact. Such reflection can be expressed in crudely anti-Islamic terms, as has recently been the case in some other European countries, but it can also lead to a recognition of Christianity's contribution to national culture which is not exclusive of other traditions. Recent events suggest that Christian Britain is not dead, but that it will continue to be reshaped and redefined in years to come.

Notes

1 Brown, *Death*, p. 8.

2 Daniel Bell, 'The Return of the Sacred? The Argument on the Future of Religion', *British Journal of Sociology*, 28 (1977), pp. 425–6.

3 Alan Gilbert, 1980, *The Making of Post-Christian Britain: A History of the Secularization of British Society*, London: Longman.

4 Bell, 'The Return of the Sacred?' p. 425.

5 See for example C. A. Bayly, 2004, *The Birth of the Modern World 1780–1914*, Oxford: Blackwell, Ch. 9; Susan Thorne, 1999, *Congregational Missions and the Making of an Imperial Culture in Nineteenth Century England*, Stanford: Stanford University Press.

6 Ian Buruma and Avishai Margalit, 2004, *Occidentalism: The West in the Eyes of its Enemies*, New York: Penguin.

Select Bibliography

Talal Asad, 1993, *Genealogies of Religion: Discipline and Reasons of Power in Christianity and Islam*, Baltimore and London: Johns Hopkins University Press.
Paul Avis (ed.), 2003, *Public Faith? The State of Religious Belief and Practice in Britain*, London: SPCK.

Edward Bailey, 1998, *Implicit Religion: An Introduction*, London: Middlesex University Press.
M. M. Bakhtin, 1981, *The Dialogical Imagination: Four Essays*, ed. Michael Holquist, trans. Caryl Emerson and Michael Holquist, Austin TX: University of Austin Press.
Zygmunt Bauman, 1998, *Globalization: The Human Consequences*, Cambridge: Polity Press.
Zygmunt Bauman, 2004, *Identity: Conversations with Benedetto Vecchi*, Cambridge: Polity Press.
Zygmunt Bauman, 2000, *Liquid Modernity*, Cambridge: Polity Press.
James A. Beckford and James T. Richardson (eds), 2003, *Challenging Religion: Essays in Honour of Eileen Barker*, London: Routledge.
Daniel Bell, 'The Return of the Sacred? The Argument on the Future of Religion', *British Journal of Sociology*, 28 (1977), 419–49.
Peter L. Berger, 1967, *The Sacred Canopy: Elements of a Sociological Theory of Religion*, Garden City, New York: Doubleday.
Peter L. Berger, 1967, *The Social Reality of Religion*, London: Faber & Faber.
Nigel Biggar, 1997, *Good Life: Reflections on What We Value Today*, London: SPCK.
Nigel Biggar and Rufus Black (eds), 2000, *The Revival of Natural Law: Philosophical, Theological and Ethical Responses to the Finnis-Grisez School*, Aldershot: Ashgate.
Pierre Bourdieu, 1991, *Language and Symbolic Power*, ed. John B. Thompson, trans. Gino Raymond and Matthew Adamson, Cambridge: Polity Press.
Callum G. Brown, 2002, *The Death of Christian Britain: Understanding Secularisation 1800–2000*, London: Routledge.
Callum G. Brown, 2006, *Religion and Society in Twentieth-Century Britain*, Harlow: Pearson.
Steve Bruce, 1999, *Choice and Religion: A Critique of Rational Choice Theory*, Oxford: Oxford University Press.
Steve Bruce, 2002, *God is Dead: Secularization in the West*, Oxford: Blackwell.
Steve Bruce, 1996, *Religion in the Modern World: From Cathedrals to Cults*, Oxford: Oxford University Press.

Steve Bruce (ed.), 1992, *Religion and Modernization: Sociologists and Historians Debate the Secularization Thesis*, Oxford: Clarendon Press.

Paul van Buren, 1963, *The Secular Meaning of the Gospel, Based on an Analysis of its Language*, London: SCM Press.

Judith Butler, 1993, *Bodies that Matter: On the Discursive Limits of 'Sex'*, New York and London: Routledge.

Judith Butler, 1990, *Gender Trouble: Feminism and the Subversion of Identity*, New York and London: Routledge.

Jeremy Carrette and Richard King, 2005, *Selling Spirituality: The Silent Takeover of Religion*, London: Routledge.

Jackson W. Carroll and Wade Clark Roof, 2002, *Bridging Divided Worlds: Generational Cultures in Congregations*, San Francisco: Jossey-Bass.

José Casanova, 1994, *Public Religions in the Modern World*, Chicago: University of Chicago Press.

Mark Chapman, 2005, *Blair's Britain: A Christian Critique*, London: Darton, Longman & Todd.

Church of England Commission on Urban Priority Areas, 1985, *Faith in the City: A Call to Action by Church and Nation*, London: Church House Publishing.

Terence Copley, 2005, *Indoctrination, Education and God: The Struggle for the Mind*, London: SPCK.

Harvey Cox, 1965, *The Secular City: Secularization and Urbanization in Theological Perspective*, New York: Macmillan.

Jeffrey Cox, 'Provincializing Christendom: The Case of Great Britain', *Church History*, 75(1) (2006), 120–30.

Roger Crisp and Michael Slote (eds), 1997, *Virtue Ethics*, Oxford: Clarendon Press.

Robert Currie, Alan Gilbert and Lee Horsley (eds), 1977, *Churches and Churchgoers: Patterns of Church Growth in the British Isles since 1700*, Oxford: Clarendon Press.

Grace Davie, 2002, *Europe: The Exceptional Case: Parameters of Faith in the Modern World*, London: Darton, Longman & Todd.

Grace Davie, 'From Obligation to Consumption: A Framework for Reflection in Northern Europe', *Political Theology*, 6(3) (2005), 281–301.

Grace Davie, 1994, *Religion in Britain since 1945: Believing without Belonging*, Oxford: Blackwell.

Grace Davie, 2000, *Religion in Modern Europe: A Memory Mutates*, Oxford: Oxford University Press.

Grace Davie, Paul Heelas and Linda Woodhead (eds), 2003, *Predicting Religion: Christian, Secular and Alternative Futures*, Aldershot: Ashgate.

John Drane, 2000, *The McDonaldization of the Church: Spirituality, Creativity, and the Future of the Church*, London: Darton, Longman & Todd.

David Fergusson, 1998, *Community, Liberalism, and Christian Ethics*, Cambridge: Cambridge University Press.

Richard W. Flory and Donald E. Miller, 2000, *GenX Religion*, London: Routledge.

Michel Foucault, 1989, *The Archaeology of Knowledge*, trans. A. M. Sheridan Smith, London: Routledge.

Hans-Georg Gadamer, 2004, *Truth and Method*, rev. edn, trans. Joel Weinsheimer and Donald G. Marshall, London and New York: Continuum.

Robert Gascoigne, 2001, *The Public Forum and Christian Ethics*, Cambridge: Cambridge University Press.

Anthony Giddens, 1991, *Modernity and Self-Identity: Self and Society in the Late Modern Age*, Cambridge: Polity Press.

Alan Gilbert, 1980, *The Making of Post-Christian Britain: A History of the Secularization of British Society*, London: Longman.

Robin Gill, 2003, *The 'Empty' Church Revisited*, Aldershot: Ashgate.

Sheridan Gilley and W. J. Sheils (eds), 1994, *A History of Religion in Britain: Practice and Belief from Pre-Roman Times to the Present*, Oxford: Blackwell.

Matthew Grimley, 2004, *Citizenship, Community and the Church of England: Liberal Anglican Theories of the State between the Wars*, Oxford: Clarendon Press.

Mathew Guest, Karin Tusting and Linda Woodhead (eds), 2004, *Congregational Studies in the UK: Christianity in a Post-Christian Context*, Aldershot: Ashgate.

Jürgen Habermas, 1984–7, *Theory of Communicative Action*, trans. Thomas McCarthy; 2 vols. Cambridge and Oxford: Polity Press.

Adrian Hastings, 2001, *A History of English Christianity 1920–2000*, London: SCM Press.

Paul Heelas and Linda Woodhead, 2005, *The Spiritual Revolution: Why Religion is Giving Way to Spirituality*, Oxford: Blackwell.

Paul Heelas, Scott Lash and Paul Morris (eds), 1996, *Detraditionalization: Critical Reflections on Authority and Identity*, Oxford: Blackwell.

Astrid Henry, 2004, *Not My Mother's Sister: Generational Conflict and Third Wave Feminism*, Indiana: Indiana University Press.

Danièle Hervieu-Léger, 2000, *Religion as a Chain of Memory*, trans. Simon Lee, Cambridge: Polity Press.

William James, 2002, *Varieties of Religious Experience: A Study in Human Nature*, Centenary Edition, London: Routledge.

Mary Kenny, 2000, *Goodbye to Catholic Ireland*, rev. edn, Dublin: New Island.

Gordon Lynch, 2002, *After Religion: 'Generation X' and the Search for Meaning*, London: Darton, Longman & Todd.

Gordon Lynch, 2005, *Understanding Theology and Popular Culture*, Oxford: Blackwell.

Alasdair MacIntyre, 1984, *After Virtue*, Notre Dame: University of Notre Dame Press.

Bernice Martin, 1981, *A Sociology of Contemporary Cultural Change*, Oxford: Basil Blackwell.

David Martin, 2002, *Christian Language and its Mutations: Essays in Sociological Understanding*, Aldershot: Ashgate.

David Martin, 1993, *A General Theory of Secularization*, rev. edn, Aldershot: Gregg Revivals.

David Martin, 2005, *On Secularization: Towards a Revised General Theory*, Aldershot: Ashgate.

Herbert McCabe, 2005, *The Good Life: Ethics and the Pursuit of Happiness*, London: Continuum.

Hugh McLeod, 'The religious crisis of the 1960s', *Journal of Modern European History*, 3(2) (2005), 205–30.

Hugh McLeod (ed.), 2006, *The Cambridge History of Christianity: Volume 9 World Christianities c.1914–c.2000*, Cambridge: Cambridge University Press.

Hugh McLeod and Werner Ustorf (eds), 2004, *The Decline of Christendom in Western Europe, 1750–2000*, Cambridge: Cambridge University Press.

Angela McRobbie, 2000, *Feminism and Youth Culture*, 2nd edn, Basingstoke: Macmillan.

Mass-Observation, 1947, *Puzzled People: A Study in Popular Attitudes to Religion, Ethics, Progress and Politics in a London Borough*, London: Victor Gollancz.

Tariq Modood, Anna Triandafyllidou and Richard Zapata-Barrero (eds), 2006, *Multiculturalism, Muslims and Citizenship: A European Approach*, London: Routledge.

R. Lawrence Moore, 1994, *Selling God: American Religion in the Marketplace*, New York and Oxford: Oxford University Press.

Jeremy Morris, 'The Strange Death of Christian Britain: A New Look at the Secularization Debate', *Historical Journal* 46 (2003), 963–76.

Martha Nussbaum and Amartya Sen, (eds), 1993, *Quality of Life*, Oxford: Clarendon Press.

Gerald Parsons (ed.), 1994, *The Growth of Religious Diversity: Britain from 1945 Vol. II: Issues*, London: Open University/Routledge.

Martyn Percy, 'Join the Dots Christianity: Assessing Alpha', *Religion and Theology*, (May) (1997), 14–8.

Martin Percy, 2004, 'Losing Our Space, Finding Our Place? The Changing Identity of the English Parish Church', in S. Coleman and P. Collins (eds), *Religion, Identity and Change: Perspectives on Global Transformations*, Aldershot: Ashgate, pp. 26–41.

Wade Clark Roof, 1999, *Spiritual Marketplace: Baby Boomers and the Remaking of American Religion*, Princeton and London: Princeton University Press.

Wade Clark Roof, Jackson W. Carroll and David A. Roosen (eds), 1996, *The Post-War Generation and Establish Religion: Cross-Cultural Perspectives*, Boulder: Westview Press.

Nikolas Rose, 1997, 'Assembling the Modern Self' in Roy Porter (ed.), *Rewriting the Self: Histories from the Renaissance to the Present*, London: Routledge.

Amartya K. Sen, 2006, *Identity and Violence: The Illusion of Destiny*. London: Allen Lane.

Richard Sennett, 2006, *The Culture of the New Capitalism*, New Haven: Yale University Press.

Richard Sennett, 1977, *The Fall of Public Man*, Cambridge: Cambridge University Press.

Julia Stapleton, 2001, *Political Intellectuals and Public Identities since 1850*, Manchester: Manchester University Press.

Rodney Stark and William Sims Bainbridge, 1985, *The Future of Religion: Secularization, Revival and Cult Formation*, Berkeley: University of California Press.

Rodney Stark and Roger Finke, 2000, *Acts of Faith: Explaining the Human Side of Religion*, Berkeley: University of California Press.

Charles Taylor, 1989, *Sources of the Self: The Making of Modern Identity*, Cambridge: Cambridge University Press.

Charles Taylor, 1991, *The Ethics of Authenticity*, Cambridge: Harvard University Press.

Charles Taylor, 2002, *Varieties of Religion Today: William James Revisited*, Cambridge: Harvard University Press.

David Voas and Steve Bruce, 'The 2001 Census and Christian Identification in Britain', *Journal of Contemporary Religion* 19(1) (2004), 23–8.

Pete Ward, 2002, *Liquid Church*, Carlisle: Paternoster Press.

Sarah Williams, 1999, *Religious Belief and Popular Culture in Southwark c.1880–1939*, Oxford: Oxford University Press.

Bryan R. Wilson, 1969, *Religion in Secular Society*, Harmondsworth: Penguin.

Bryan R. Wilson (ed.), 1992, *Religion: Contemporary Issues: The All Souls Seminars in the Sociology of Religion*, London: Bellew.

Wolffe, John (ed.), 2004, *Religion in History: Conflict, Conversion and Coexistence*, Manchester: Manchester University Press.

Index of Names and Subjects